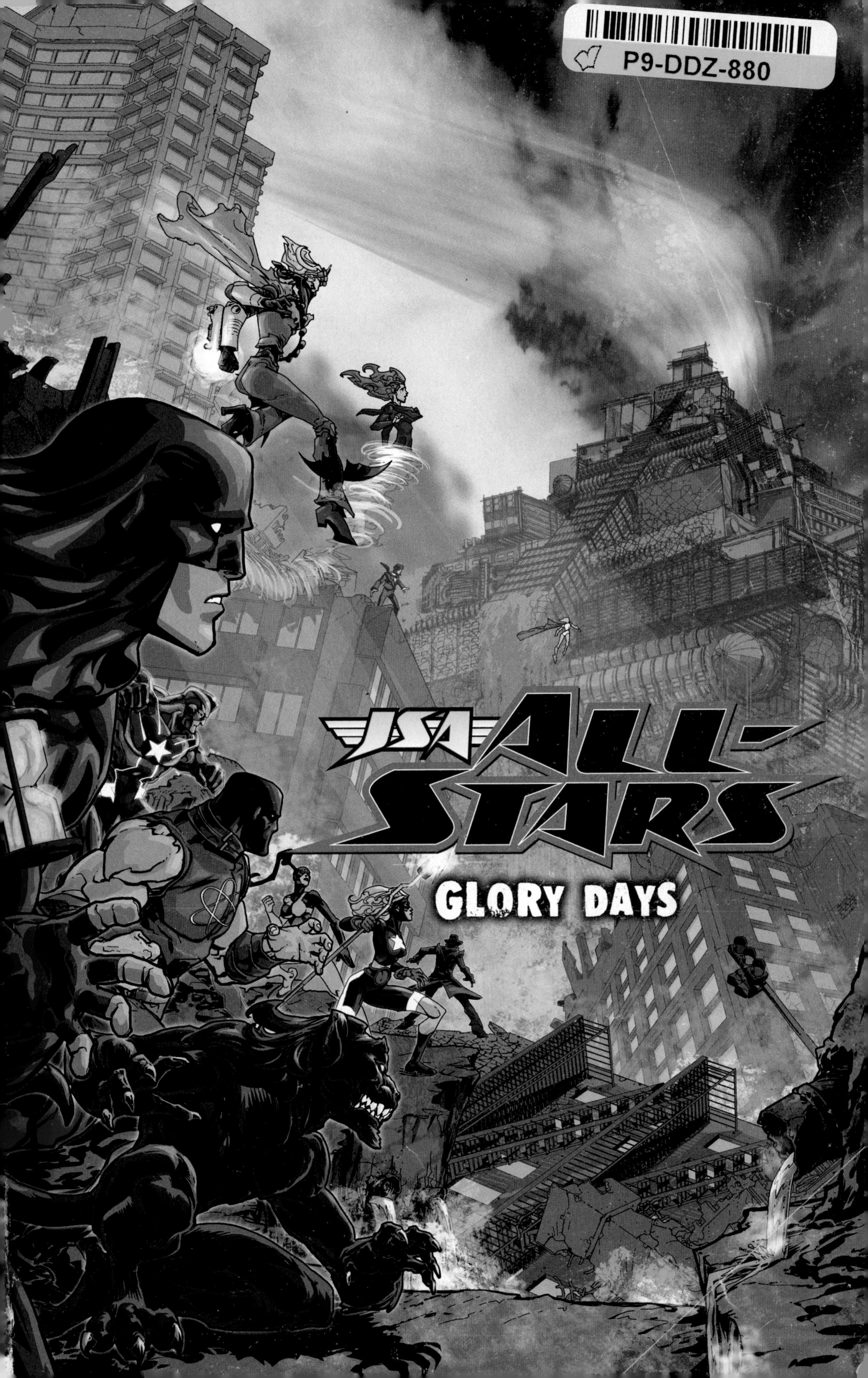
JSA
ALL-STARS
GLORY DAYS

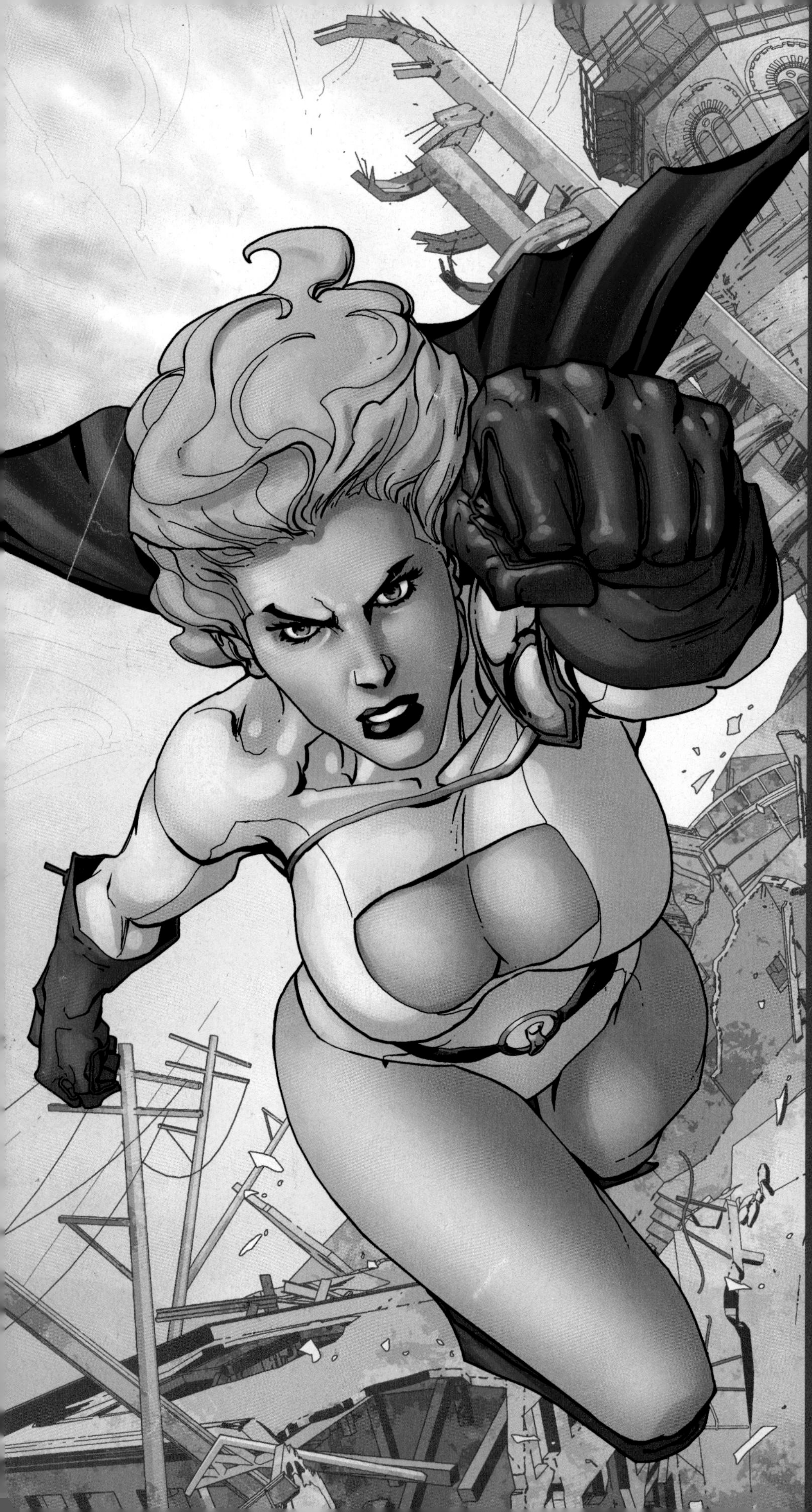

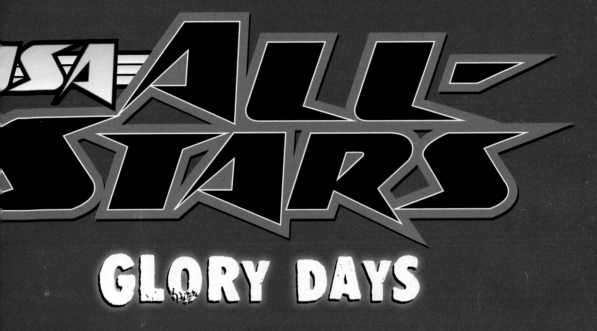

GLORY DAYS

Written by **Matthew Sturges**
Art by **Freddie Williams II & Howard Porter**
Inks by **Freddie Williams II & Art Thibert**
Colors by **Richard and Tanya Horie & Chris Sotomayor**
Letters by **Patrick Brosseau**
Covers by **Freddie Williams II**

Mike Carlin Editor – Original Series
Rachel Gluckstern Associate Editor – Original Series
Ian Sattler Director Editorial, Special Projects and Archival Editions
Robbin Brosterman Design Director – Books

Eddie Berganza Executive Editor
Bob Harras VP – Editor in Chief

Diane Nelson President
Dan DiDio and **Jim Lee** Co-Publishers
Geoff Johns Chief Creative Officer
John Rood Executive VP – Sales, Marketing and Business Development
Amy Genkins Senior VP – Business and Legal Affairs
Nairi Gardiner Senior VP – Finance
Jeff Boison VP – Publishing Operations
Mark Chiarello VP – Art Direction and Design
John Cunningham VP – Marketing
Terri Cunningham VP – Talent Relations and Services
Alison Gill Senior VP – Manufacturing and Operations
David Hyde VP – Publicity
Hank Kanalz Senior VP – Digital
Jay Kogan VP – Business and Legal Affairs, Publishing
Jack Mahan VP – Business Affairs, Talent
Nick Napolitano VP – Manufacturing Administration
Ron Perazza VP – Online
Sue Pohja VP – Book Sales
Courtney Simmons Senior VP – Publicity
Bob Wayne Senior VP – Sales

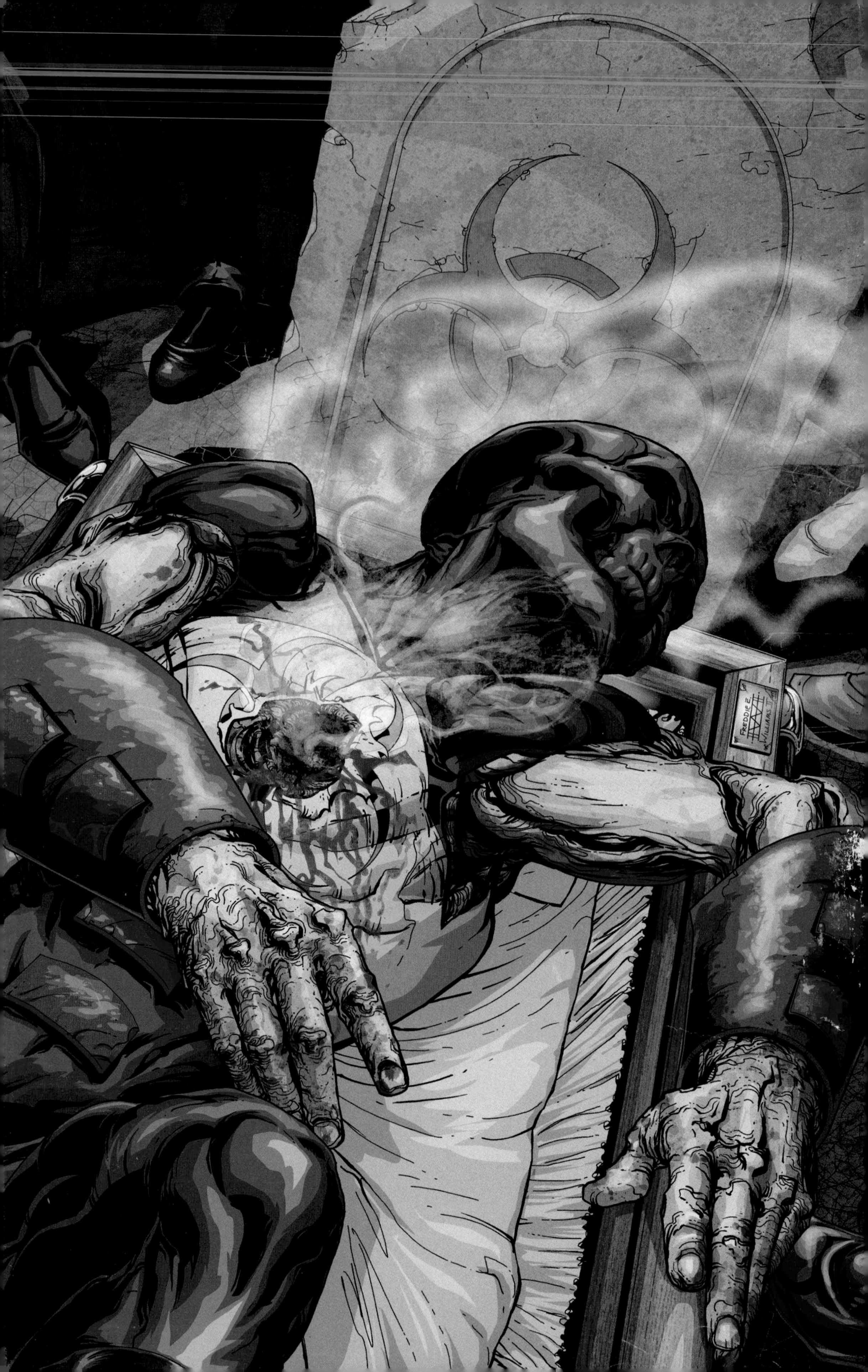
FREDDIE E.
WILLIAMS II

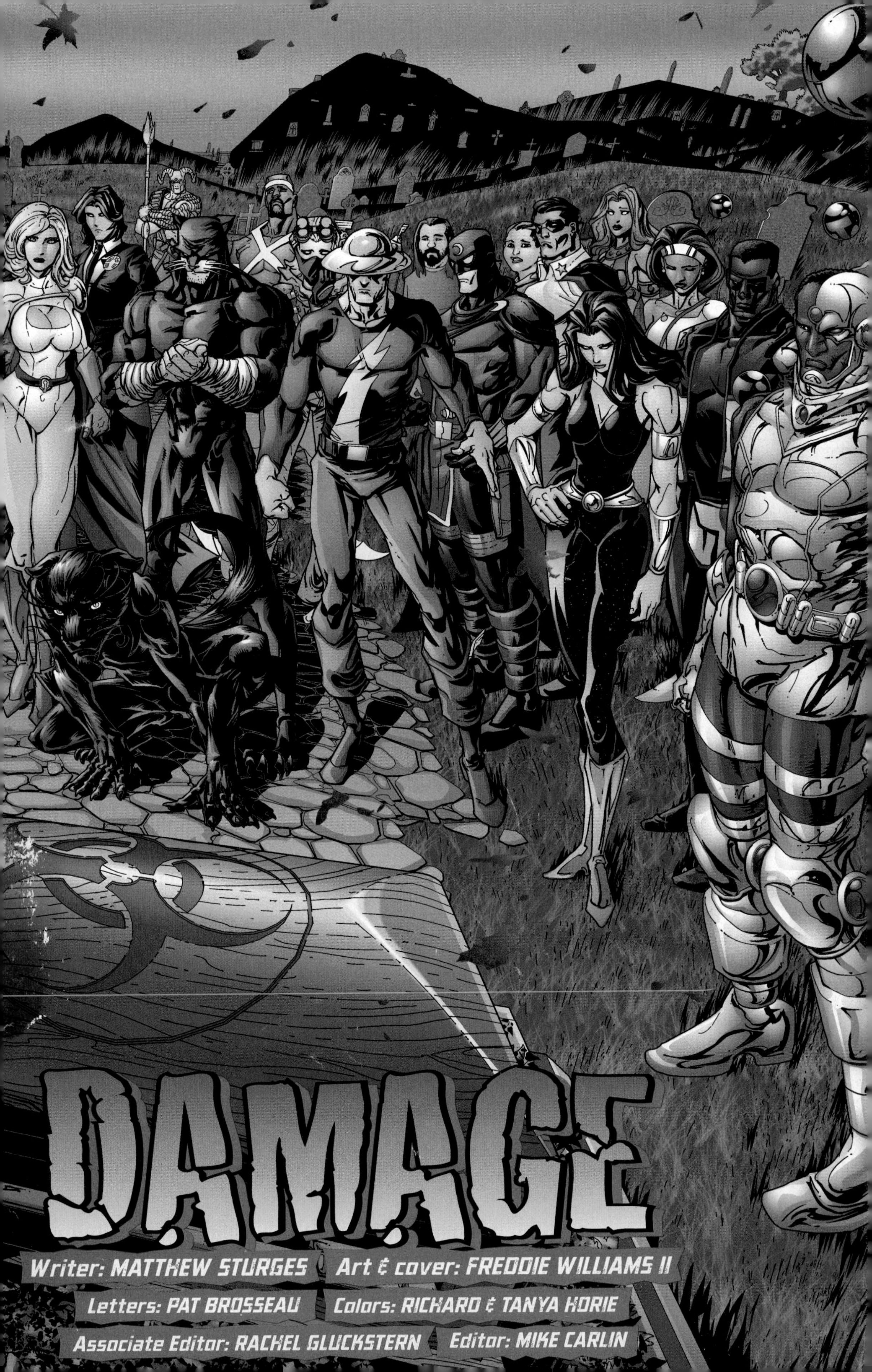
DAMAGE
Writer: MATTHEW STURGES
Art & cover: FREDDIE WILLIAMS II
Letters: PAT BROSSEAU
Colors: RICHARD & TANYA HORIE
Associate Editor: RACHEL GLUCKSTERN
Editor: MIKE CARLIN

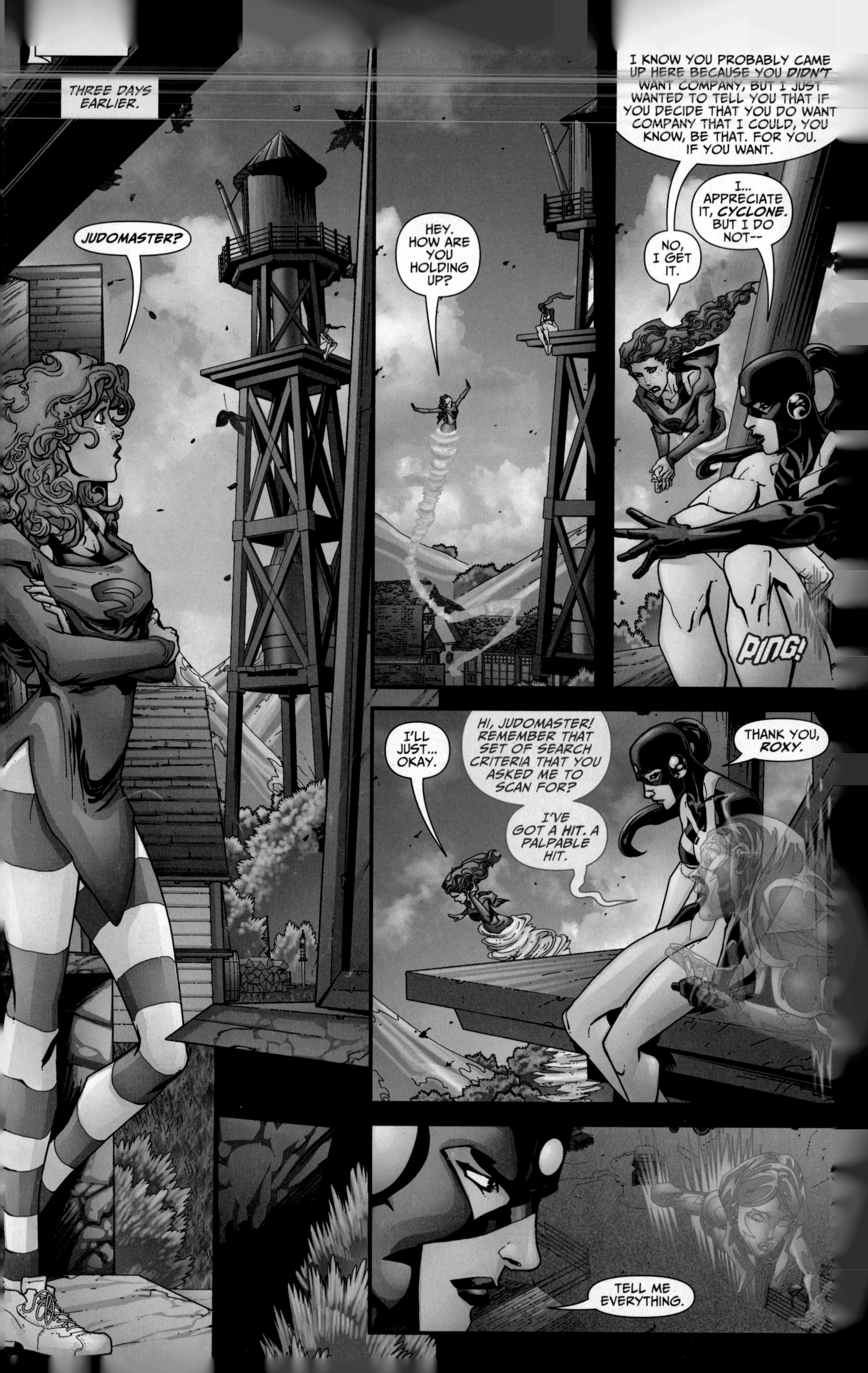
THREE DAYS EARLIER.
JUDOMASTER?
HEY. HOW ARE YOU HOLDING UP?
I KNOW YOU PROBABLY CAME UP HERE BECAUSE YOU DIDN'T WANT COMPANY, BUT I JUST WANTED TO TELL YOU THAT IF YOU DECIDE THAT YOU DO WANT COMPANY THAT I COULD, YOU KNOW, BE THAT. FOR YOU. IF YOU WANT.
I... APPRECIATE IT, CYCLONE. BUT I DO NOT--
NO, I GET IT.
PING!
I'LL JUST... OKAY.
HI, JUDOMASTER! REMEMBER THAT SET OF SEARCH CRITERIA THAT YOU ASKED ME TO SCAN FOR?
I'VE GOT A HIT. A PALPABLE HIT.
THANK YOU, ROXY.
TELL ME EVERYTHING.

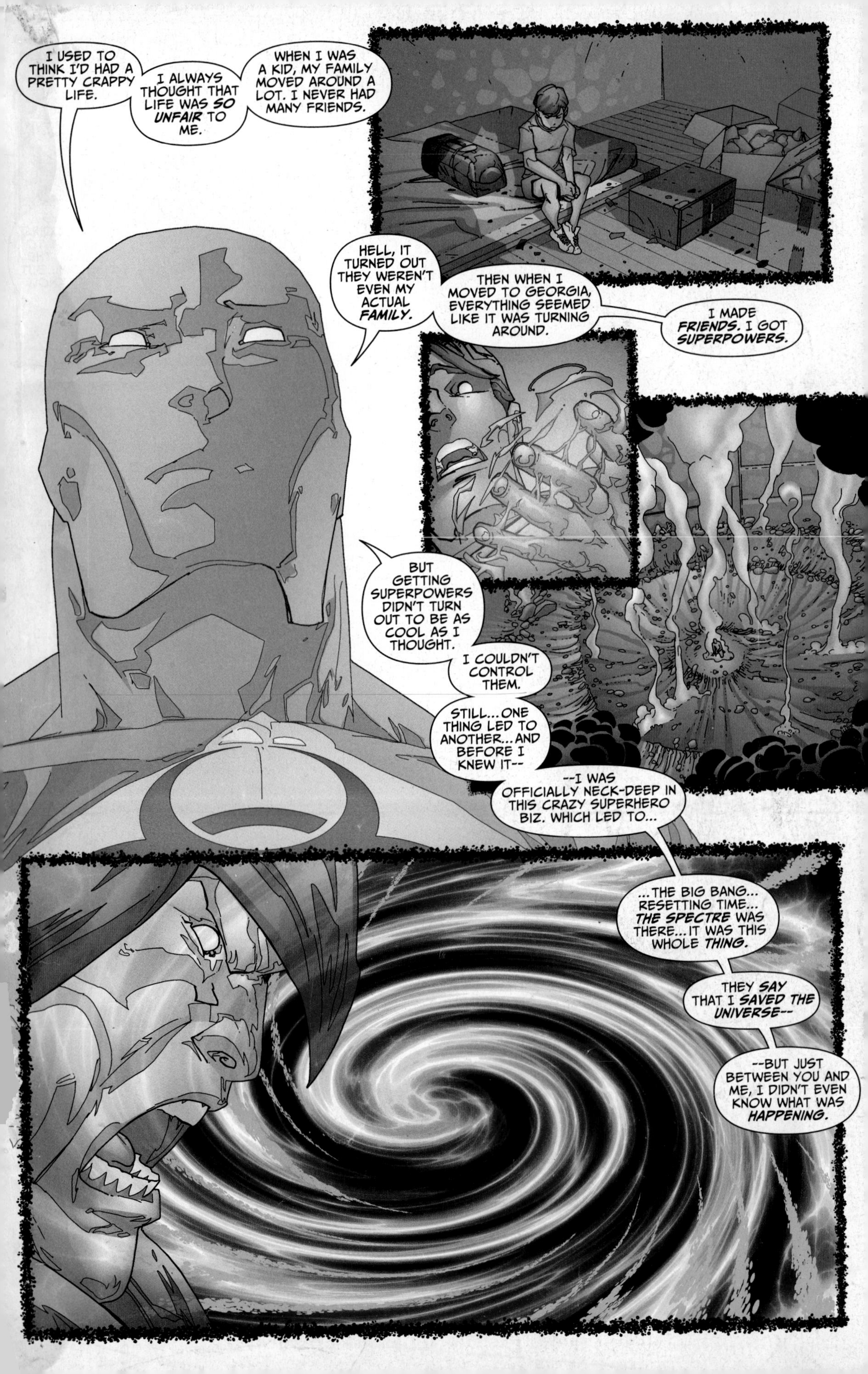

I USED TO THINK I'D HAD A PRETTY CRAPPY LIFE.
I ALWAYS THOUGHT THAT LIFE WAS SO UNFAIR TO ME.
WHEN I WAS A KID, MY FAMILY MOVED AROUND A LOT. I NEVER HAD MANY FRIENDS.
HELL, IT TURNED OUT THEY WEREN'T EVEN MY ACTUAL FAMILY.
THEN WHEN I MOVED TO GEORGIA, EVERYTHING SEEMED LIKE IT WAS TURNING AROUND.
I MADE FRIENDS. I GOT SUPERPOWERS.
BUT GETTING SUPERPOWERS DIDN'T TURN OUT TO BE AS COOL AS I THOUGHT.
I COULDN'T CONTROL THEM.
STILL...ONE THING LED TO ANOTHER...AND BEFORE I KNEW IT--
--I WAS OFFICIALLY NECK-DEEP IN THIS CRAZY SUPERHERO BIZ. WHICH LED TO...
...THE BIG BANG... RESETTING TIME... THE SPECTRE WAS THERE...IT WAS THIS WHOLE THING.
THEY SAY THAT I SAVED THE UNIVERSE--
--BUT JUST BETWEEN YOU AND ME, I DIDN'T EVEN KNOW WHAT WAS HAPPENING.

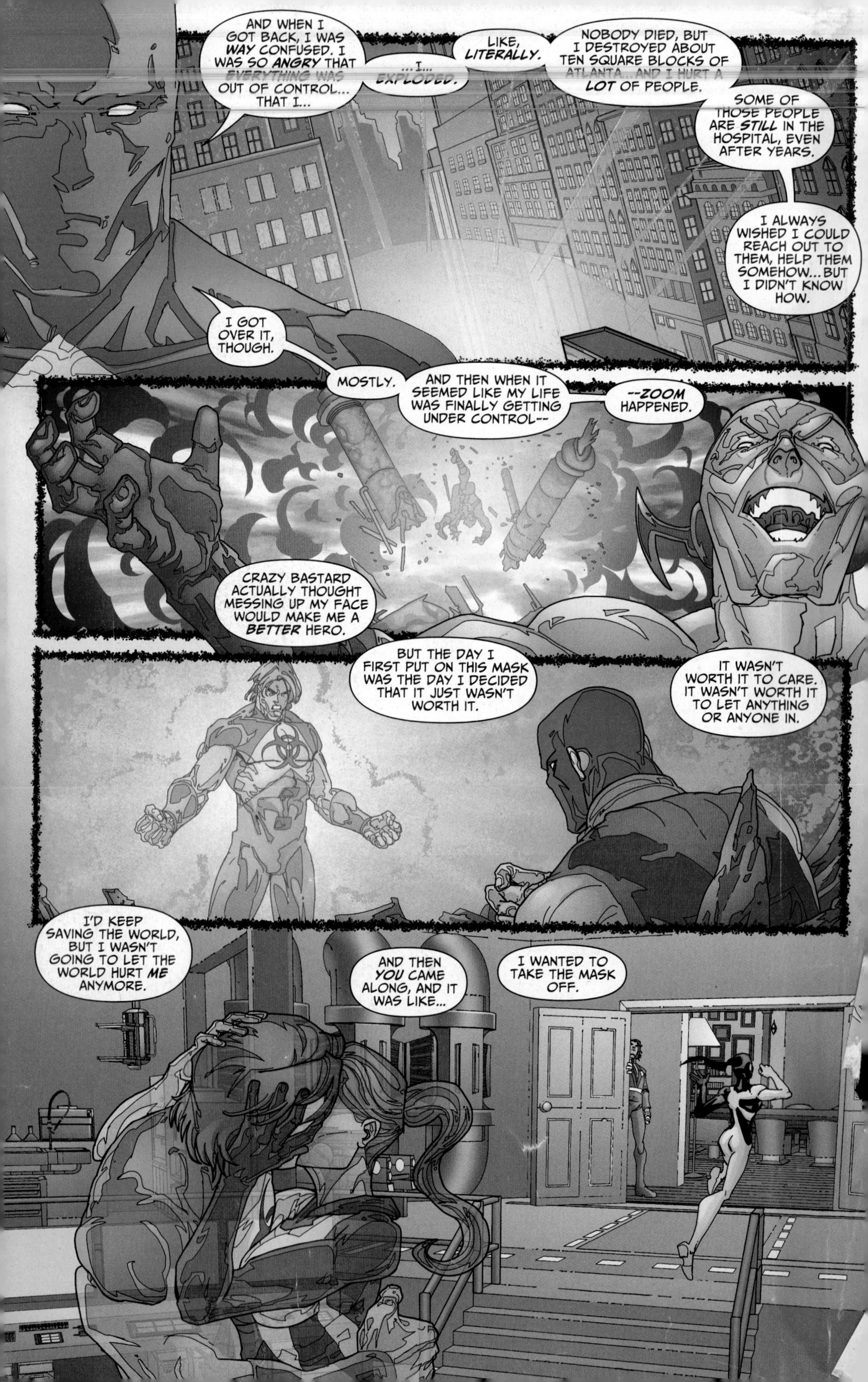

AND WHEN I GOT BACK, I WAS WAY CONFUSED. I WAS SO ANGRY THAT EVERYTHING WAS OUT OF CONTROL... THAT I...
...I... EXPLODED.
LIKE, LITERALLY.
NOBODY DIED, BUT I DESTROYED ABOUT TEN SQUARE BLOCKS OF ATLANTA...AND I HURT A LOT OF PEOPLE.
SOME OF THOSE PEOPLE ARE STILL IN THE HOSPITAL, EVEN AFTER YEARS.
I ALWAYS WISHED I COULD REACH OUT TO THEM, HELP THEM SOMEHOW...BUT I DIDN'T KNOW HOW.
I GOT OVER IT, THOUGH.
MOSTLY.
AND THEN WHEN IT SEEMED LIKE MY LIFE WAS FINALLY GETTING UNDER CONTROL--
--ZOOM HAPPENED.
CRAZY BASTARD ACTUALLY THOUGHT MESSING UP MY FACE WOULD MAKE ME A BETTER HERO.
BUT THE DAY I FIRST PUT ON THIS MASK WAS THE DAY I DECIDED THAT IT JUST WASN'T WORTH IT.
IT WASN'T WORTH IT TO CARE. IT WASN'T WORTH IT TO LET ANYTHING OR ANYONE IN.
I'D KEEP SAVING THE WORLD, BUT I WASN'T GOING TO LET THE WORLD HURT ME ANYMORE.
AND THEN YOU CAME ALONG, AND IT WAS LIKE...
I WANTED TO TAKE THE MASK OFF.

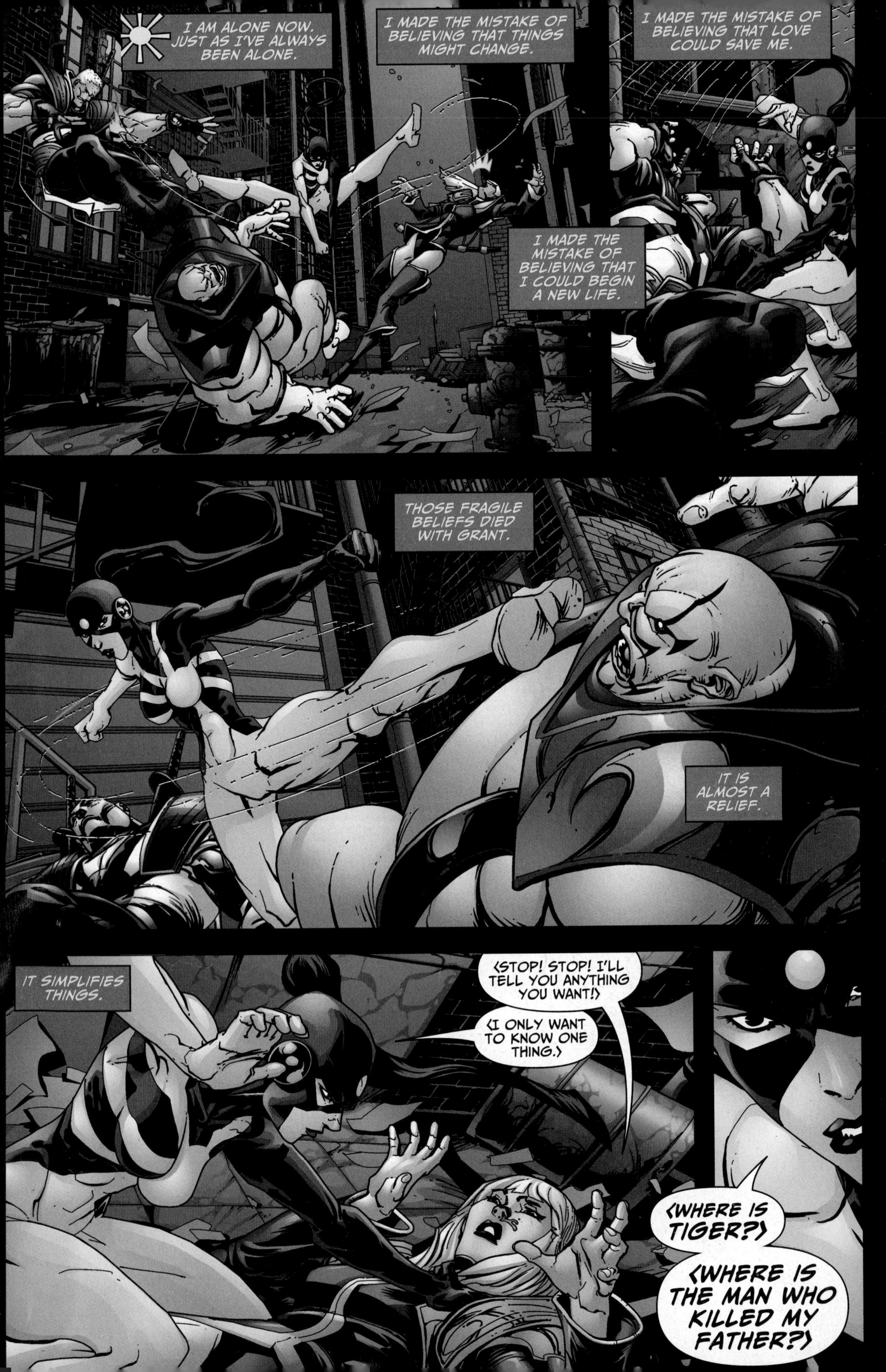
I AM ALONE NOW. JUST AS I'VE ALWAYS BEEN ALONE.
I MADE THE MISTAKE OF BELIEVING THAT THINGS MIGHT CHANGE.
I MADE THE MISTAKE OF BELIEVING THAT LOVE COULD SAVE ME.
I MADE THE MISTAKE OF BELIEVING THAT I COULD BEGIN A NEW LIFE.
THOSE FRAGILE BELIEFS DIED WITH GRANT.
IT IS ALMOST A RELIEF.
IT SIMPLIFIES THINGS.
‹STOP! STOP! I'LL TELL YOU ANYTHING YOU WANT!›
‹I ONLY WANT TO KNOW ONE THING.›
‹WHERE IS TIGER?›
‹WHERE IS THE MAN WHO KILLED MY FATHER?›

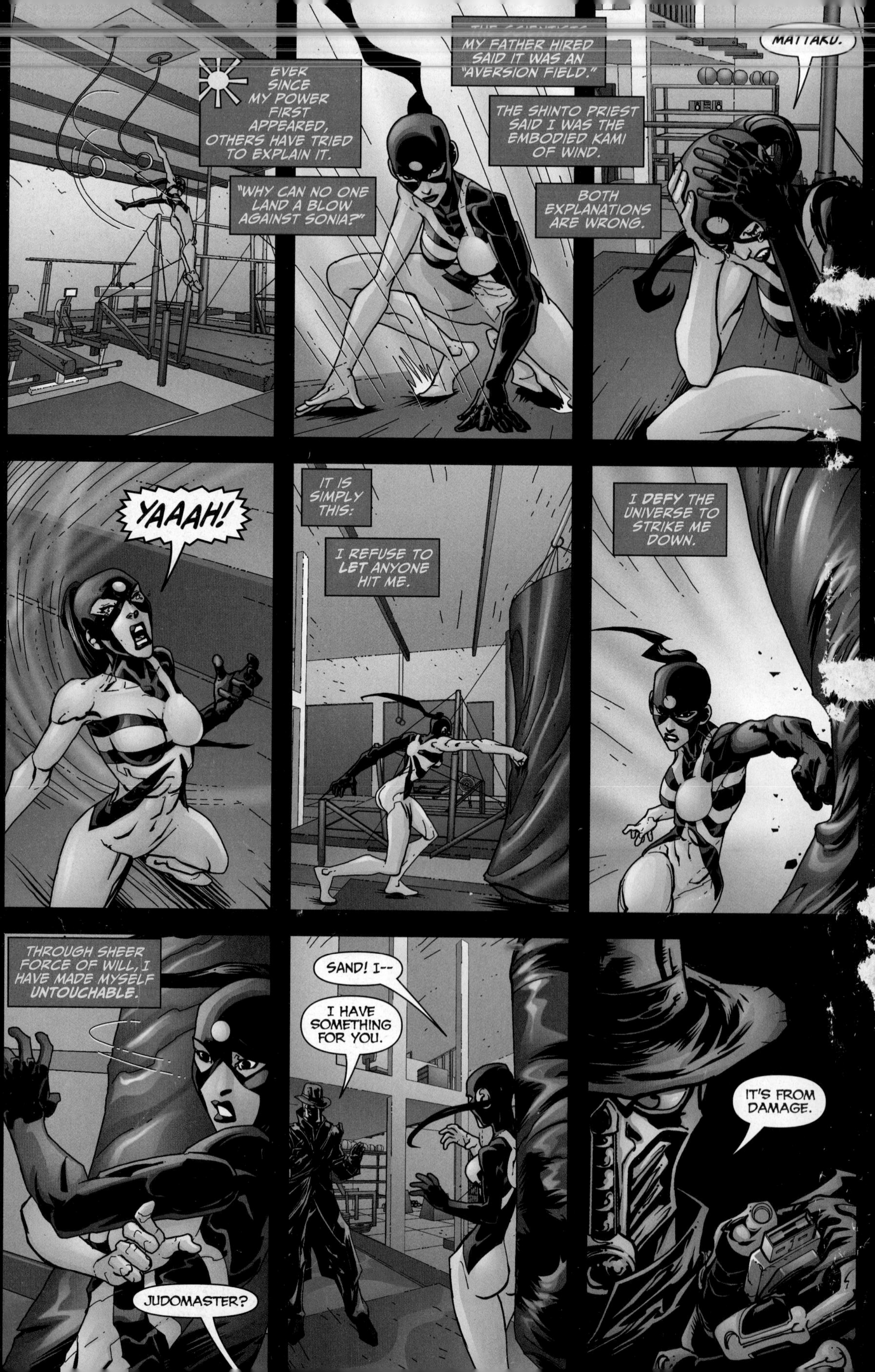
EVER SINCE MY POWER FIRST APPEARED, OTHERS HAVE TRIED TO EXPLAIN IT.
"WHY CAN NO ONE LAND A BLOW AGAINST SONIA?"
MY FATHER HIRED SAID IT WAS AN "AVERSION FIELD."
THE SHINTO PRIEST SAID I WAS THE EMBODIED KAMI OF WIND.
BOTH EXPLANATIONS ARE WRONG.
MATTAKU.
YAAAH!
IT IS SIMPLY THIS:
I REFUSE TO LET ANYONE HIT ME.
I DEFY THE UNIVERSE TO STRIKE ME DOWN.
THROUGH SHEER FORCE OF WILL, I HAVE MADE MYSELF UNTOUCHABLE.
JUDOMASTER?
SAND! I--
I HAVE SOMETHING FOR YOU.
IT'S FROM DAMAGE.

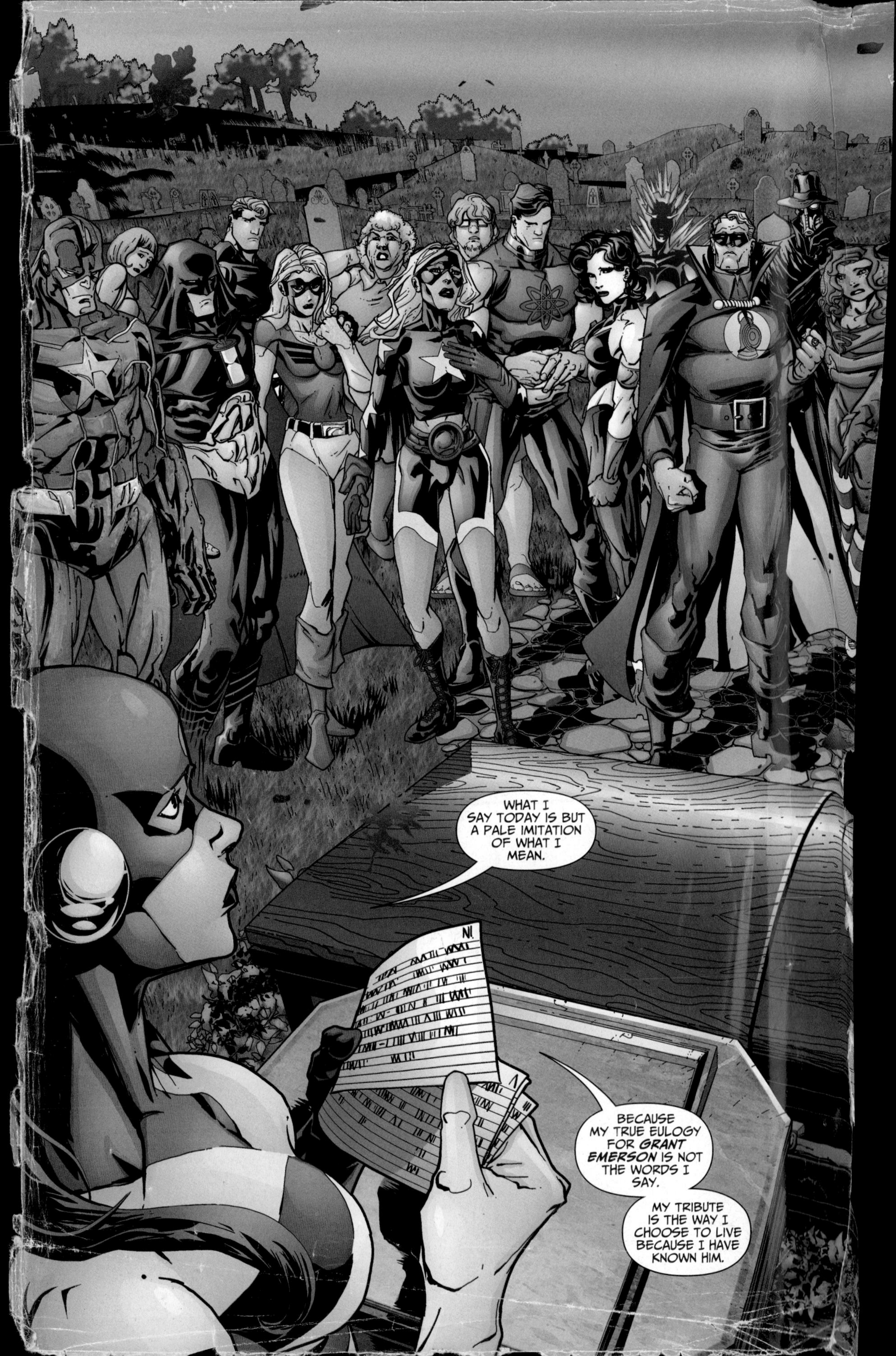
WHAT I SAY TODAY IS BUT A PALE IMITATION OF WHAT I MEAN.
BECAUSE MY TRUE EULOGY FOR GRANT EMERSON IS NOT THE WORDS I SAY.
MY TRIBUTE IS THE WAY I CHOOSE TO LIVE BECAUSE I HAVE KNOWN HIM.

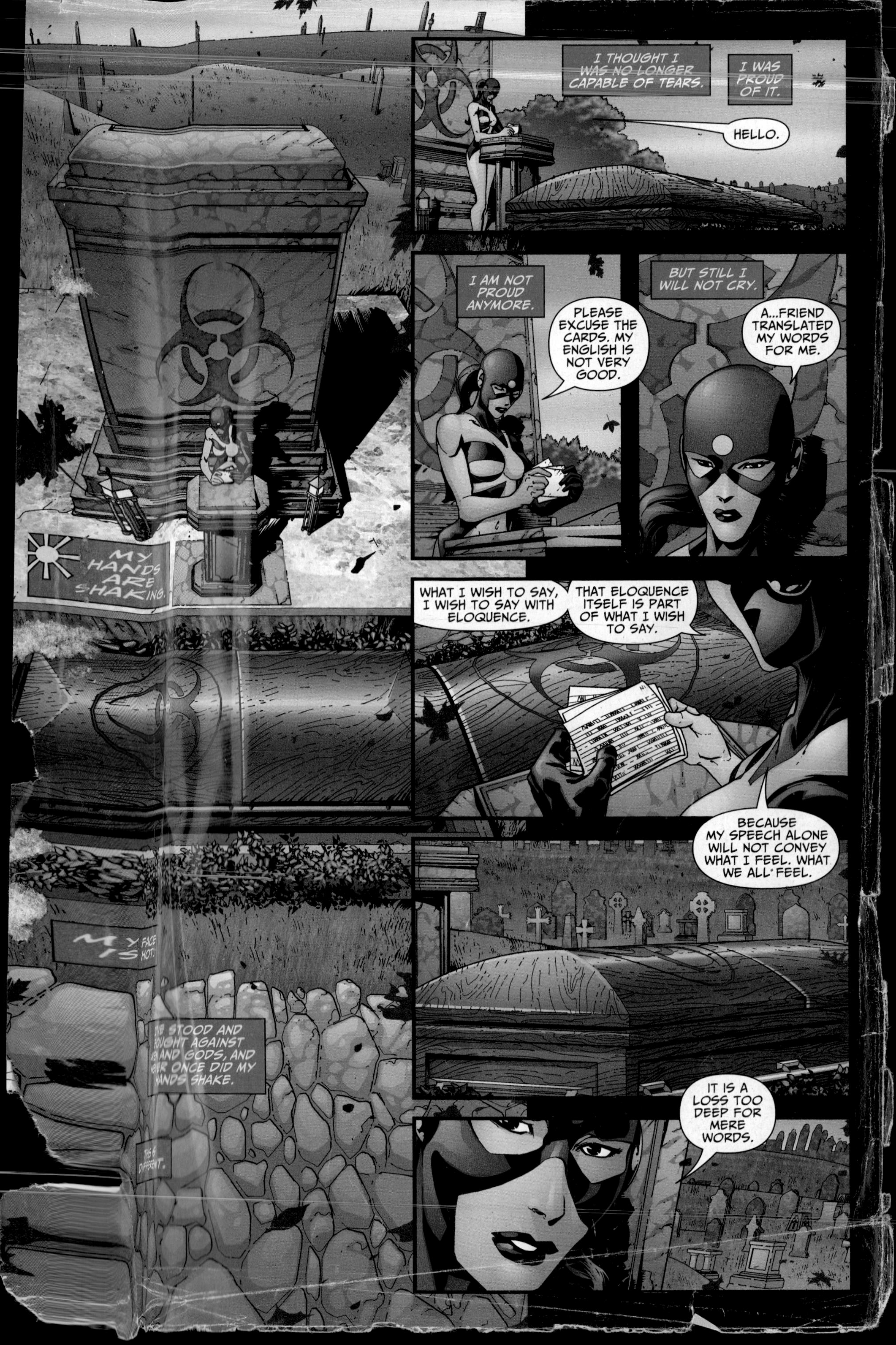
I THOUGHT I WAS NO LONGER CAPABLE OF TEARS.
I WAS PROUD OF IT.
HELLO.
I AM NOT PROUD ANYMORE.
PLEASE EXCUSE THE CARDS. MY ENGLISH IS NOT VERY GOOD.
BUT STILL I WILL NOT CRY.
A...FRIEND TRANSLATED MY WORDS FOR ME.
WHAT I WISH TO SAY, I WISH TO SAY WITH ELOQUENCE.
THAT ELOQUENCE ITSELF IS PART OF WHAT I WISH TO SAY.
BECAUSE MY SPEECH ALONE WILL NOT CONVEY WHAT I FEEL. WHAT WE ALL FEEL.
IT IS A LOSS TOO DEEP FOR MERE WORDS.
MY HANDS ARE SHAKING.
MY FACE IS HOT.
I'VE STOOD AND FOUGHT AGAINST MEN AND GODS, AND NEVER ONCE DID MY HANDS SHAKE.
THIS IS DIFFERENT.

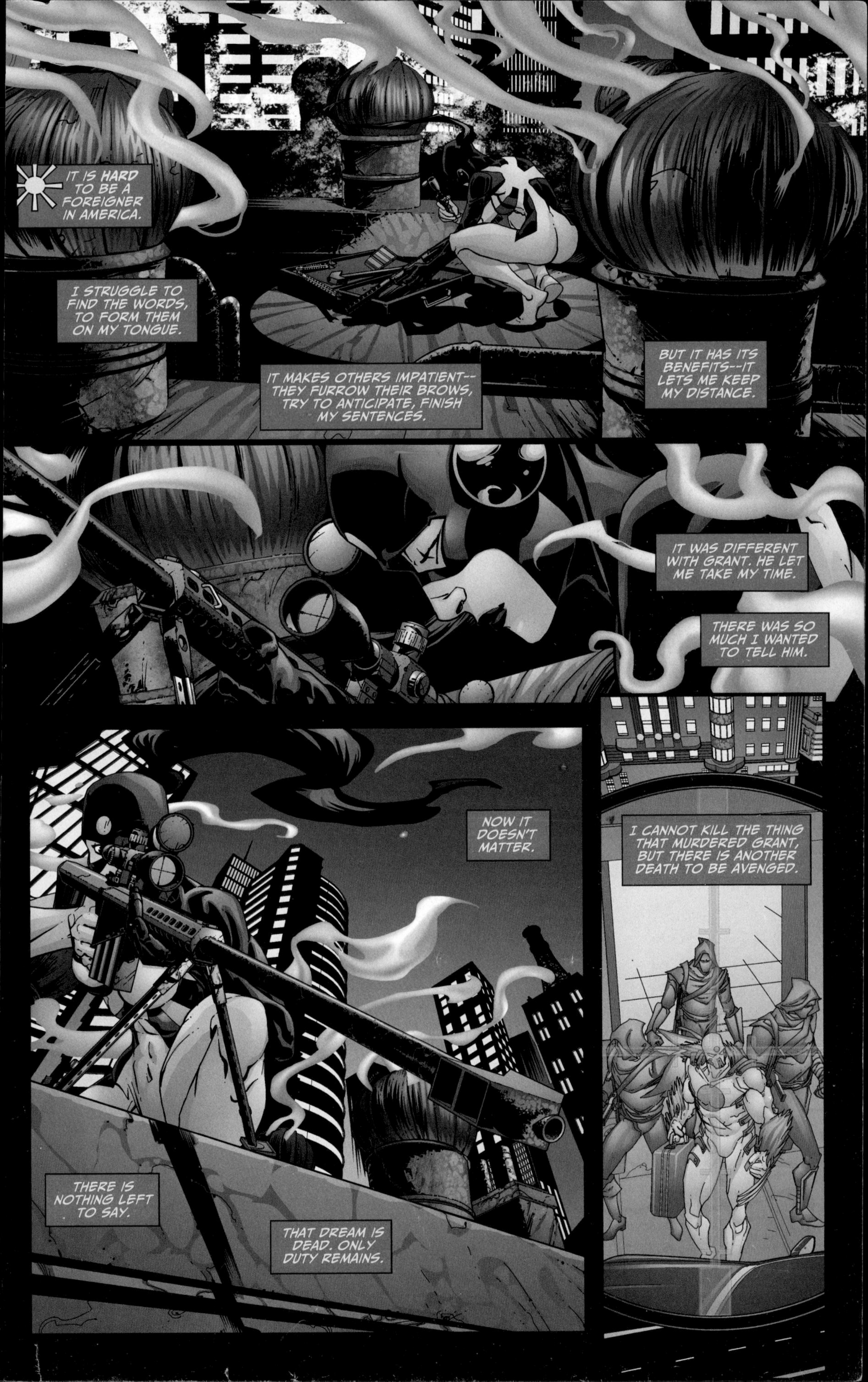
IT IS HARD TO BE A FOREIGNER IN AMERICA.
I STRUGGLE TO FIND THE WORDS, TO FORM THEM ON MY TONGUE.
IT MAKES OTHERS IMPATIENT-- THEY FURROW THEIR BROWS, TRY TO ANTICIPATE, FINISH MY SENTENCES.
BUT IT HAS ITS BENEFITS--IT LETS ME KEEP MY DISTANCE.
IT WAS DIFFERENT WITH GRANT. HE LET ME TAKE MY TIME.
THERE WAS SO MUCH I WANTED TO TELL HIM.
NOW IT DOESN'T MATTER.
THERE IS NOTHING LEFT TO SAY.
THAT DREAM IS DEAD. ONLY DUTY REMAINS.
I CANNOT KILL THE THING THAT MURDERED GRANT, BUT THERE IS ANOTHER DEATH TO BE AVENGED.

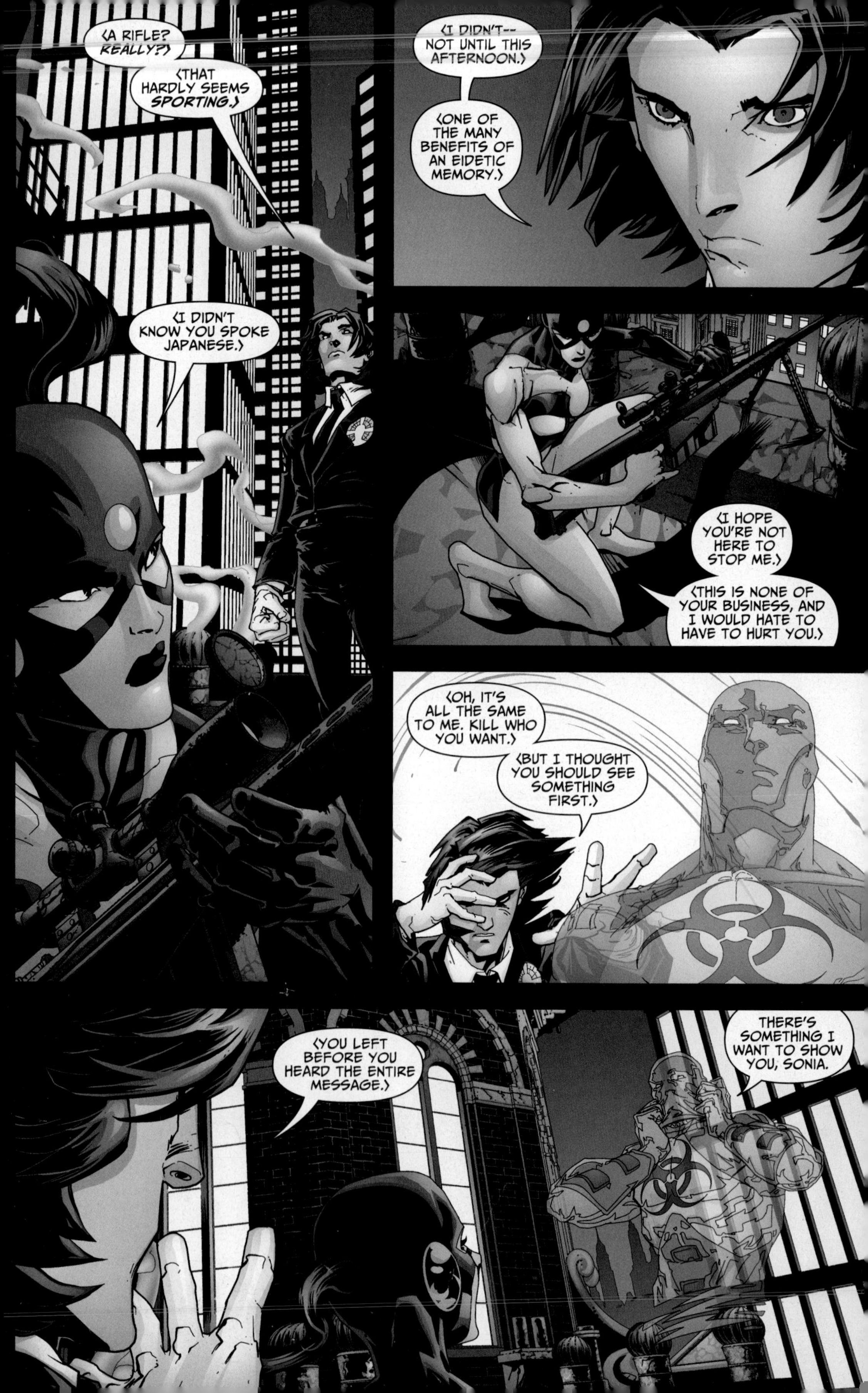

‹A RIFLE? REALLY?›
‹THAT HARDLY SEEMS SPORTING.›
‹I DIDN'T KNOW YOU SPOKE JAPANESE.›
‹I DIDN'T-- NOT UNTIL THIS AFTERNOON.›
‹ONE OF THE MANY BENEFITS OF AN EIDETIC MEMORY.›
‹I HOPE YOU'RE NOT HERE TO STOP ME.›
‹THIS IS NONE OF YOUR BUSINESS, AND I WOULD HATE TO HAVE TO HURT YOU.›
‹OH, IT'S ALL THE SAME TO ME. KILL WHO YOU WANT.›
‹BUT I THOUGHT YOU SHOULD SEE SOMETHING FIRST.›
‹YOU LEFT BEFORE YOU HEARD THE ENTIRE MESSAGE.›
THERE'S SOMETHING I WANT TO SHOW YOU, SONIA.

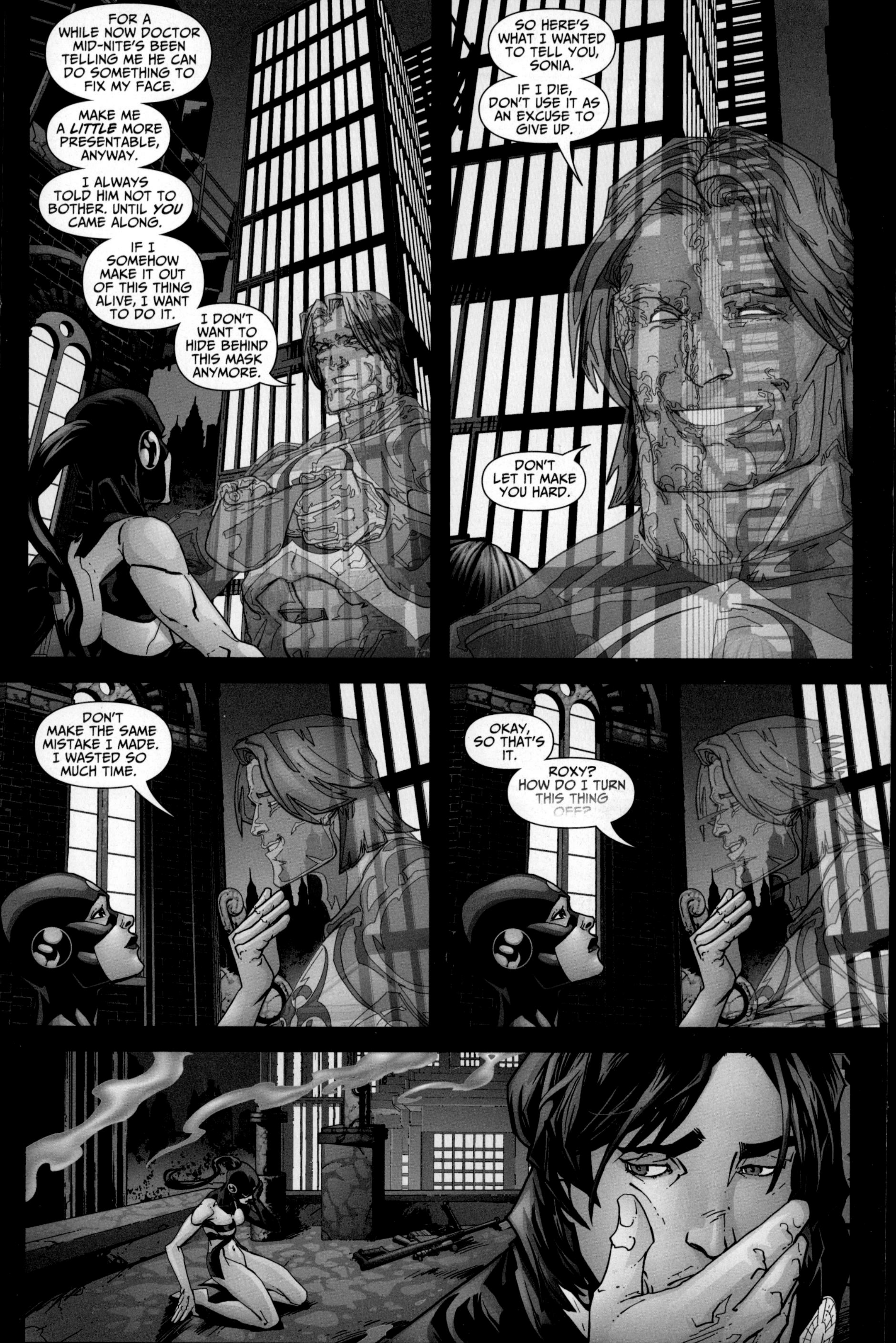
FOR A WHILE NOW DOCTOR MID-NITE'S BEEN TELLING ME HE CAN DO SOMETHING TO FIX MY FACE.
MAKE ME A *LITTLE* MORE PRESENTABLE, ANYWAY.
I ALWAYS TOLD HIM NOT TO BOTHER. UNTIL *YOU* CAME ALONG.
IF I SOMEHOW MAKE IT OUT OF THIS THING ALIVE, I WANT TO DO IT.
I DON'T WANT TO HIDE BEHIND THIS MASK ANYMORE.
SO HERE'S WHAT I WANTED TO TELL YOU, SONIA.
IF I DIE, DON'T USE IT AS AN EXCUSE TO GIVE UP.
DON'T LET IT MAKE YOU HARD.
DON'T MAKE THE SAME MISTAKE I MADE. I WASTED SO MUCH TIME.
OKAY, SO THAT'S IT.
ROXY? HOW DO I TURN THIS THING OFF?

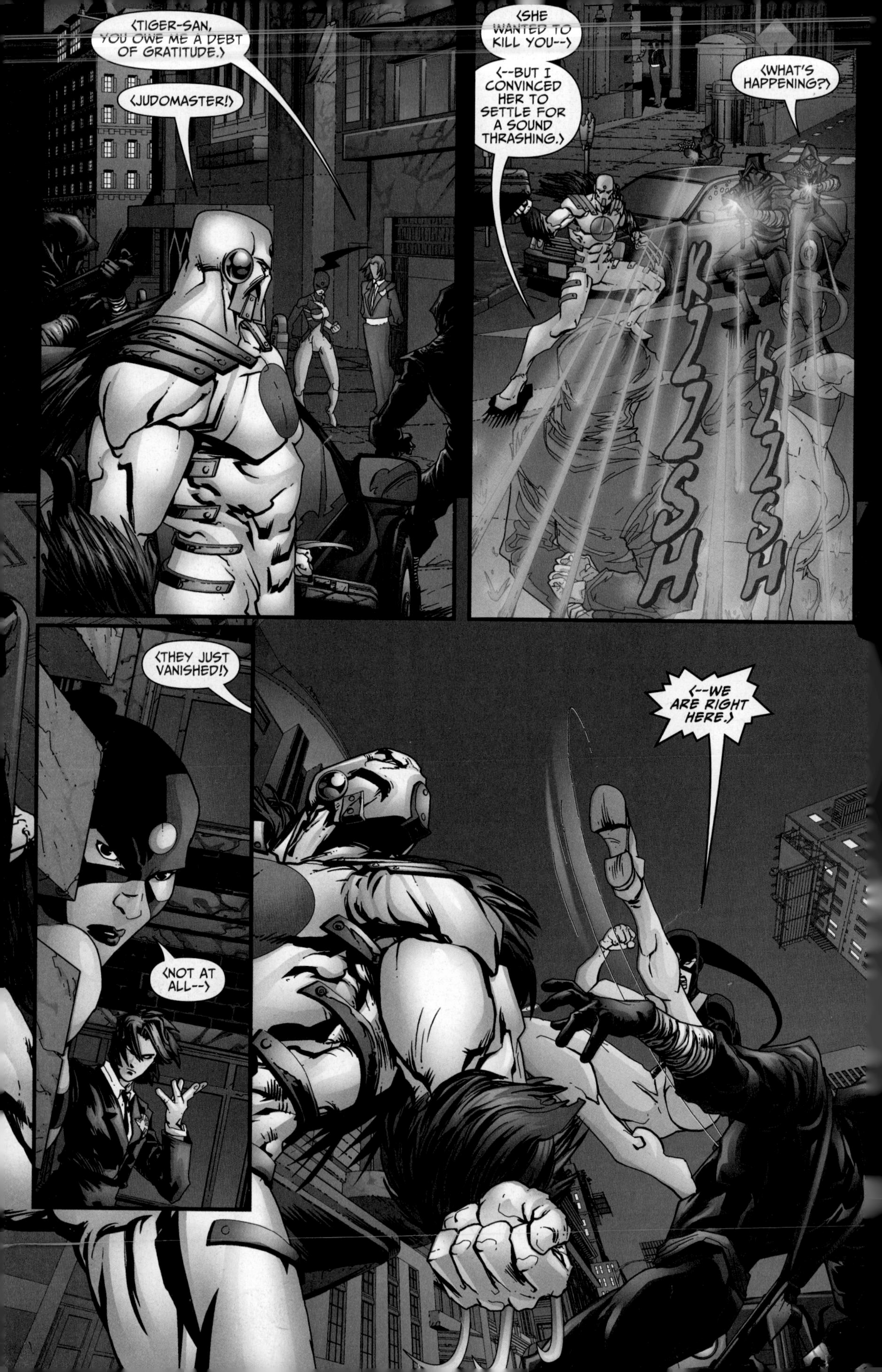

<TIGER-SAN, YOU OWE ME A DEBT OF GRATITUDE.>
<JUDOMASTER!>
<SHE WANTED TO KILL YOU-->
<--BUT I CONVINCED HER TO SETTLE FOR A SOUND THRASHING.>
<WHAT'S HAPPENING?>
KZZSH
KZZSH
<THEY JUST VANISHED!>
<NOT AT ALL-->
<--WE ARE RIGHT HERE.>

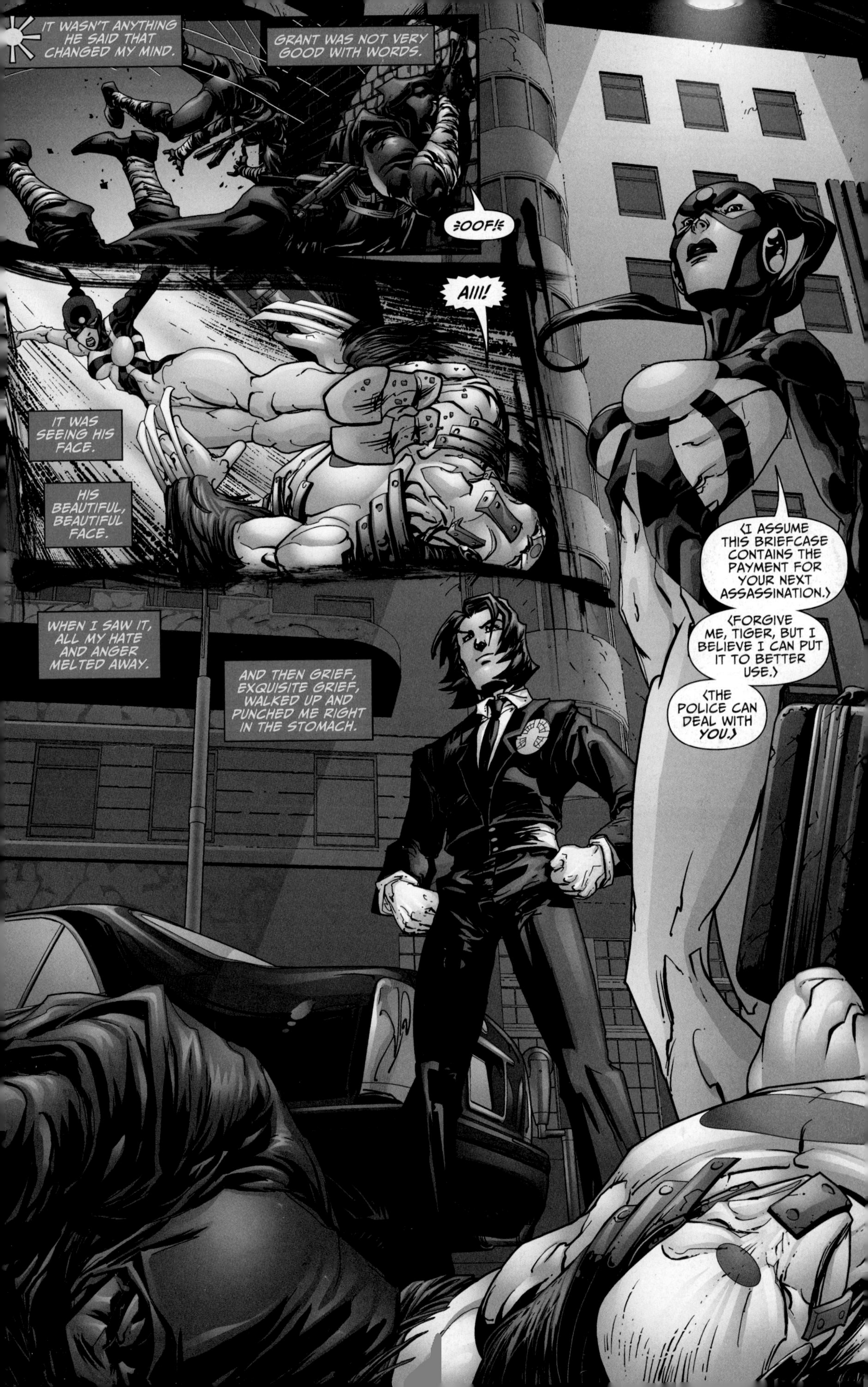
IT WASN'T ANYTHING HE SAID THAT CHANGED MY MIND.
GRANT WAS NOT VERY GOOD WITH WORDS.
OOF!
AIII!
IT WAS SEEING HIS FACE.
HIS BEAUTIFUL, BEAUTIFUL FACE.
WHEN I SAW IT, ALL MY HATE AND ANGER MELTED AWAY.
AND THEN GRIEF, EXQUISITE GRIEF, WALKED UP AND PUNCHED ME RIGHT IN THE STOMACH.
<I ASSUME THIS BRIEFCASE CONTAINS THE PAYMENT FOR YOUR NEXT ASSASSINATION.>
<FORGIVE ME, TIGER, BUT I BELIEVE I CAN PUT IT TO BETTER USE.>
<THE POLICE CAN DEAL WITH YOU.>

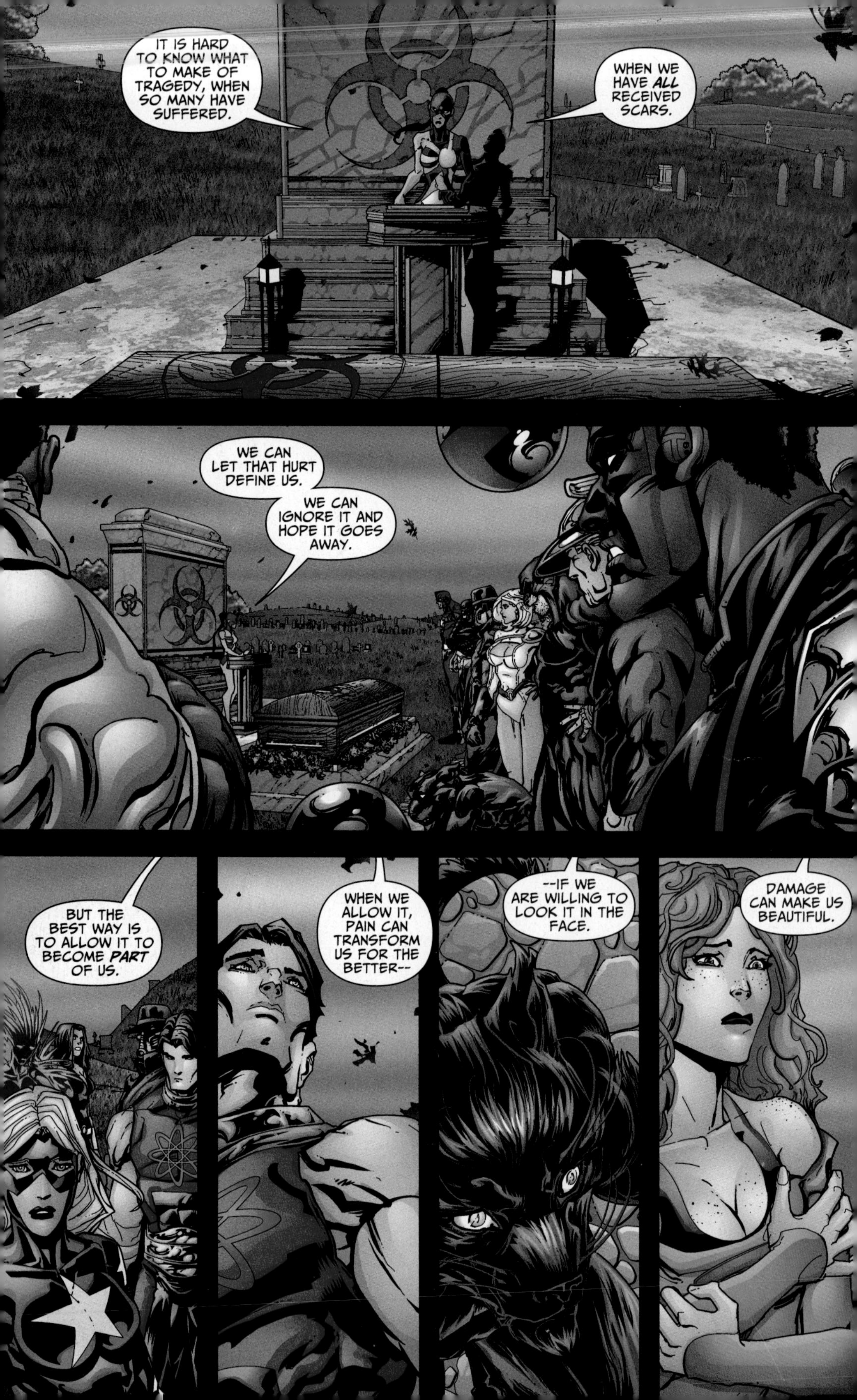
IT IS HARD TO KNOW WHAT TO MAKE OF TRAGEDY, WHEN SO MANY HAVE SUFFERED.
WHEN WE HAVE ALL RECEIVED SCARS.
WE CAN LET THAT HURT DEFINE US.
WE CAN IGNORE IT AND HOPE IT GOES AWAY.
BUT THE BEST WAY IS TO ALLOW IT TO BECOME PART OF US.
WHEN WE ALLOW IT, PAIN CAN TRANSFORM US FOR THE BETTER--
--IF WE ARE WILLING TO LOOK IT IN THE FACE.
DAMAGE CAN MAKE US BEAUTIFUL.

MY HANDS ARE STILL SHAKING.

THERE IS MUCH THAT GRANT EMERSON HAS LEFT ME.

MY EYES STING WITH TEARS AND I WILL LET THEM FLOW.

BUT THERE IS ONE THING FOR WHICH I WILL ALWAYS BE GRATEFUL.

I CAN BARELY SPEAK, BUT I WILL SPEAK.

BEFORE I MET HIM, LOVE WAS A FOREIGN LANGUAGE TO ME.

DAMAGE TAUGHT ME TO SPEAK IT.

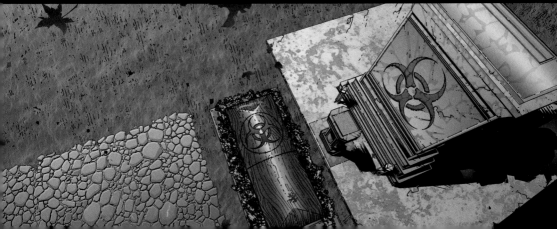

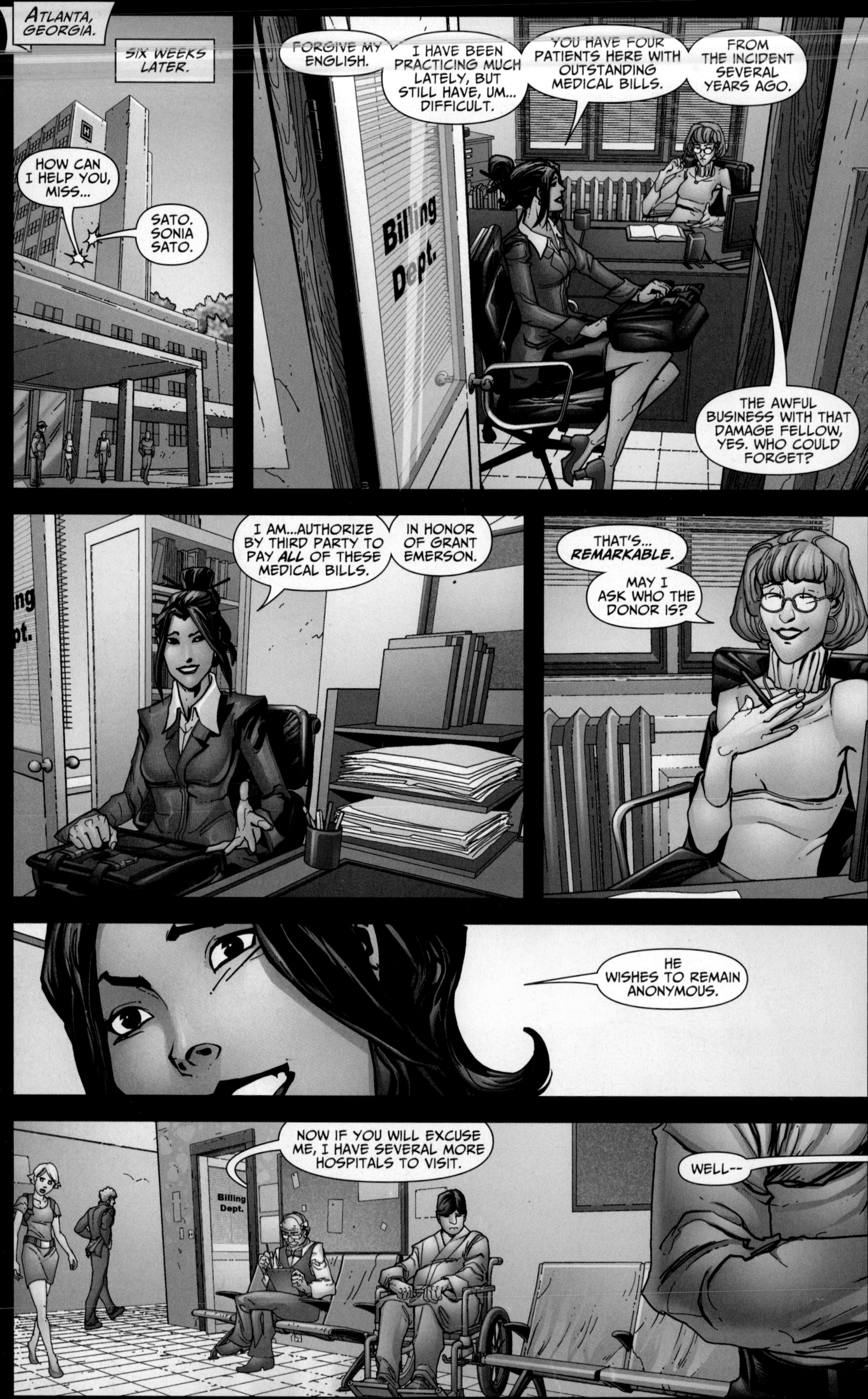
ATLANTA, GEORGIA.
SIX WEEKS LATER.
HOW CAN I HELP YOU, MISS...
SATO. SONIA SATO.
FORGIVE MY ENGLISH.
I HAVE BEEN PRACTICING MUCH LATELY, BUT STILL HAVE, UM... DIFFICULT.
YOU HAVE FOUR PATIENTS HERE WITH OUTSTANDING MEDICAL BILLS.
FROM THE INCIDENT SEVERAL YEARS AGO.
Billing Dept.
THE AWFUL BUSINESS WITH THAT DAMAGE FELLOW, YES. WHO COULD FORGET?
I AM...AUTHORIZE BY THIRD PARTY TO PAY ALL OF THESE MEDICAL BILLS.
IN HONOR OF GRANT EMERSON.
THAT'S... REMARKABLE.
MAY I ASK WHO THE DONOR IS?
HE WISHES TO REMAIN ANONYMOUS.
NOW IF YOU WILL EXCUSE ME, I HAVE SEVERAL MORE HOSPITALS TO VISIT.
Billing Dept.
WELL--

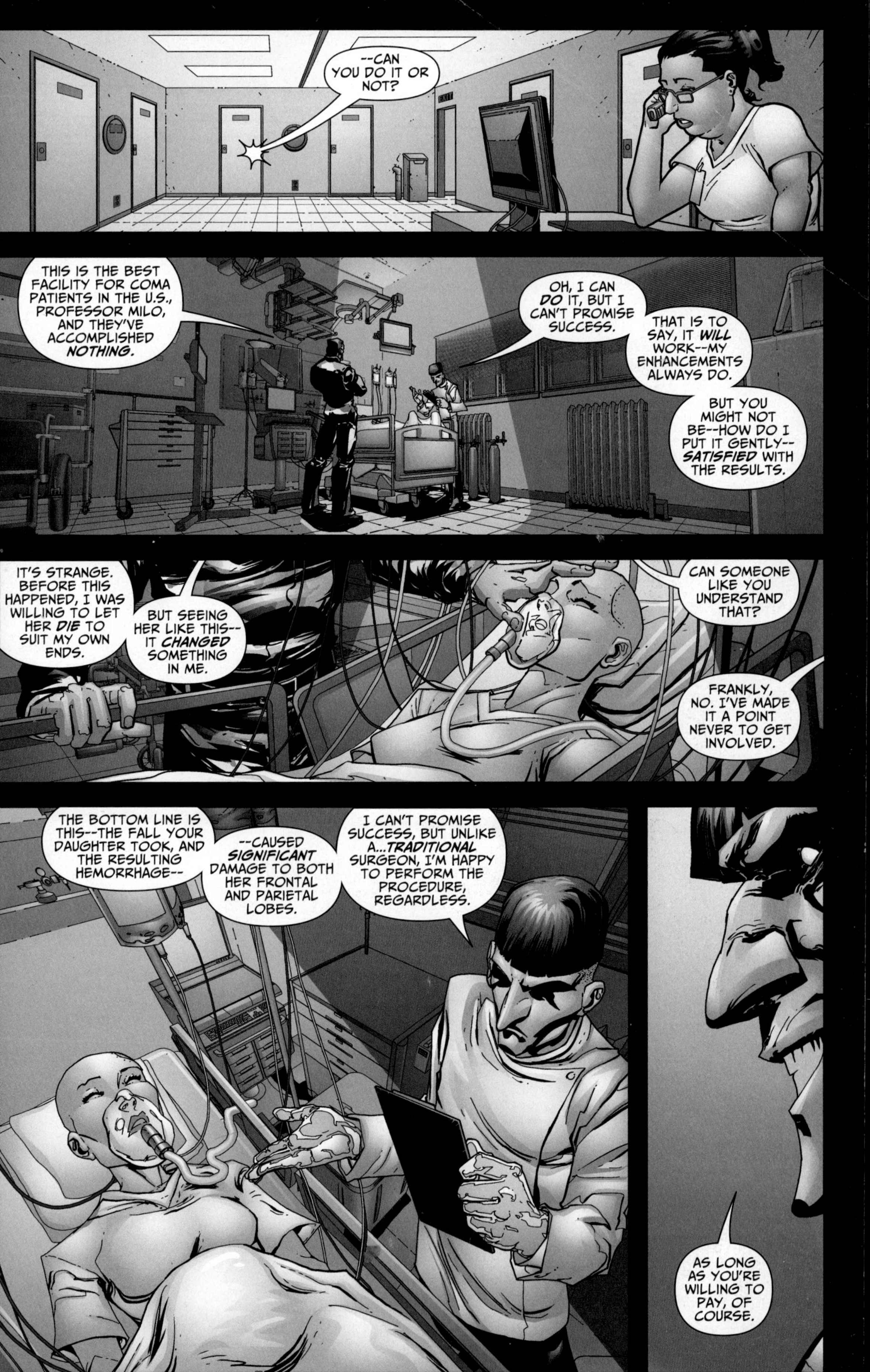
--CAN YOU DO IT OR NOT?
THIS IS THE BEST FACILITY FOR COMA PATIENTS IN THE U.S., PROFESSOR MILO, AND THEY'VE ACCOMPLISHED NOTHING.
OH, I CAN DO IT, BUT I CAN'T PROMISE SUCCESS.
THAT IS TO SAY, IT WILL WORK--MY ENHANCEMENTS ALWAYS DO.
BUT YOU MIGHT NOT BE--HOW DO I PUT IT GENTLY--SATISFIED WITH THE RESULTS.
IT'S STRANGE. BEFORE THIS HAPPENED, I WAS WILLING TO LET HER DIE TO SUIT MY OWN ENDS.
BUT SEEING HER LIKE THIS--IT CHANGED SOMETHING IN ME.
CAN SOMEONE LIKE YOU UNDERSTAND THAT?
FRANKLY, NO. I'VE MADE IT A POINT NEVER TO GET INVOLVED.
THE BOTTOM LINE IS THIS--THE FALL YOUR DAUGHTER TOOK, AND THE RESULTING HEMORRHAGE--
--CAUSED SIGNIFICANT DAMAGE TO BOTH HER FRONTAL AND PARIETAL LOBES.
I CAN'T PROMISE SUCCESS, BUT UNLIKE A...TRADITIONAL SURGEON, I'M HAPPY TO PERFORM THE PROCEDURE, REGARDLESS.
AS LONG AS YOU'RE WILLING TO PAY, OF COURSE.

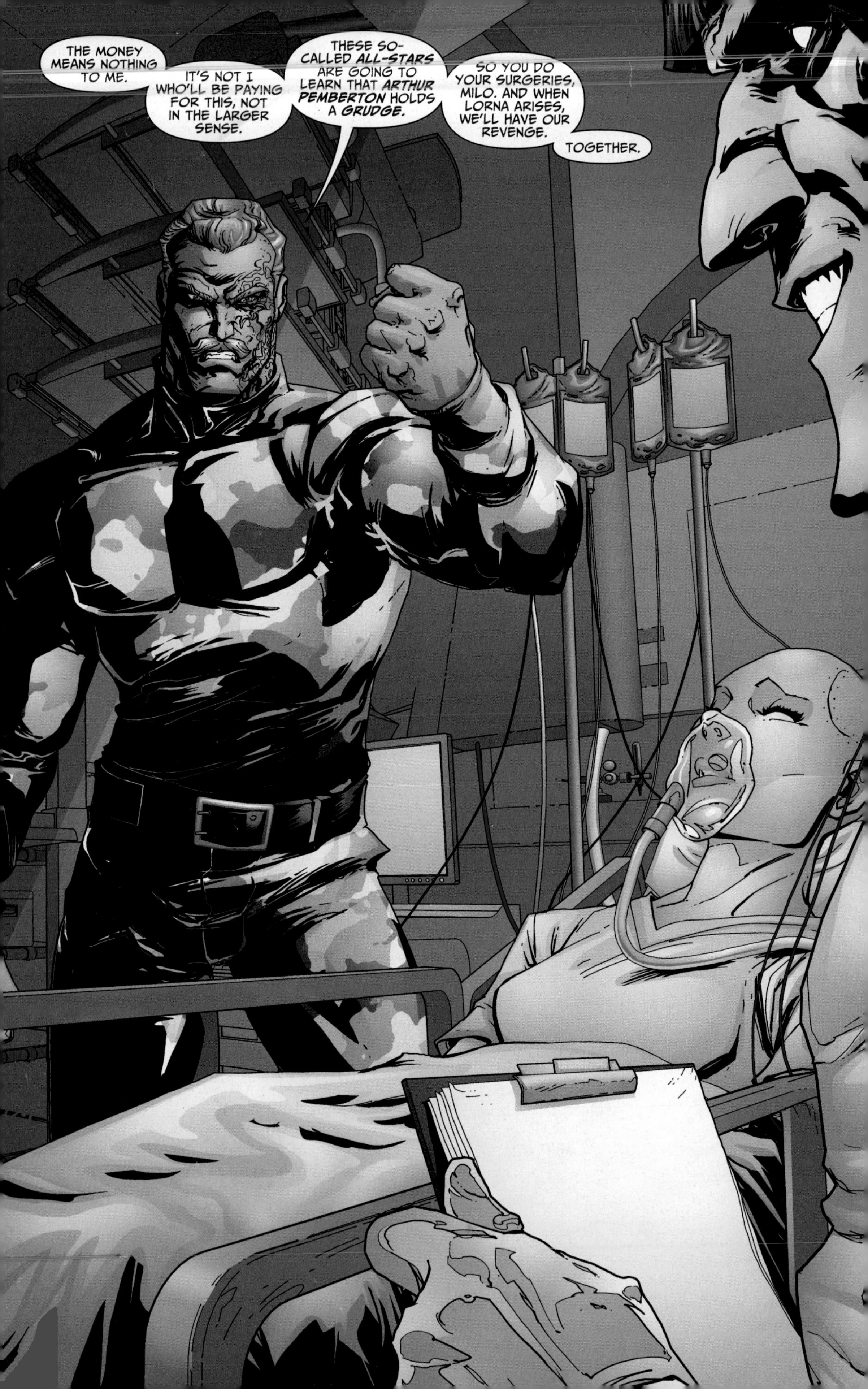
THE MONEY MEANS NOTHING TO ME.
IT'S NOT I WHO'LL BE PAYING FOR THIS, NOT IN THE LARGER SENSE.
THESE SO-CALLED ALL-STARS ARE GOING TO LEARN THAT ARTHUR PEMBERTON HOLDS A GRUDGE.
SO YOU DO YOUR SURGERIES, MILO. AND WHEN LORNA ARISES, WE'LL HAVE OUR REVENGE.
TOGETHER.

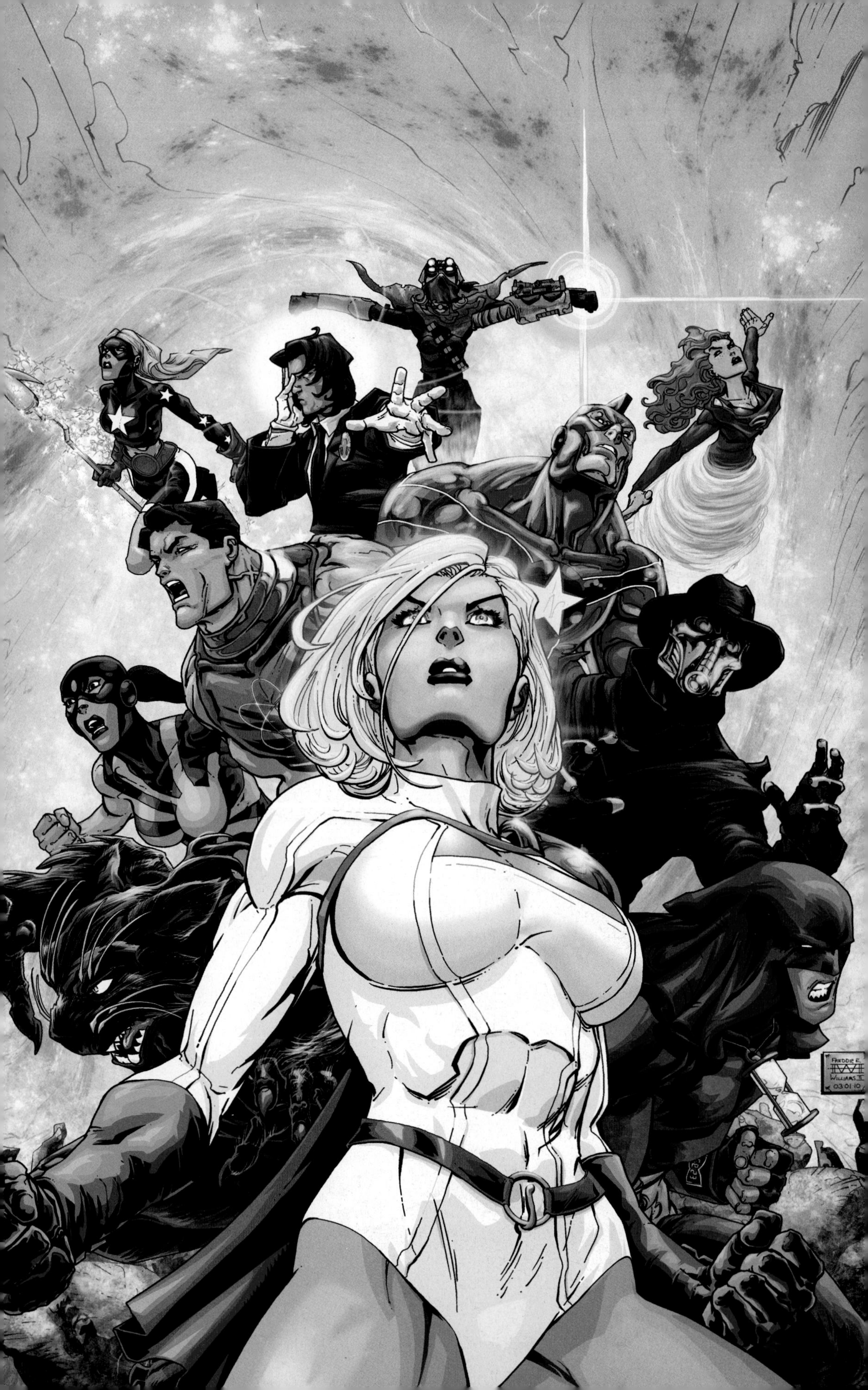
FREDDIE E.
WILLIAMS II
03.01.10

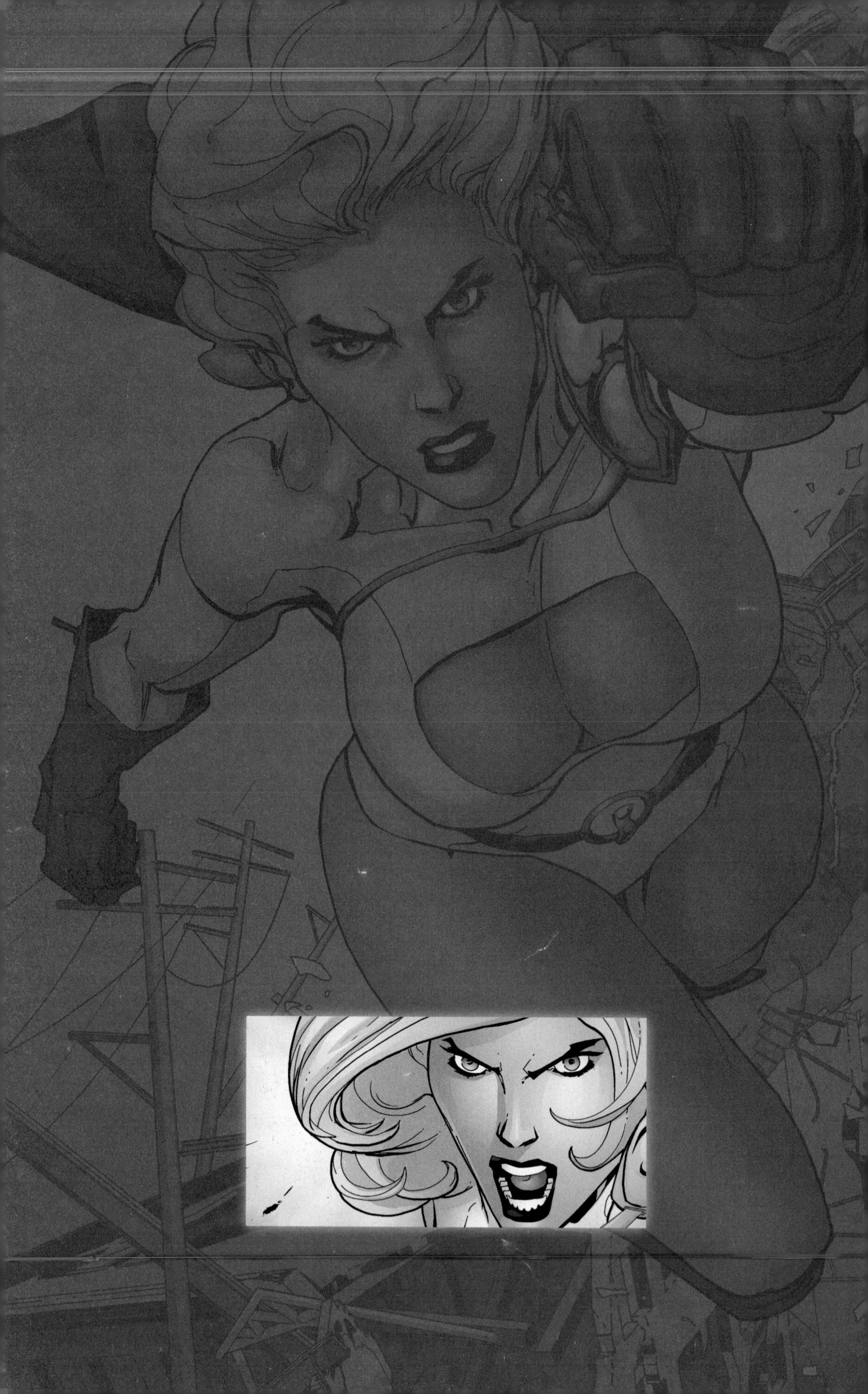

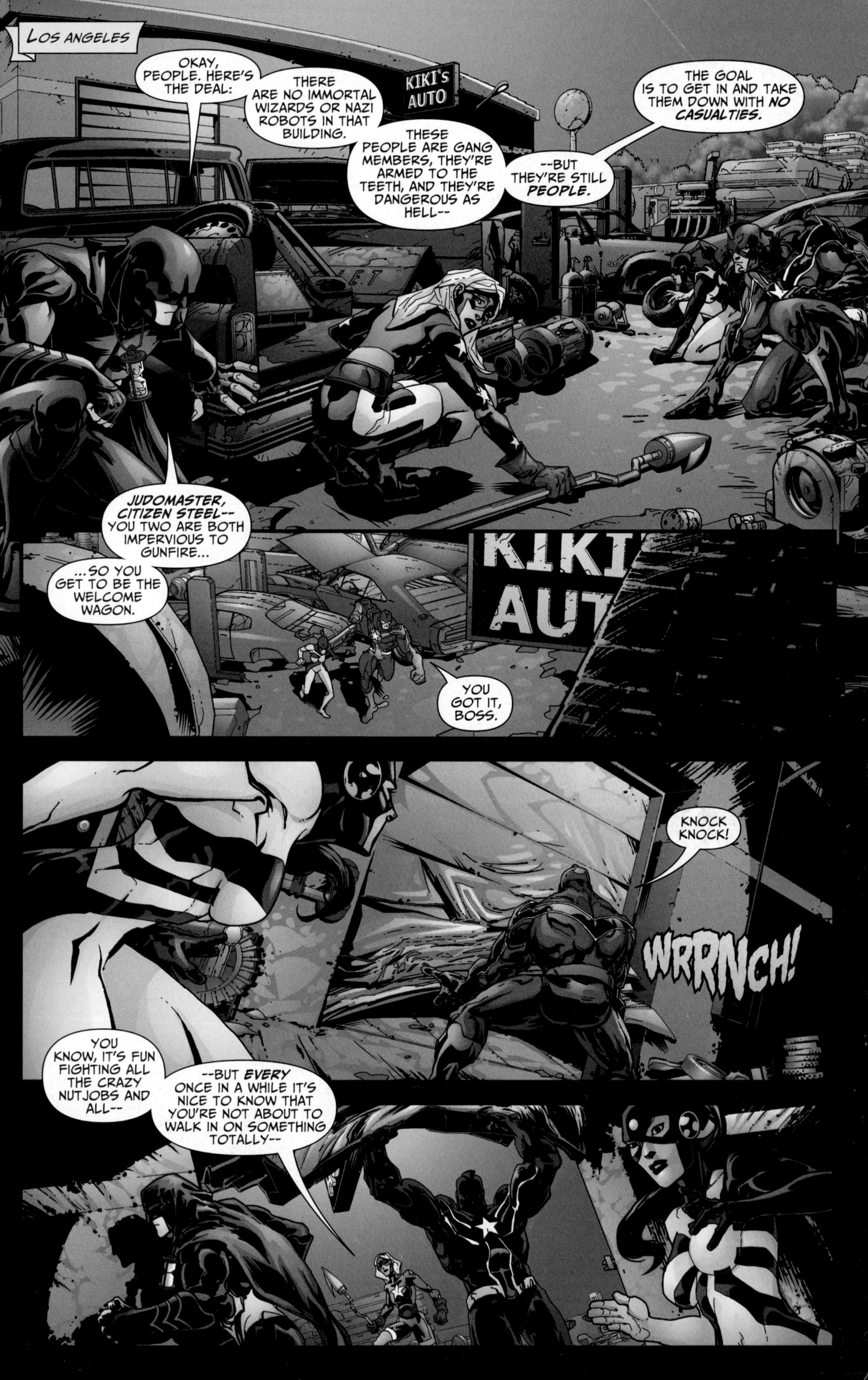

LOS ANGELES
OKAY, PEOPLE. HERE'S THE DEAL:
THERE ARE NO IMMORTAL WIZARDS OR NAZI ROBOTS IN THAT BUILDING.
KIKI's AUTO
THESE PEOPLE ARE GANG MEMBERS, THEY'RE ARMED TO THE TEETH, AND THEY'RE DANGEROUS AS HELL--
--BUT THEY'RE STILL *PEOPLE.*
THE GOAL IS TO GET IN AND TAKE THEM DOWN WITH *NO CASUALTIES.*
JUDOMASTER, CITIZEN STEEL-- YOU TWO ARE BOTH IMPERVIOUS TO GUNFIRE...
...SO YOU GET TO BE THE WELCOME WAGON.
KIKI AUT
YOU GOT IT, BOSS.
KNOCK KNOCK!
WRRNCH!
YOU KNOW, IT'S FUN FIGHTING ALL THE CRAZY NUTJOBS AND ALL--
--BUT *EVERY* ONCE IN A WHILE IT'S NICE TO KNOW THAT YOU'RE NOT ABOUT TO WALK IN ON SOMETHING TOTALLY--

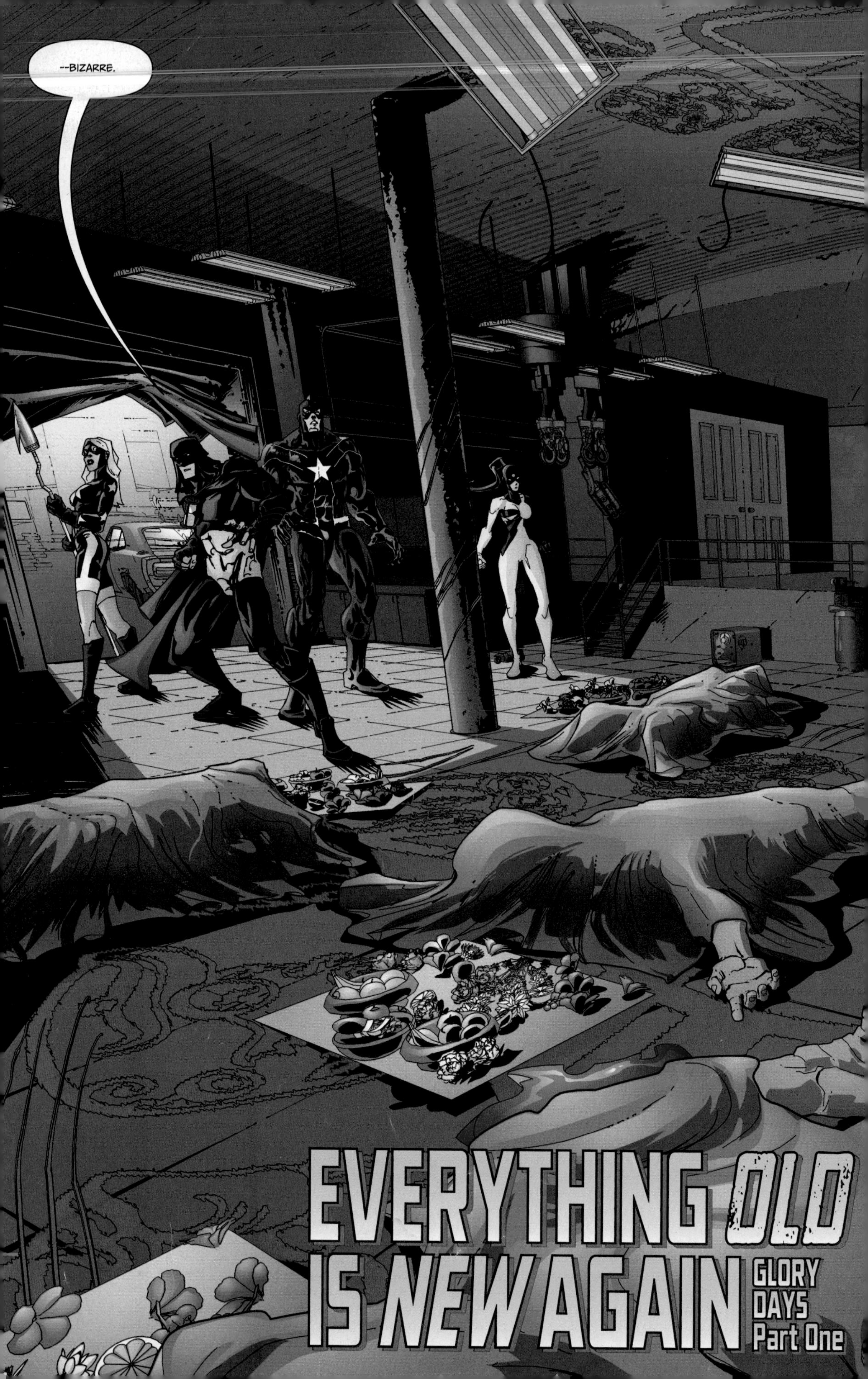
--BIZARRE.
EVERYTHING OLD IS NEW AGAIN
GLORY DAYS Part One

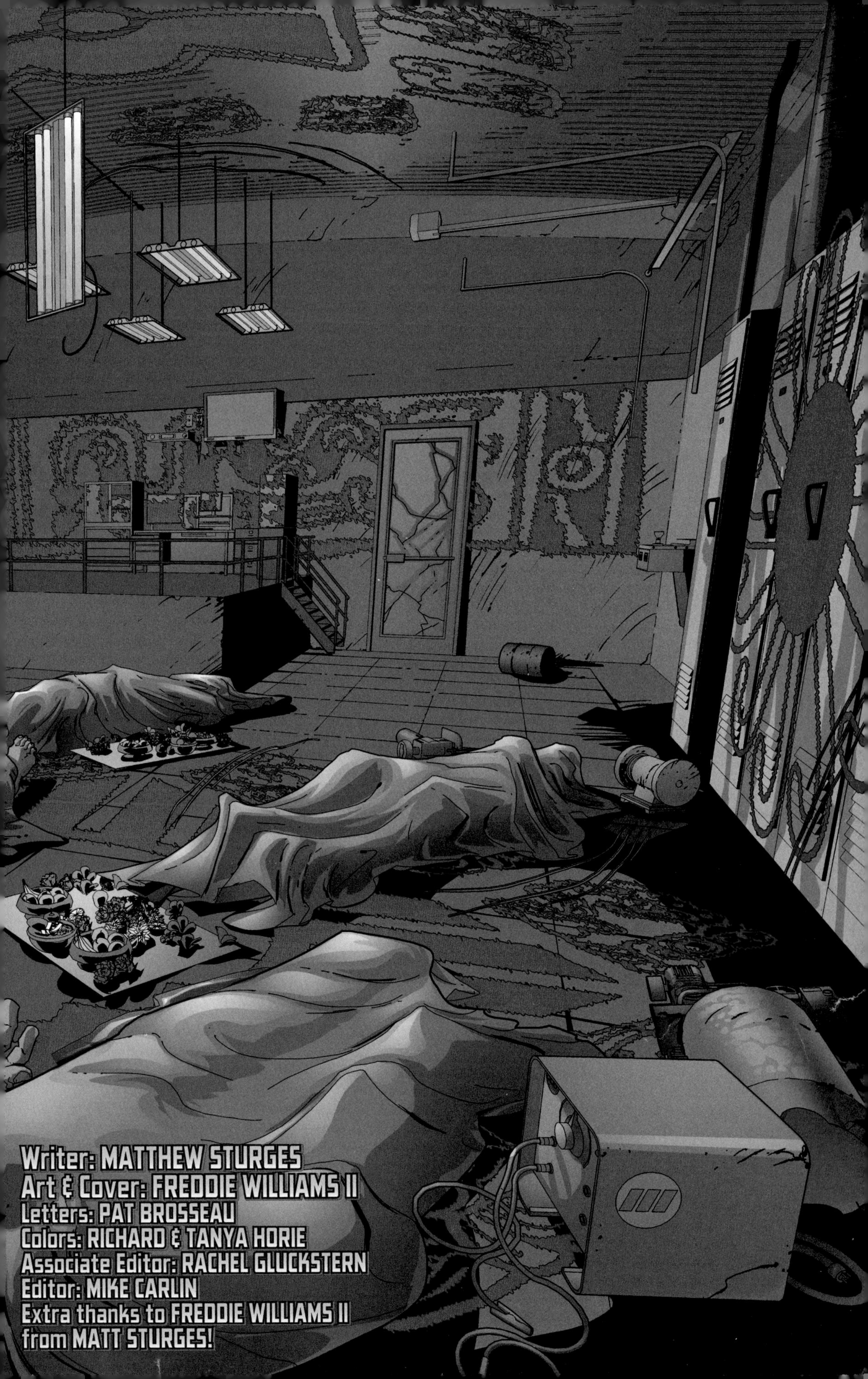
Writer: MATTHEW STURGES
Art & Cover: FREDDIE WILLIAMS II
Letters: PAT BROSSEAU
Colors: RICHARD & TANYA HORIE
Associate Editor: RACHEL GLUCKSTERN
Editor: MIKE CARLIN
Extra thanks to FREDDIE WILLIAMS II
from MATT STURGES!

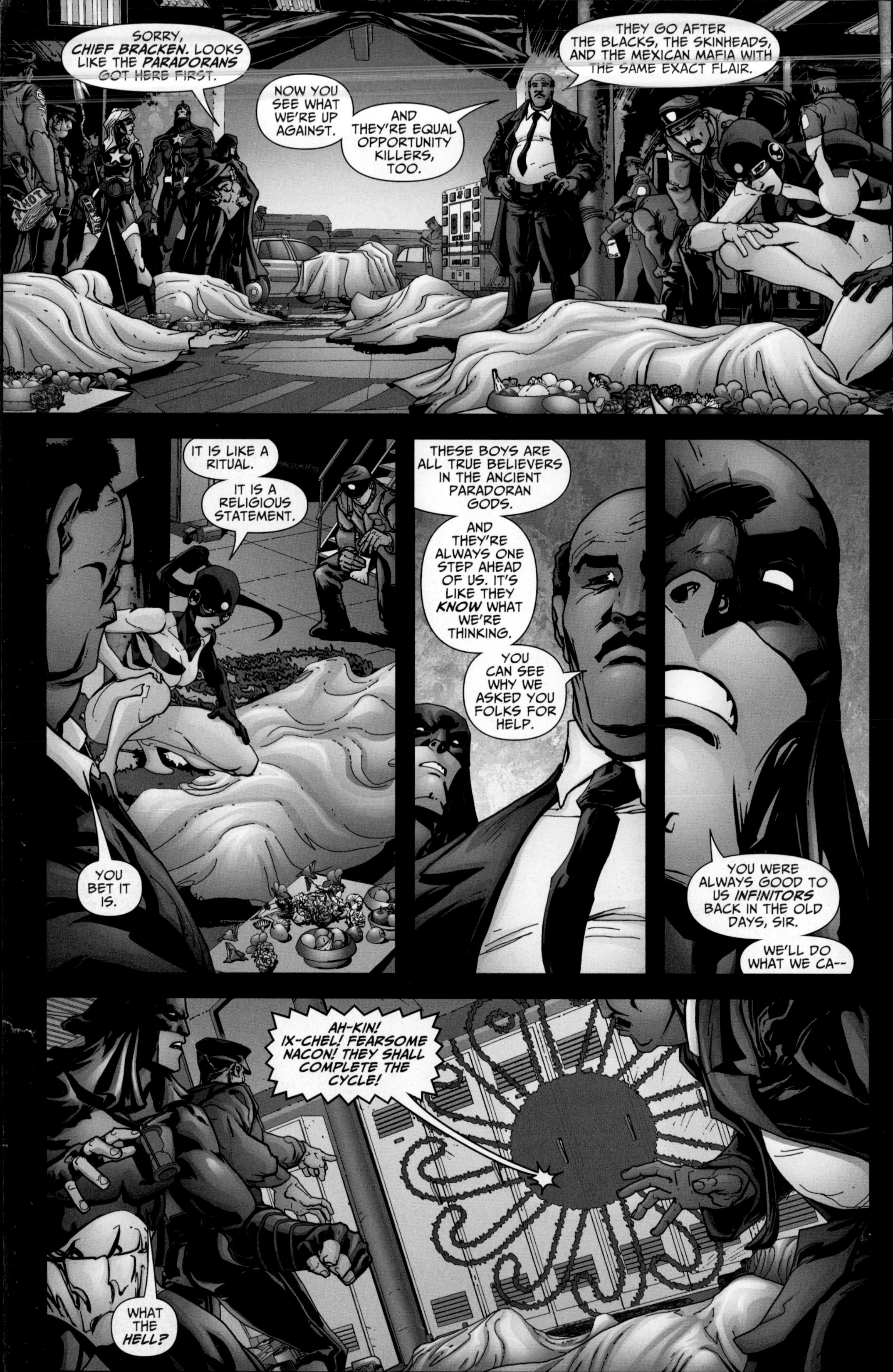
SORRY, CHIEF BRACKEN. LOOKS LIKE THE PARADORANS GOT HERE FIRST.
NOW YOU SEE WHAT WE'RE UP AGAINST.
AND THEY'RE EQUAL OPPORTUNITY KILLERS, TOO.
THEY GO AFTER THE BLACKS, THE SKINHEADS, AND THE MEXICAN MAFIA WITH THE SAME EXACT FLAIR.
IT IS LIKE A RITUAL.
IT IS A RELIGIOUS STATEMENT.
YOU BET IT IS.
THESE BOYS ARE ALL TRUE BELIEVERS IN THE ANCIENT PARADORAN GODS.
AND THEY'RE ALWAYS ONE STEP AHEAD OF US. IT'S LIKE THEY KNOW WHAT WE'RE THINKING.
YOU CAN SEE WHY WE ASKED YOU FOLKS FOR HELP.
YOU WERE ALWAYS GOOD TO US INFINITORS BACK IN THE OLD DAYS, SIR.
WE'LL DO WHAT WE CA--
AH-KIN! IX-CHEL! FEARSOME NACON! THEY SHALL COMPLETE THE CYCLE!
WHAT THE HELL?

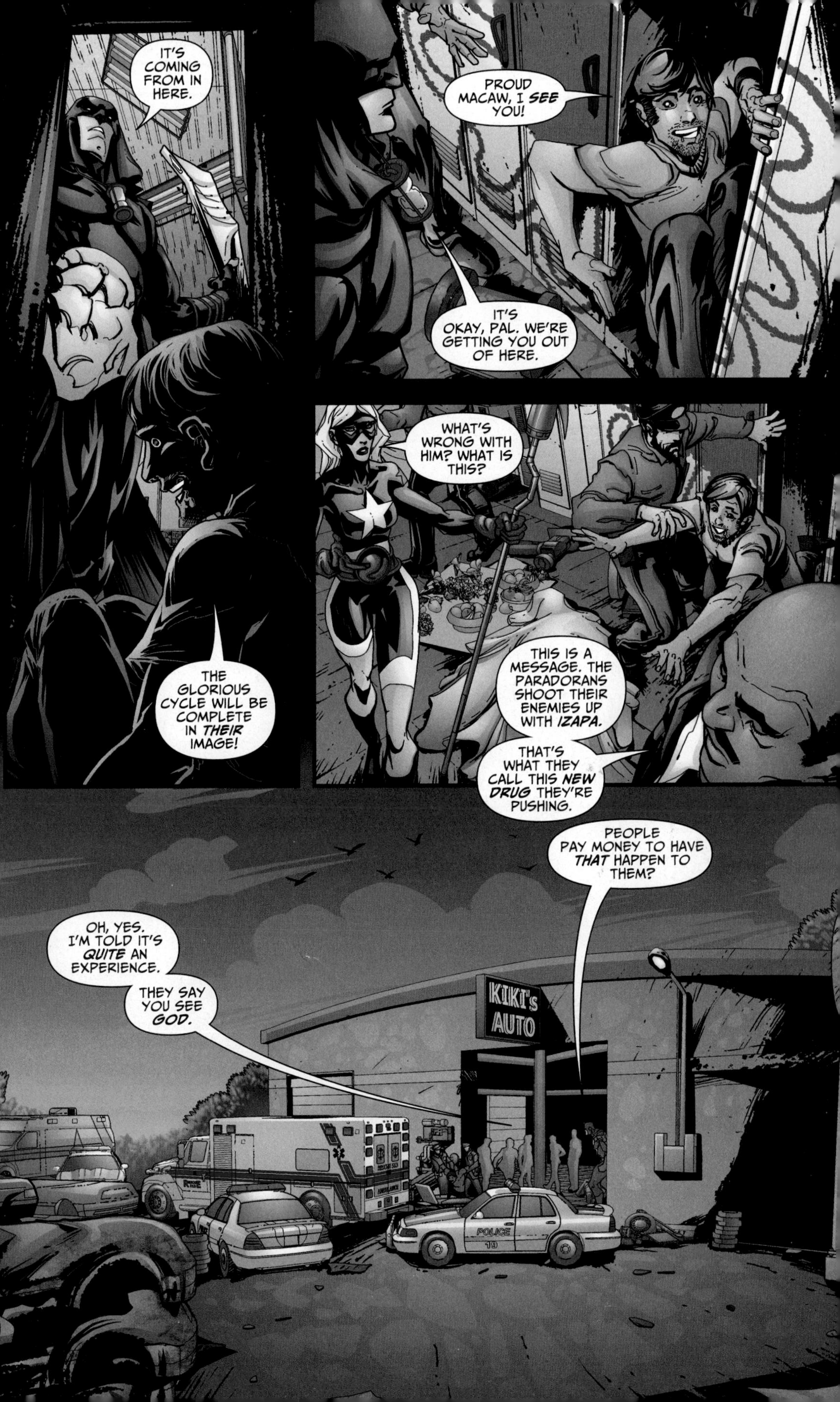

IT'S COMING FROM IN HERE.
PROUD MACAW, I *SEE* YOU!
IT'S OKAY, PAL. WE'RE GETTING YOU OUT OF HERE.
THE GLORIOUS CYCLE WILL BE COMPLETE IN *THEIR* IMAGE!
WHAT'S WRONG WITH HIM? WHAT IS THIS?
THIS IS A MESSAGE. THE PARADORANS SHOOT THEIR ENEMIES UP WITH *IZAPA.*
THAT'S WHAT THEY CALL THIS *NEW DRUG* THEY'RE PUSHING.
PEOPLE PAY MONEY TO HAVE *THAT* HAPPEN TO THEM?
OH, YES. I'M TOLD IT'S *QUITE* AN EXPERIENCE.
THEY SAY YOU SEE *GOD.*
KIKI's AUTO
POLICE

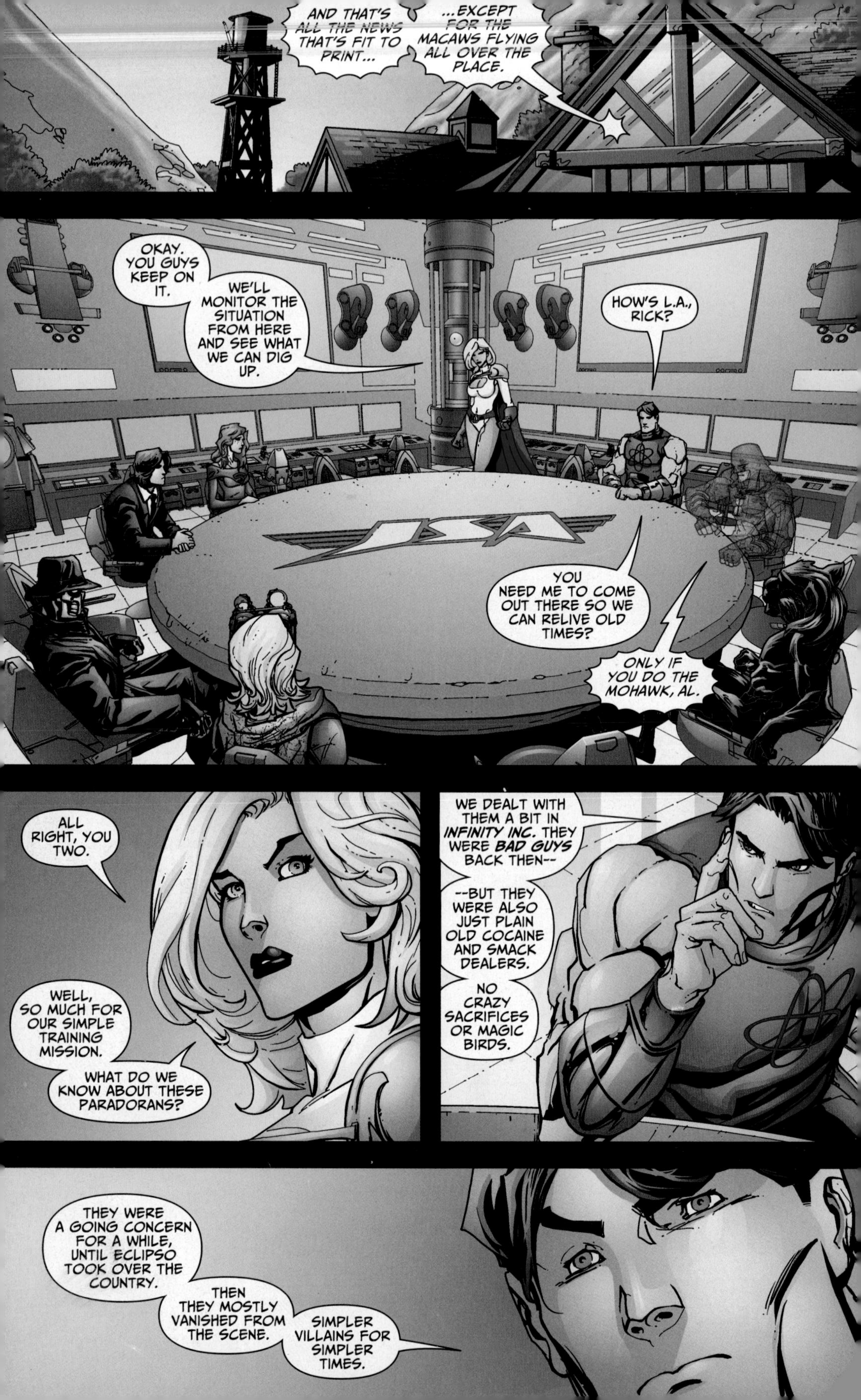
AND THAT'S ALL THE NEWS THAT'S FIT TO PRINT...
...EXCEPT FOR THE MACAWS FLYING ALL OVER THE PLACE.
OKAY. YOU GUYS KEEP ON IT.
WE'LL MONITOR THE SITUATION FROM HERE AND SEE WHAT WE CAN DIG UP.
HOW'S L.A., RICK?
YOU NEED ME TO COME OUT THERE SO WE CAN RELIVE OLD TIMES?
ONLY IF YOU DO THE MOHAWK, AL.
ALL RIGHT, YOU TWO.
WELL, SO MUCH FOR OUR SIMPLE TRAINING MISSION.
WHAT DO WE KNOW ABOUT THESE PARADORANS?
WE DEALT WITH THEM A BIT IN *INFINITY INC.* THEY WERE *BAD GUYS* BACK THEN--
--BUT THEY WERE ALSO JUST PLAIN OLD COCAINE AND SMACK DEALERS.
NO CRAZY SACRIFICES OR MAGIC BIRDS.
THEY WERE A GOING CONCERN FOR A WHILE, UNTIL ECLIPSO TOOK OVER THE COUNTRY.
THEN THEY MOSTLY VANISHED FROM THE SCENE.
SIMPLER VILLAINS FOR SIMPLER TIMES.

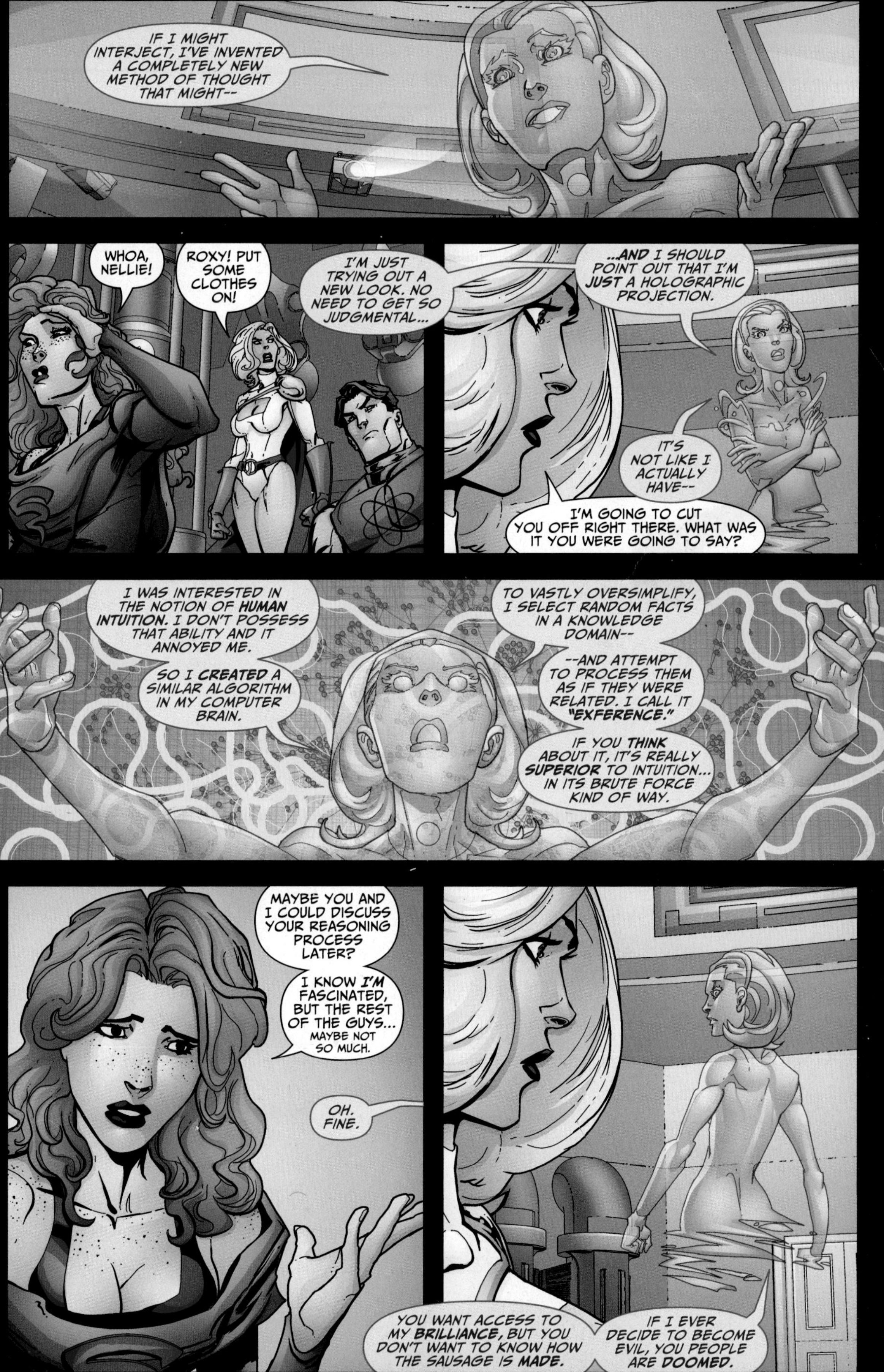
IF I MIGHT INTERJECT, I'VE INVENTED A COMPLETELY NEW METHOD OF THOUGHT THAT MIGHT--
WHOA, NELLIE!
ROXY! PUT SOME CLOTHES ON!
I'M JUST TRYING OUT A NEW LOOK. NO NEED TO GET SO JUDGMENTAL...
...AND I SHOULD POINT OUT THAT I'M JUST A HOLOGRAPHIC PROJECTION.
IT'S NOT LIKE I ACTUALLY HAVE--
I'M GOING TO CUT YOU OFF RIGHT THERE. WHAT WAS IT YOU WERE GOING TO SAY?
I WAS INTERESTED IN THE NOTION OF HUMAN INTUITION. I DON'T POSSESS THAT ABILITY AND IT ANNOYED ME.
SO I CREATED A SIMILAR ALGORITHM IN MY COMPUTER BRAIN.
TO VASTLY OVERSIMPLIFY, I SELECT RANDOM FACTS IN A KNOWLEDGE DOMAIN--
--AND ATTEMPT TO PROCESS THEM AS IF THEY WERE RELATED. I CALL IT "EXFERENCE."
IF YOU THINK ABOUT IT, IT'S REALLY SUPERIOR TO INTUITION... IN ITS BRUTE FORCE KIND OF WAY.
MAYBE YOU AND I COULD DISCUSS YOUR REASONING PROCESS LATER?
I KNOW I'M FASCINATED, BUT THE REST OF THE GUYS... MAYBE NOT SO MUCH.
OH. FINE.
YOU WANT ACCESS TO MY BRILLIANCE, BUT YOU DON'T WANT TO KNOW HOW THE SAUSAGE IS MADE.
IF I EVER DECIDE TO BECOME EVIL, YOU PEOPLE ARE DOOMED.

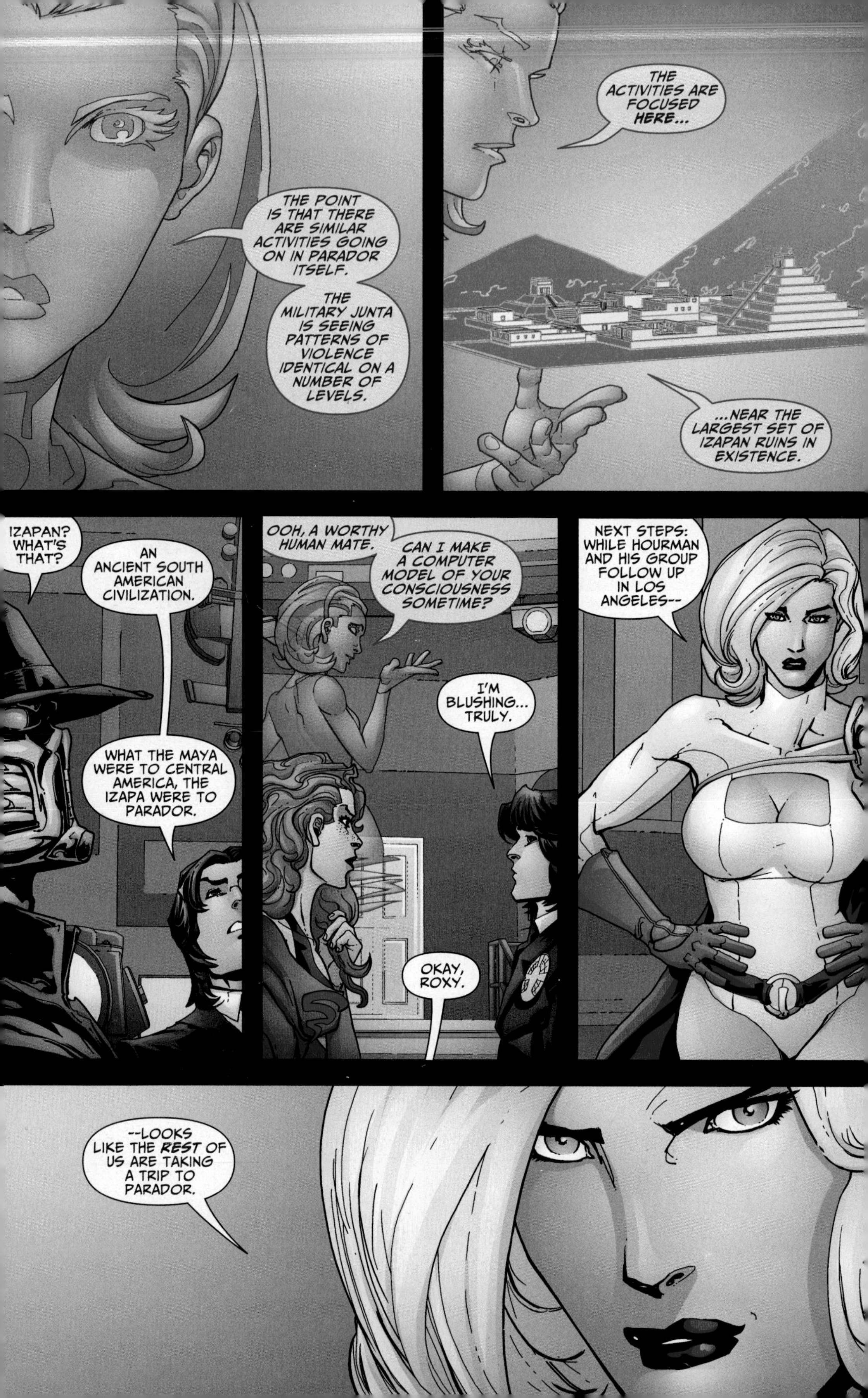
THE POINT IS THAT THERE ARE SIMILAR ACTIVITIES GOING ON IN PARADOR ITSELF.
THE MILITARY JUNTA IS SEEING PATTERNS OF VIOLENCE IDENTICAL ON A NUMBER OF LEVELS.
THE ACTIVITIES ARE FOCUSED HERE...
...NEAR THE LARGEST SET OF IZAPAN RUINS IN EXISTENCE.
IZAPAN? WHAT'S THAT?
AN ANCIENT SOUTH AMERICAN CIVILIZATION.
WHAT THE MAYA WERE TO CENTRAL AMERICA, THE IZAPA WERE TO PARADOR.
OOH, A WORTHY HUMAN MATE.
CAN I MAKE A COMPUTER MODEL OF YOUR CONSCIOUSNESS SOMETIME?
I'M BLUSHING... TRULY.
OKAY, ROXY.
NEXT STEPS: WHILE HOURMAN AND HIS GROUP FOLLOW UP IN LOS ANGELES--
--LOOKS LIKE THE REST OF US ARE TAKING A TRIP TO PARADOR.

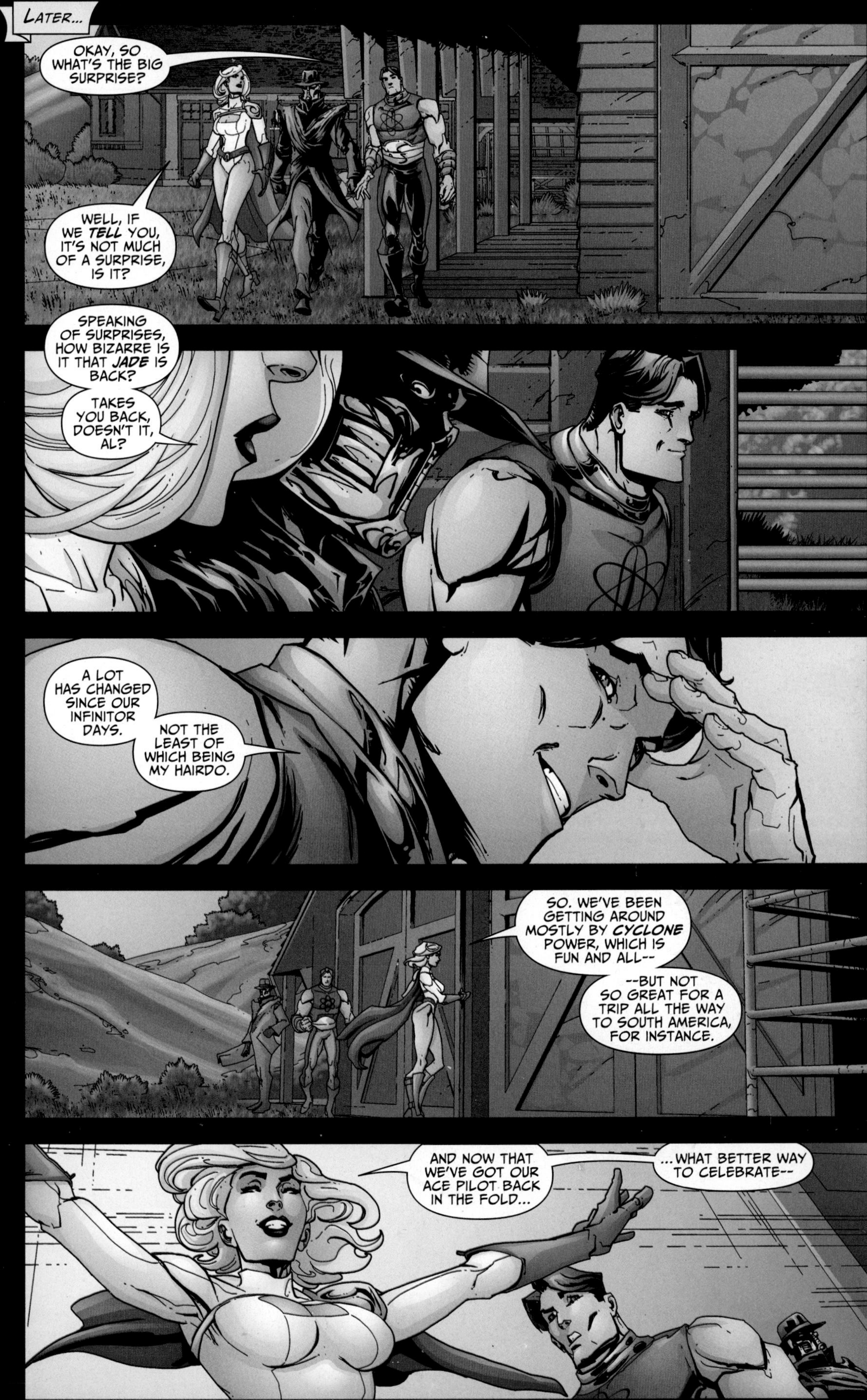
LATER...
OKAY, SO WHAT'S THE BIG SURPRISE?
WELL, IF WE TELL YOU, IT'S NOT MUCH OF A SURPRISE, IS IT?
SPEAKING OF SURPRISES, HOW BIZARRE IS IT THAT JADE IS BACK?
TAKES YOU BACK, DOESN'T IT, AL?
A LOT HAS CHANGED SINCE OUR INFINITOR DAYS.
NOT THE LEAST OF WHICH BEING MY HAIRDO.
SO. WE'VE BEEN GETTING AROUND MOSTLY BY CYCLONE POWER, WHICH IS FUN AND ALL--
--BUT NOT SO GREAT FOR A TRIP ALL THE WAY TO SOUTH AMERICA, FOR INSTANCE.
AND NOW THAT WE'VE GOT OUR ACE PILOT BACK IN THE FOLD...
...WHAT BETTER WAY TO CELEBRATE--

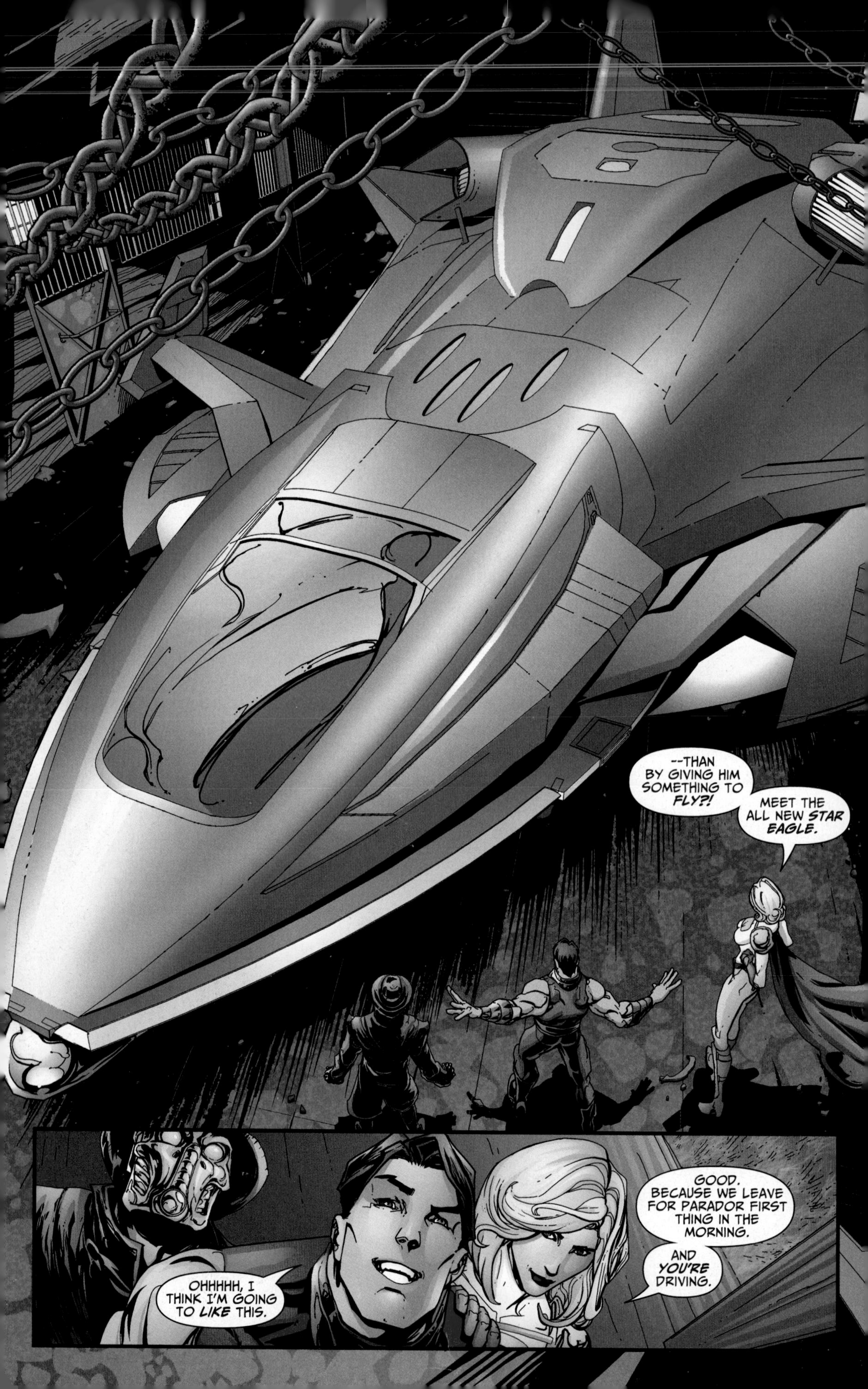
--THAN BY GIVING HIM SOMETHING TO FLY?!
MEET THE ALL NEW STAR EAGLE.
GOOD. BECAUSE WE LEAVE FOR PARADOR FIRST THING IN THE MORNING.
AND YOU'RE DRIVING.
OHHHHH, I THINK I'M GOING TO LIKE THIS.

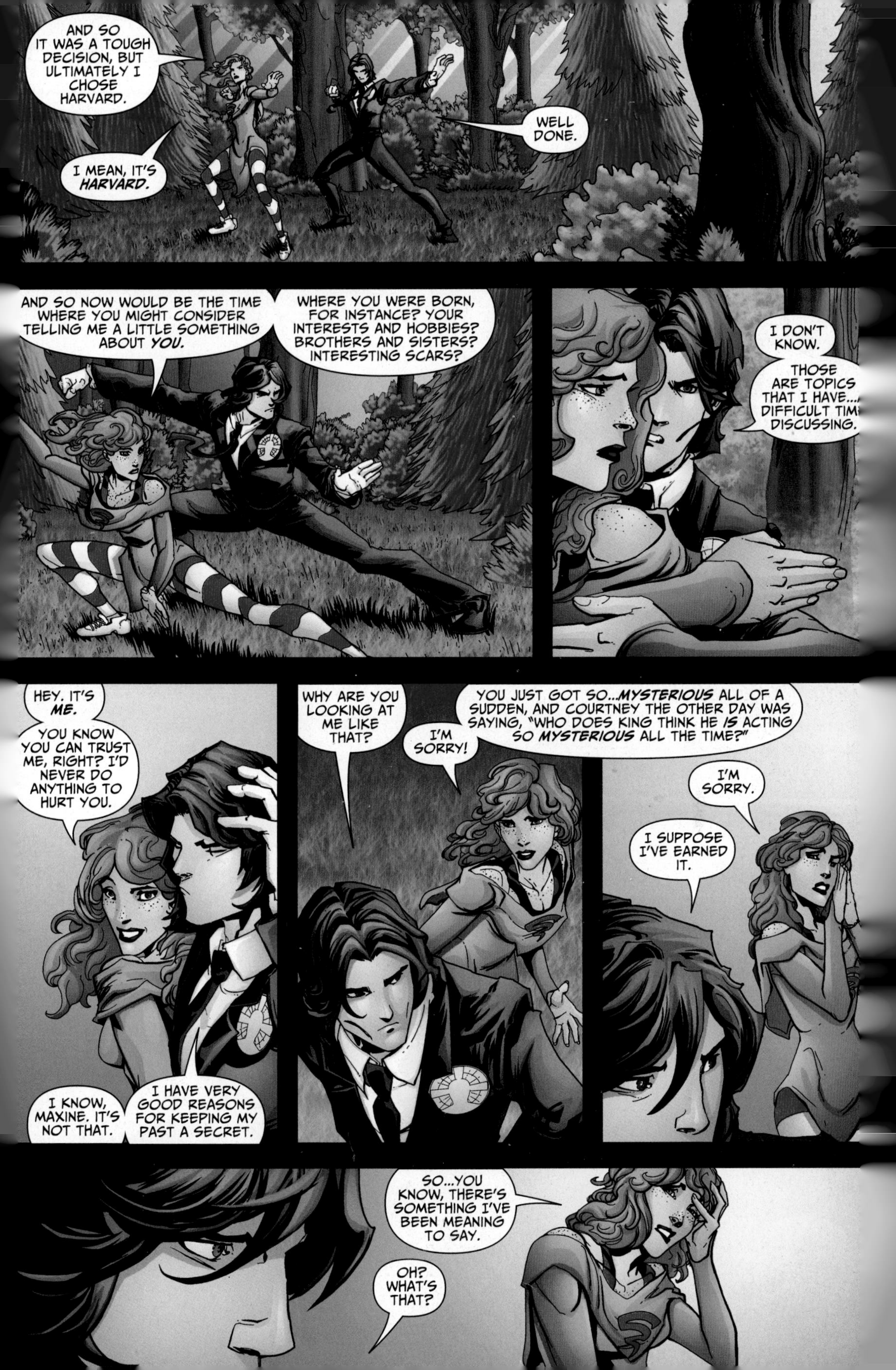
AND SO IT WAS A TOUGH DECISION, BUT ULTIMATELY I CHOSE HARVARD.
I MEAN, IT'S *HARVARD.*
WELL DONE.
AND SO NOW WOULD BE THE TIME WHERE YOU MIGHT CONSIDER TELLING ME A LITTLE SOMETHING ABOUT *YOU.*
WHERE YOU WERE BORN, FOR INSTANCE? YOUR INTERESTS AND HOBBIES? BROTHERS AND SISTERS? INTERESTING SCARS?
I DON'T KNOW.
THOSE ARE TOPICS THAT I HAVE... DIFFICULT TIM DISCUSSING.
HEY. IT'S *ME.*
YOU KNOW YOU CAN TRUST ME, RIGHT? I'D NEVER DO ANYTHING TO HURT YOU.
I KNOW, MAXINE. IT'S NOT THAT.
I HAVE VERY GOOD REASONS FOR KEEPING MY PAST A SECRET.
WHY ARE YOU LOOKING AT ME LIKE THAT?
I'M SORRY!
YOU JUST GOT SO...*MYSTERIOUS* ALL OF A SUDDEN, AND COURTNEY THE OTHER DAY WAS SAYING, "WHO DOES KING THINK HE *IS* ACTING SO *MYSTERIOUS* ALL THE TIME?"
I'M SORRY.
I SUPPOSE I'VE EARNED IT.
SO...YOU KNOW, THERE'S SOMETHING I'VE BEEN MEANING TO SAY.
OH? WHAT'S THAT?

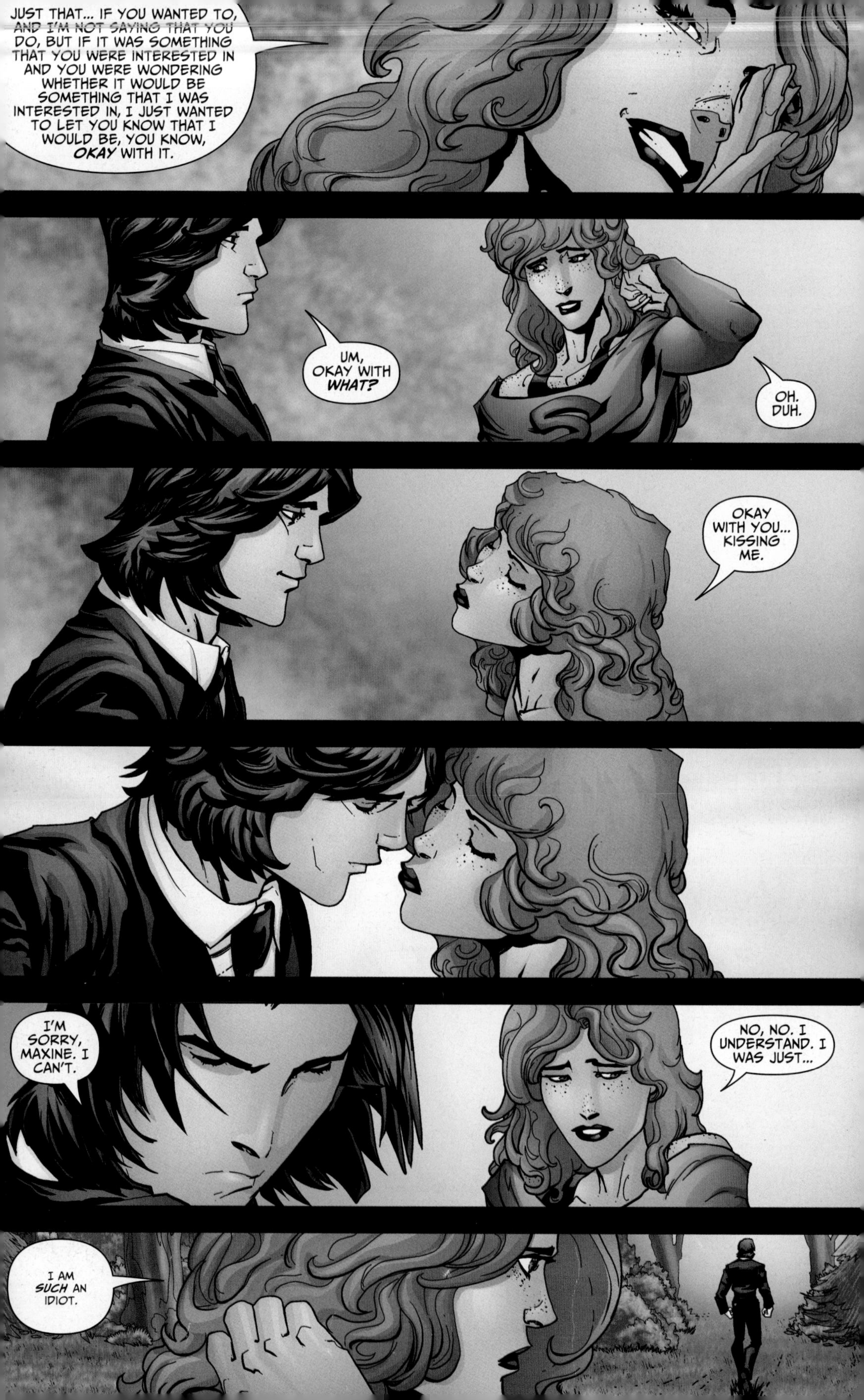
JUST THAT... IF YOU WANTED TO, AND I'M NOT SAYING THAT YOU DO, BUT IF IT WAS SOMETHING THAT YOU WERE INTERESTED IN AND YOU WERE WONDERING WHETHER IT WOULD BE SOMETHING THAT I WAS INTERESTED IN, I JUST WANTED TO LET YOU KNOW THAT I WOULD BE, YOU KNOW, OKAY WITH IT.
UM, OKAY WITH WHAT?
OH. DUH.
OKAY WITH YOU... KISSING ME.
I'M SORRY, MAXINE. I CAN'T.
NO, NO. I UNDERSTAND. I WAS JUST...
I AM SUCH AN IDIOT.

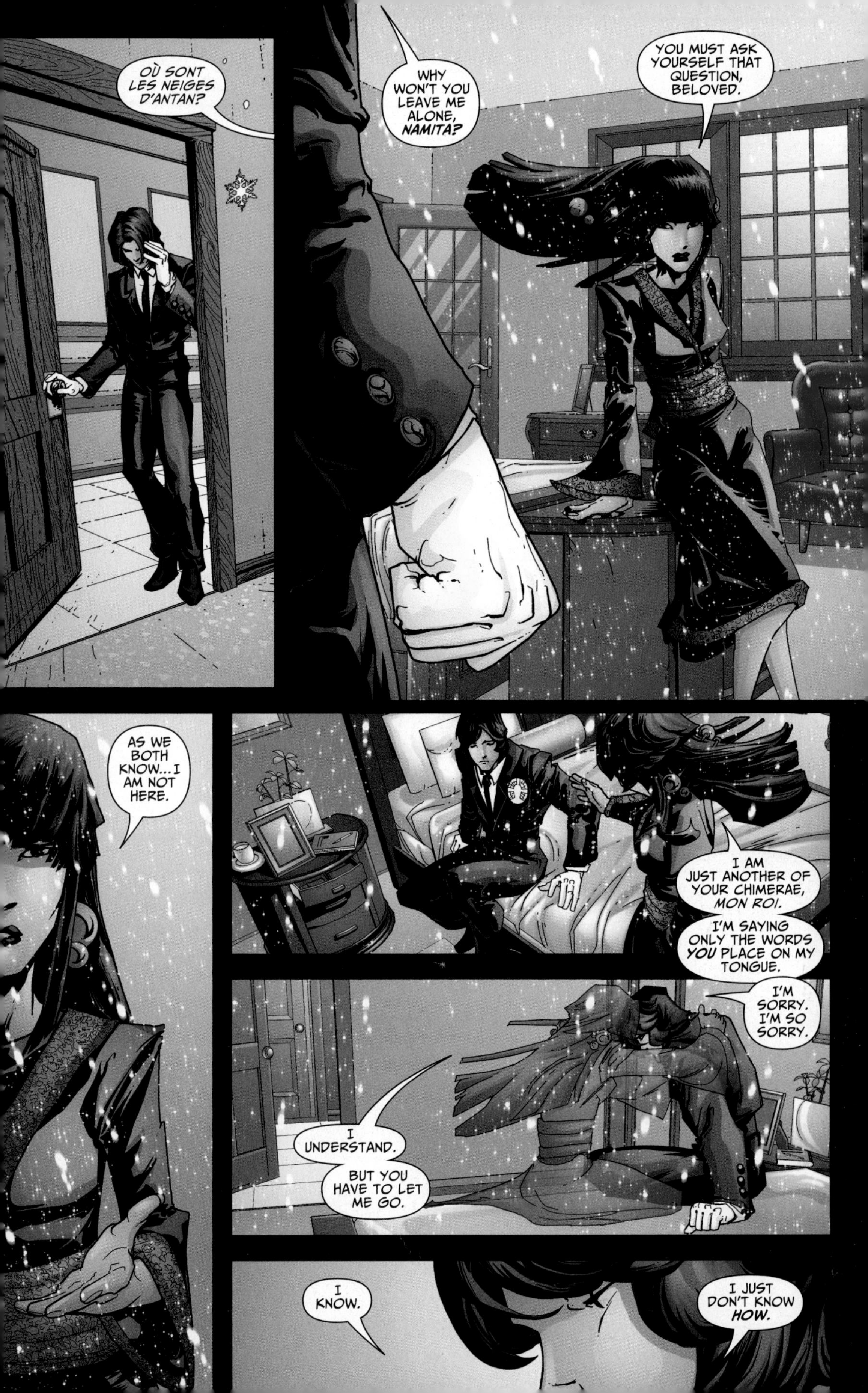
OÙ SONT LES NEIGES D'ANTAN?
WHY WON'T YOU LEAVE ME ALONE, NAMITA?
YOU MUST ASK YOURSELF THAT QUESTION, BELOVED.
AS WE BOTH KNOW... I AM NOT HERE.
I AM JUST ANOTHER OF YOUR CHIMERAE, MON ROI.
I'M SAYING ONLY THE WORDS YOU PLACE ON MY TONGUE.
I'M SORRY. I'M SO SORRY.
I UNDERSTAND.
BUT YOU HAVE TO LET ME GO.
I KNOW.
I JUST DON'T KNOW HOW.

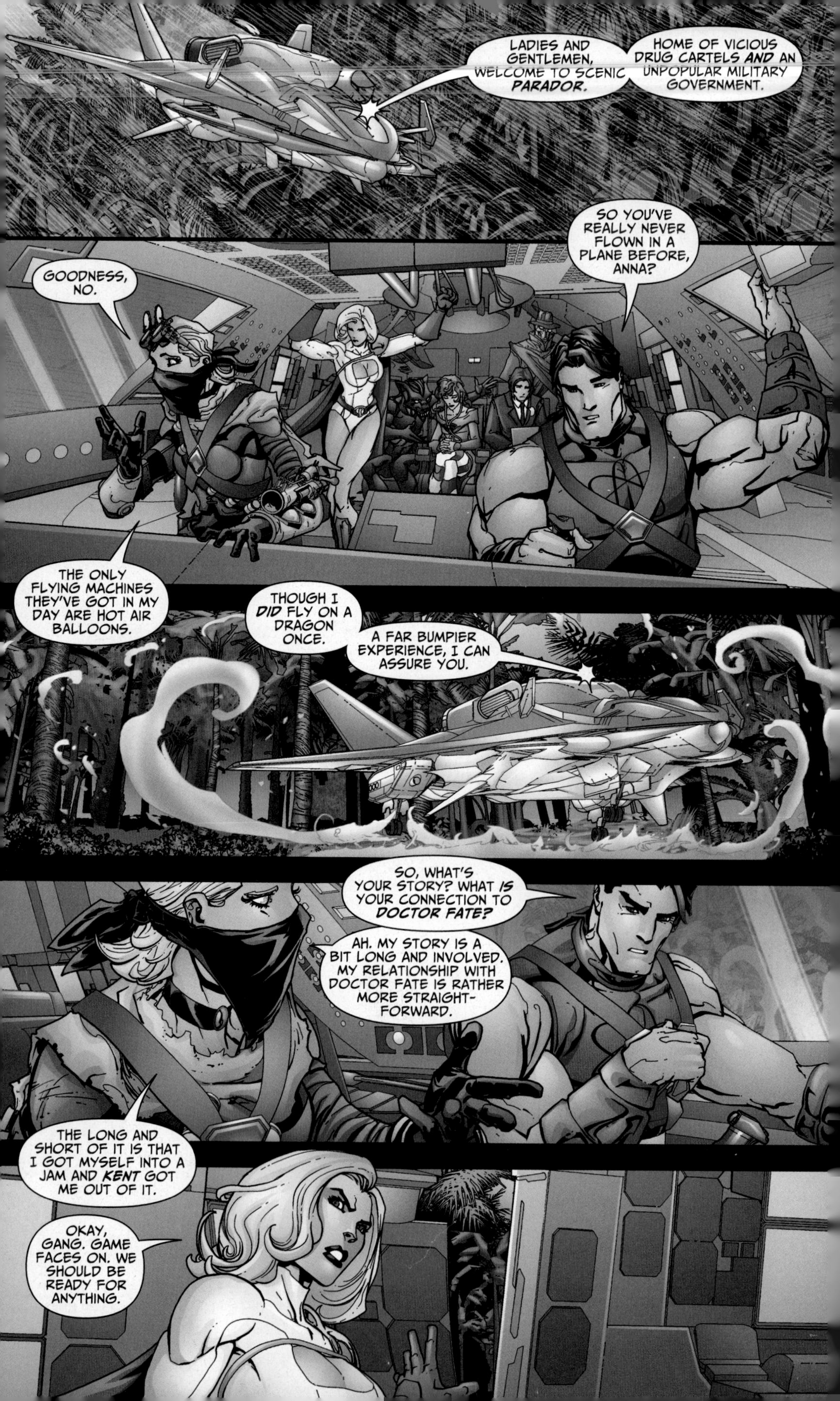
LADIES AND GENTLEMEN, WELCOME TO SCENIC PARADOR.
HOME OF VICIOUS DRUG CARTELS AND AN UNPOPULAR MILITARY GOVERNMENT.
SO YOU'VE REALLY NEVER FLOWN IN A PLANE BEFORE, ANNA?
GOODNESS, NO.
THE ONLY FLYING MACHINES THEY'VE GOT IN MY DAY ARE HOT AIR BALLOONS.
THOUGH I DID FLY ON A DRAGON ONCE.
A FAR BUMPIER EXPERIENCE, I CAN ASSURE YOU.
SO, WHAT'S YOUR STORY? WHAT IS YOUR CONNECTION TO DOCTOR FATE?
AH. MY STORY IS A BIT LONG AND INVOLVED. MY RELATIONSHIP WITH DOCTOR FATE IS RATHER MORE STRAIGHT-FORWARD.
THE LONG AND SHORT OF IT IS THAT I GOT MYSELF INTO A JAM AND KENT GOT ME OUT OF IT.
OKAY, GANG. GAME FACES ON. WE SHOULD BE READY FOR ANYTHING.

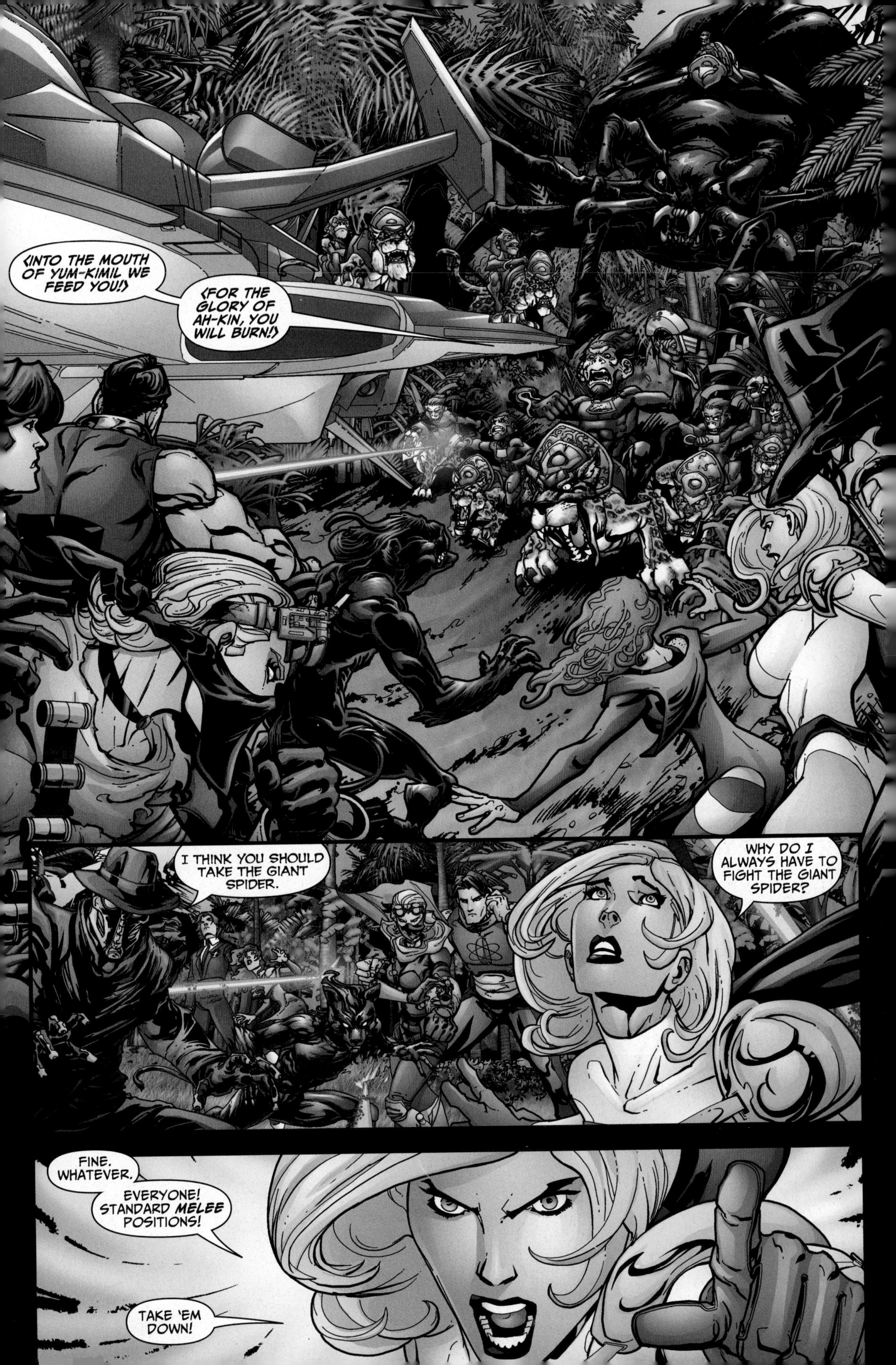
<INTO THE MOUTH OF YUM-KIMIL WE FEED YOU!>
<FOR THE GLORY OF AH-KIN, YOU WILL BURN!>
I THINK YOU SHOULD TAKE THE GIANT SPIDER.
WHY DO I ALWAYS HAVE TO FIGHT THE GIANT SPIDER?
FINE. WHATEVER.
EVERYONE! STANDARD MELEE POSITIONS!
TAKE 'EM DOWN!

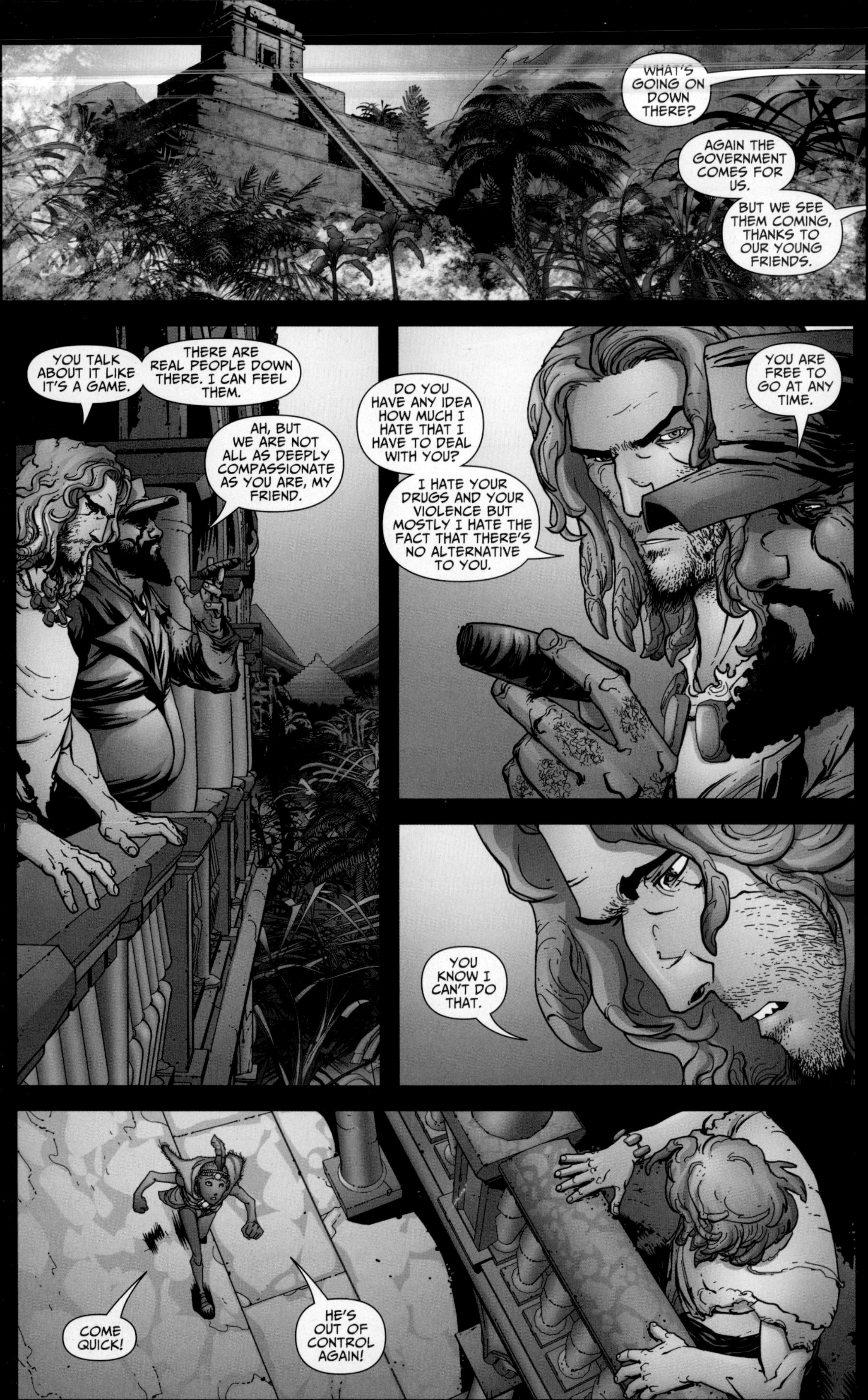
WHAT'S GOING ON DOWN THERE?
AGAIN THE GOVERNMENT COMES FOR US.
BUT WE SEE THEM COMING, THANKS TO OUR YOUNG FRIENDS.
YOU TALK ABOUT IT LIKE IT'S A GAME.
THERE ARE REAL PEOPLE DOWN THERE. I CAN FEEL THEM.
AH, BUT WE ARE NOT ALL AS DEEPLY COMPASSIONATE AS YOU ARE, MY FRIEND.
DO YOU HAVE ANY IDEA HOW MUCH I HATE THAT I HAVE TO DEAL WITH YOU?
I HATE YOUR DRUGS AND YOUR VIOLENCE BUT MOSTLY I HATE THE FACT THAT THERE'S NO ALTERNATIVE TO YOU.
YOU ARE FREE TO GO AT ANY TIME.
YOU KNOW I CAN'T DO THAT.
COME QUICK!
HE'S OUT OF CONTROL AGAIN!

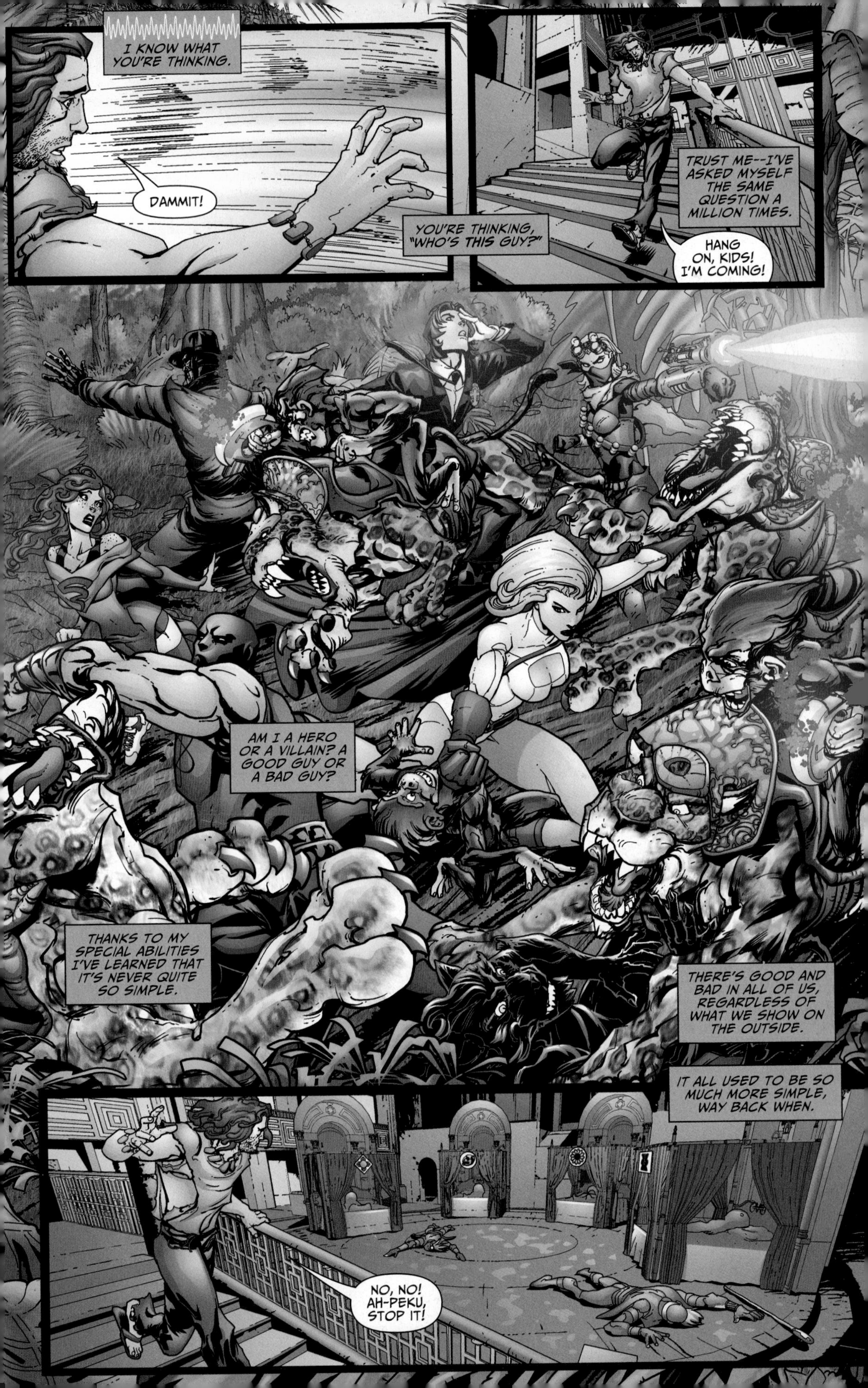
I KNOW WHAT YOU'RE THINKING.
DAMMIT!
YOU'RE THINKING, "WHO'S THIS GUY?"
TRUST ME--I'VE ASKED MYSELF THE SAME QUESTION A MILLION TIMES.
HANG ON, KIDS! I'M COMING!
AM I A HERO OR A VILLAIN? A GOOD GUY OR A BAD GUY?
THANKS TO MY SPECIAL ABILITIES I'VE LEARNED THAT IT'S NEVER QUITE SO SIMPLE.
THERE'S GOOD AND BAD IN ALL OF US, REGARDLESS OF WHAT WE SHOW ON THE OUTSIDE.
IT ALL USED TO BE SO MUCH MORE SIMPLE, WAY BACK WHEN.
NO, NO! AH-PEKU, STOP IT!

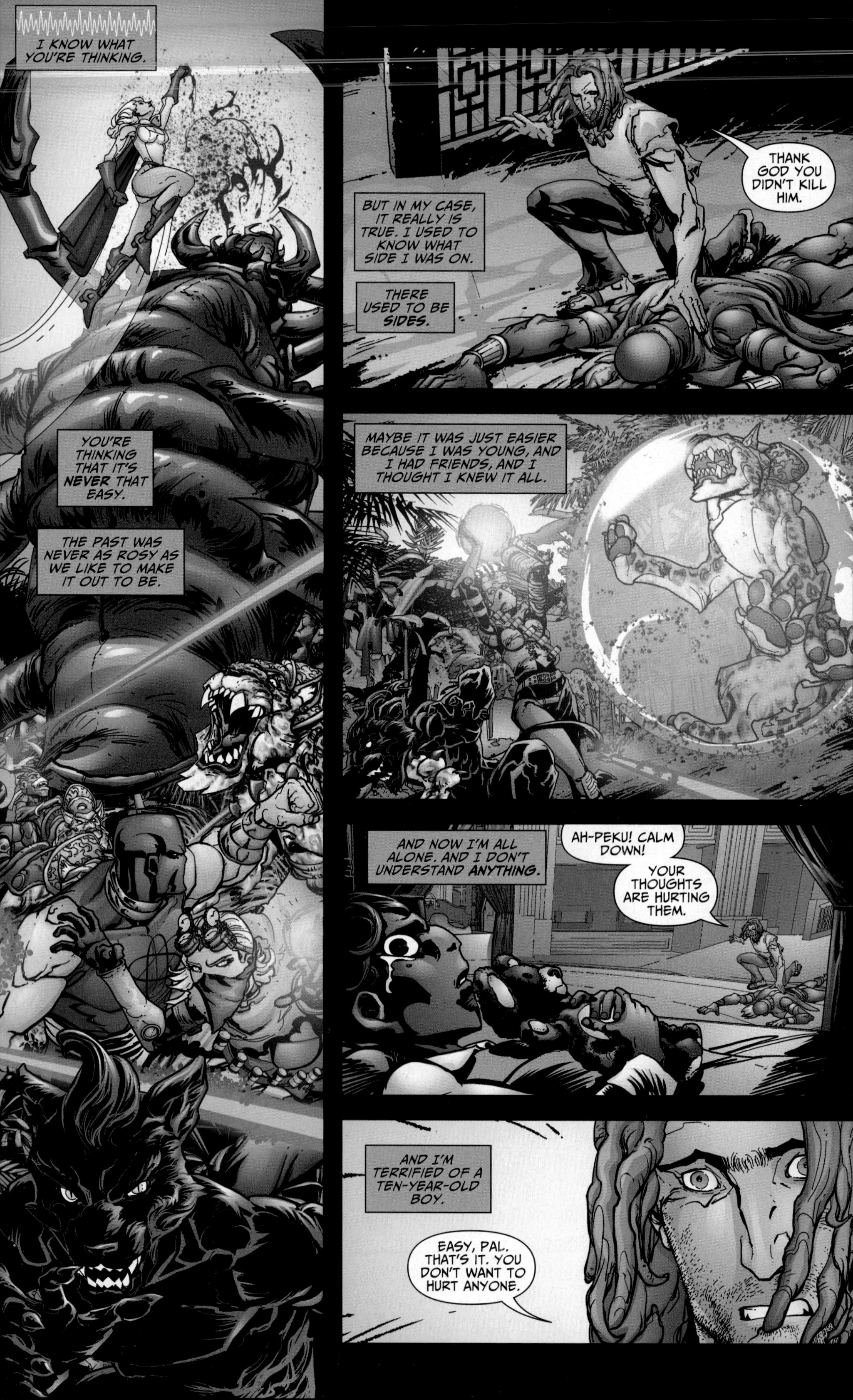
I KNOW WHAT YOU'RE THINKING.
YOU'RE THINKING THAT IT'S NEVER THAT EASY.
THE PAST WAS NEVER AS ROSY AS WE LIKE TO MAKE IT OUT TO BE.
BUT IN MY CASE, IT REALLY IS TRUE. I USED TO KNOW WHAT SIDE I WAS ON.
THERE USED TO BE SIDES.
THANK GOD YOU DIDN'T KILL HIM.
MAYBE IT WAS JUST EASIER BECAUSE I WAS YOUNG, AND I HAD FRIENDS, AND I THOUGHT I KNEW IT ALL.
AND NOW I'M ALL ALONE. AND I DON'T UNDERSTAND ANYTHING.
AH-PEKU! CALM DOWN!
YOUR THOUGHTS ARE HURTING THEM.
AND I'M TERRIFIED OF A TEN-YEAR-OLD BOY.
EASY, PAL. THAT'S IT. YOU DON'T WANT TO HURT ANYONE.

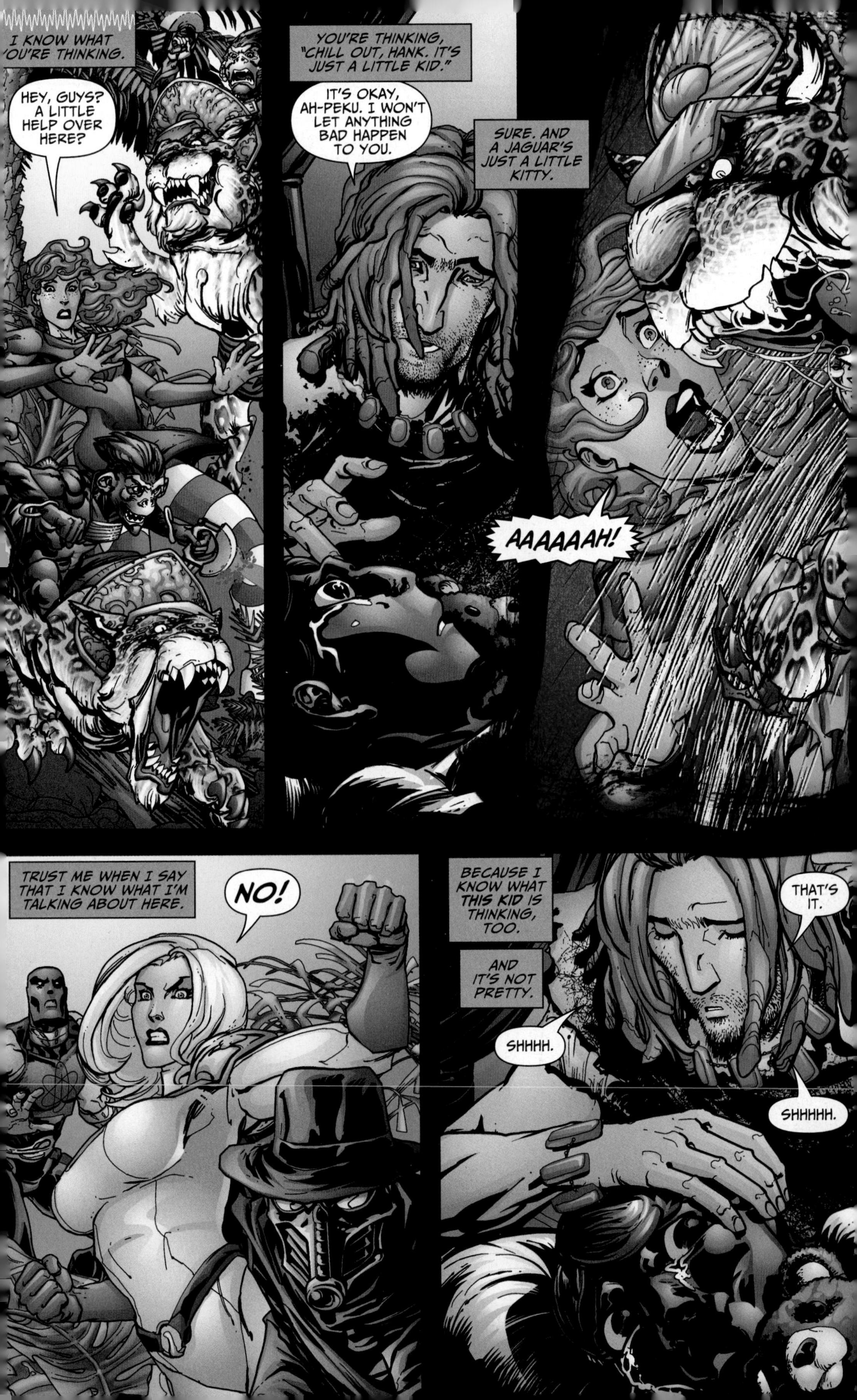
I KNOW WHAT YOU'RE THINKING.
HEY, GUYS? A LITTLE HELP OVER HERE?
YOU'RE THINKING, "CHILL OUT, HANK. IT'S JUST A LITTLE KID."
IT'S OKAY, AH-PEKU. I WON'T LET ANYTHING BAD HAPPEN TO YOU.
SURE. AND A JAGUAR'S JUST A LITTLE KITTY.
AAAAAAH!
TRUST ME WHEN I SAY THAT I KNOW WHAT I'M TALKING ABOUT HERE.
NO!
BECAUSE I KNOW WHAT THIS KID IS THINKING, TOO.
AND IT'S NOT PRETTY.
THAT'S IT.
SHHHH.
SHHHHH.

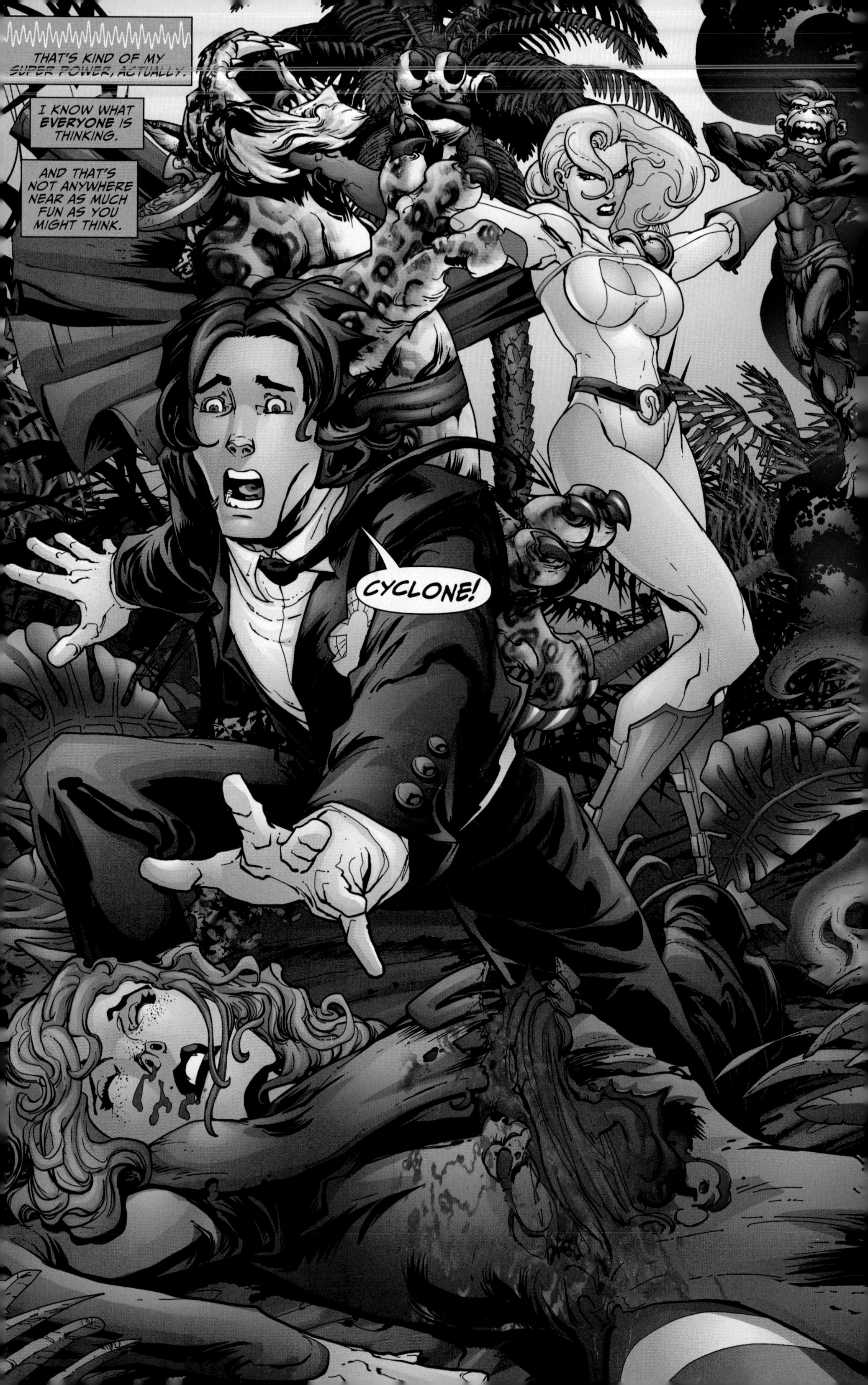
THAT'S KIND OF MY SUPER POWER, ACTUALLY.
I KNOW WHAT EVERYONE IS THINKING.
AND THAT'S NOT ANYWHERE NEAR AS MUCH FUN AS YOU MIGHT THINK.
CYCLONE!

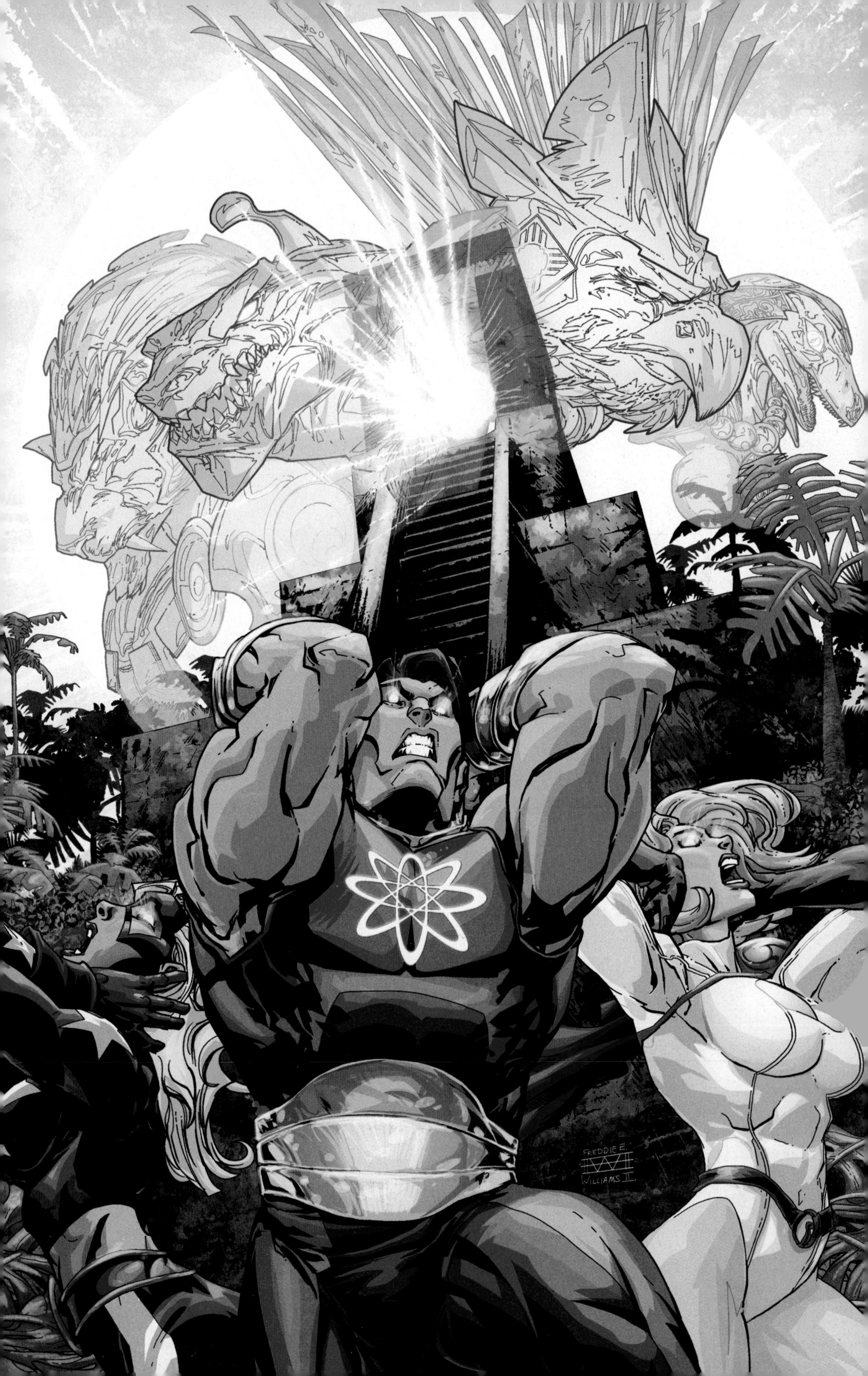
FREDDIE E.
WILLIAMS II.

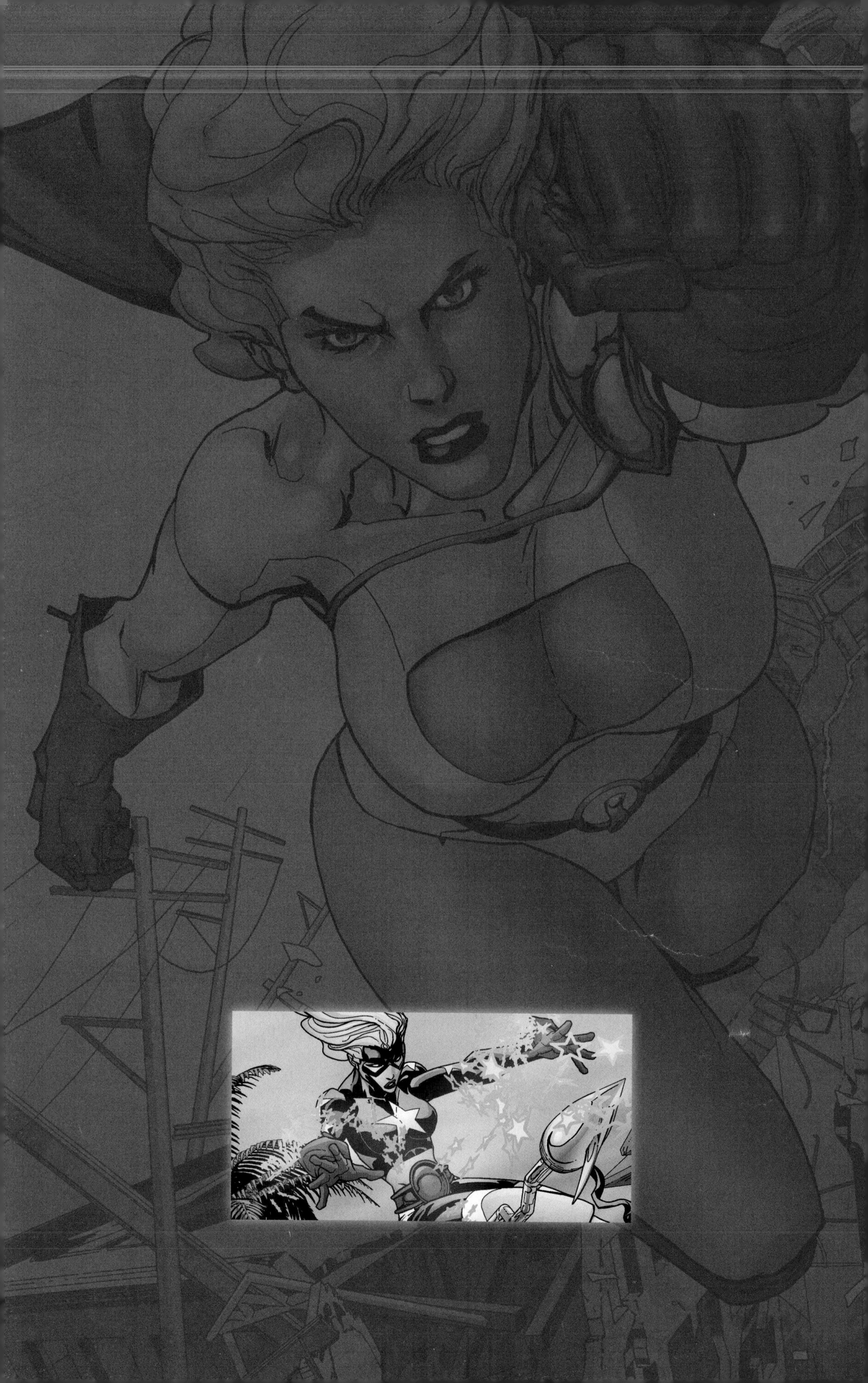

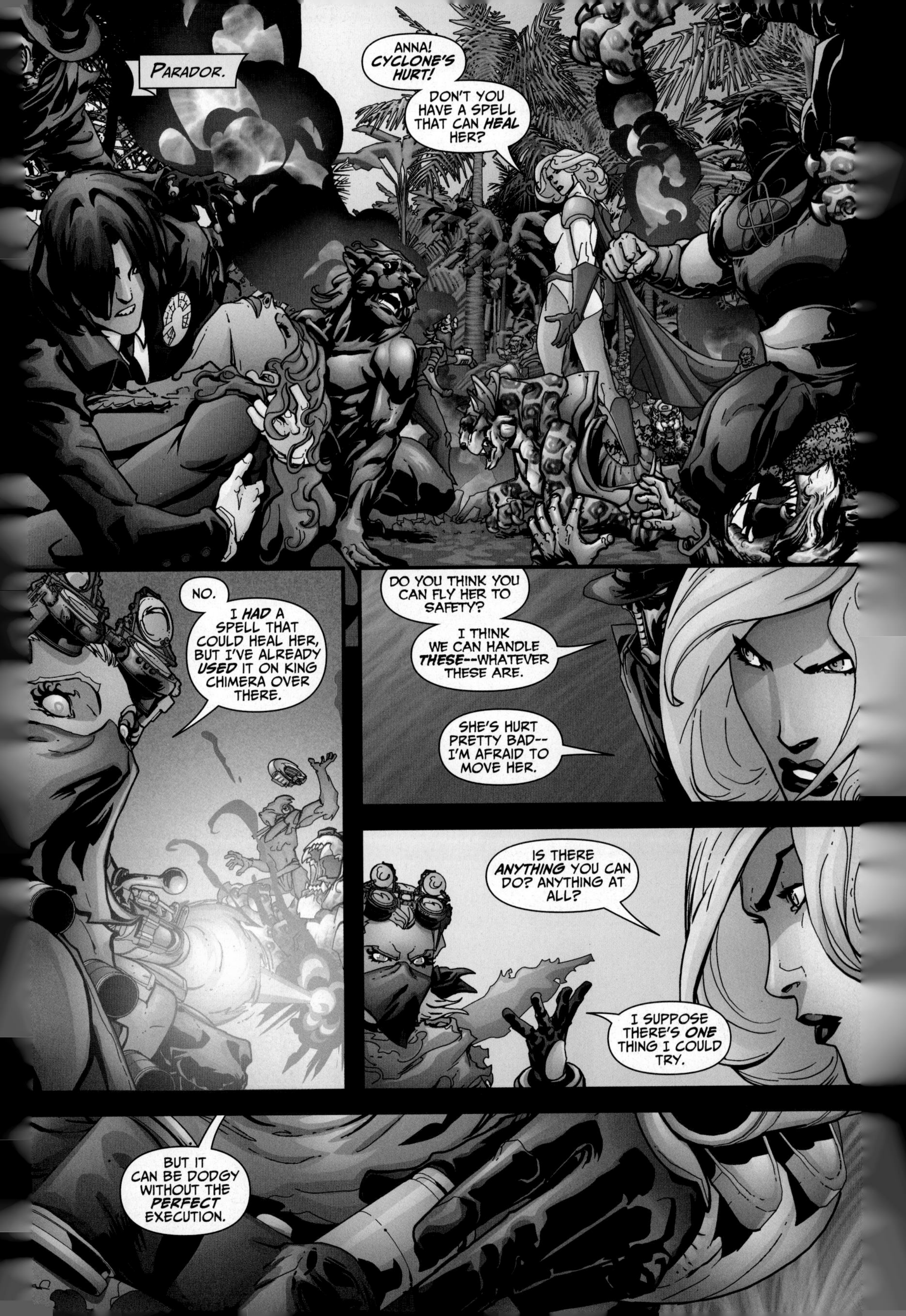
PARADOR.
ANNA! CYCLONE'S HURT!
DON'T YOU HAVE A SPELL THAT CAN HEAL HER?
NO.
I HAD A SPELL THAT COULD HEAL HER, BUT I'VE ALREADY USED IT ON KING CHIMERA OVER THERE.
DO YOU THINK YOU CAN FLY HER TO SAFETY?
I THINK WE CAN HANDLE THESE--WHATEVER THESE ARE.
SHE'S HURT PRETTY BAD-- I'M AFRAID TO MOVE HER.
IS THERE ANYTHING YOU CAN DO? ANYTHING AT ALL?
I SUPPOSE THERE'S ONE THING I COULD TRY.
BUT IT CAN BE DODGY WITHOUT THE PERFECT EXECUTION.

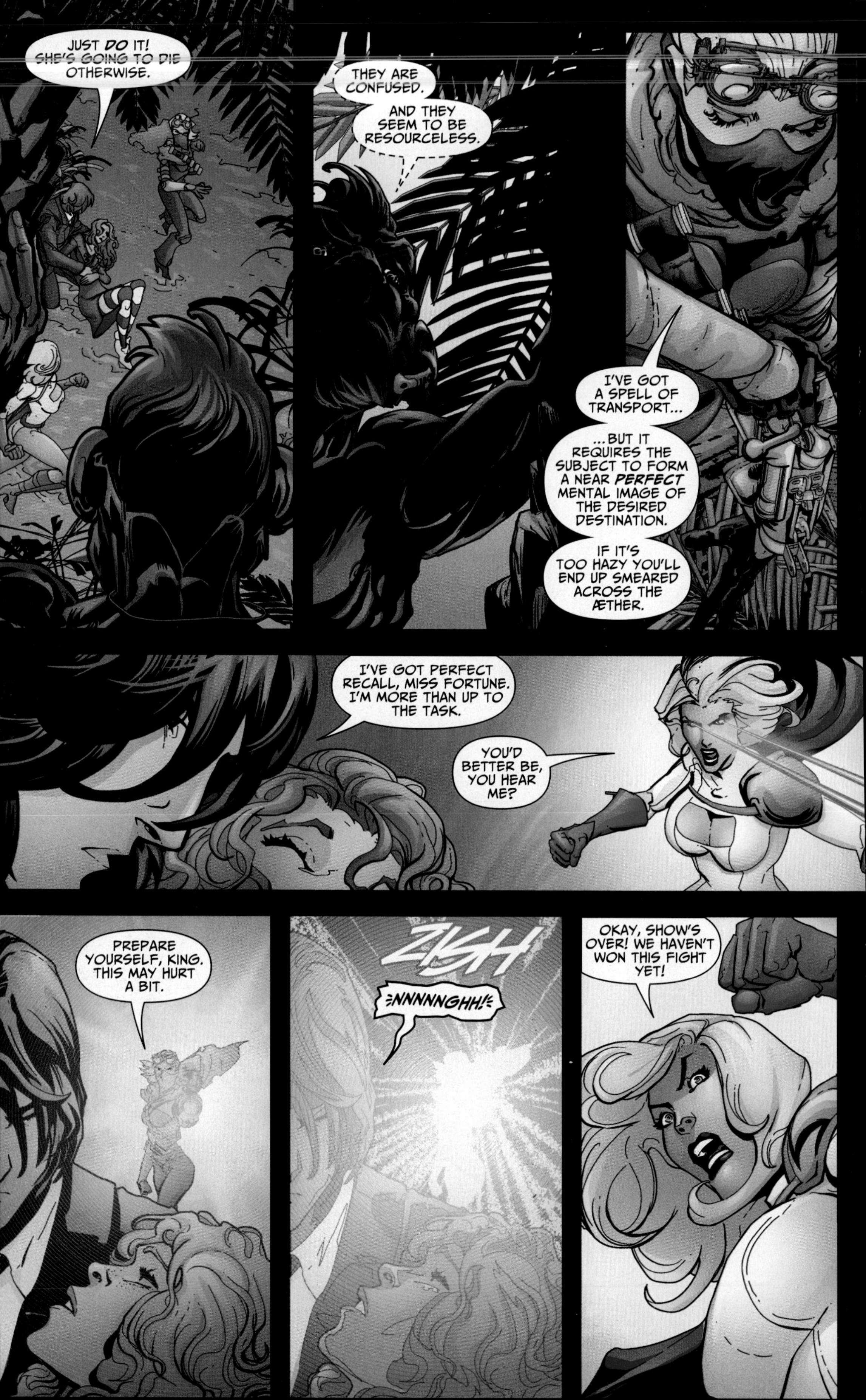
JUST DO IT! SHE'S GOING TO DIE OTHERWISE.
THEY ARE CONFUSED.
AND THEY SEEM TO BE RESOURCELESS.
I'VE GOT A SPELL OF TRANSPORT...
...BUT IT REQUIRES THE SUBJECT TO FORM A NEAR PERFECT MENTAL IMAGE OF THE DESIRED DESTINATION.
IF IT'S TOO HAZY YOU'LL END UP SMEARED ACROSS THE ÆTHER.
I'VE GOT PERFECT RECALL, MISS FORTUNE. I'M MORE THAN UP TO THE TASK.
YOU'D BETTER BE, YOU HEAR ME?
PREPARE YOURSELF, KING. THIS MAY HURT A BIT.
ZISH
NNNNNGHH!
OKAY, SHOW'S OVER! WE HAVEN'T WON THIS FIGHT YET!

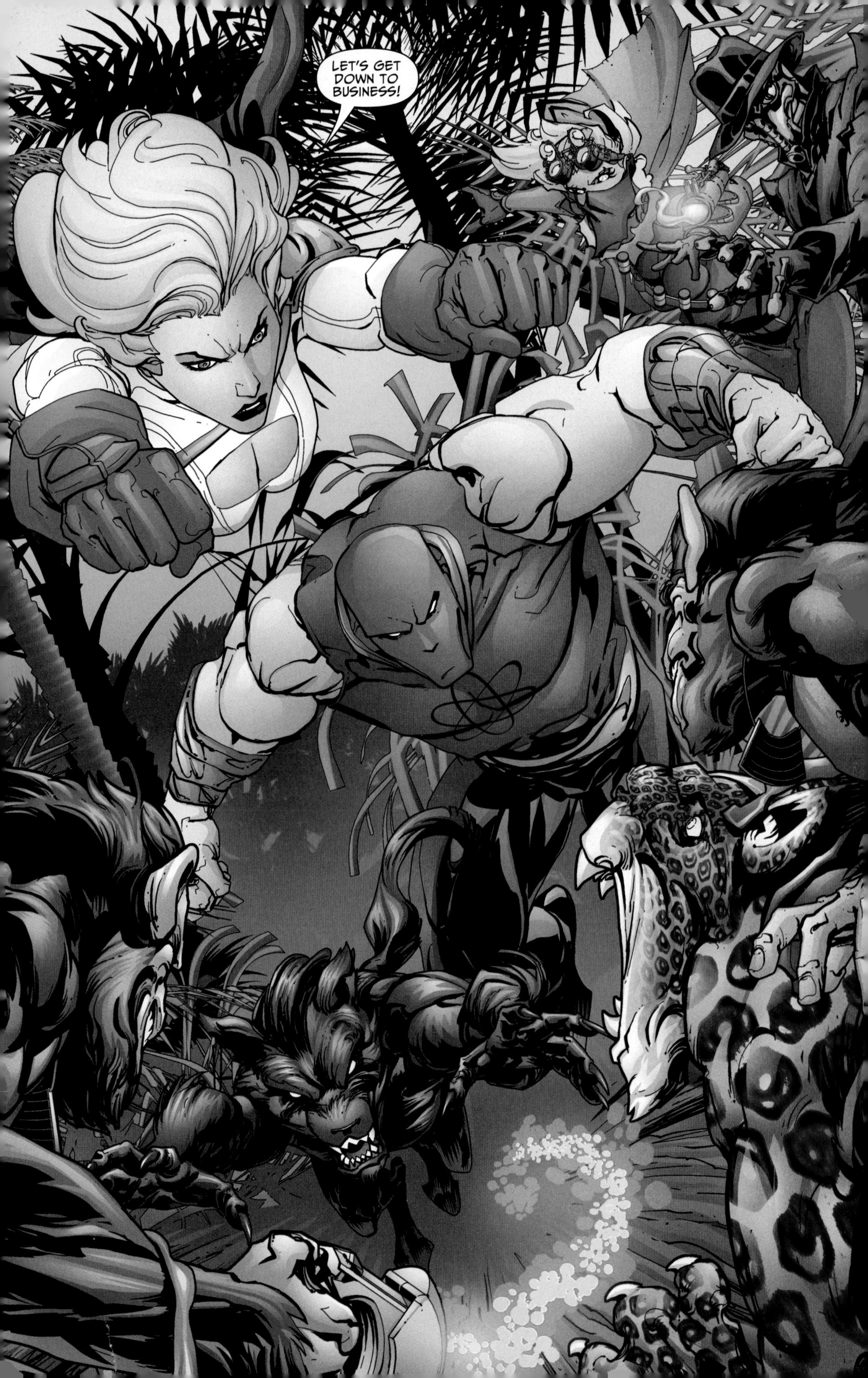
LET'S GET DOWN TO BUSINESS!

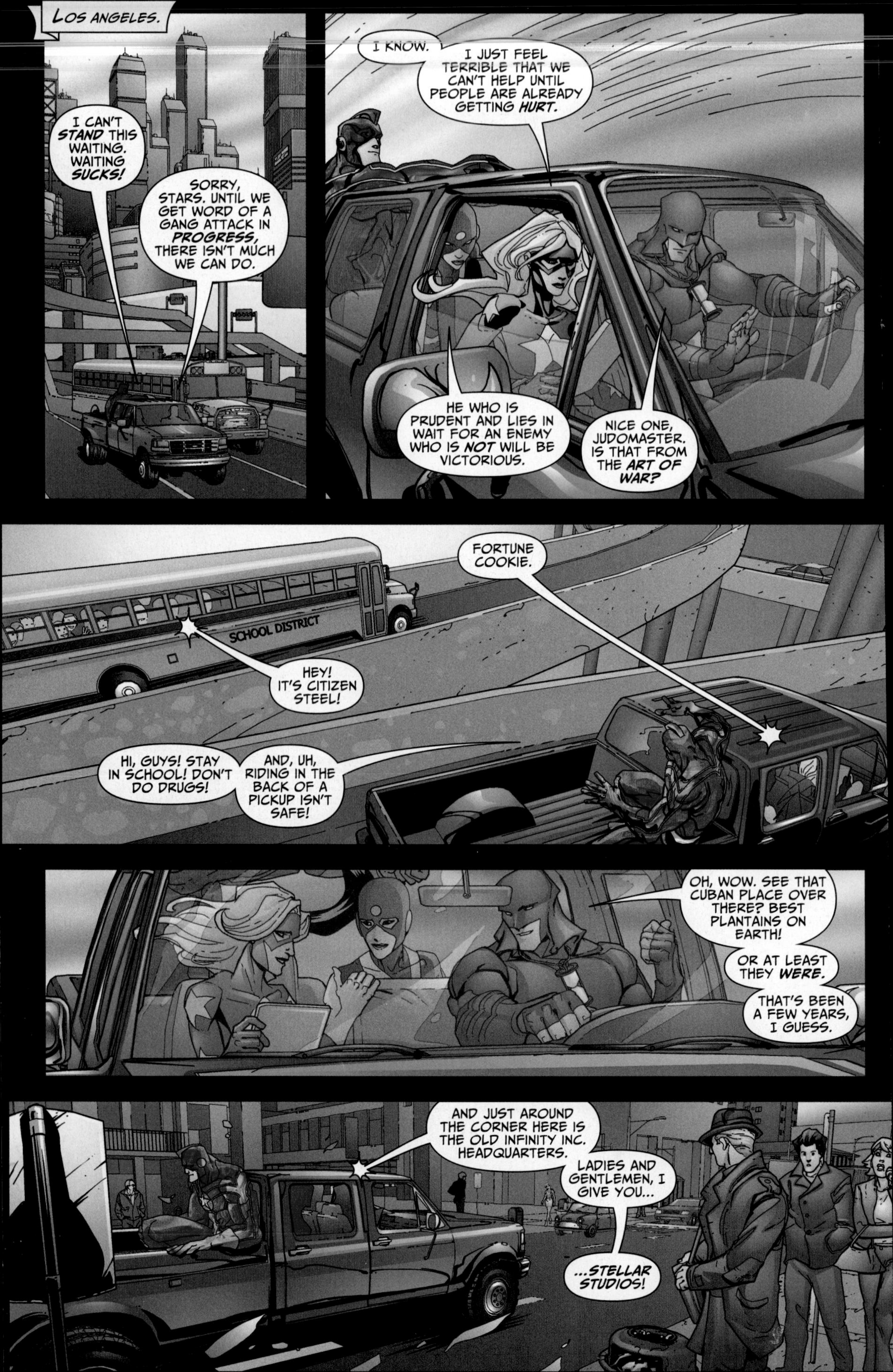
LOS ANGELES.
I CAN'T STAND THIS WAITING. WAITING SUCKS!
SORRY, STARS. UNTIL WE GET WORD OF A GANG ATTACK IN PROGRESS, THERE ISN'T MUCH WE CAN DO.
I KNOW.
I JUST FEEL TERRIBLE THAT WE CAN'T HELP UNTIL PEOPLE ARE ALREADY GETTING HURT.
HE WHO IS PRUDENT AND LIES IN WAIT FOR AN ENEMY WHO IS NOT WILL BE VICTORIOUS.
NICE ONE, JUDOMASTER. IS THAT FROM THE ART OF WAR?
FORTUNE COOKIE.
SCHOOL DISTRICT
HEY! IT'S CITIZEN STEEL!
HI, GUYS! STAY IN SCHOOL! DON'T DO DRUGS!
AND, UH, RIDING IN THE BACK OF A PICKUP ISN'T SAFE!
OH, WOW. SEE THAT CUBAN PLACE OVER THERE? BEST PLANTAINS ON EARTH!
OR AT LEAST THEY WERE.
THAT'S BEEN A FEW YEARS, I GUESS.
AND JUST AROUND THE CORNER HERE IS THE OLD INFINITY INC. HEADQUARTERS.
LADIES AND GENTLEMEN, I GIVE YOU...
...STELLAR STUDIOS!

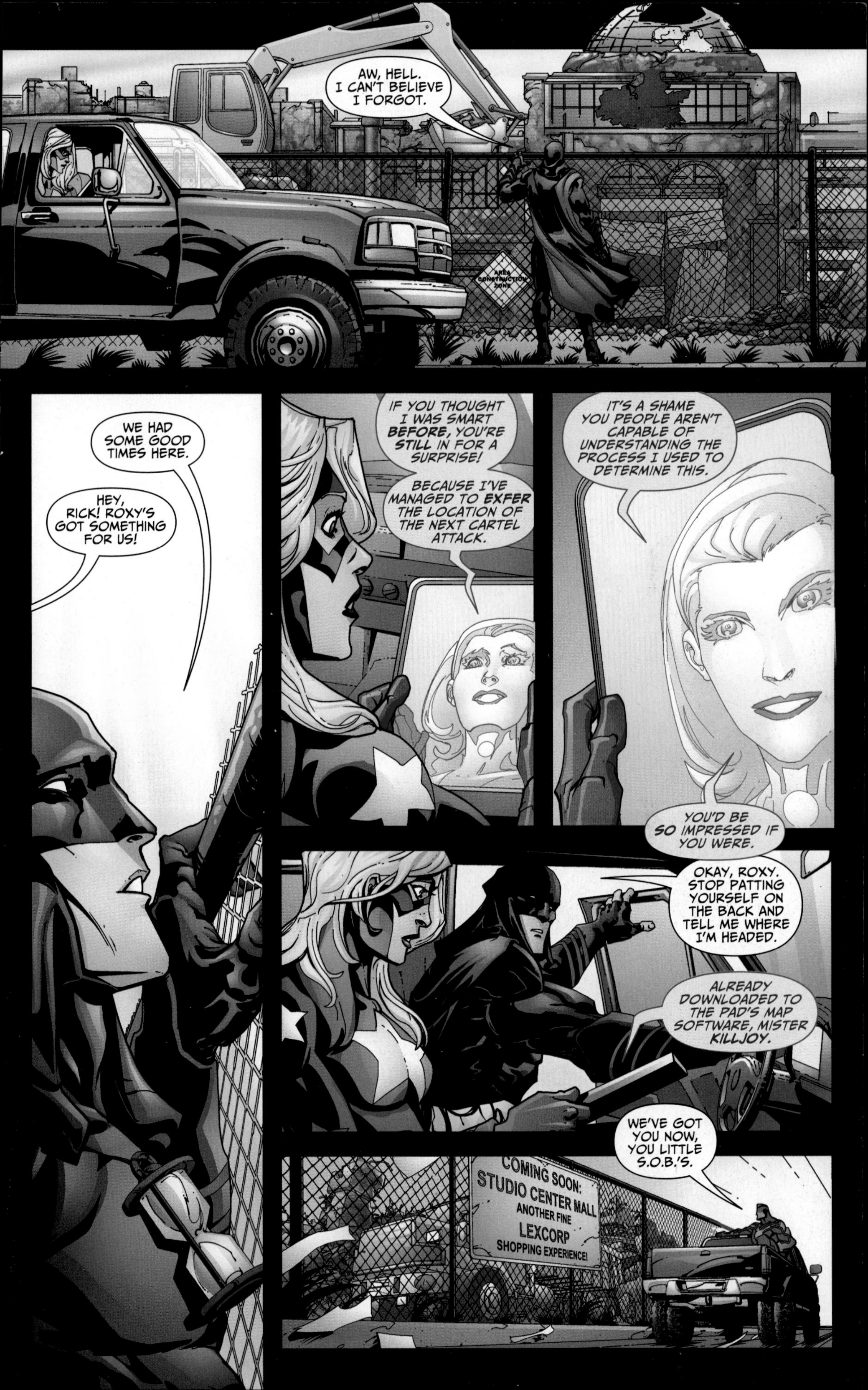
AW, HELL. I CAN'T BELIEVE I FORGOT.
AREA CONSTRUCTION ZONE
WE HAD SOME GOOD TIMES HERE.
HEY, RICK! ROXY'S GOT SOMETHING FOR US!
IF YOU THOUGHT I WAS SMART BEFORE, YOU'RE STILL IN FOR A SURPRISE!
BECAUSE I'VE MANAGED TO EXFER THE LOCATION OF THE NEXT CARTEL ATTACK.
IT'S A SHAME YOU PEOPLE AREN'T CAPABLE OF UNDERSTANDING THE PROCESS I USED TO DETERMINE THIS.
YOU'D BE SO IMPRESSED IF YOU WERE.
OKAY, ROXY. STOP PATTING YOURSELF ON THE BACK AND TELL ME WHERE I'M HEADED.
ALREADY DOWNLOADED TO THE PAD'S MAP SOFTWARE, MISTER KILLJOY.
WE'VE GOT YOU NOW, YOU LITTLE S.O.B.'S.
COMING SOON: STUDIO CENTER MALL ANOTHER FINE LEXCORP SHOPPING EXPERIENCE!

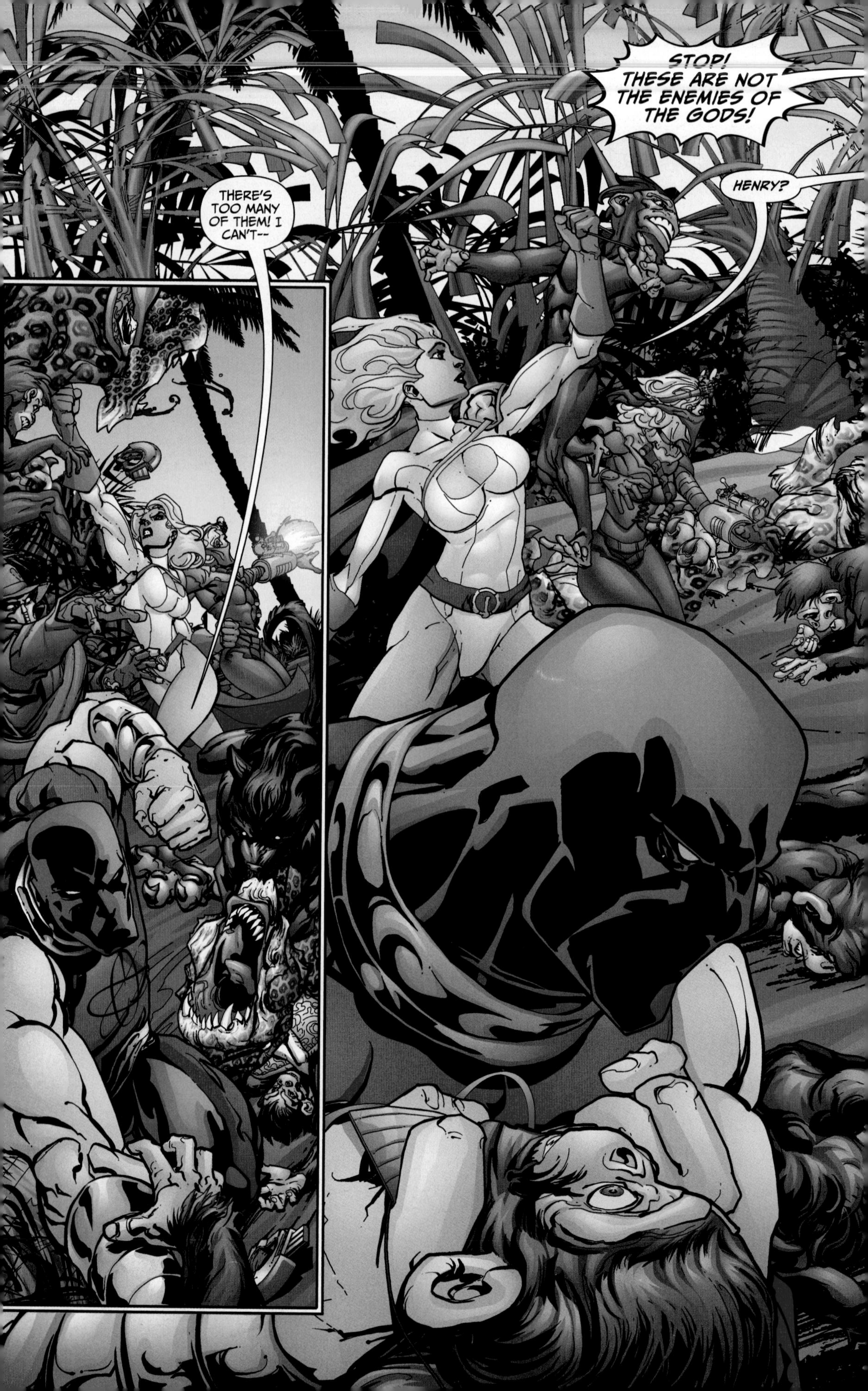
STOP! THESE ARE NOT THE ENEMIES OF THE GODS!
HENRY?
THERE'S TOO MANY OF THEM! I CAN'T--

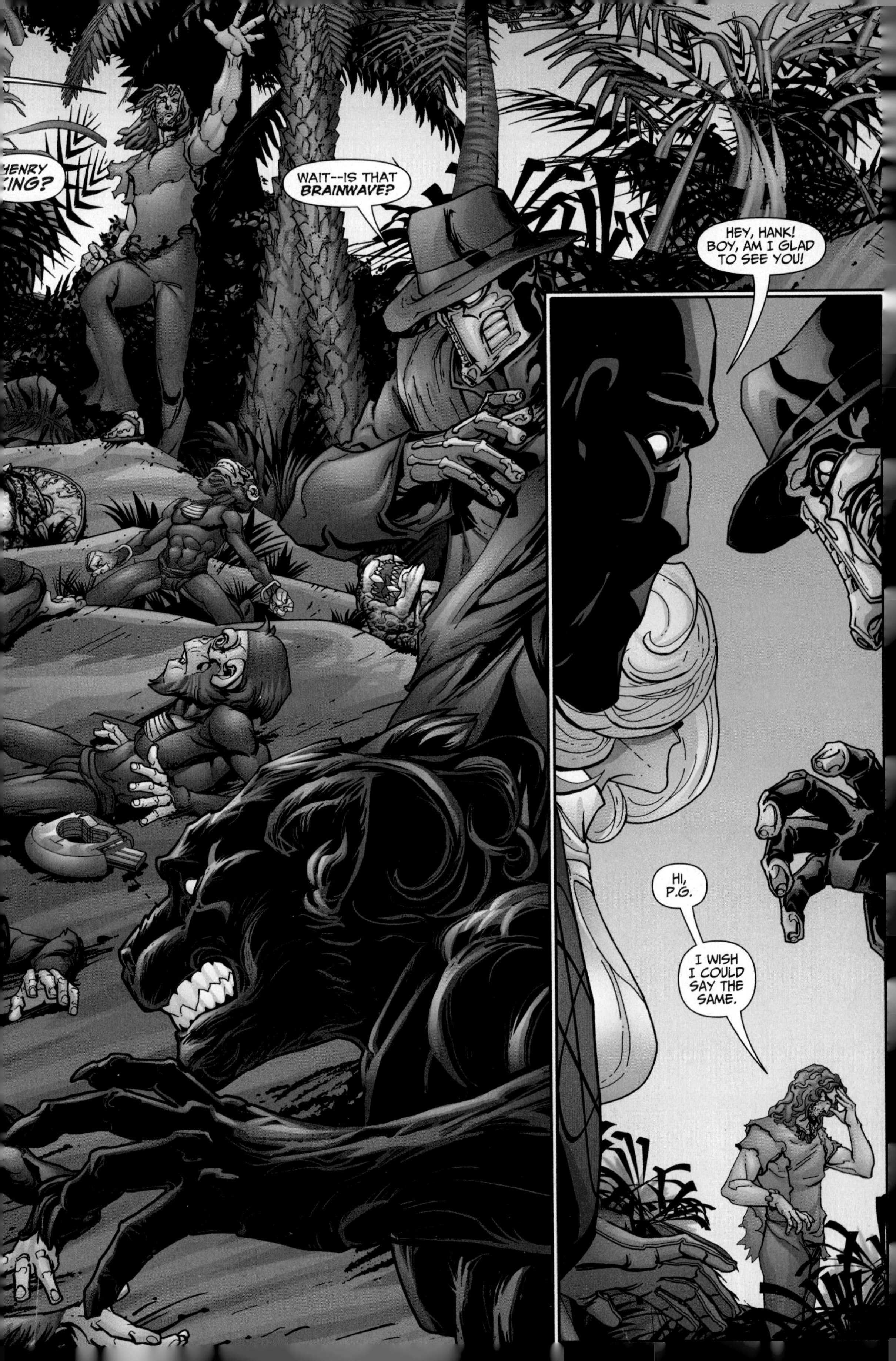
HENRY
KING?
WAIT--IS THAT BRAINWAVE?
HEY, HANK! BOY, AM I GLAD TO SEE YOU!
HI, P.G.
I WISH I COULD SAY THE SAME.

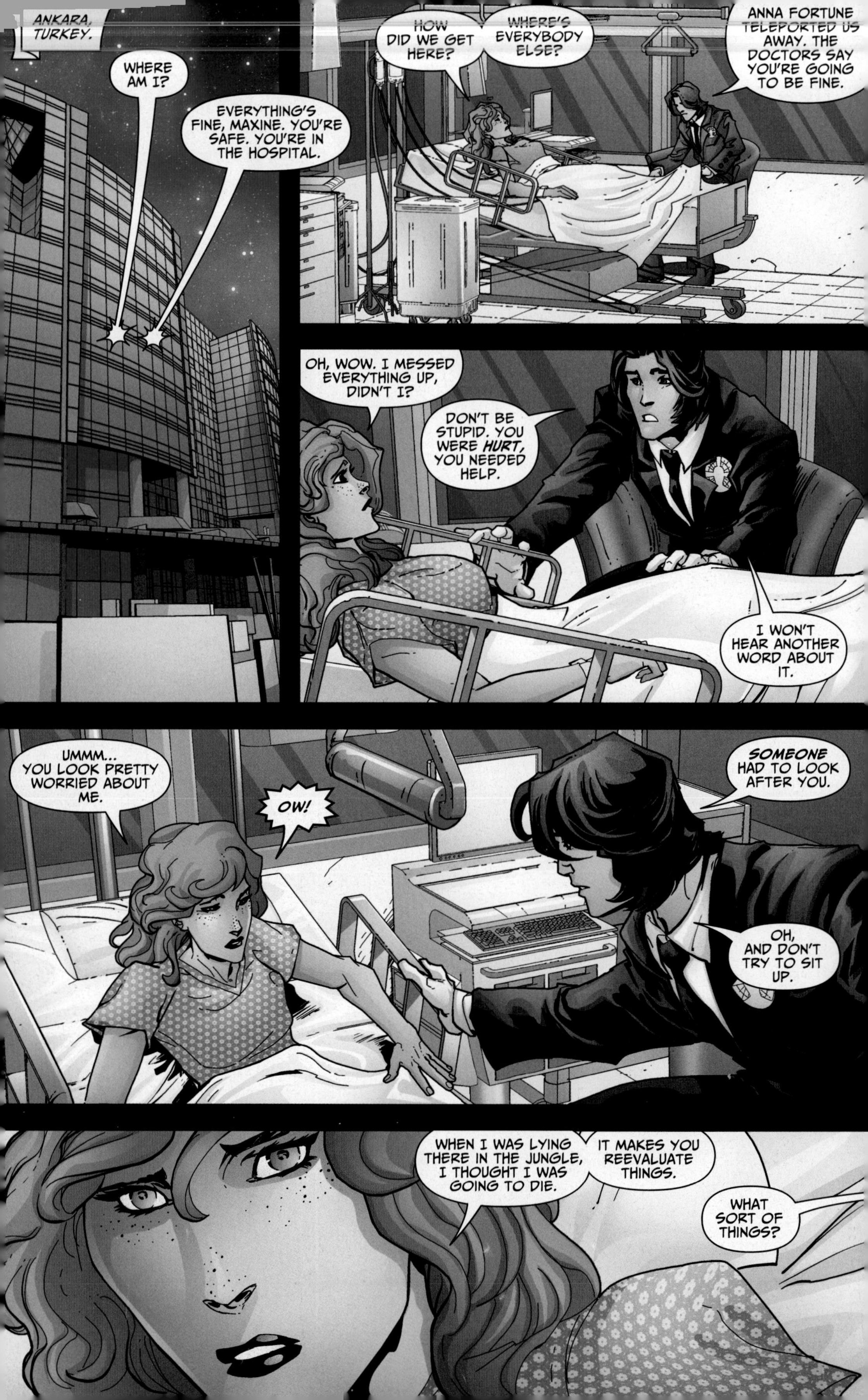
ANKARA, TURKEY.
WHERE AM I?
EVERYTHING'S FINE, MAXINE. YOU'RE SAFE. YOU'RE IN THE HOSPITAL.
HOW DID WE GET HERE?
WHERE'S EVERYBODY ELSE?
ANNA FORTUNE TELEPORTED US AWAY. THE DOCTORS SAY YOU'RE GOING TO BE FINE.
OH, WOW. I MESSED EVERYTHING UP, DIDN'T I?
DON'T BE STUPID. YOU WERE HURT, YOU NEEDED HELP.
I WON'T HEAR ANOTHER WORD ABOUT IT.
UMMM... YOU LOOK PRETTY WORRIED ABOUT ME.
OW!
SOMEONE HAD TO LOOK AFTER YOU.
OH, AND DON'T TRY TO SIT UP.
WHEN I WAS LYING THERE IN THE JUNGLE, I THOUGHT I WAS GOING TO DIE.
IT MAKES YOU REEVALUATE THINGS.
WHAT SORT OF THINGS?

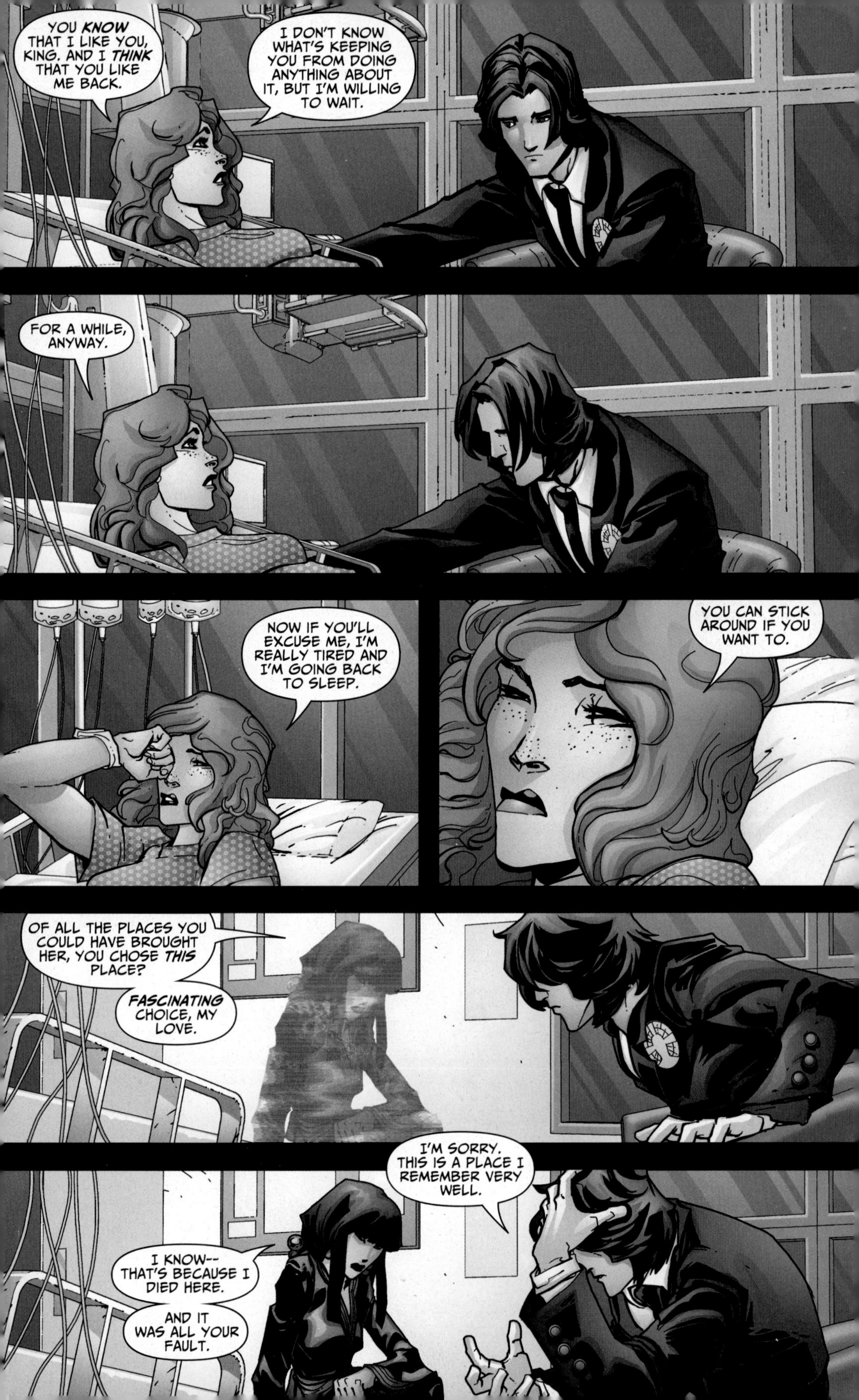
YOU KNOW THAT I LIKE YOU, KING. AND I THINK THAT YOU LIKE ME BACK.
I DON'T KNOW WHAT'S KEEPING YOU FROM DOING ANYTHING ABOUT IT, BUT I'M WILLING TO WAIT.
FOR A WHILE, ANYWAY.
NOW IF YOU'LL EXCUSE ME, I'M REALLY TIRED AND I'M GOING BACK TO SLEEP.
YOU CAN STICK AROUND IF YOU WANT TO.
OF ALL THE PLACES YOU COULD HAVE BROUGHT HER, YOU CHOSE THIS PLACE?
FASCINATING CHOICE, MY LOVE.
I'M SORRY. THIS IS A PLACE I REMEMBER VERY WELL.
I KNOW-- THAT'S BECAUSE I DIED HERE.
AND IT WAS ALL YOUR FAULT.

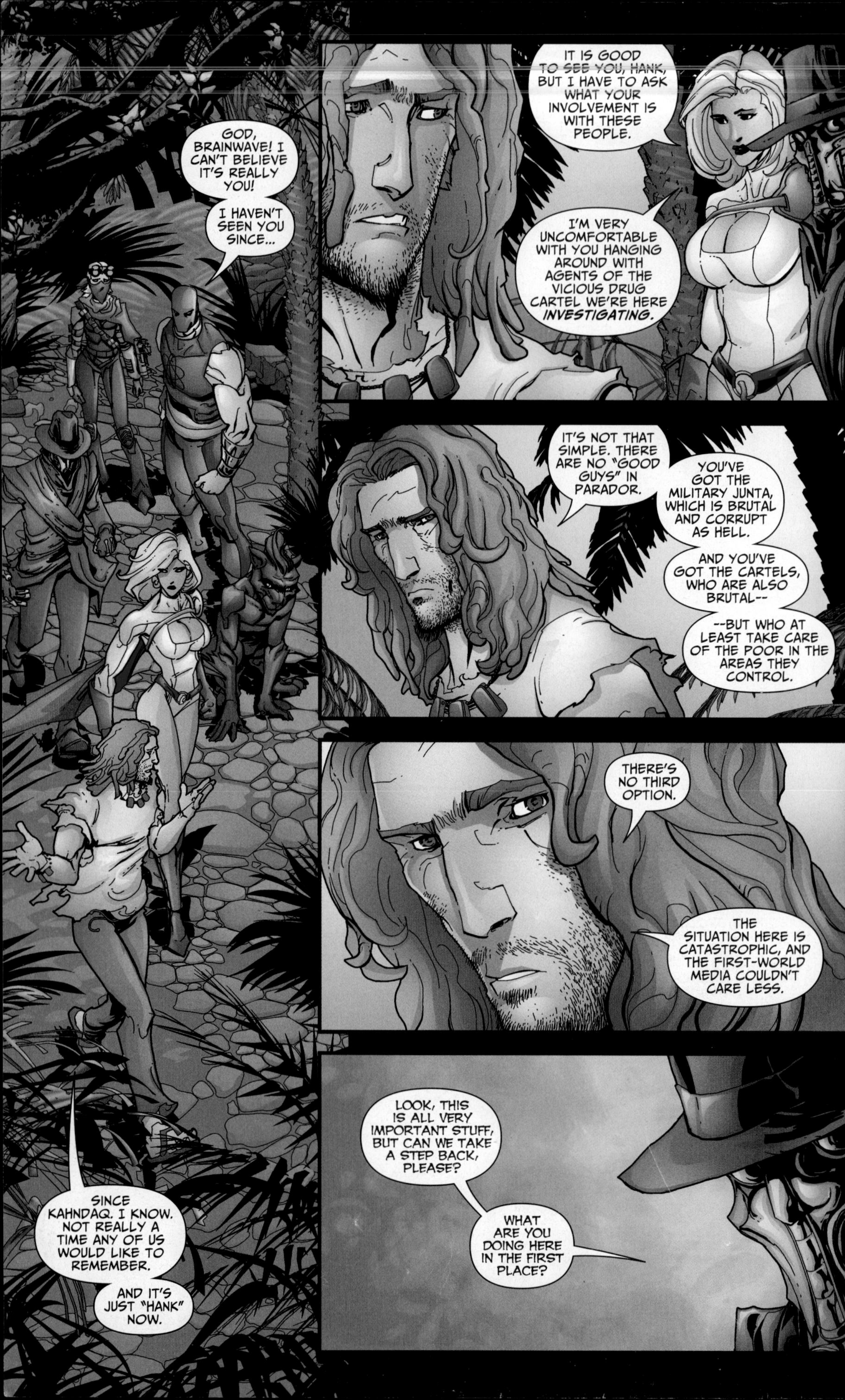
GOD, BRAINWAVE! I CAN'T BELIEVE IT'S REALLY YOU!
I HAVEN'T SEEN YOU SINCE...
SINCE KAHNDAQ. I KNOW. NOT REALLY A TIME ANY OF US WOULD LIKE TO REMEMBER.
AND IT'S JUST "HANK" NOW.
IT IS GOOD TO SEE YOU, HANK, BUT I HAVE TO ASK WHAT YOUR INVOLVEMENT IS WITH THESE PEOPLE.
I'M VERY UNCOMFORTABLE WITH YOU HANGING AROUND WITH AGENTS OF THE VICIOUS DRUG CARTEL WE'RE HERE *INVESTIGATING.*
IT'S NOT THAT SIMPLE. THERE ARE NO "GOOD GUYS" IN PARADOR.
YOU'VE GOT THE MILITARY JUNTA, WHICH IS BRUTAL AND CORRUPT AS HELL.
AND YOU'VE GOT THE CARTELS, WHO ARE ALSO BRUTAL--
--BUT WHO AT LEAST TAKE CARE OF THE POOR IN THE AREAS THEY CONTROL.
THERE'S NO THIRD OPTION.
THE SITUATION HERE IS CATASTROPHIC, AND THE FIRST-WORLD MEDIA COULDN'T CARE LESS.
LOOK, THIS IS ALL VERY IMPORTANT STUFF, BUT CAN WE TAKE A STEP BACK, PLEASE?
WHAT ARE YOU DOING HERE IN THE FIRST PLACE?

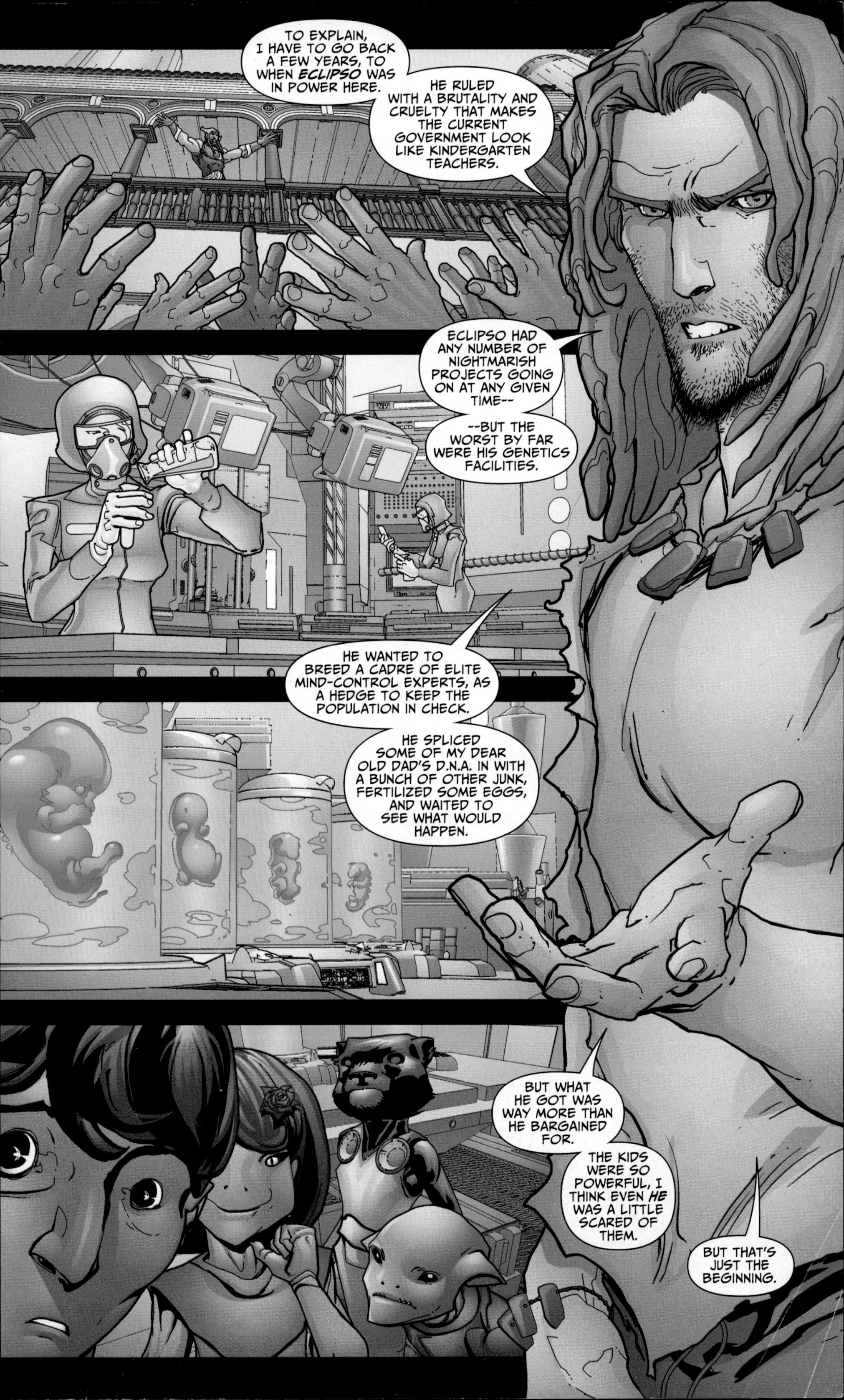
TO EXPLAIN, I HAVE TO GO BACK A FEW YEARS, TO WHEN ECLIPSO WAS IN POWER HERE.
HE RULED WITH A BRUTALITY AND CRUELTY THAT MAKES THE CURRENT GOVERNMENT LOOK LIKE KINDERGARTEN TEACHERS.
ECLIPSO HAD ANY NUMBER OF NIGHTMARISH PROJECTS GOING ON AT ANY GIVEN TIME--
--BUT THE WORST BY FAR WERE HIS GENETICS FACILITIES.
HE WANTED TO BREED A CADRE OF ELITE MIND-CONTROL EXPERTS, AS A HEDGE TO KEEP THE POPULATION IN CHECK.
HE SPLICED SOME OF MY DEAR OLD DAD'S D.N.A. IN WITH A BUNCH OF OTHER JUNK, FERTILIZED SOME EGGS, AND WAITED TO SEE WHAT WOULD HAPPEN.
BUT WHAT HE GOT WAS WAY MORE THAN HE BARGAINED FOR.
THE KIDS WERE SO POWERFUL, I THINK EVEN HE WAS A LITTLE SCARED OF THEM.
BUT THAT'S JUST THE BEGINNING.

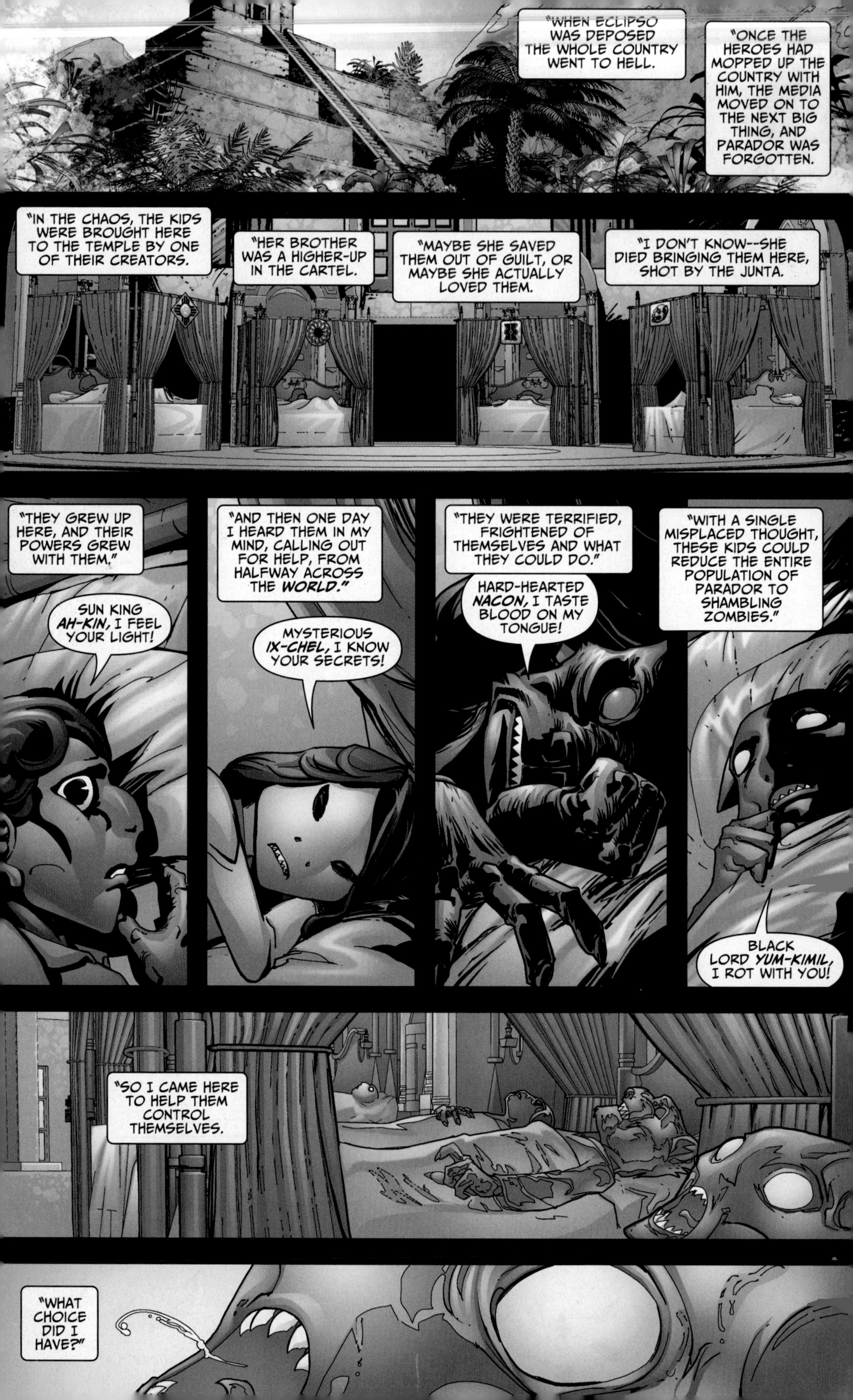
"WHEN ECLIPSO WAS DEPOSED THE WHOLE COUNTRY WENT TO HELL.
"ONCE THE HEROES HAD MOPPED UP THE COUNTRY WITH HIM, THE MEDIA MOVED ON TO THE NEXT BIG THING, AND PARADOR WAS FORGOTTEN.
"IN THE CHAOS, THE KIDS WERE BROUGHT HERE TO THE TEMPLE BY ONE OF THEIR CREATORS.
"HER BROTHER WAS A HIGHER-UP IN THE CARTEL.
"MAYBE SHE SAVED THEM OUT OF GUILT, OR MAYBE SHE ACTUALLY LOVED THEM.
"I DON'T KNOW--SHE DIED BRINGING THEM HERE, SHOT BY THE JUNTA.
"THEY GREW UP HERE, AND THEIR POWERS GREW WITH THEM."
SUN KING AH-KIN, I FEEL YOUR LIGHT!
"AND THEN ONE DAY I HEARD THEM IN MY MIND, CALLING OUT FOR HELP, FROM HALFWAY ACROSS THE WORLD."
MYSTERIOUS IX-CHEL, I KNOW YOUR SECRETS!
"THEY WERE TERRIFIED, FRIGHTENED OF THEMSELVES AND WHAT THEY COULD DO."
HARD-HEARTED NACON, I TASTE BLOOD ON MY TONGUE!
"WITH A SINGLE MISPLACED THOUGHT, THESE KIDS COULD REDUCE THE ENTIRE POPULATION OF PARADOR TO SHAMBLING ZOMBIES."
BLACK LORD YUM-KIMIL, I ROT WITH YOU!
"SO I CAME HERE TO HELP THEM CONTROL THEMSELVES.
"WHAT CHOICE DID I HAVE?"

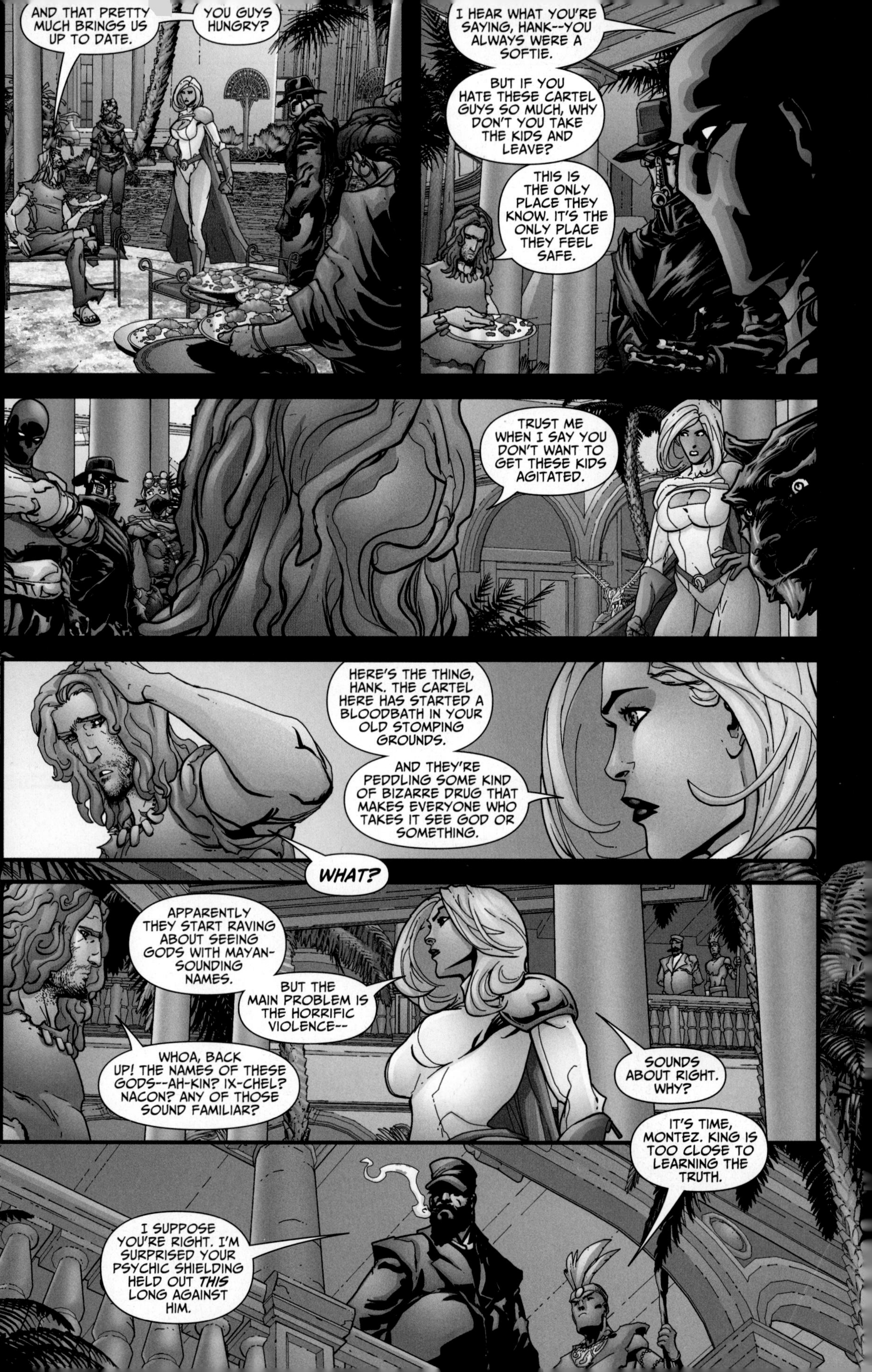
AND THAT PRETTY MUCH BRINGS US UP TO DATE.
YOU GUYS HUNGRY?
I HEAR WHAT YOU'RE SAYING, HANK--YOU ALWAYS WERE A SOFTIE.
BUT IF YOU HATE THESE CARTEL GUYS SO MUCH, WHY DON'T YOU TAKE THE KIDS AND LEAVE?
THIS IS THE ONLY PLACE THEY KNOW. IT'S THE ONLY PLACE THEY FEEL SAFE.
TRUST ME WHEN I SAY YOU DON'T WANT TO GET THESE KIDS AGITATED.
HERE'S THE THING, HANK. THE CARTEL HERE HAS STARTED A BLOODBATH IN YOUR OLD STOMPING GROUNDS.
AND THEY'RE PEDDLING SOME KIND OF BIZARRE DRUG THAT MAKES EVERYONE WHO TAKES IT SEE GOD OR SOMETHING.
WHAT?
APPARENTLY THEY START RAVING ABOUT SEEING GODS WITH MAYAN-SOUNDING NAMES.
BUT THE MAIN PROBLEM IS THE HORRIFIC VIOLENCE--
WHOA, BACK UP! THE NAMES OF THESE GODS--AH-KIN? IX-CHEL? NACON? ANY OF THOSE SOUND FAMILIAR?
SOUNDS ABOUT RIGHT. WHY?
IT'S TIME, MONTEZ. KING IS TOO CLOSE TO LEARNING THE TRUTH.
I SUPPOSE YOU'RE RIGHT. I'M SURPRISED YOUR PSYCHIC SHIELDING HELD OUT *THIS* LONG AGAINST HIM.

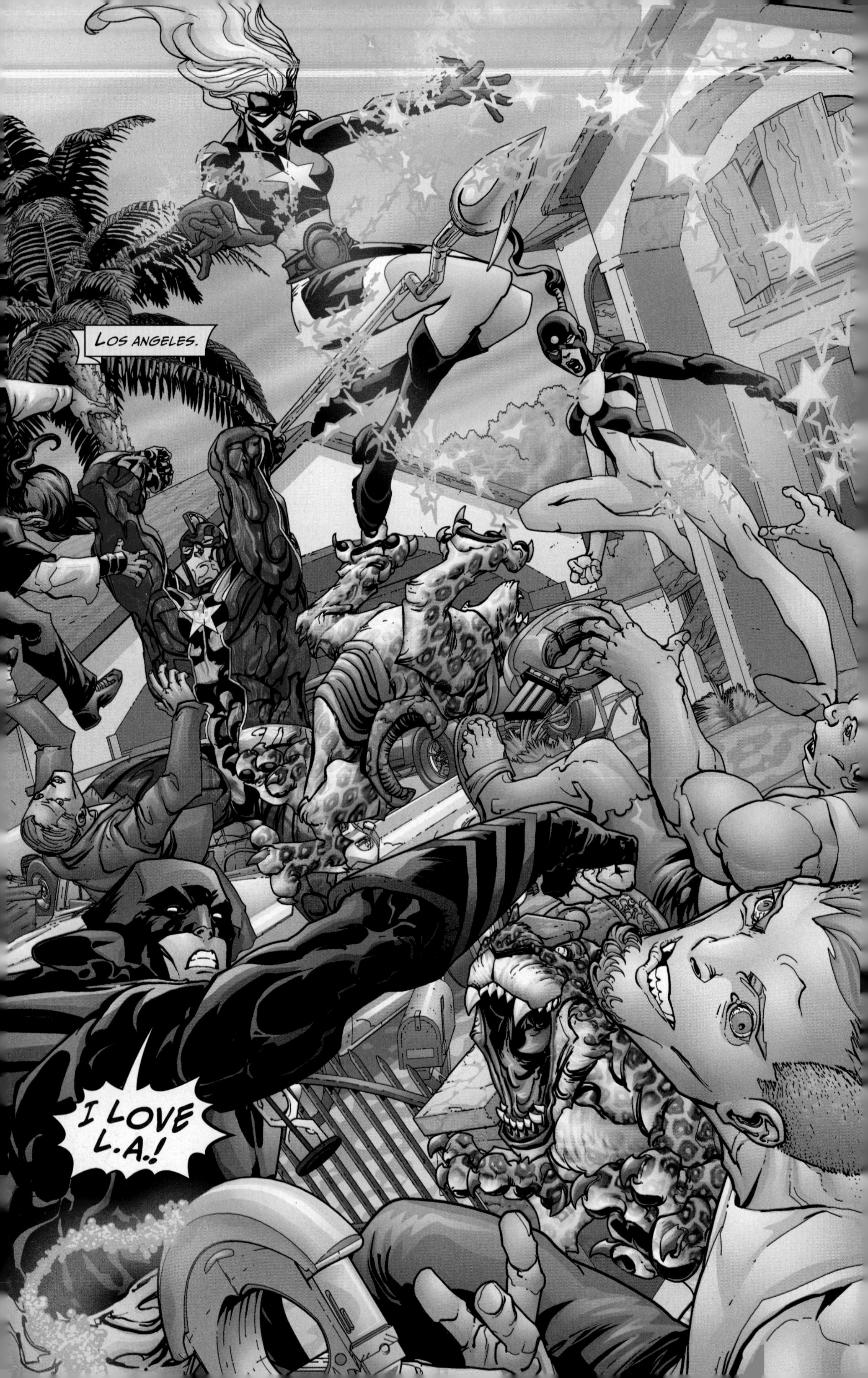
LOS ANGELES.
I LOVE L.A.!

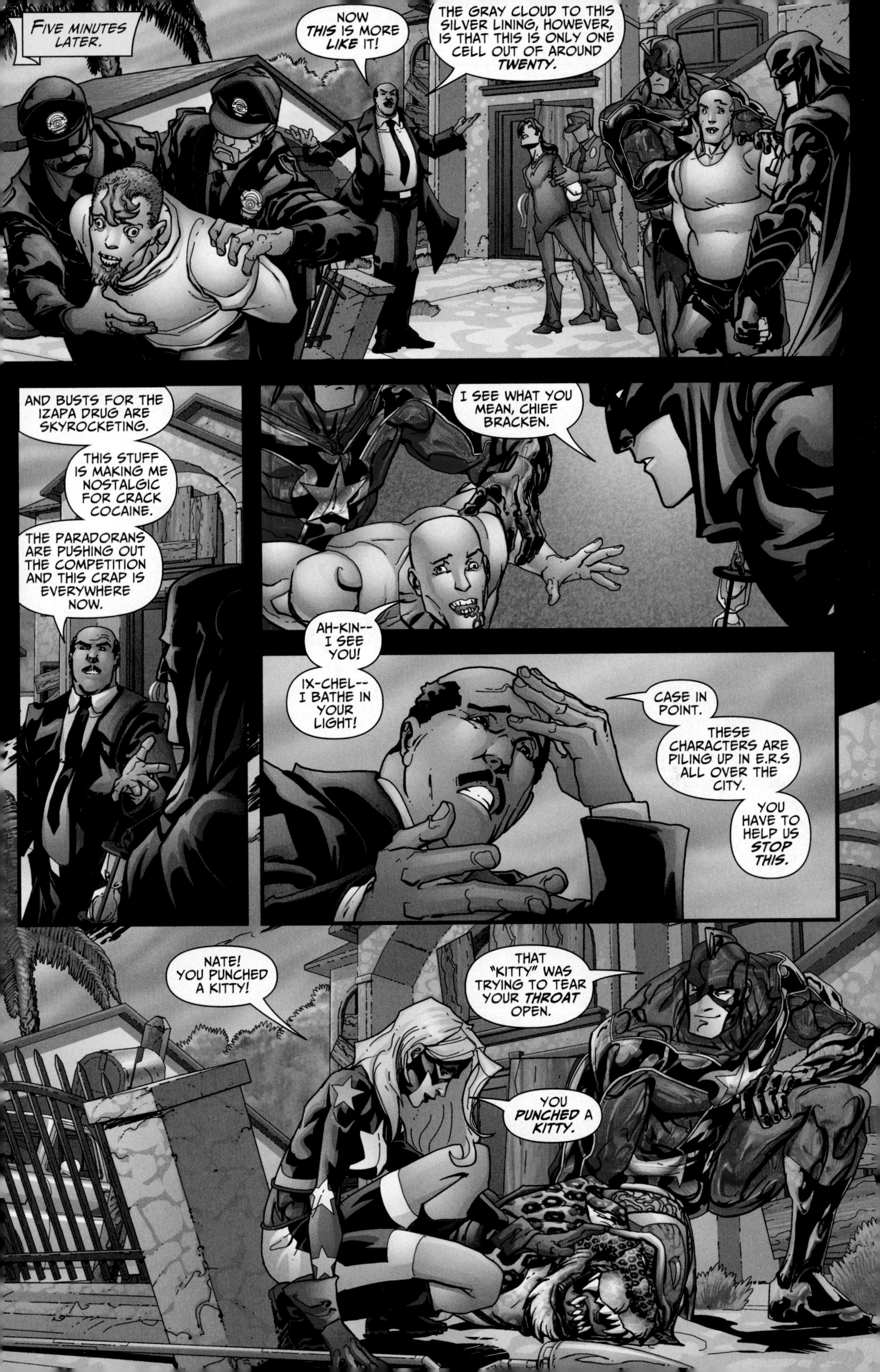
FIVE MINUTES LATER.
NOW THIS IS MORE LIKE IT!
THE GRAY CLOUD TO THIS SILVER LINING, HOWEVER, IS THAT THIS IS ONLY ONE CELL OUT OF AROUND TWENTY.
AND BUSTS FOR THE IZAPA DRUG ARE SKYROCKETING.
THIS STUFF IS MAKING ME NOSTALGIC FOR CRACK COCAINE.
THE PARADORANS ARE PUSHING OUT THE COMPETITION AND THIS CRAP IS EVERYWHERE NOW.
I SEE WHAT YOU MEAN, CHIEF BRACKEN.
AH-KIN-- I SEE YOU!
IX-CHEL-- I BATHE IN YOUR LIGHT!
CASE IN POINT.
THESE CHARACTERS ARE PILING UP IN E.R.S ALL OVER THE CITY.
YOU HAVE TO HELP US STOP THIS.
NATE! YOU PUNCHED A KITTY!
THAT "KITTY" WAS TRYING TO TEAR YOUR THROAT OPEN.
YOU PUNCHED A KITTY.

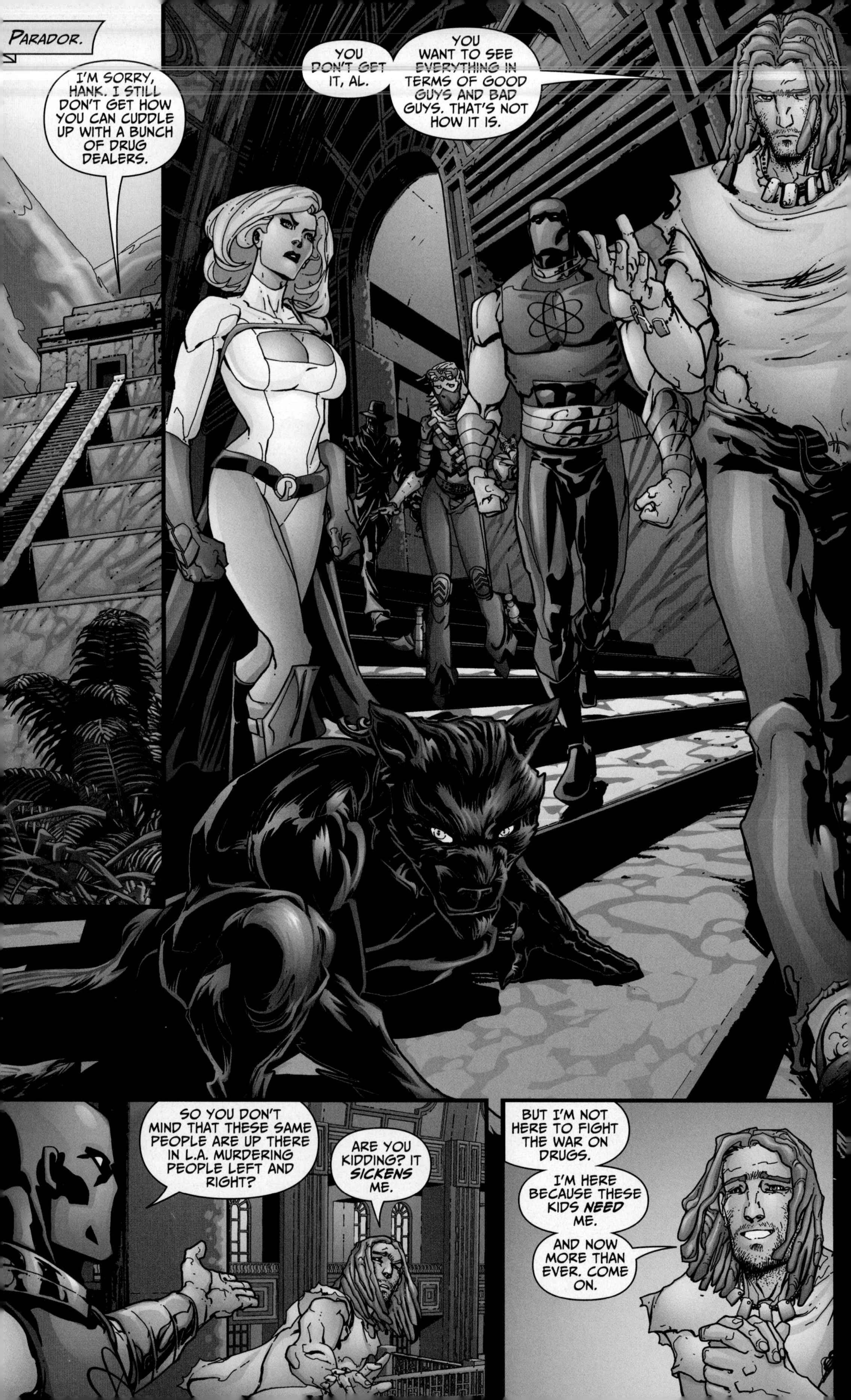
PARADOR.
I'M SORRY, HANK. I STILL DON'T GET HOW YOU CAN CUDDLE UP WITH A BUNCH OF DRUG DEALERS.
YOU DON'T GET IT, AL.
YOU WANT TO SEE EVERYTHING IN TERMS OF GOOD GUYS AND BAD GUYS. THAT'S NOT HOW IT IS.
SO YOU DON'T MIND THAT THESE SAME PEOPLE ARE UP THERE IN L.A. MURDERING PEOPLE LEFT AND RIGHT?
ARE YOU KIDDING? IT SICKENS ME.
BUT I'M NOT HERE TO FIGHT THE WAR ON DRUGS.
I'M HERE BECAUSE THESE KIDS NEED ME.
AND NOW MORE THAN EVER. COME ON.

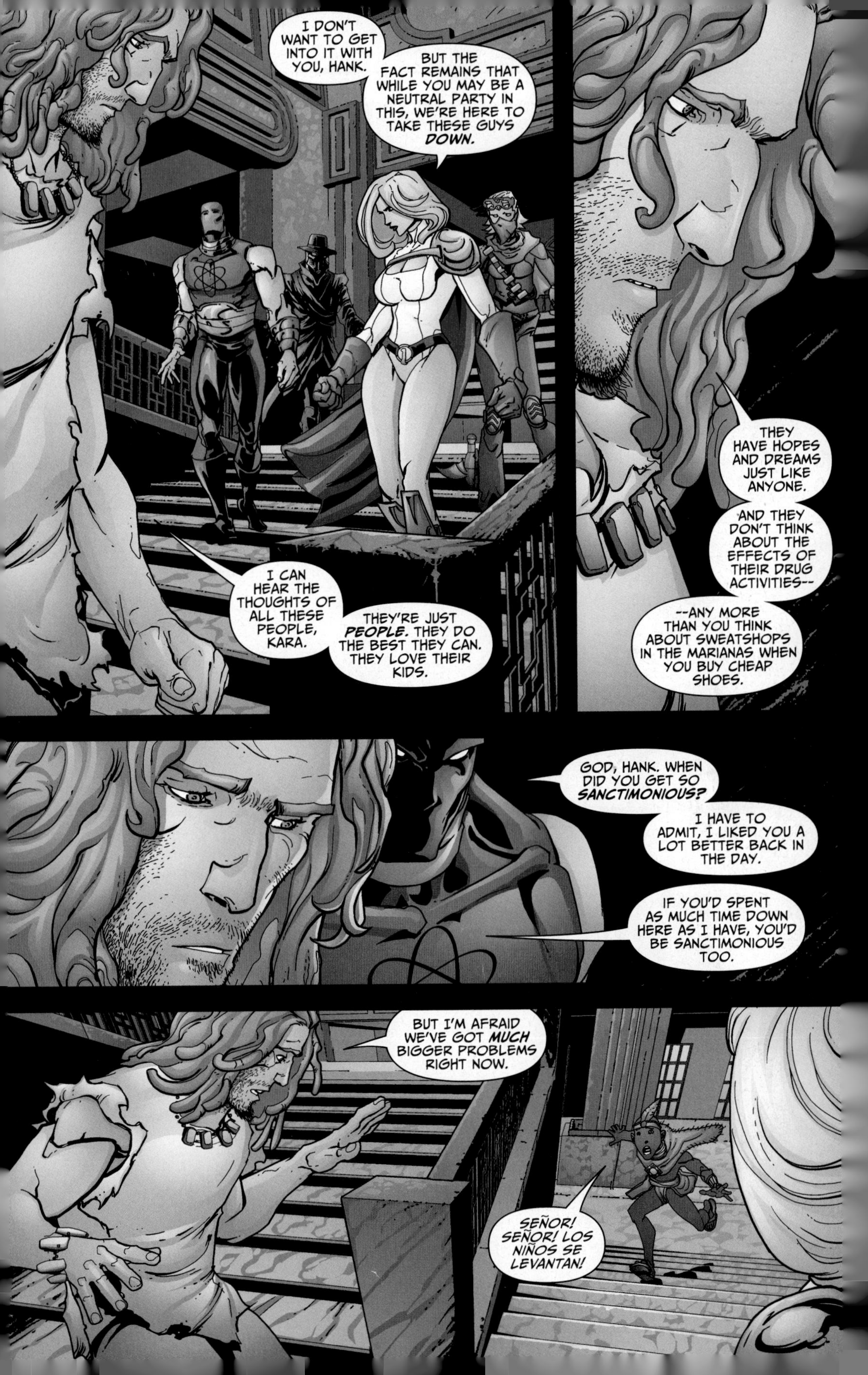
I DON'T WANT TO GET INTO IT WITH YOU, HANK.
BUT THE FACT REMAINS THAT WHILE YOU MAY BE A NEUTRAL PARTY IN THIS, WE'RE HERE TO TAKE THESE GUYS DOWN.
I CAN HEAR THE THOUGHTS OF ALL THESE PEOPLE, KARA.
THEY'RE JUST PEOPLE. THEY DO THE BEST THEY CAN. THEY LOVE THEIR KIDS.
THEY HAVE HOPES AND DREAMS JUST LIKE ANYONE.
AND THEY DON'T THINK ABOUT THE EFFECTS OF THEIR DRUG ACTIVITIES--
--ANY MORE THAN YOU THINK ABOUT SWEATSHOPS IN THE MARIANAS WHEN YOU BUY CHEAP SHOES.
GOD, HANK. WHEN DID YOU GET SO SANCTIMONIOUS?
I HAVE TO ADMIT, I LIKED YOU A LOT BETTER BACK IN THE DAY.
IF YOU'D SPENT AS MUCH TIME DOWN HERE AS I HAVE, YOU'D BE SANCTIMONIOUS TOO.
BUT I'M AFRAID WE'VE GOT MUCH BIGGER PROBLEMS RIGHT NOW.
SEÑOR! SEÑOR! LOS NIÑOS SE LEVANTAN!

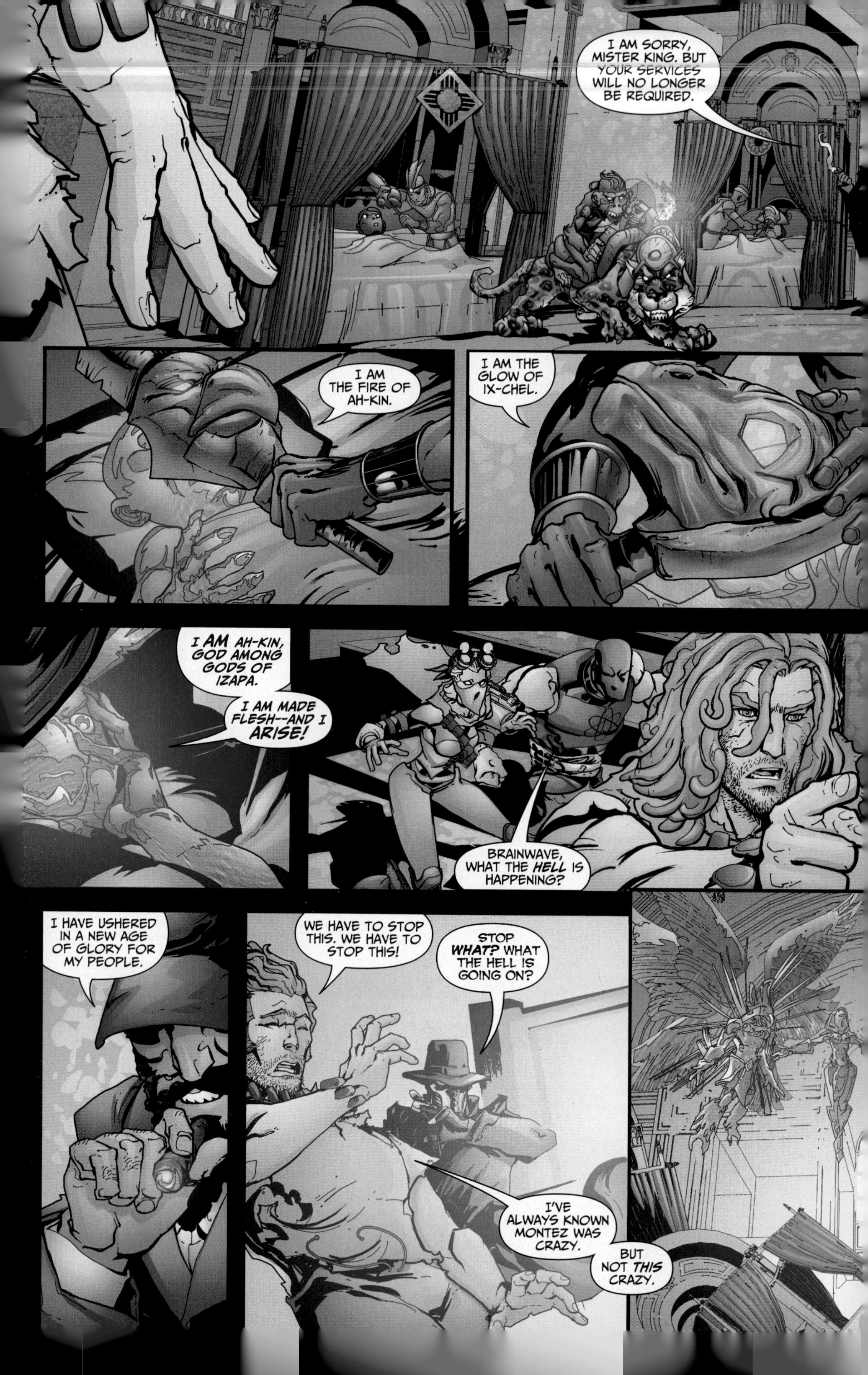
I AM SORRY, MISTER KING. BUT YOUR SERVICES WILL NO LONGER BE REQUIRED.
I AM THE FIRE OF AH-KIN.
I AM THE GLOW OF IX-CHEL.
I AM AH-KIN, GOD AMONG GODS OF IZAPA.
I AM MADE FLESH--AND I ARISE!
BRAINWAVE, WHAT THE HELL IS HAPPENING?
I HAVE USHERED IN A NEW AGE OF GLORY FOR MY PEOPLE.
WE HAVE TO STOP THIS. WE HAVE TO STOP THIS!
STOP WHAT? WHAT THE HELL IS GOING ON?
I'VE ALWAYS KNOWN MONTEZ WAS CRAZY.
BUT NOT THIS CRAZY.

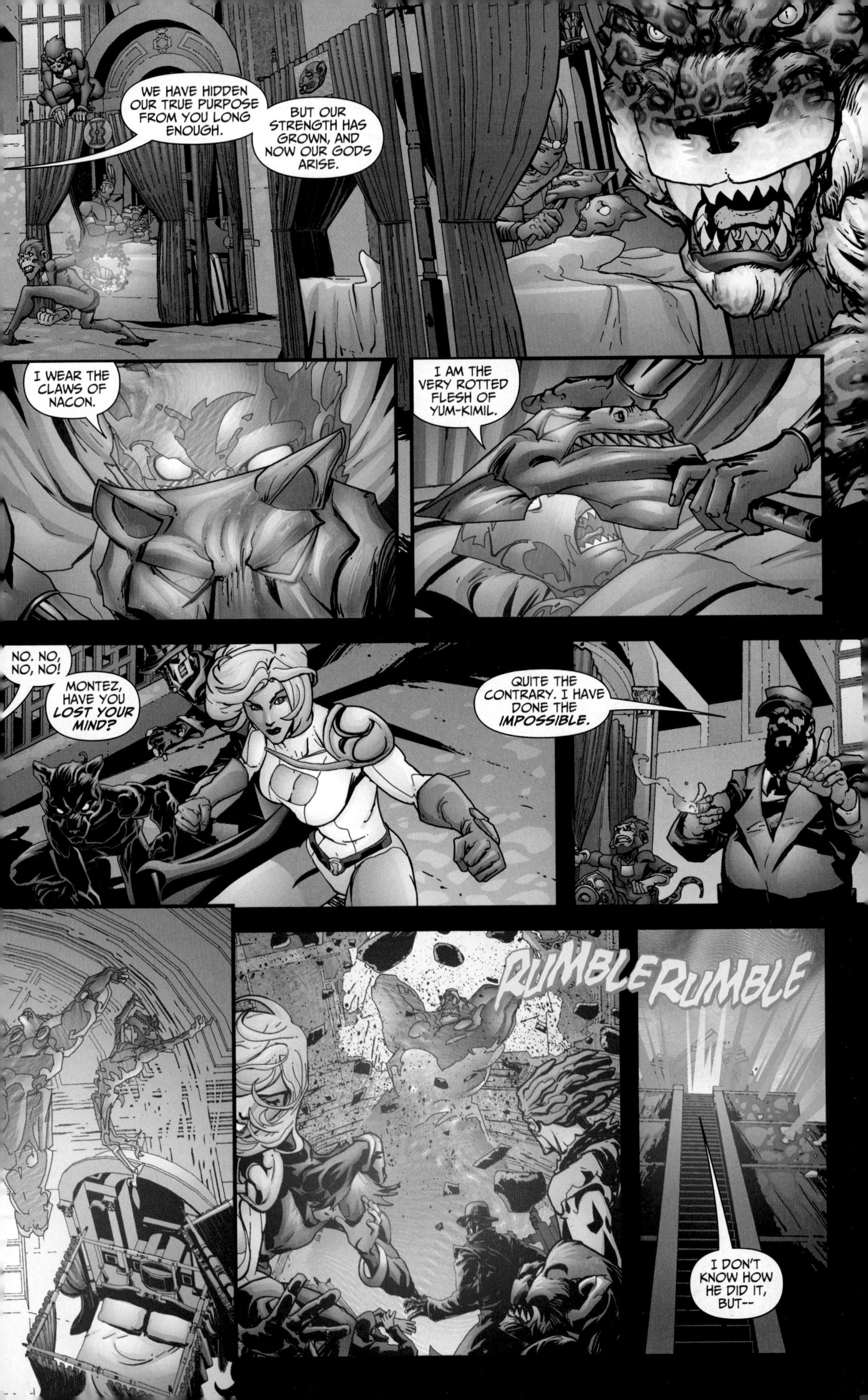
WE HAVE HIDDEN OUR TRUE PURPOSE FROM YOU LONG ENOUGH.
BUT OUR STRENGTH HAS GROWN, AND NOW OUR GODS ARISE.
I WEAR THE CLAWS OF NACON.
I AM THE VERY ROTTED FLESH OF YUM-KIMIL.
NO. NO, NO, NO!
MONTEZ, HAVE YOU LOST YOUR MIND?
QUITE THE CONTRARY. I HAVE DONE THE IMPOSSIBLE.
RUMBLE RUMBLE
I DON'T KNOW HOW HE DID IT, BUT--

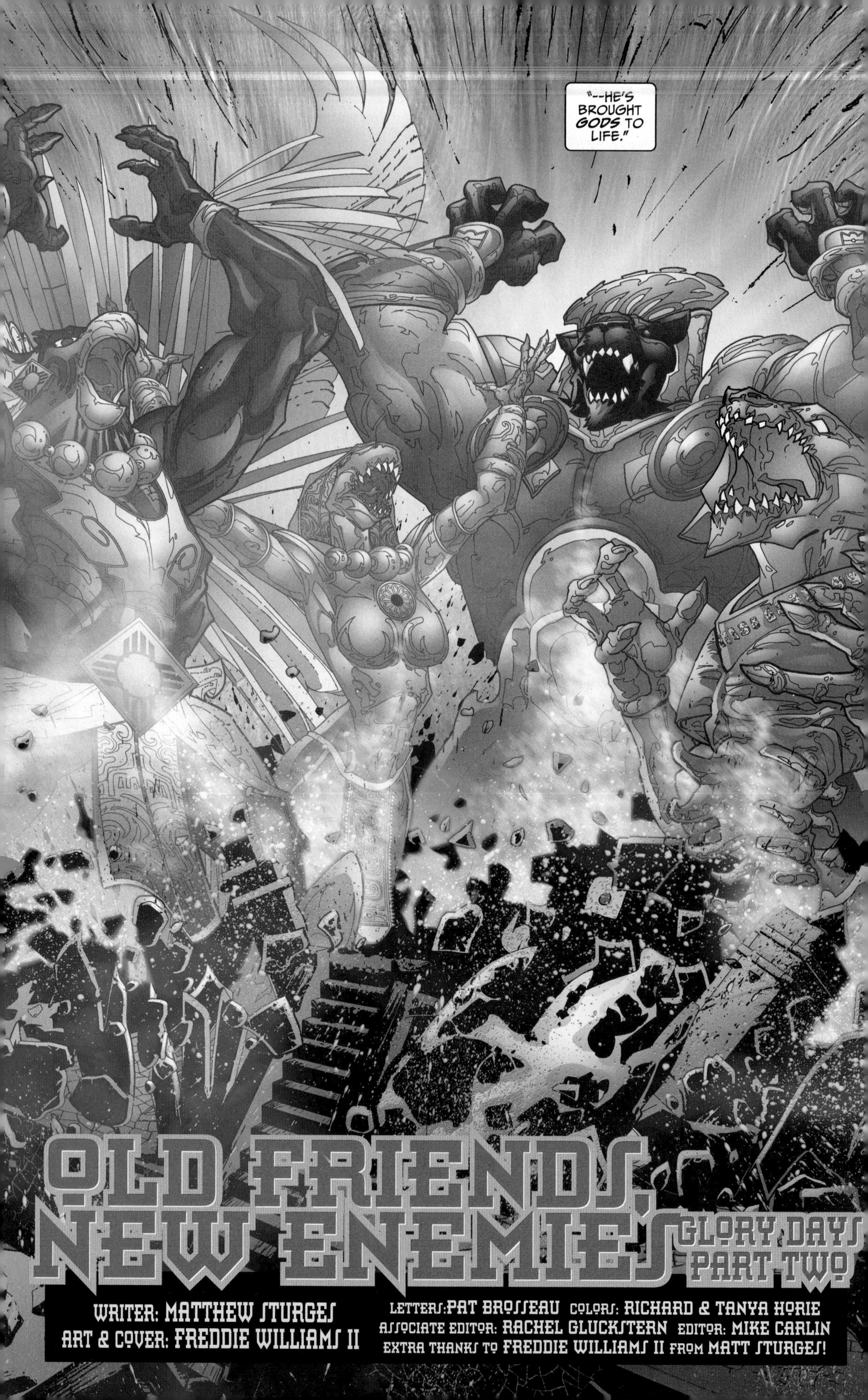
"--HE'S BROUGHT GODS TO LIFE."
OLD FRIENDS, NEW ENEMIES
GLORY DAYS PART TWO
WRITER: MATTHEW STURGES
ART & COVER: FREDDIE WILLIAMS II
LETTERS: PAT BROSSEAU COLORS: RICHARD & TANYA HORIE
ASSOCIATE EDITOR: RACHEL GLUCKSTERN EDITOR: MIKE CARLIN
EXTRA THANKS TO FREDDIE WILLIAMS II FROM MATT STURGES!

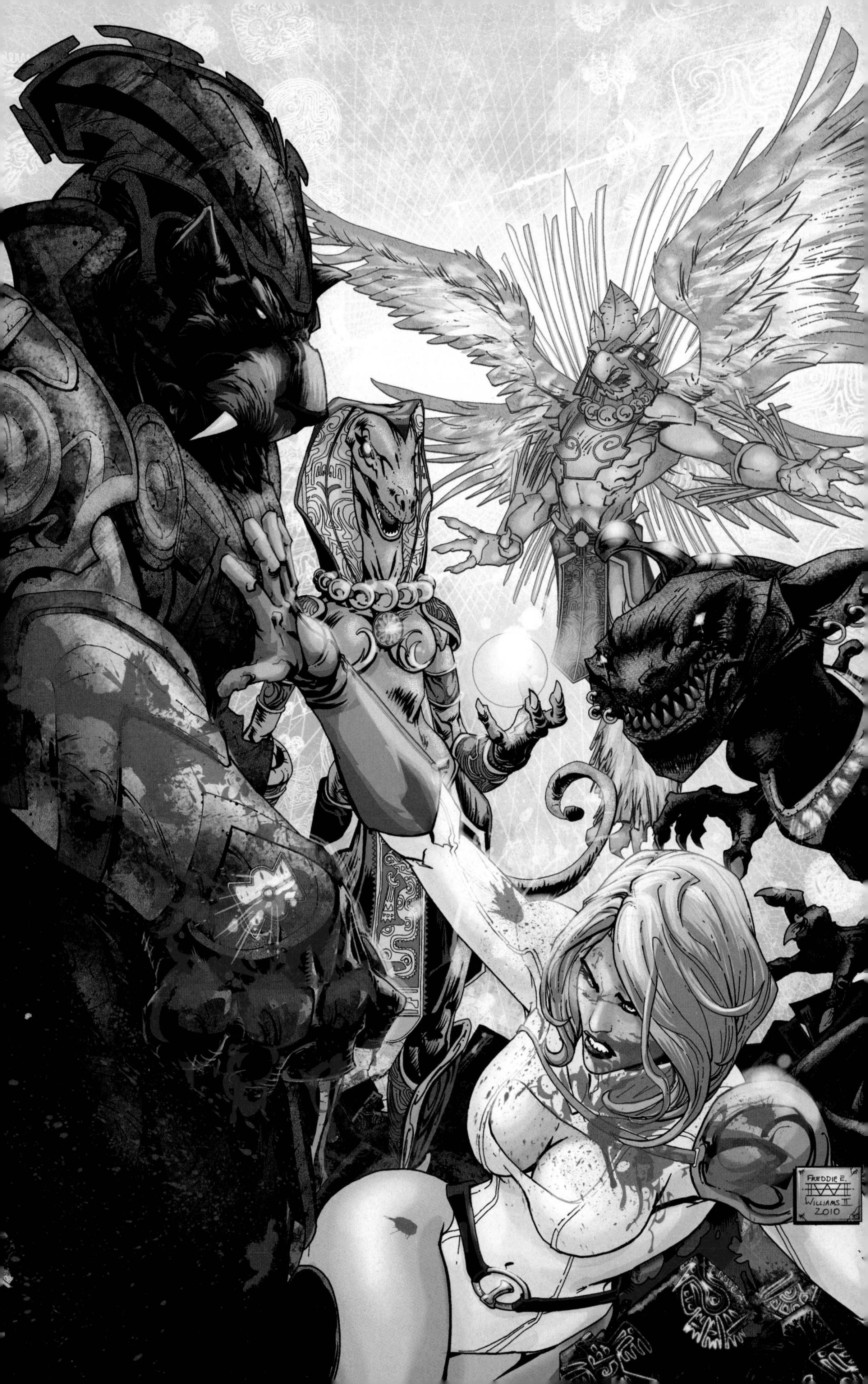
FREDDIE E.
WILLIAMS II
2010

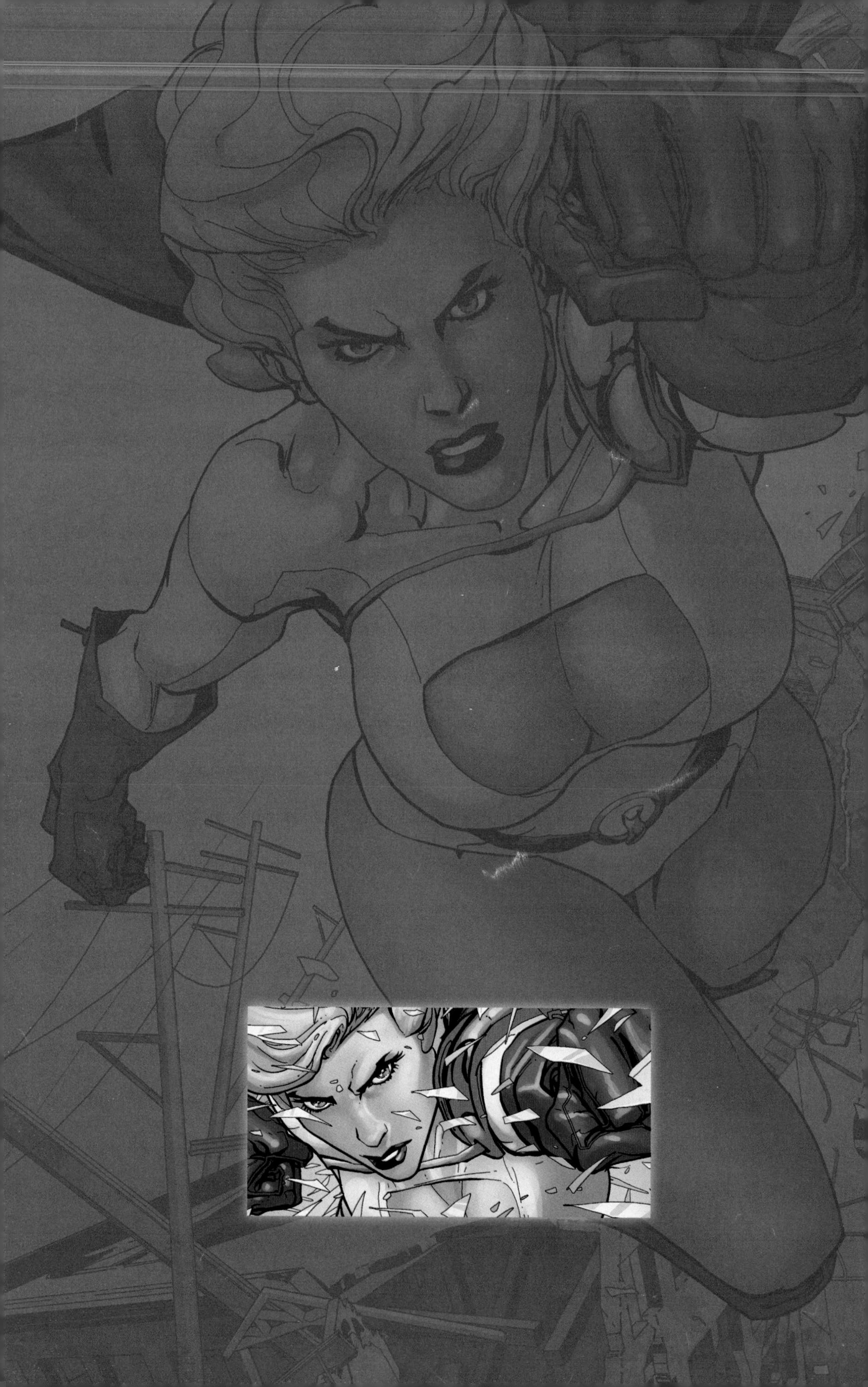

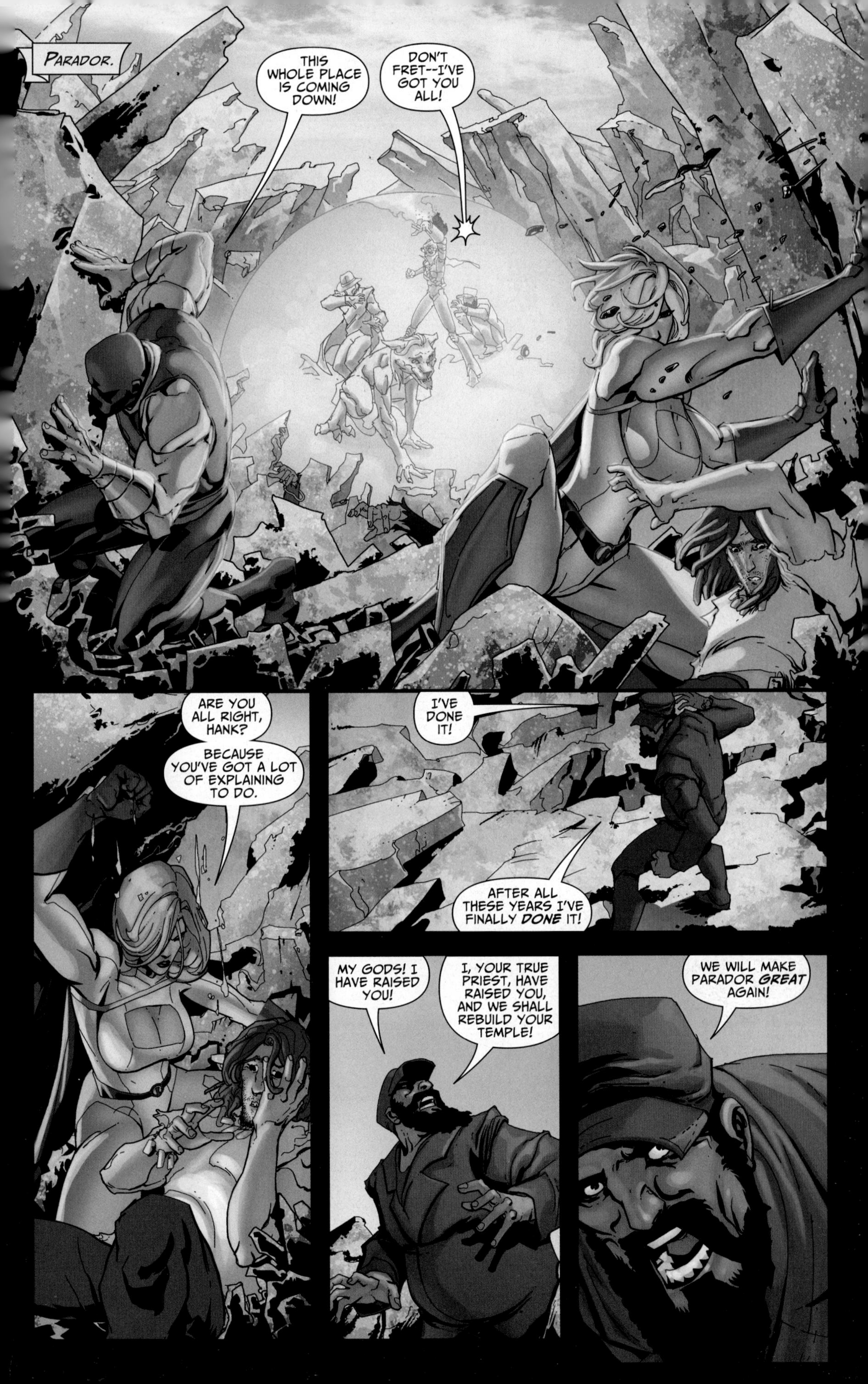
PARADOR.
THIS WHOLE PLACE IS COMING DOWN!
DON'T FRET--I'VE GOT YOU ALL!
ARE YOU ALL RIGHT, HANK?
BECAUSE YOU'VE GOT A LOT OF EXPLAINING TO DO.
I'VE DONE IT!
AFTER ALL THESE YEARS I'VE FINALLY DONE IT!
MY GODS! I HAVE RAISED YOU!
I, YOUR TRUE PRIEST, HAVE RAISED YOU, AND WE SHALL REBUILD YOUR TEMPLE!
WE WILL MAKE PARADOR GREAT AGAIN!

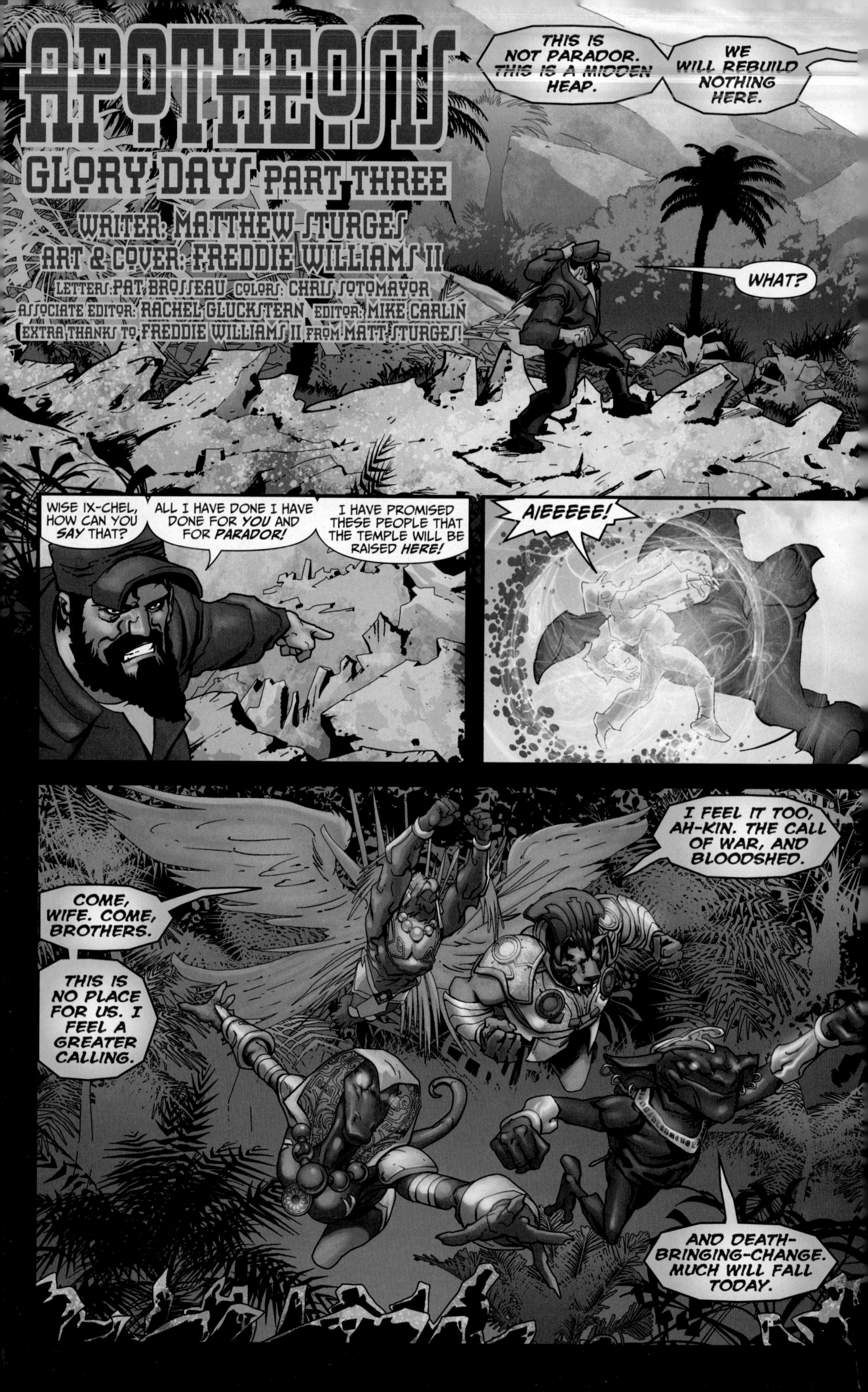
APOTHEOSIS
GLORY DAYS PART THREE
WRITER: MATTHEW STURGES
ART & COVER: FREDDIE WILLIAMS II
LETTERS: PAT BROSSEAU COLORS: CHRIS SOTOMAYOR
ASSOCIATE EDITOR: RACHEL GLUCKSTERN EDITOR: MIKE CARLIN
EXTRA THANKS TO FREDDIE WILLIAMS II FROM MATT STURGES!
THIS IS NOT PARADOR. THIS IS A MIDDEN HEAP.
WE WILL REBUILD NOTHING HERE.
WHAT?
WISE IX-CHEL, HOW CAN YOU SAY THAT?
ALL I HAVE DONE I HAVE DONE FOR YOU AND FOR PARADOR!
I HAVE PROMISED THESE PEOPLE THAT THE TEMPLE WILL BE RAISED HERE!
AIEEEEE!
COME, WIFE. COME, BROTHERS.
THIS IS NO PLACE FOR US. I FEEL A GREATER CALLING.
I FEEL IT TOO, AH-KIN. THE CALL OF WAR, AND BLOODSHED.
AND DEATH-BRINGING-CHANGE. MUCH WILL FALL TODAY.

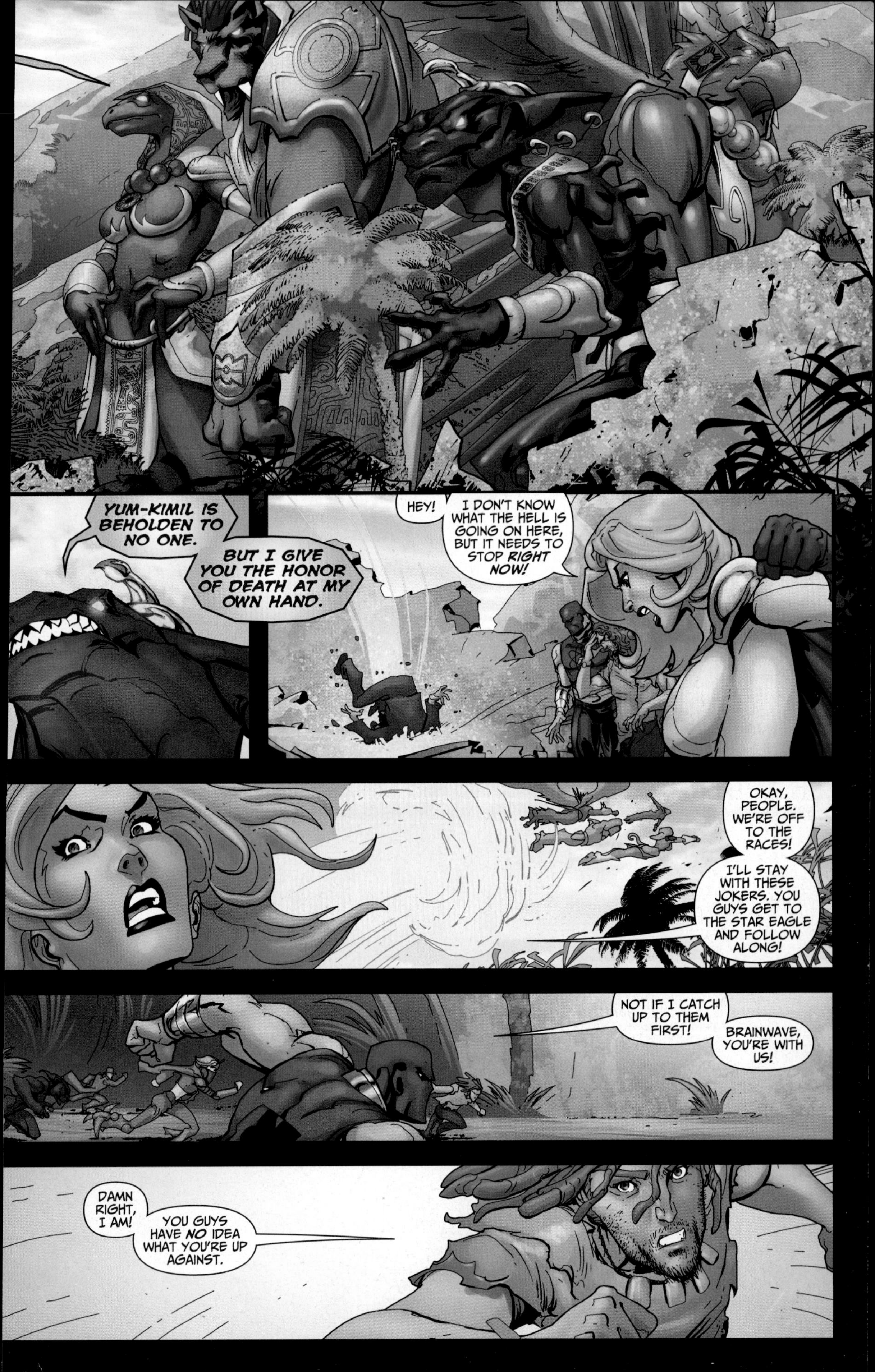
YUM-KIMIL IS BEHOLDEN TO NO ONE.
BUT I GIVE YOU THE HONOR OF DEATH AT MY OWN HAND.
HEY!
I DON'T KNOW WHAT THE HELL IS GOING ON HERE, BUT IT NEEDS TO STOP RIGHT NOW!
OKAY, PEOPLE. WE'RE OFF TO THE RACES!
I'LL STAY WITH THESE JOKERS. YOU GUYS GET TO THE STAR EAGLE AND FOLLOW ALONG!
NOT IF I CATCH UP TO THEM FIRST!
BRAINWAVE, YOU'RE WITH US!
DAMN RIGHT, I AM!
YOU GUYS HAVE NO IDEA WHAT YOU'RE UP AGAINST.

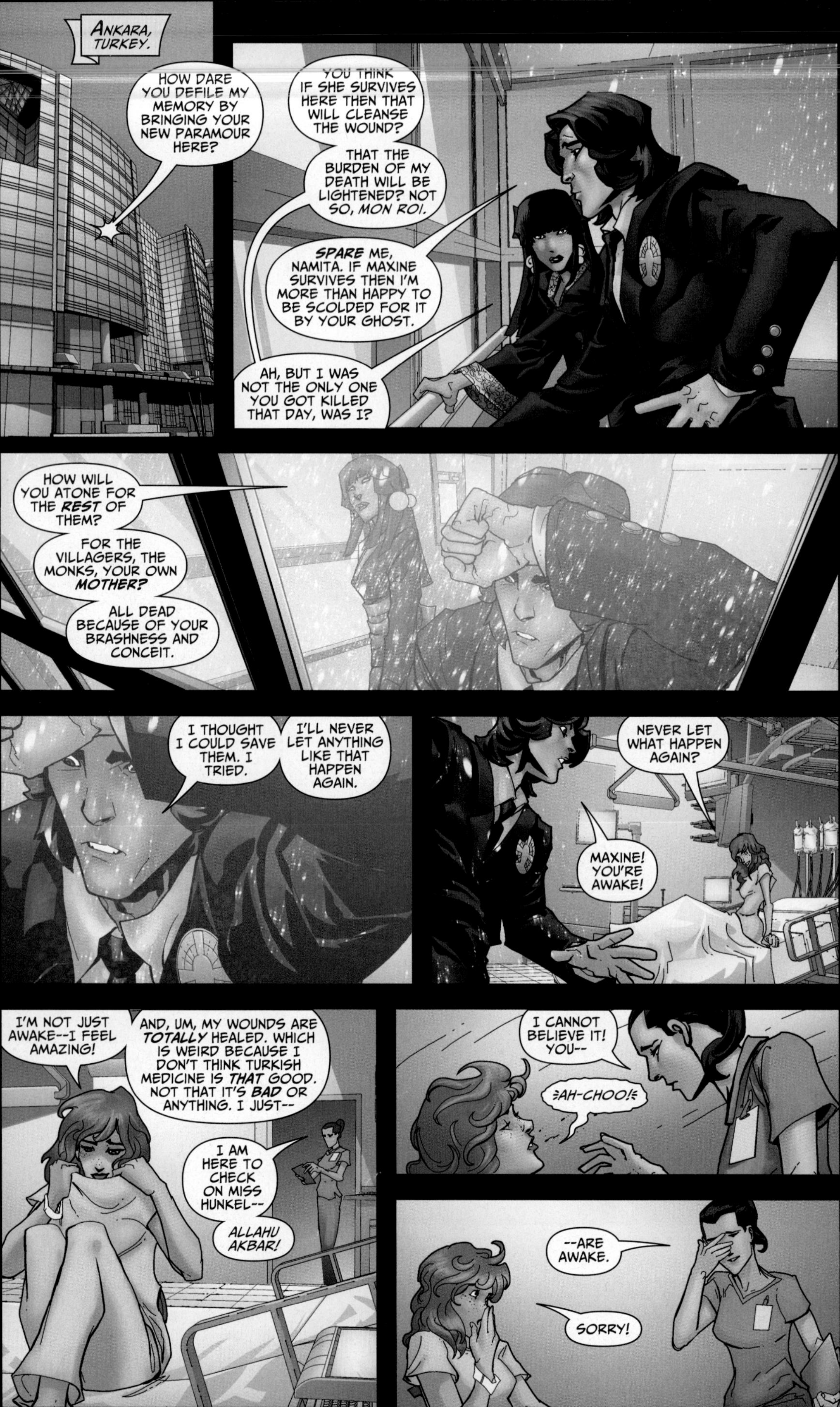

ANKARA, TURKEY.
HOW DARE YOU DEFILE MY MEMORY BY BRINGING YOUR NEW PARAMOUR HERE?
YOU THINK IF SHE SURVIVES HERE THEN THAT WILL CLEANSE THE WOUND?
THAT THE BURDEN OF MY DEATH WILL BE LIGHTENED? NOT SO, MON ROI.
SPARE ME, NAMITA. IF MAXINE SURVIVES THEN I'M MORE THAN HAPPY TO BE SCOLDED FOR IT BY YOUR GHOST.
AH, BUT I WAS NOT THE ONLY ONE YOU GOT KILLED THAT DAY, WAS I?
HOW WILL YOU ATONE FOR THE REST OF THEM?
FOR THE VILLAGERS, THE MONKS, YOUR OWN MOTHER?
ALL DEAD BECAUSE OF YOUR BRASHNESS AND CONCEIT.
I THOUGHT I COULD SAVE THEM. I TRIED.
I'LL NEVER LET ANYTHING LIKE THAT HAPPEN AGAIN.
NEVER LET WHAT HAPPEN AGAIN?
MAXINE! YOU'RE AWAKE!
I'M NOT JUST AWAKE--I FEEL AMAZING!
AND, UM, MY WOUNDS ARE TOTALLY HEALED. WHICH IS WEIRD BECAUSE I DON'T THINK TURKISH MEDICINE IS THAT GOOD. NOT THAT IT'S BAD OR ANYTHING. I JUST--
I AM HERE TO CHECK ON MISS HUNKEL--
ALLAHU AKBAR!
I CANNOT BELIEVE IT! YOU--
AH-CHOO!
--ARE AWAKE.
SORRY!

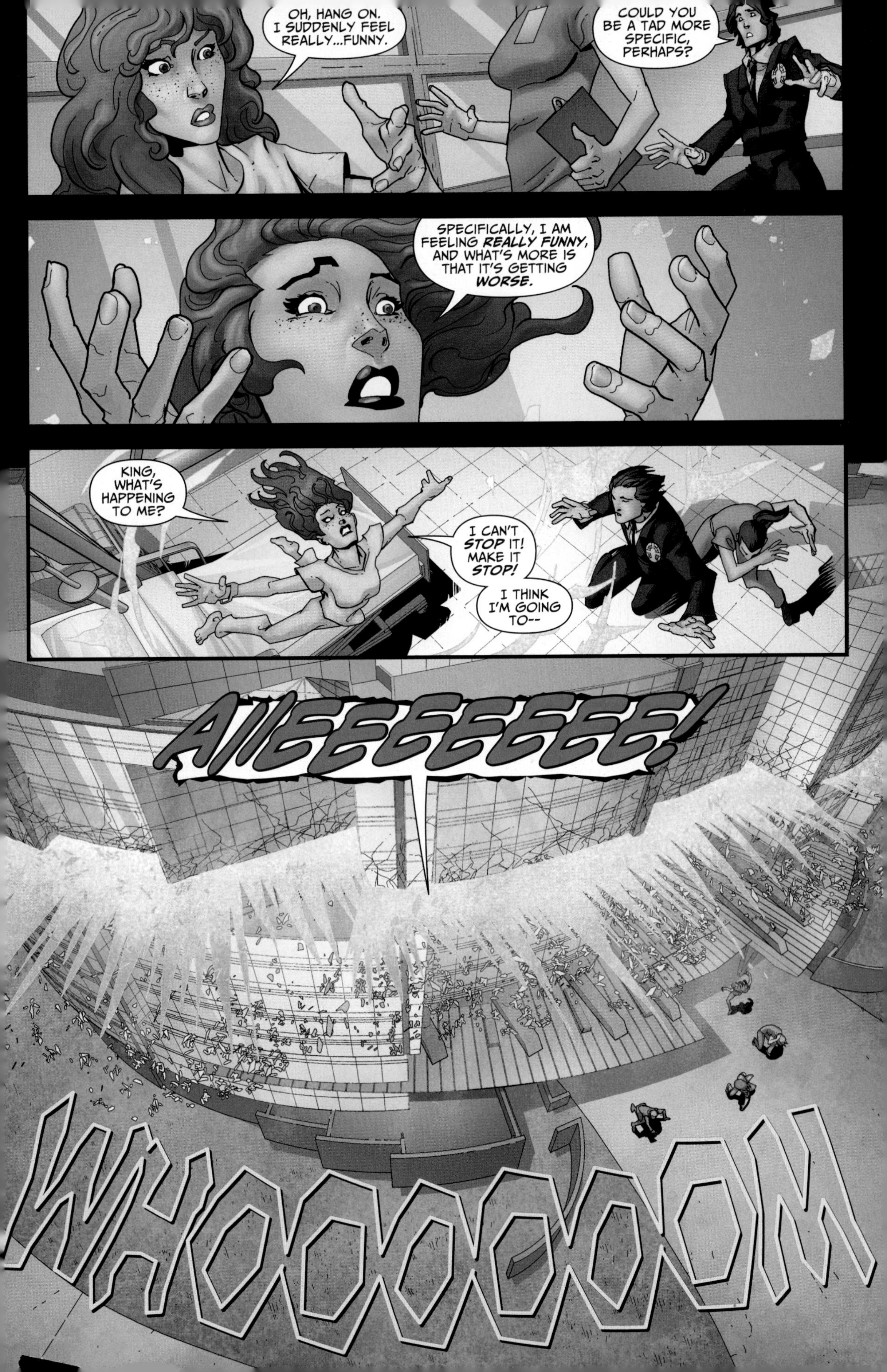
OH, HANG ON. I SUDDENLY FEEL REALLY...FUNNY.
COULD YOU BE A TAD MORE SPECIFIC, PERHAPS?
SPECIFICALLY, I AM FEELING REALLY FUNNY, AND WHAT'S MORE IS THAT IT'S GETTING WORSE.
KING, WHAT'S HAPPENING TO ME?
I CAN'T STOP IT! MAKE IT STOP!
I THINK I'M GOING TO--
AIIEEEEEEEE!
WHOOOOOOOM

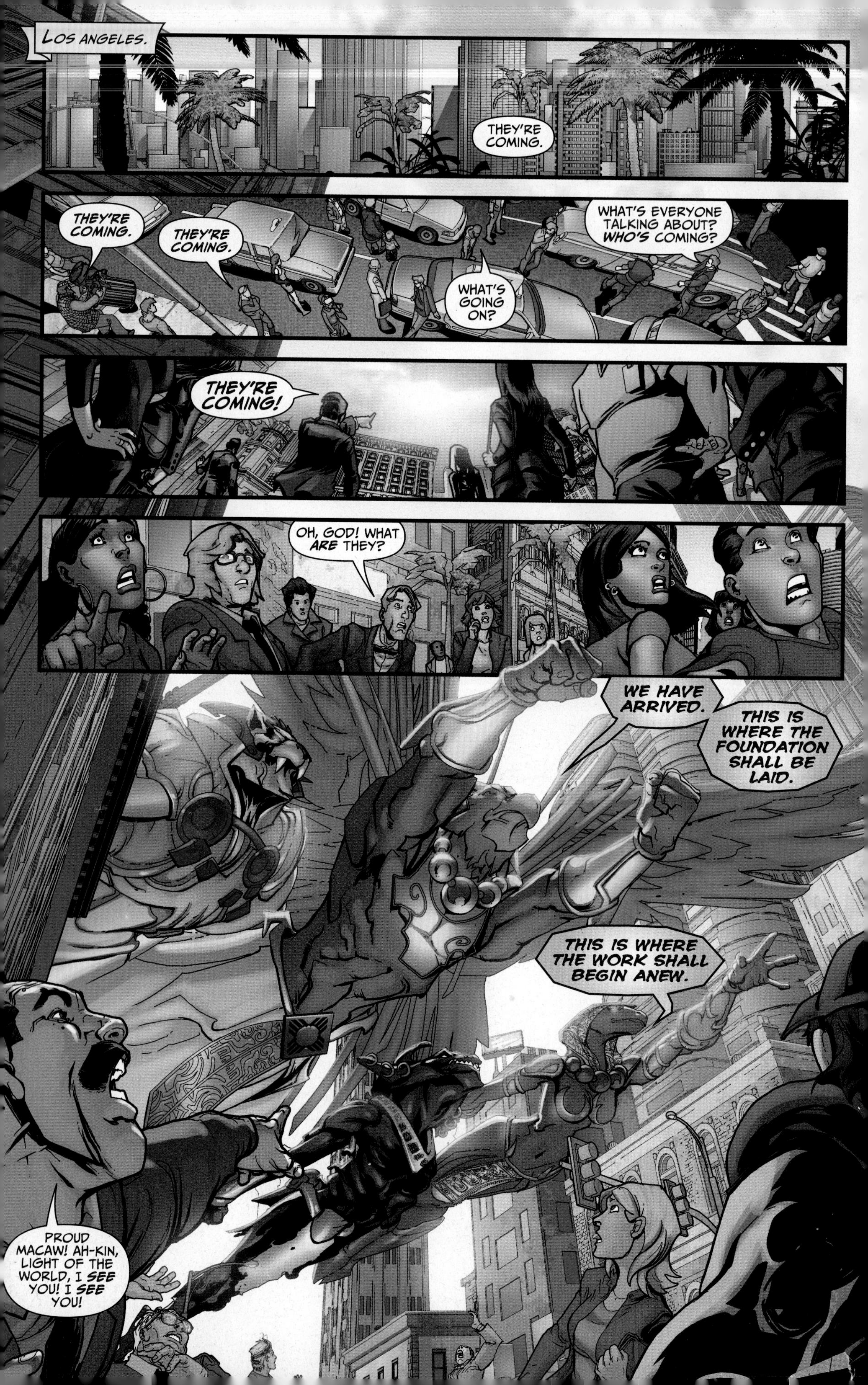
LOS ANGELES.
THEY'RE COMING.
THEY'RE COMING.
THEY'RE COMING.
WHAT'S GOING ON?
WHAT'S EVERYONE TALKING ABOUT? WHO'S COMING?
THEY'RE COMING!
OH, GOD! WHAT ARE THEY?
WE HAVE ARRIVED.
THIS IS WHERE THE FOUNDATION SHALL BE LAID.
THIS IS WHERE THE WORK SHALL BEGIN ANEW.
PROUD MACAW! AH-KIN, LIGHT OF THE WORLD, I SEE YOU! I SEE YOU!

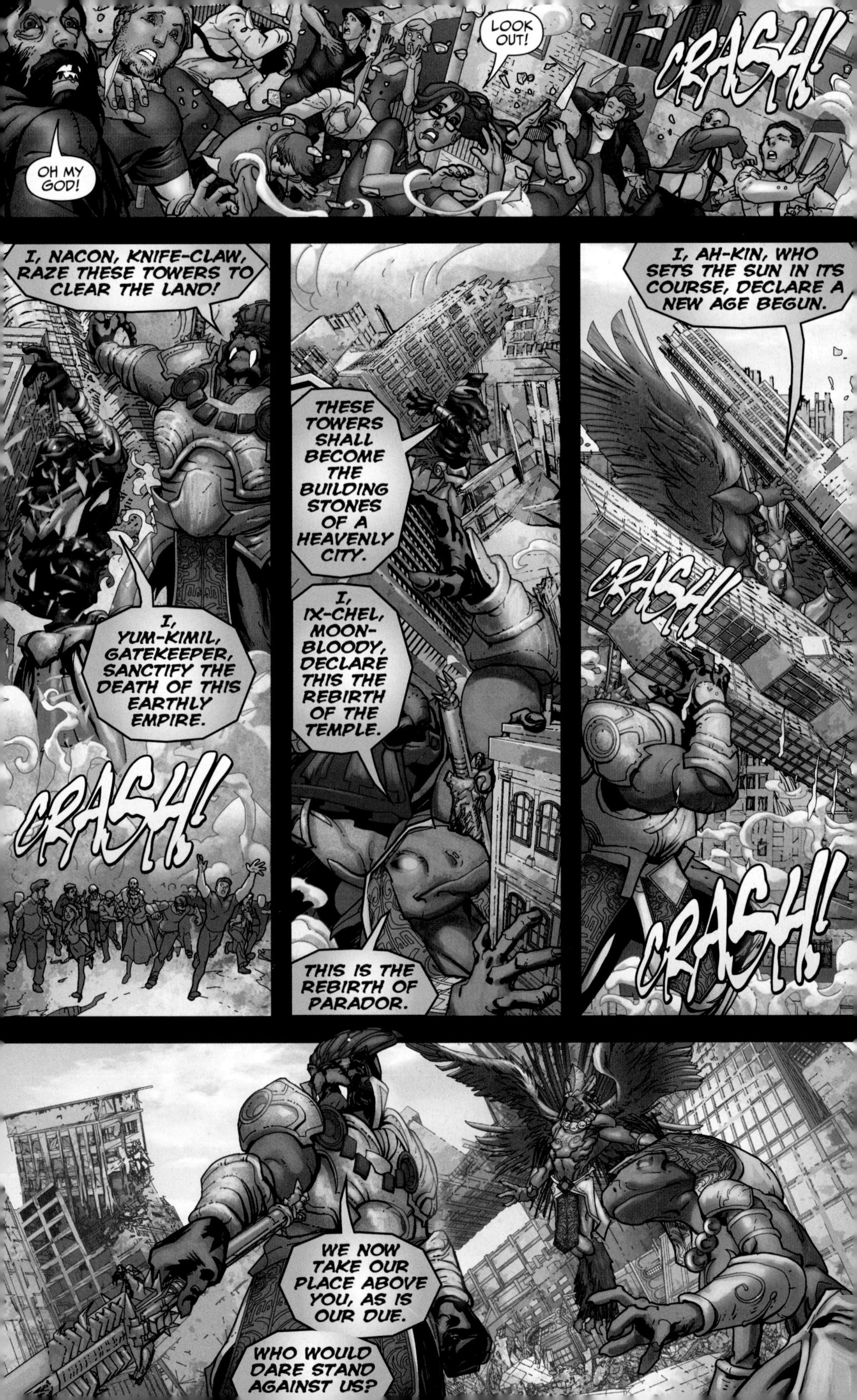
LOOK OUT!
CRASH!
OH MY GOD!
I, NACON, KNIFE-CLAW, RAZE THESE TOWERS TO CLEAR THE LAND!
I, YUM-KIMIL, GATEKEEPER, SANCTIFY THE DEATH OF THIS EARTHLY EMPIRE.
CRASH!
THESE TOWERS SHALL BECOME THE BUILDING STONES OF A HEAVENLY CITY.
I, IX-CHEL, MOON-BLOODY, DECLARE THIS THE REBIRTH OF THE TEMPLE.
THIS IS THE REBIRTH OF PARADOR.
I, AH-KIN, WHO SETS THE SUN IN ITS COURSE, DECLARE A NEW AGE BEGUN.
CRASH!
CRASH!
WE NOW TAKE OUR PLACE ABOVE YOU, AS IS OUR DUE.
WHO WOULD DARE STAND AGAINST US?

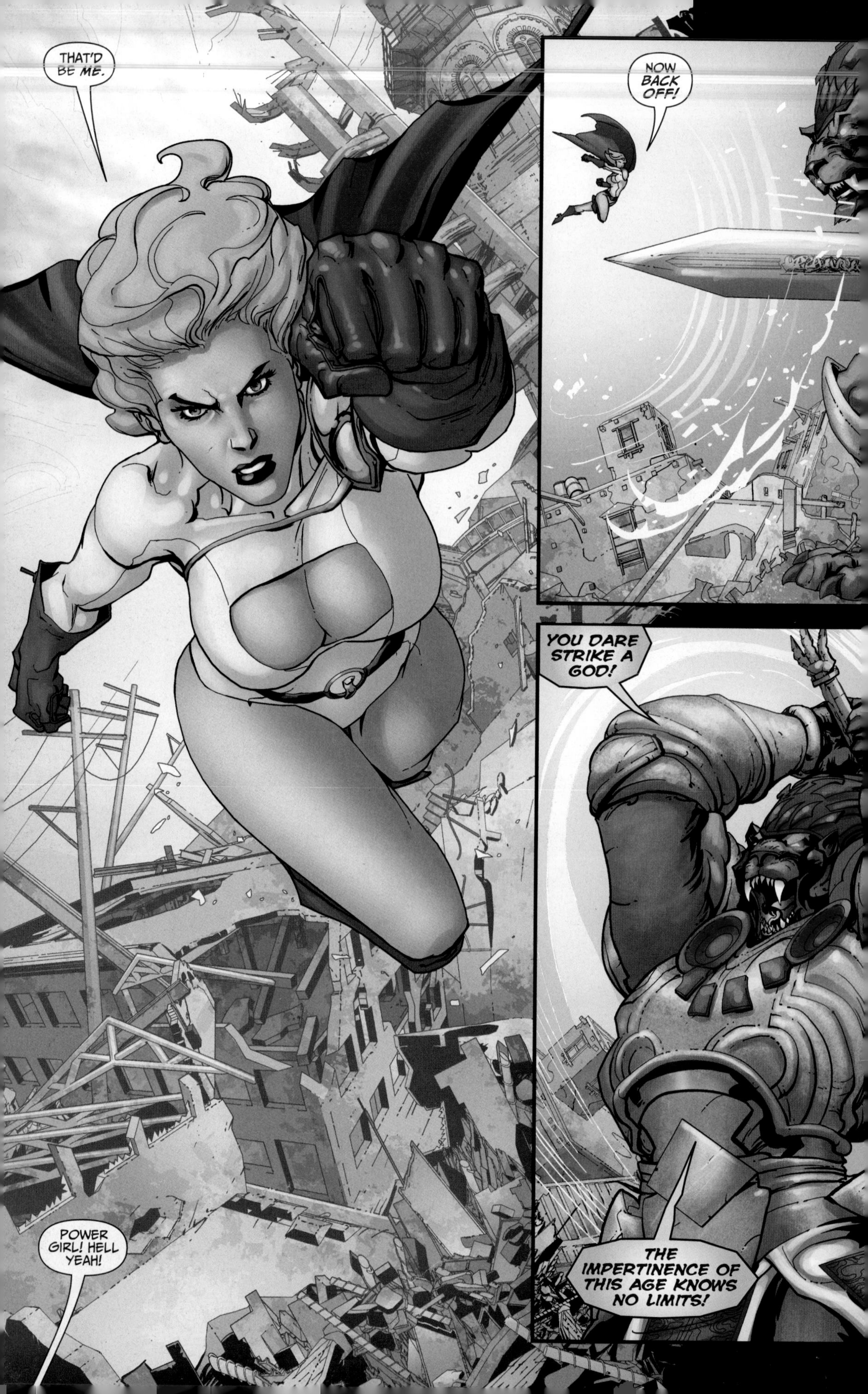
THAT'D BE ME.
NOW BACK OFF!
YOU DARE STRIKE A GOD!
POWER GIRL! HELL YEAH!
THE IMPERTINENCE OF THIS AGE KNOWS NO LIMITS!

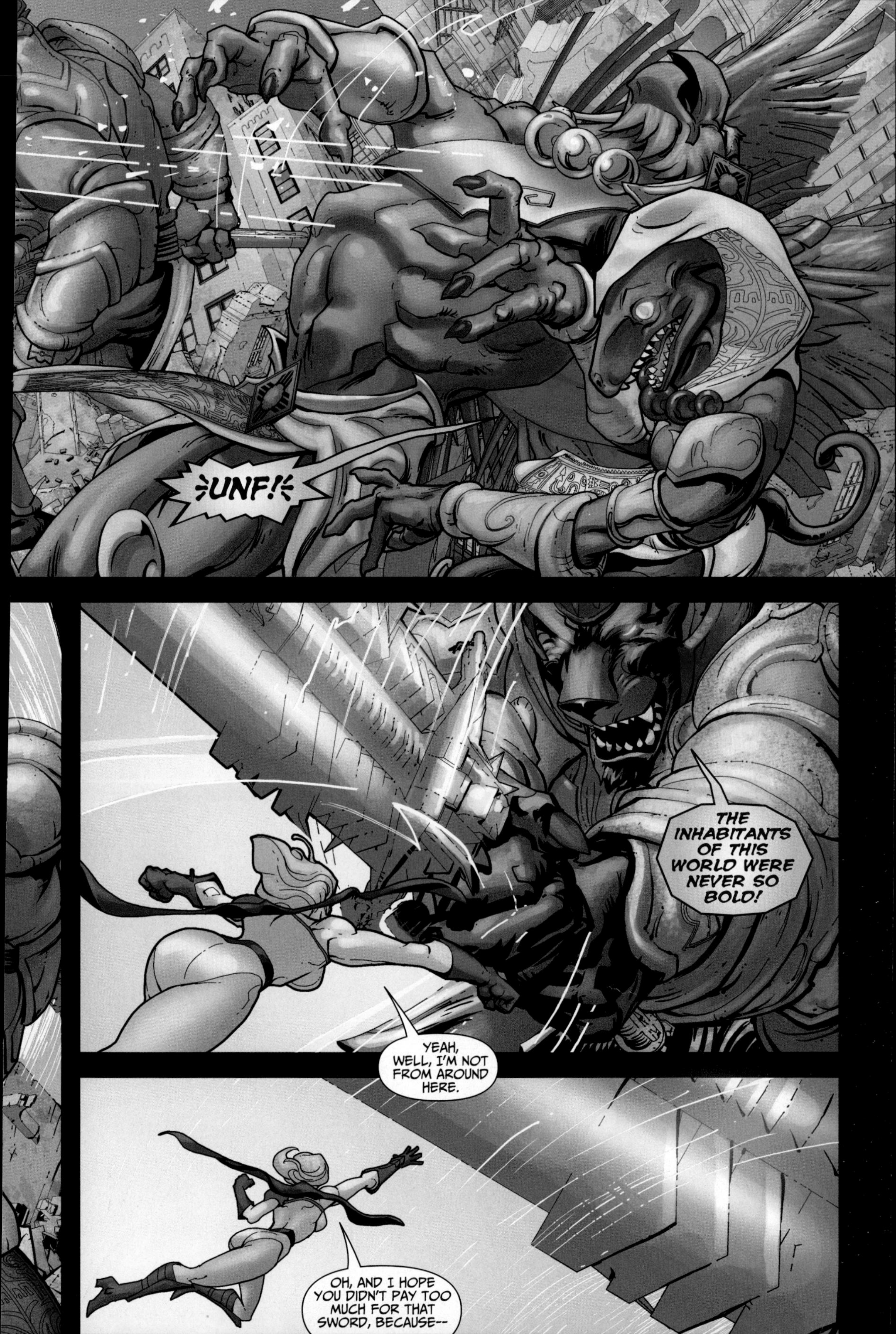
UNF!
THE INHABITANTS OF THIS WORLD WERE NEVER SO BOLD!
YEAH, WELL, I'M NOT FROM AROUND HERE.
OH, AND I HOPE YOU DIDN'T PAY TOO MUCH FOR THAT SWORD, BECAUSE--

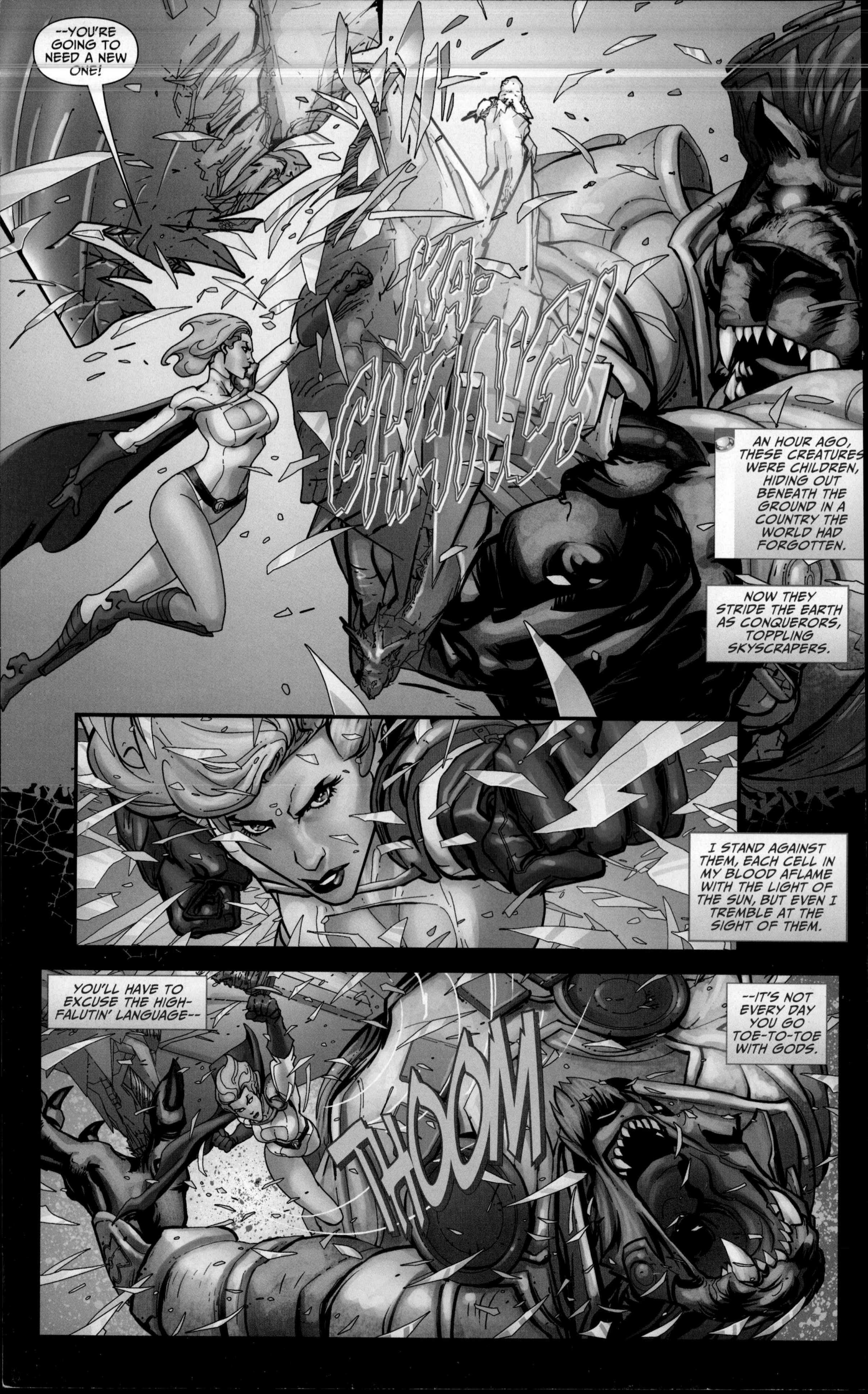
--YOU'RE GOING TO NEED A NEW ONE!
KA-CHANNG!
AN HOUR AGO, THESE CREATURES WERE CHILDREN, HIDING OUT BENEATH THE GROUND IN A COUNTRY THE WORLD HAD FORGOTTEN.
NOW THEY STRIDE THE EARTH AS CONQUERORS, TOPPLING SKYSCRAPERS.
I STAND AGAINST THEM, EACH CELL IN MY BLOOD AFLAME WITH THE LIGHT OF THE SUN, BUT EVEN I TREMBLE AT THE SIGHT OF THEM.
YOU'LL HAVE TO EXCUSE THE HIGH-FALUTIN' LANGUAGE--
--IT'S NOT EVERY DAY YOU GO TOE-TO-TOE WITH GODS.
THOOM

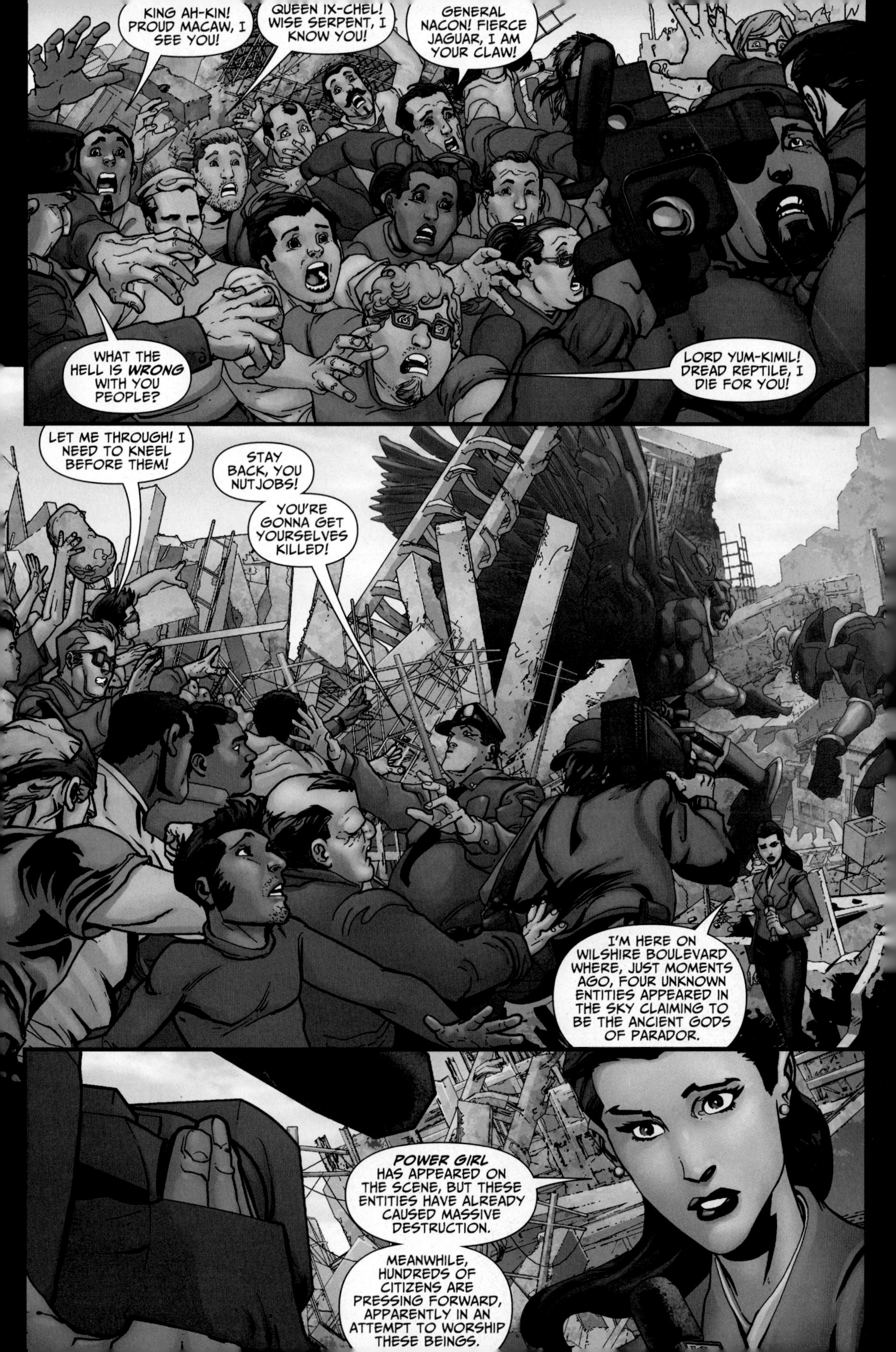
KING AH-KIN! PROUD MACAW, I SEE YOU!
QUEEN IX-CHEL! WISE SERPENT, I KNOW YOU!
GENERAL NACON! FIERCE JAGUAR, I AM YOUR CLAW!
WHAT THE HELL IS *WRONG* WITH YOU PEOPLE?
LORD YUM-KIMIL! DREAD REPTILE, I DIE FOR YOU!
LET ME THROUGH! I NEED TO KNEEL BEFORE THEM!
STAY BACK, YOU NUTJOBS!
YOU'RE GONNA GET YOURSELVES KILLED!
I'M HERE ON WILSHIRE BOULEVARD WHERE, JUST MOMENTS AGO, FOUR UNKNOWN ENTITIES APPEARED IN THE SKY CLAIMING TO BE THE ANCIENT GODS OF PARADOR.
POWER GIRL HAS APPEARED ON THE SCENE, BUT THESE ENTITIES HAVE ALREADY CAUSED MASSIVE DESTRUCTION.
MEANWHILE, HUNDREDS OF CITIZENS ARE PRESSING FORWARD, APPARENTLY IN AN ATTEMPT TO WORSHIP THESE BEINGS.

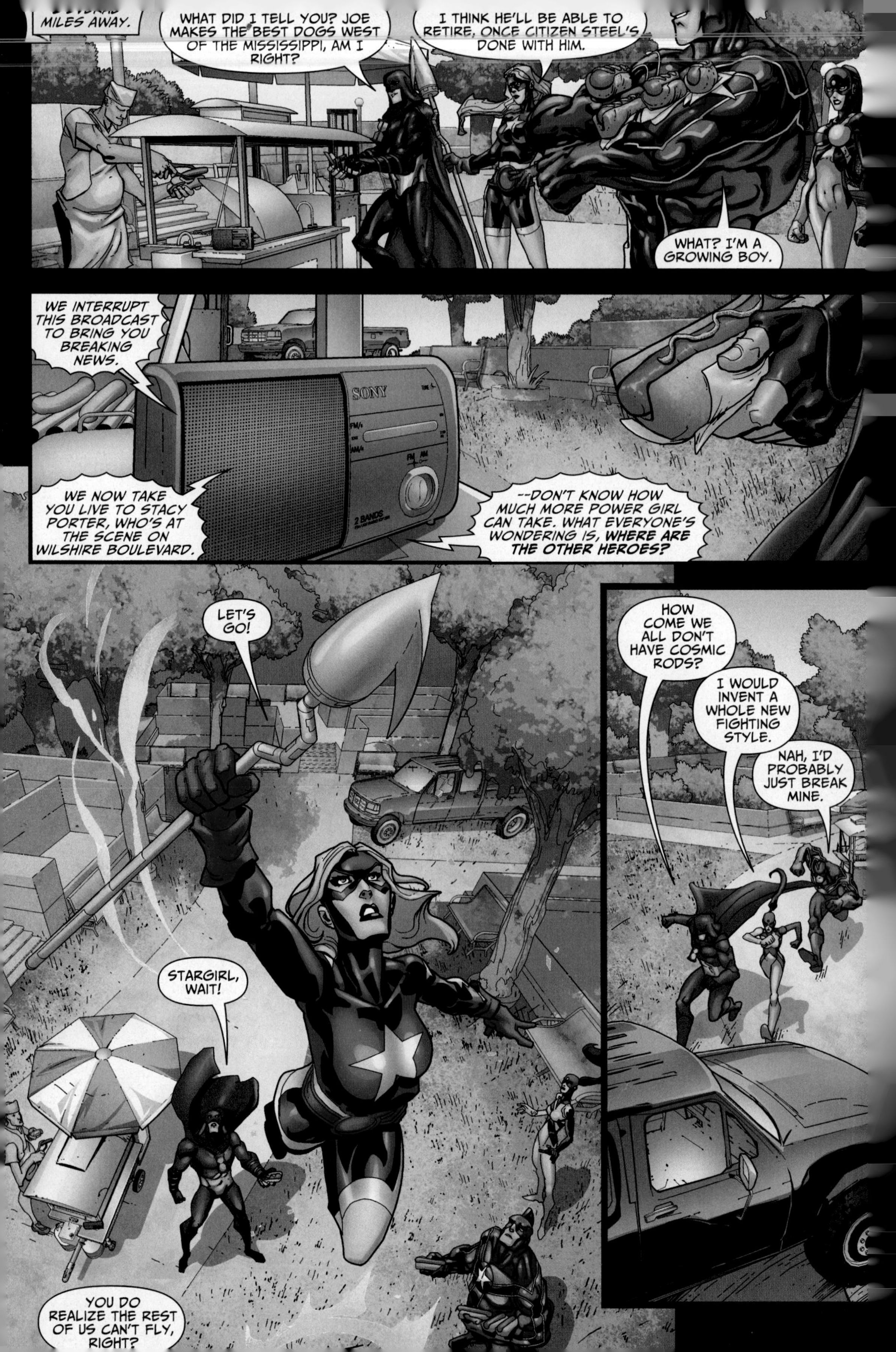

MILES AWAY.
WHAT DID I TELL YOU? JOE MAKES THE BEST DOGS WEST OF THE MISSISSIPPI, AM I RIGHT?
I THINK HE'LL BE ABLE TO RETIRE, ONCE CITIZEN STEEL'S DONE WITH HIM.
WHAT? I'M A GROWING BOY.
WE INTERRUPT THIS BROADCAST TO BRING YOU BREAKING NEWS.
SONY
WE NOW TAKE YOU LIVE TO STACY PORTER, WHO'S AT THE SCENE ON WILSHIRE BOULEVARD.
--DON'T KNOW HOW MUCH MORE POWER GIRL CAN TAKE. WHAT EVERYONE'S WONDERING IS, **WHERE ARE THE OTHER HEROES?**
LET'S GO!
STARGIRL, WAIT!
YOU DO REALIZE THE REST OF US CAN'T FLY, RIGHT?
HOW COME WE ALL DON'T HAVE COSMIC RODS?
I WOULD INVENT A WHOLE NEW FIGHTING STYLE.
NAH, I'D PROBABLY JUST BREAK MINE.

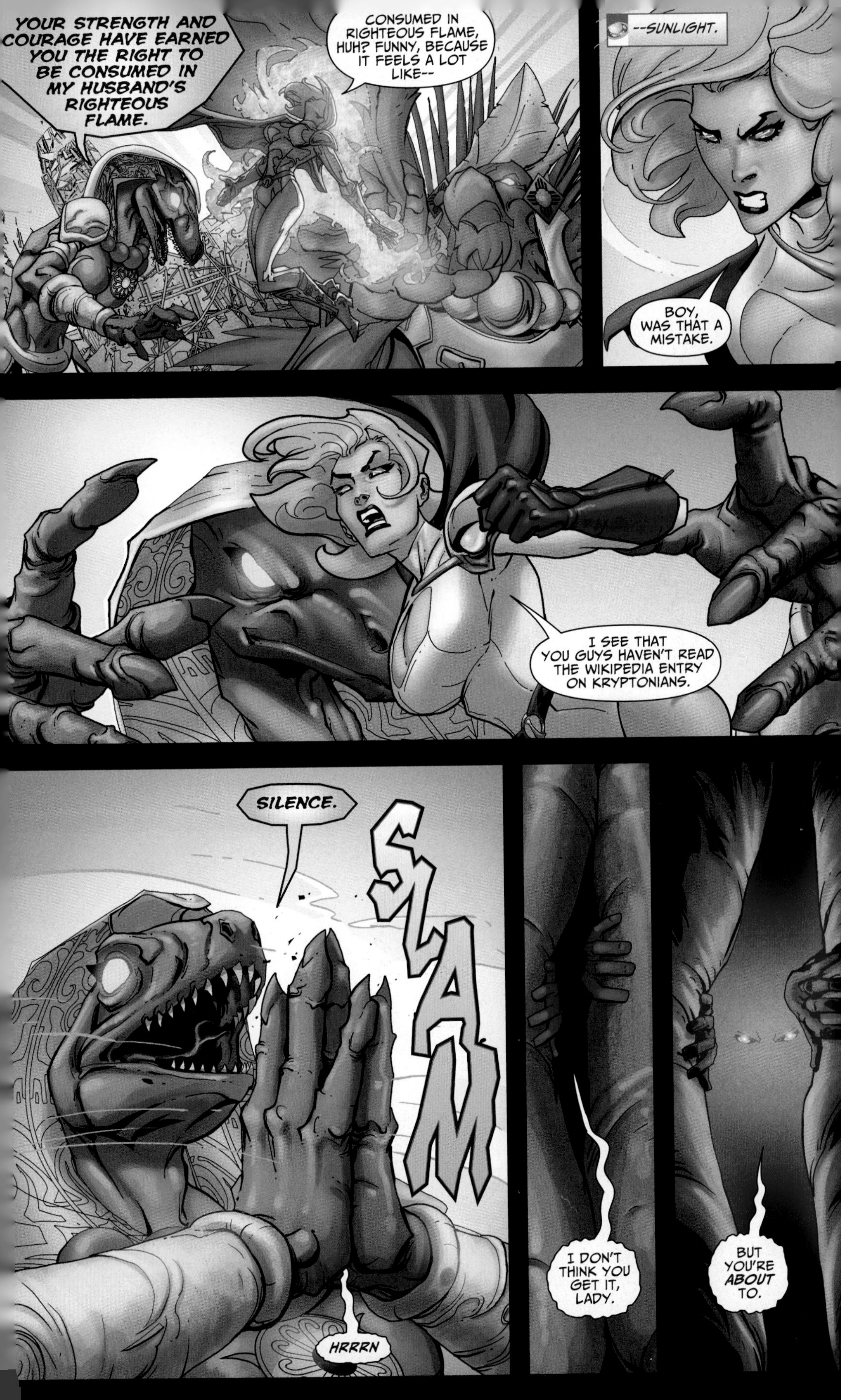
YOUR STRENGTH AND COURAGE HAVE EARNED YOU THE RIGHT TO BE CONSUMED IN MY HUSBAND'S RIGHTEOUS FLAME.
CONSUMED IN RIGHTEOUS FLAME, HUH? FUNNY, BECAUSE IT FEELS A LOT LIKE--
--SUNLIGHT.
BOY, WAS THAT A MISTAKE.
I SEE THAT YOU GUYS HAVEN'T READ THE WIKIPEDIA ENTRY ON KRYPTONIANS.
SILENCE.
SLAM
HRRRN
I DON'T THINK YOU GET IT, LADY.
BUT YOU'RE ABOUT TO.

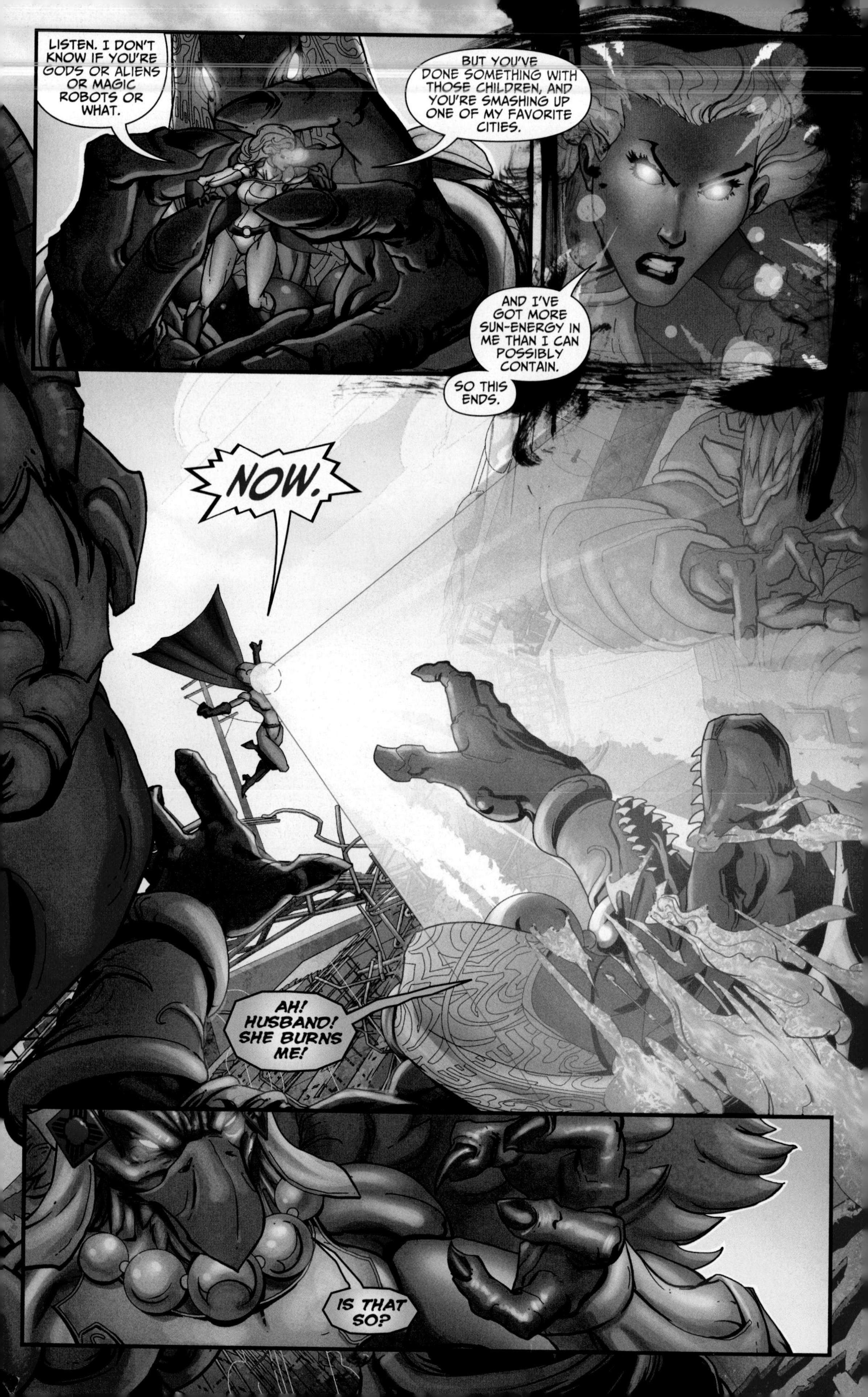
LISTEN. I DON'T KNOW IF YOU'RE GODS OR ALIENS OR MAGIC ROBOTS OR WHAT.
BUT YOU'VE DONE SOMETHING WITH THOSE CHILDREN, AND YOU'RE SMASHING UP ONE OF MY FAVORITE CITIES.
AND I'VE GOT MORE SUN-ENERGY IN ME THAN I CAN POSSIBLY CONTAIN.
SO THIS ENDS.
NOW.
AH! HUSBAND! SHE BURNS ME!
IS THAT SO?

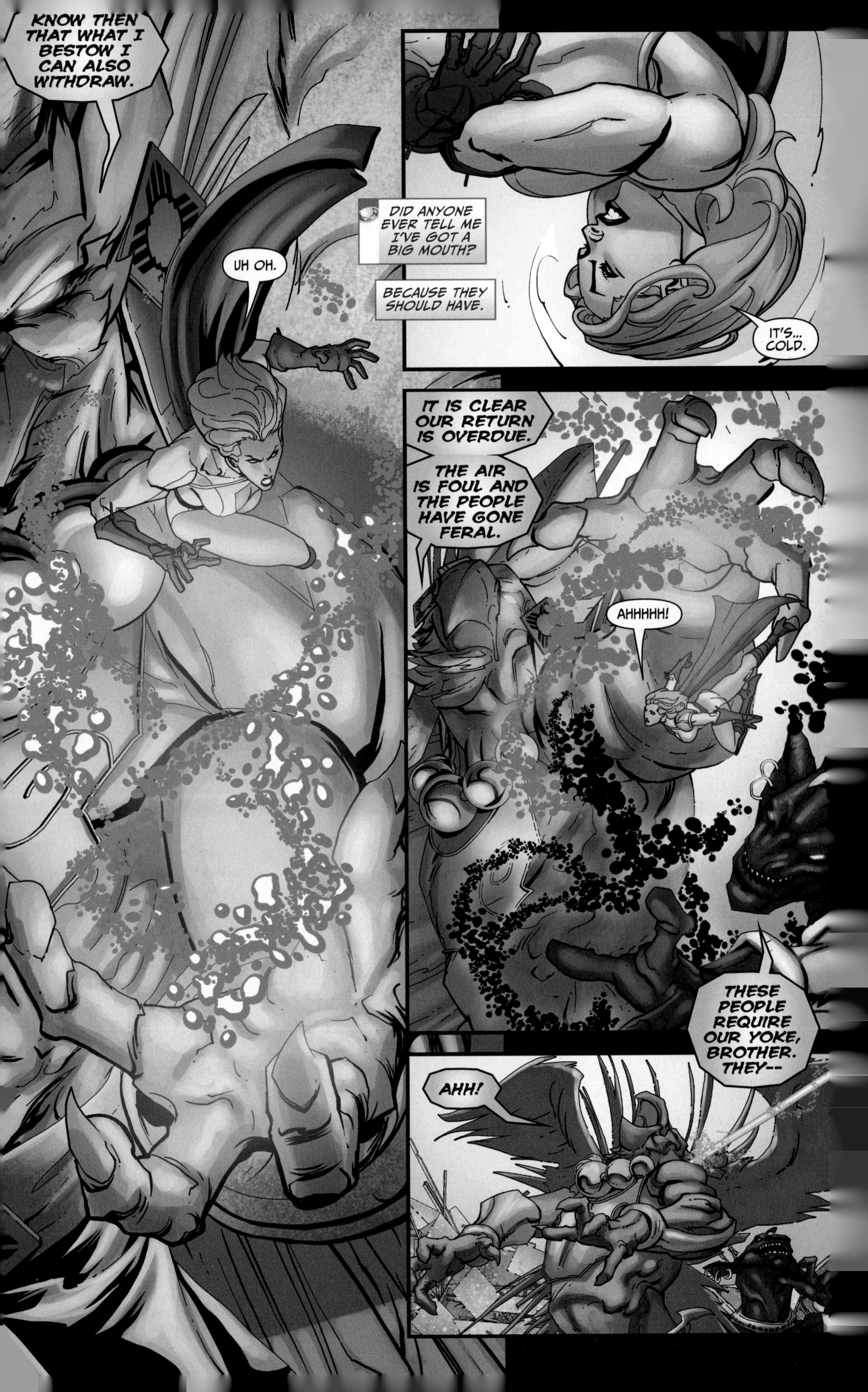
KNOW THEN THAT WHAT I BESTOW I CAN ALSO WITHDRAW.
UH OH.
DID ANYONE EVER TELL ME I'VE GOT A BIG MOUTH?
BECAUSE THEY SHOULD HAVE.
IT'S... COLD.
IT IS CLEAR OUR RETURN IS OVERDUE.
THE AIR IS FOUL AND THE PEOPLE HAVE GONE FERAL.
AHHHHH!
THESE PEOPLE REQUIRE OUR YOKE, BROTHER. THEY--
AHH!

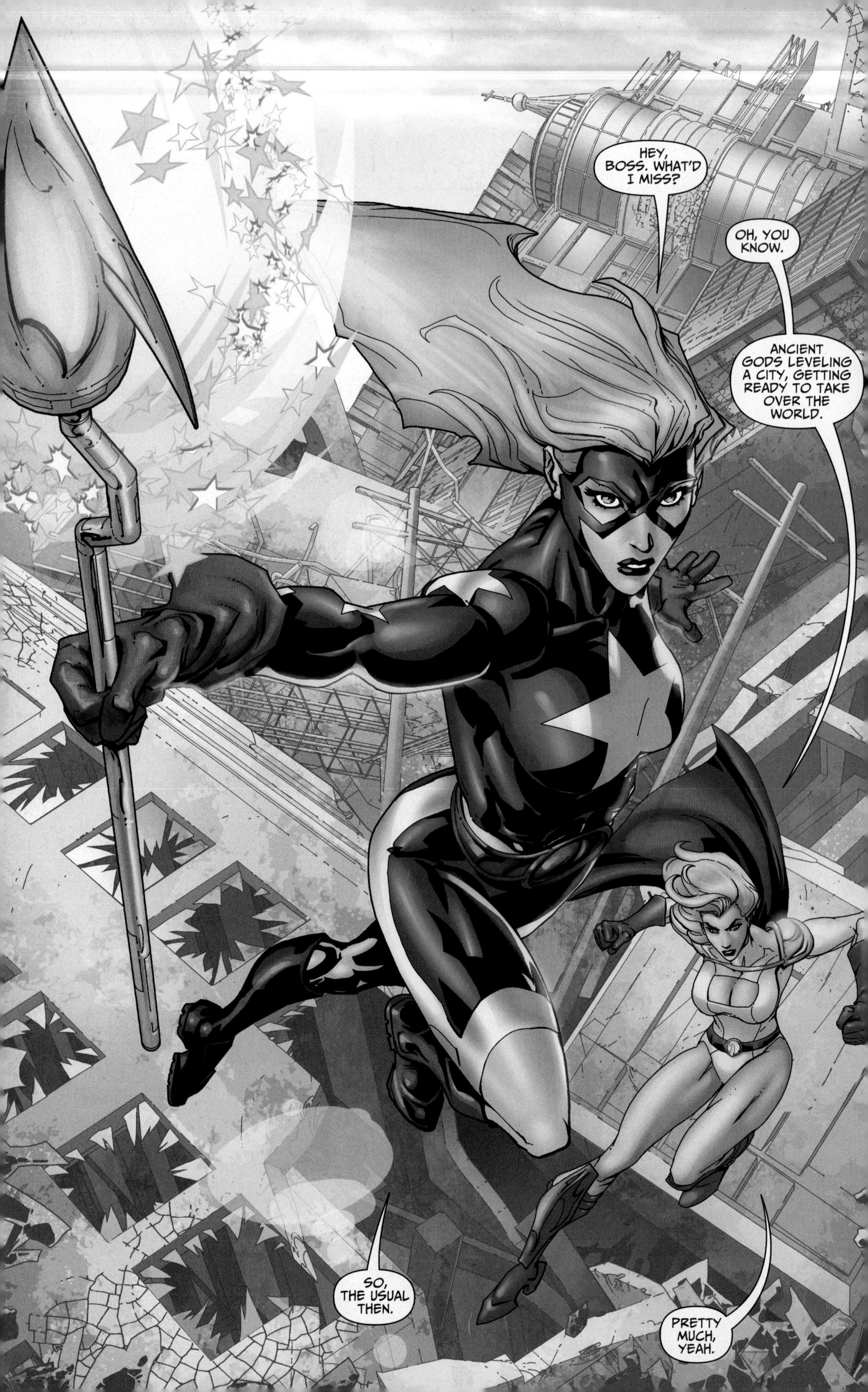
HEY, BOSS. WHAT'D I MISS?
OH, YOU KNOW.
ANCIENT GODS LEVELING A CITY, GETTING READY TO TAKE OVER THE WORLD.
SO, THE USUAL THEN.
PRETTY MUCH, YEAH.

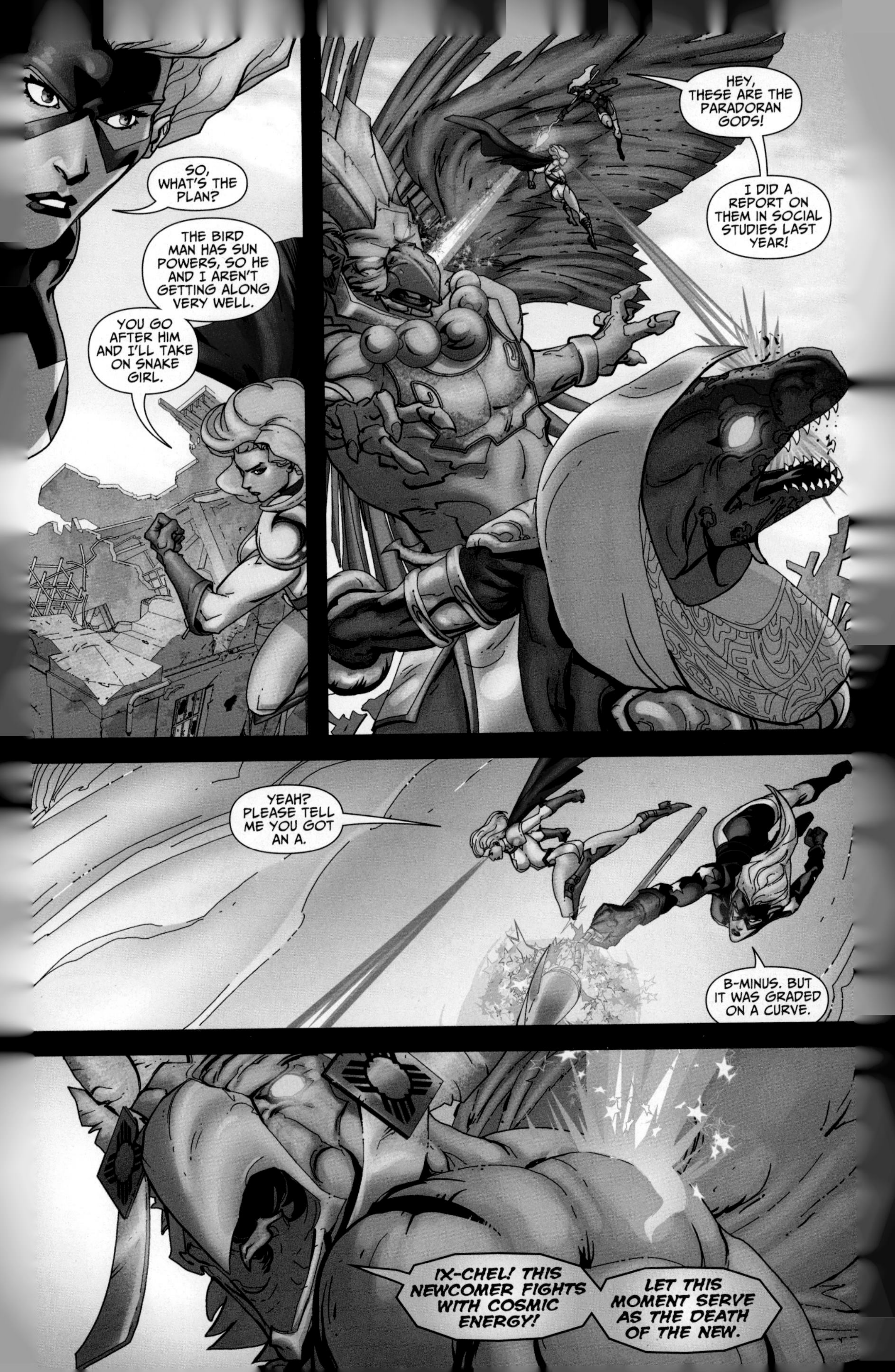
SO, WHAT'S THE PLAN?
THE BIRD MAN HAS SUN POWERS, SO HE AND I AREN'T GETTING ALONG VERY WELL.
YOU GO AFTER HIM AND I'LL TAKE ON SNAKE GIRL.
HEY, THESE ARE THE PARADORAN GODS!
I DID A REPORT ON THEM IN SOCIAL STUDIES LAST YEAR!
YEAH? PLEASE TELL ME YOU GOT AN A.
B-MINUS. BUT IT WAS GRADED ON A CURVE.
IX-CHEL! THIS NEWCOMER FIGHTS WITH COSMIC ENERGY!
LET THIS MOMENT SERVE AS THE DEATH OF THE NEW.

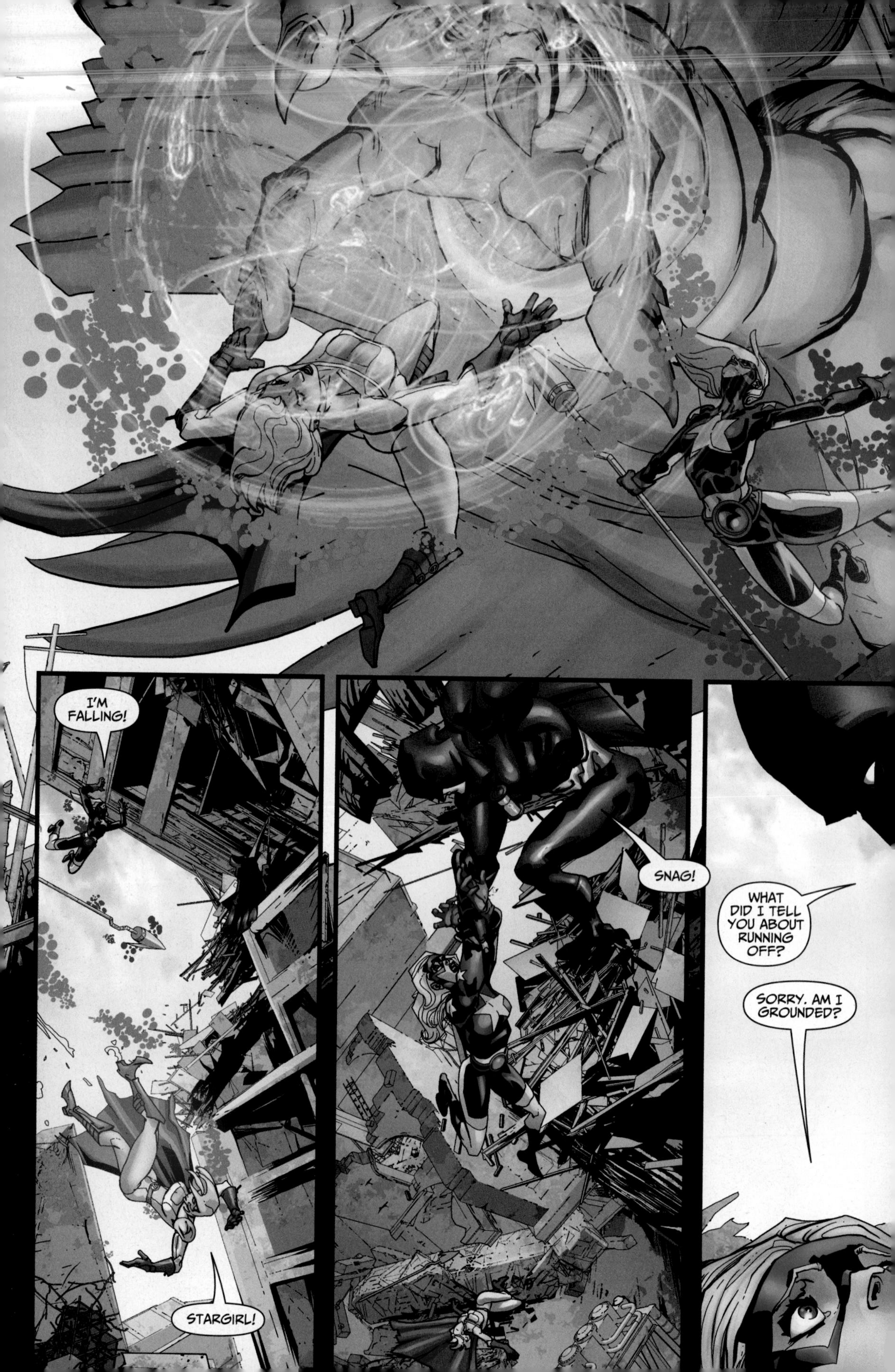
I'M FALLING!
STARGIRL!
SNAG!
WHAT DID I TELL YOU ABOUT RUNNING OFF?
SORRY. AM I GROUNDED?

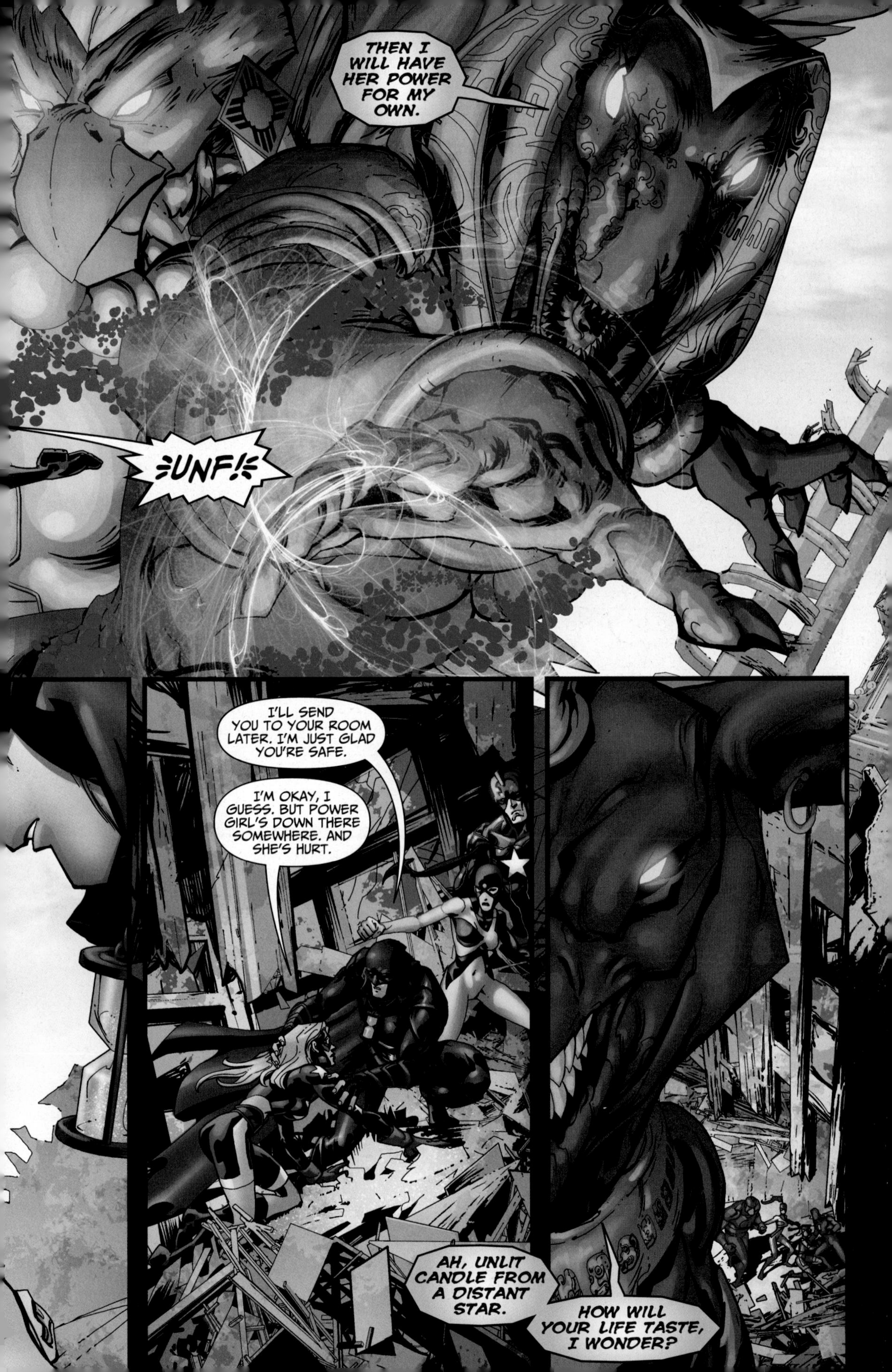
THEN I WILL HAVE HER POWER FOR MY OWN.
UNF!
I'LL SEND YOU TO YOUR ROOM LATER. I'M JUST GLAD YOU'RE SAFE.
I'M OKAY, I GUESS. BUT POWER GIRL'S DOWN THERE SOMEWHERE. AND SHE'S HURT.
AH, UNLIT CANDLE FROM A DISTANT STAR.
HOW WILL YOUR LIFE TASTE, I WONDER?

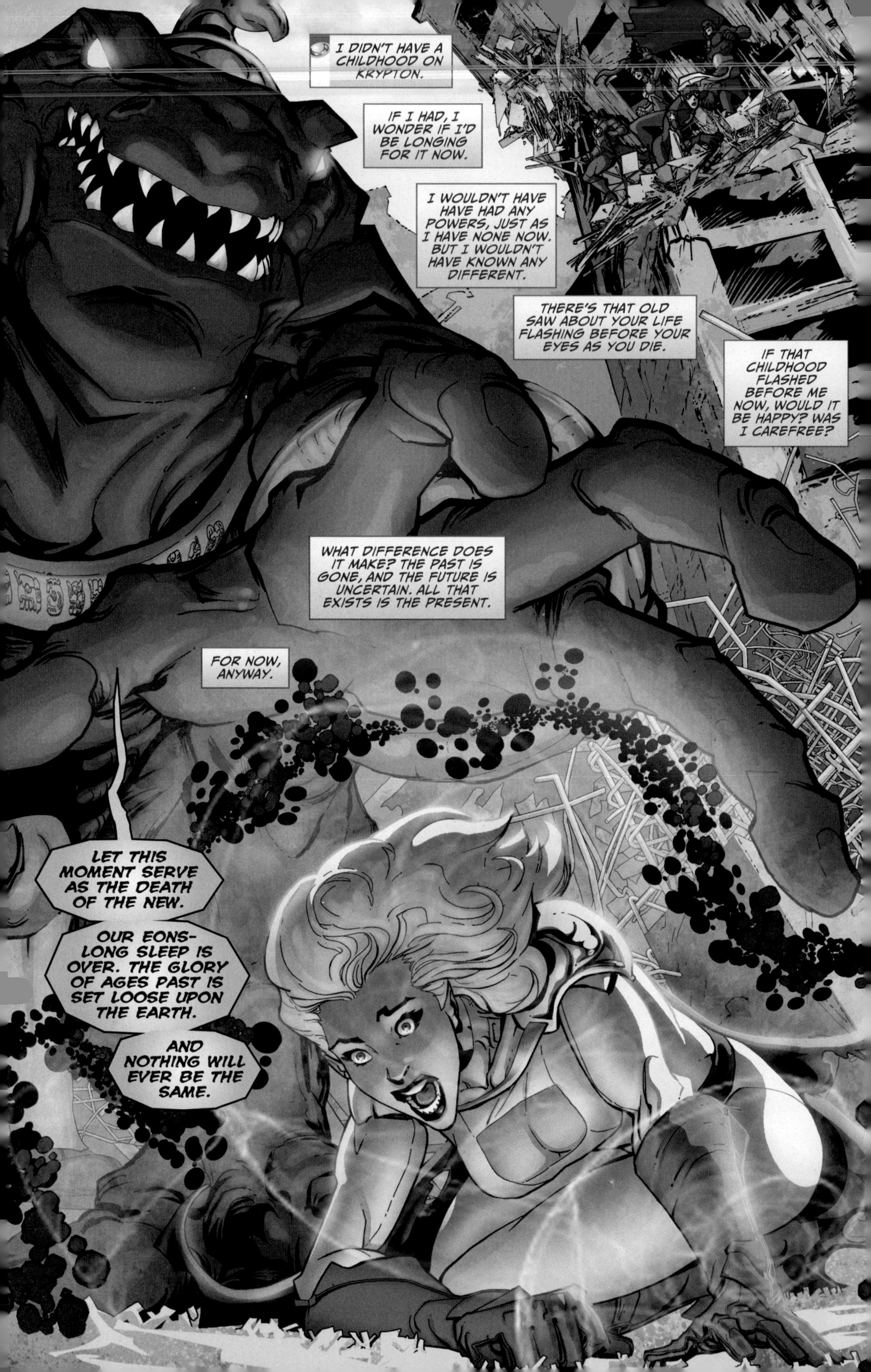
I DIDN'T HAVE A CHILDHOOD ON KRYPTON.
IF I HAD, I WONDER IF I'D BE LONGING FOR IT NOW.
I WOULDN'T HAVE HAVE HAD ANY POWERS, JUST AS I HAVE NONE NOW. BUT I WOULDN'T HAVE KNOWN ANY DIFFERENT.
THERE'S THAT OLD SAW ABOUT YOUR LIFE FLASHING BEFORE YOUR EYES AS YOU DIE.
IF THAT CHILDHOOD FLASHED BEFORE ME NOW, WOULD IT BE HAPPY? WAS I CAREFREE?
WHAT DIFFERENCE DOES IT MAKE? THE PAST IS GONE, AND THE FUTURE IS UNCERTAIN. ALL THAT EXISTS IS THE PRESENT.
FOR NOW, ANYWAY.
LET THIS MOMENT SERVE AS THE DEATH OF THE NEW.
OUR EONS-LONG SLEEP IS OVER. THE GLORY OF AGES PAST IS SET LOOSE UPON THE EARTH.
AND NOTHING WILL EVER BE THE SAME.

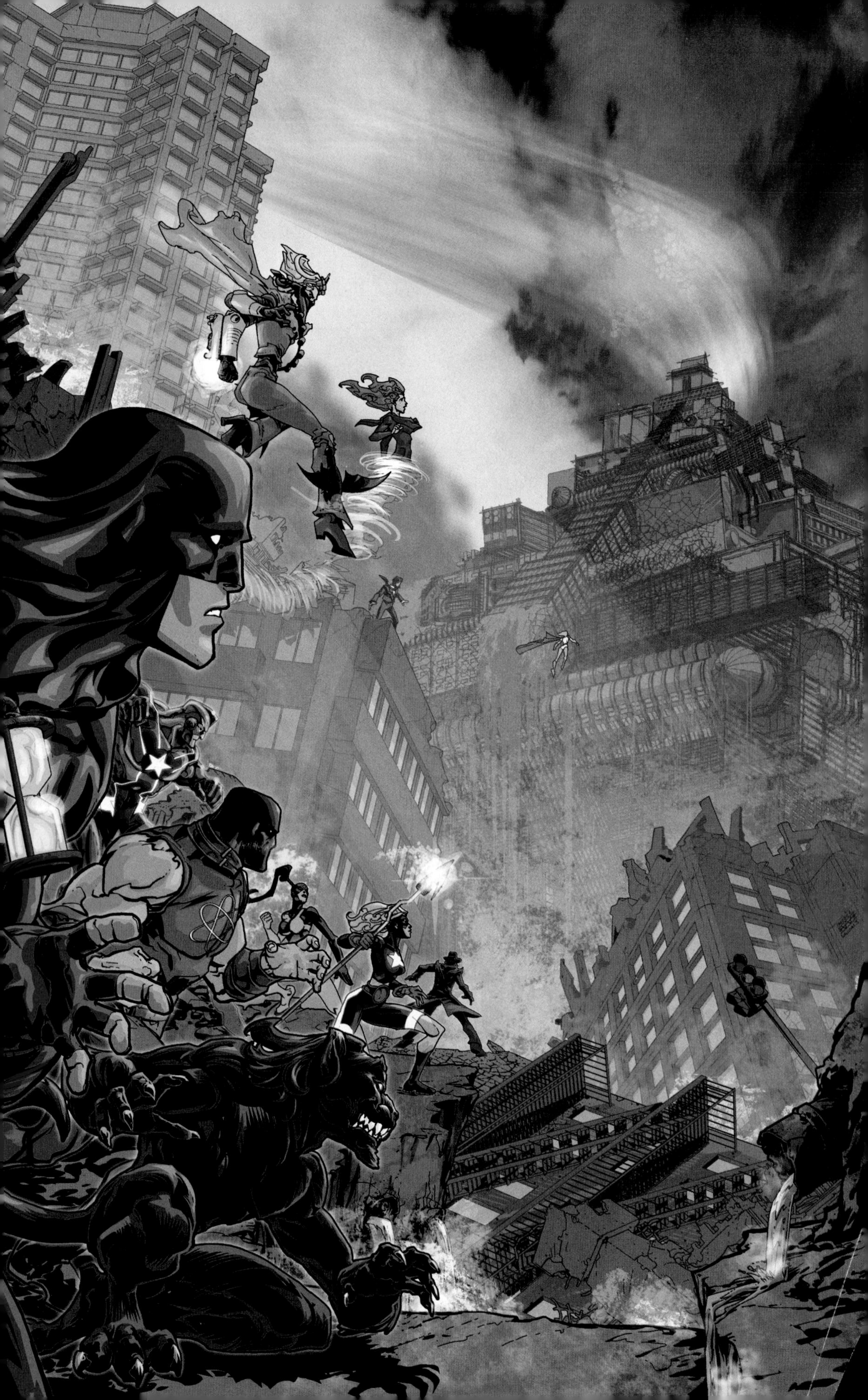

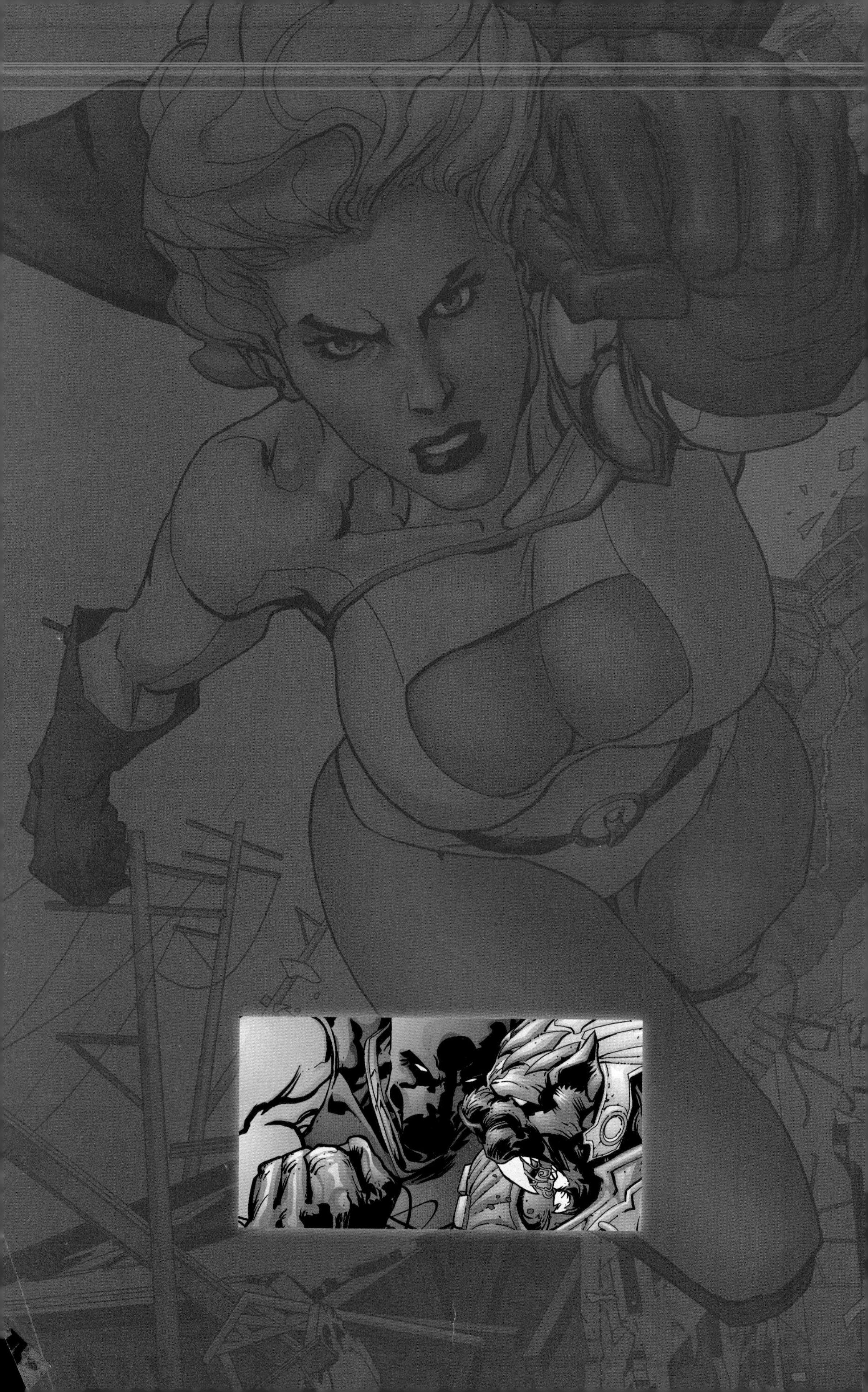

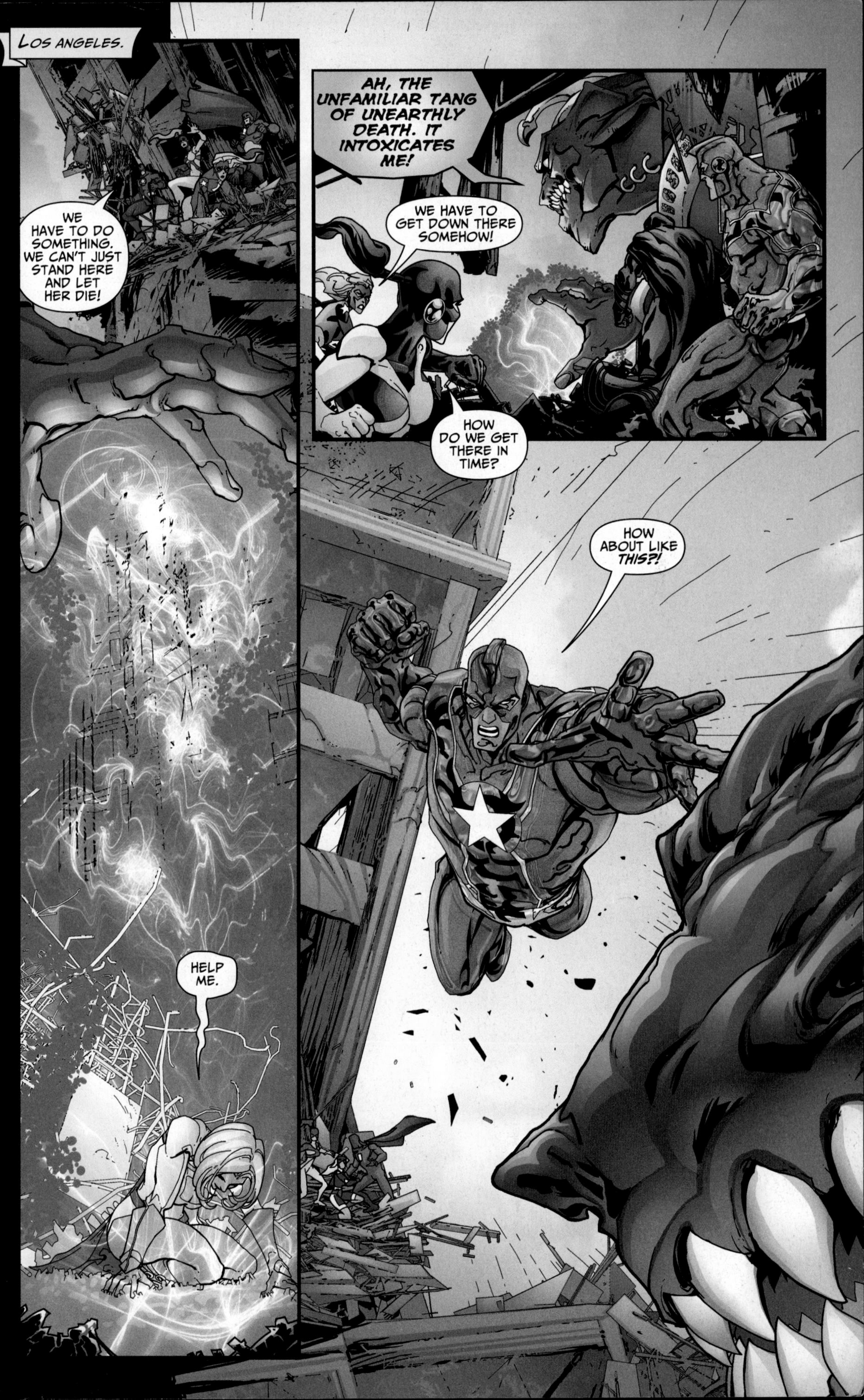
LOS ANGELES.
WE HAVE TO DO SOMETHING. WE CAN'T JUST STAND HERE AND LET HER DIE!
AH, THE UNFAMILIAR TANG OF UNEARTHLY DEATH. IT INTOXICATES ME!
WE HAVE TO GET DOWN THERE SOMEHOW!
HOW DO WE GET THERE IN TIME?
HOW ABOUT LIKE *THIS?!*
HELP ME.

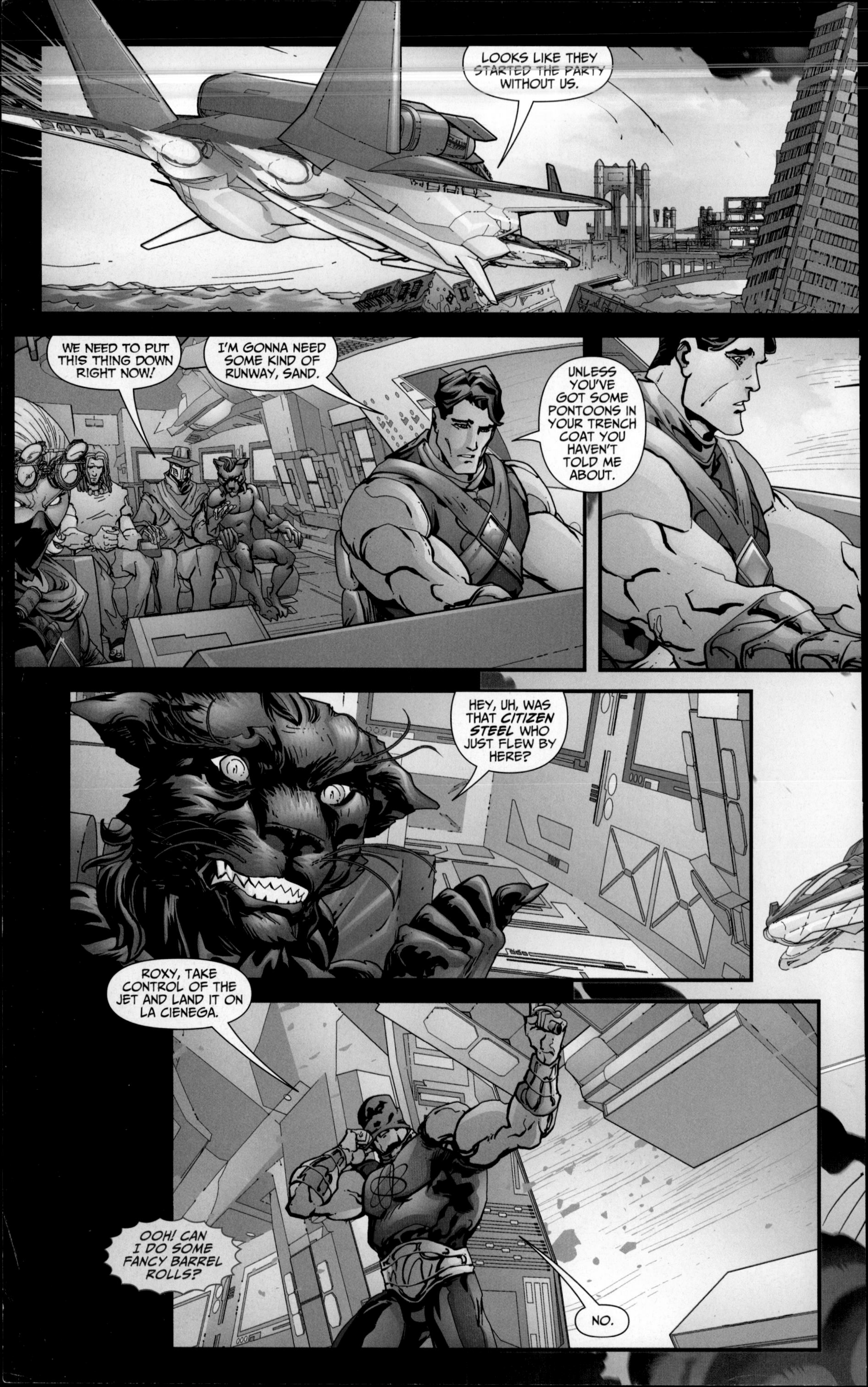
LOOKS LIKE THEY STARTED THE PARTY WITHOUT US.
WE NEED TO PUT THIS THING DOWN RIGHT NOW!
I'M GONNA NEED SOME KIND OF RUNWAY, SAND.
UNLESS YOU'VE GOT SOME PONTOONS IN YOUR TRENCH COAT YOU HAVEN'T TOLD ME ABOUT.
HEY, UH, WAS THAT *CITIZEN STEEL* WHO JUST FLEW BY HERE?
ROXY, TAKE CONTROL OF THE JET AND LAND IT ON LA CIENEGA.
OOH! CAN I DO SOME FANCY BARREL ROLLS?
NO.

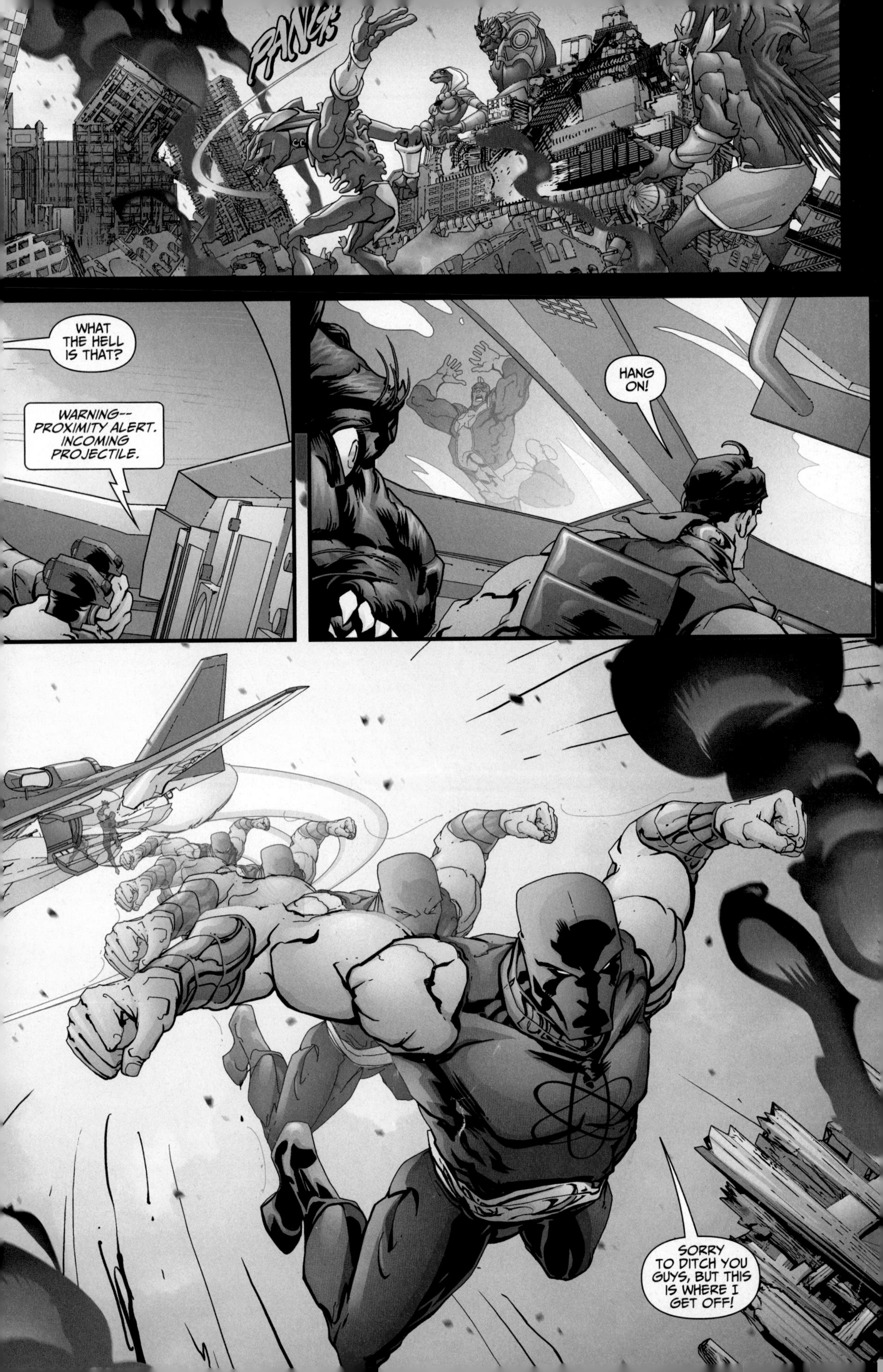
PANG
WHAT THE HELL IS THAT?
WARNING-- PROXIMITY ALERT. INCOMING PROJECTILE.
HANG ON!
SORRY TO DITCH YOU GUYS, BUT THIS IS WHERE I GET OFF!

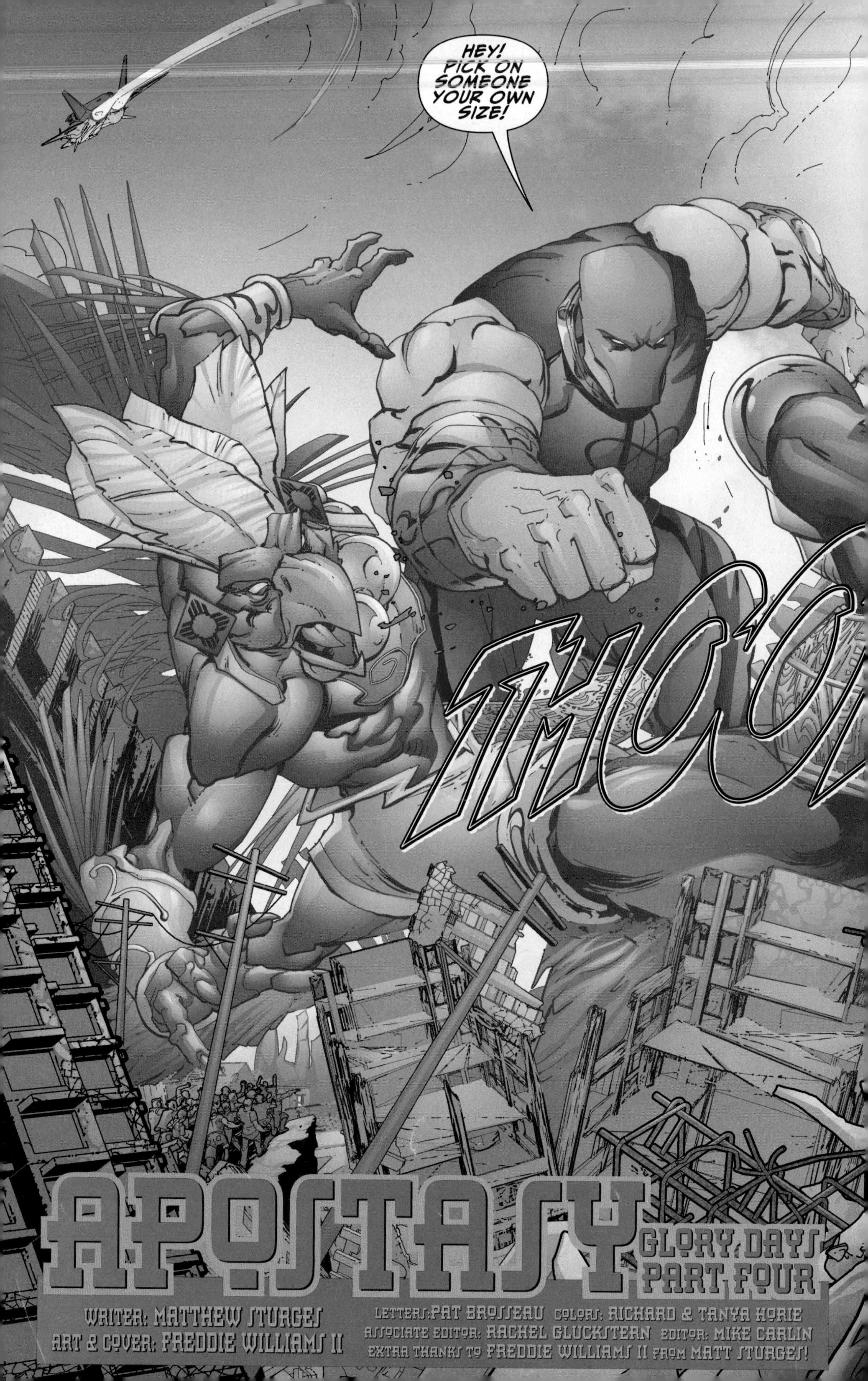
HEY! PICK ON SOMEONE YOUR OWN SIZE!
APOSTASY
GLORY DAYS PART FOUR
WRITER: MATTHEW STURGES
ART & COVER: FREDDIE WILLIAMS II
LETTERS: PAT BROSSEAU
COLORS: RICHARD & TANYA HORIE
ASSOCIATE EDITOR: RACHEL GLUCKSTERN
EDITOR: MIKE CARLIN
EXTRA THANKS TO FREDDIE WILLIAMS II FROM MATT STURGES!

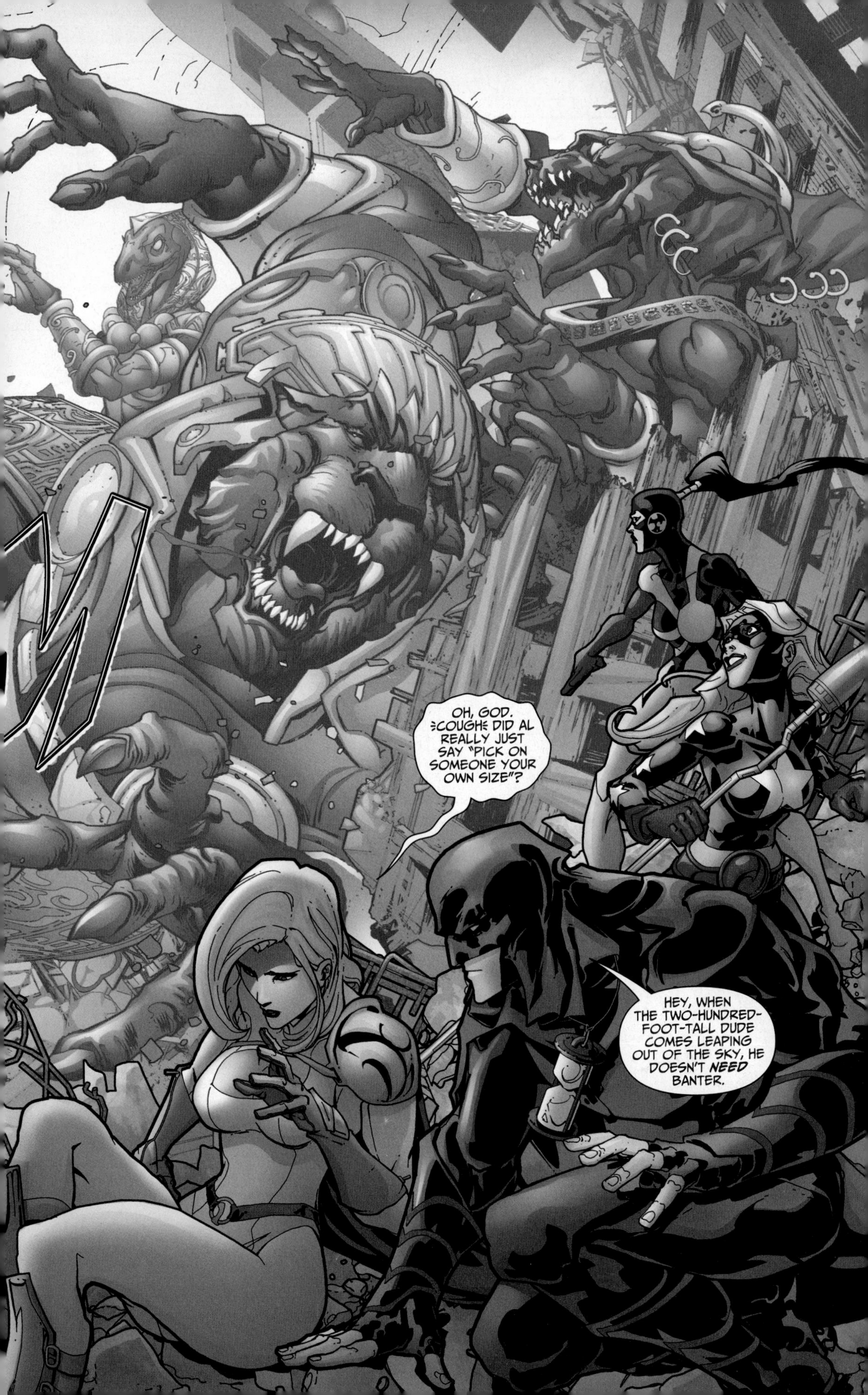
OH, GOD. ≷COUGH≶ DID AL REALLY JUST SAY "PICK ON SOMEONE YOUR OWN SIZE"?
HEY, WHEN THE TWO-HUNDRED-FOOT-TALL DUDE COMES LEAPING OUT OF THE SKY, HE DOESN'T **NEED** BANTER.

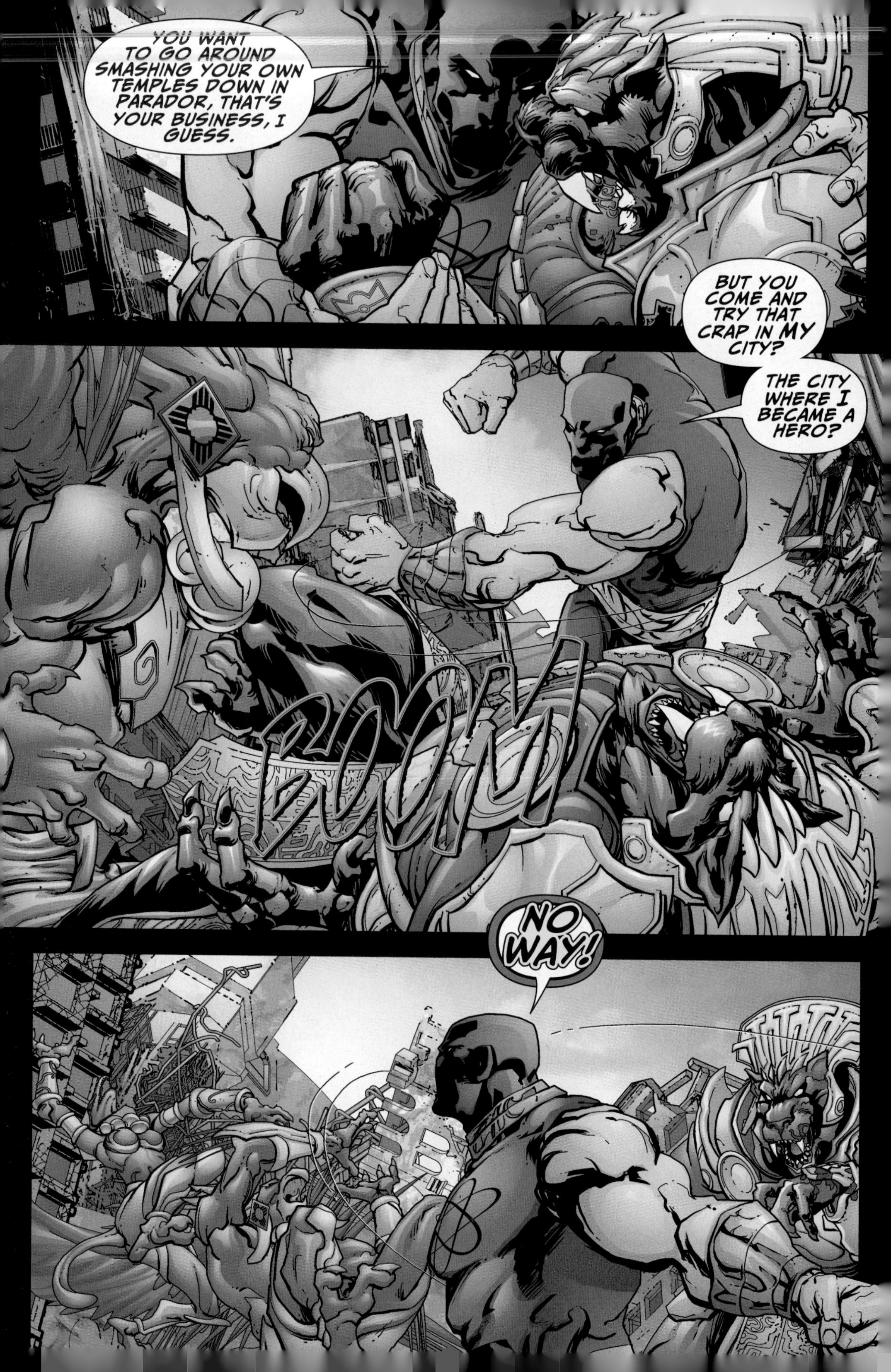
YOU WANT TO GO AROUND SMASHING YOUR OWN TEMPLES DOWN IN PARADOR, THAT'S YOUR BUSINESS, I GUESS.
BUT YOU COME AND TRY THAT CRAP IN MY CITY?
THE CITY WHERE I BECAME A HERO?
BOOM
NO WAY!

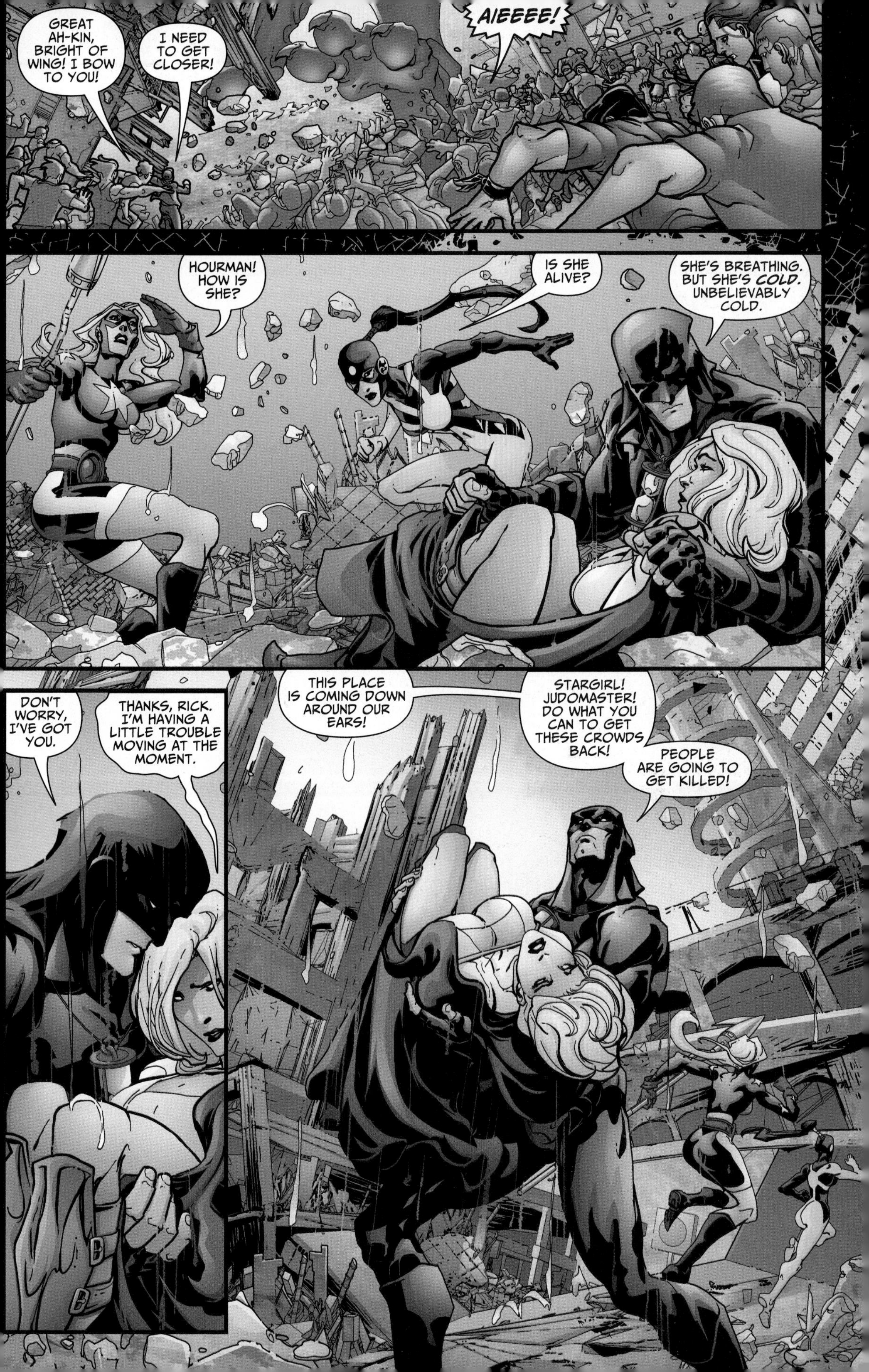
GREAT AH-KIN, BRIGHT OF WING! I BOW TO YOU!
I NEED TO GET CLOSER!
AIEEEE!
HOURMAN! HOW IS SHE?
IS SHE ALIVE?
SHE'S BREATHING. BUT SHE'S COLD. UNBELIEVABLY COLD.
DON'T WORRY, I'VE GOT YOU.
THANKS, RICK. I'M HAVING A LITTLE TROUBLE MOVING AT THE MOMENT.
THIS PLACE IS COMING DOWN AROUND OUR EARS!
STARGIRL! JUDOMASTER! DO WHAT YOU CAN TO GET THESE CROWDS BACK!
PEOPLE ARE GOING TO GET KILLED!

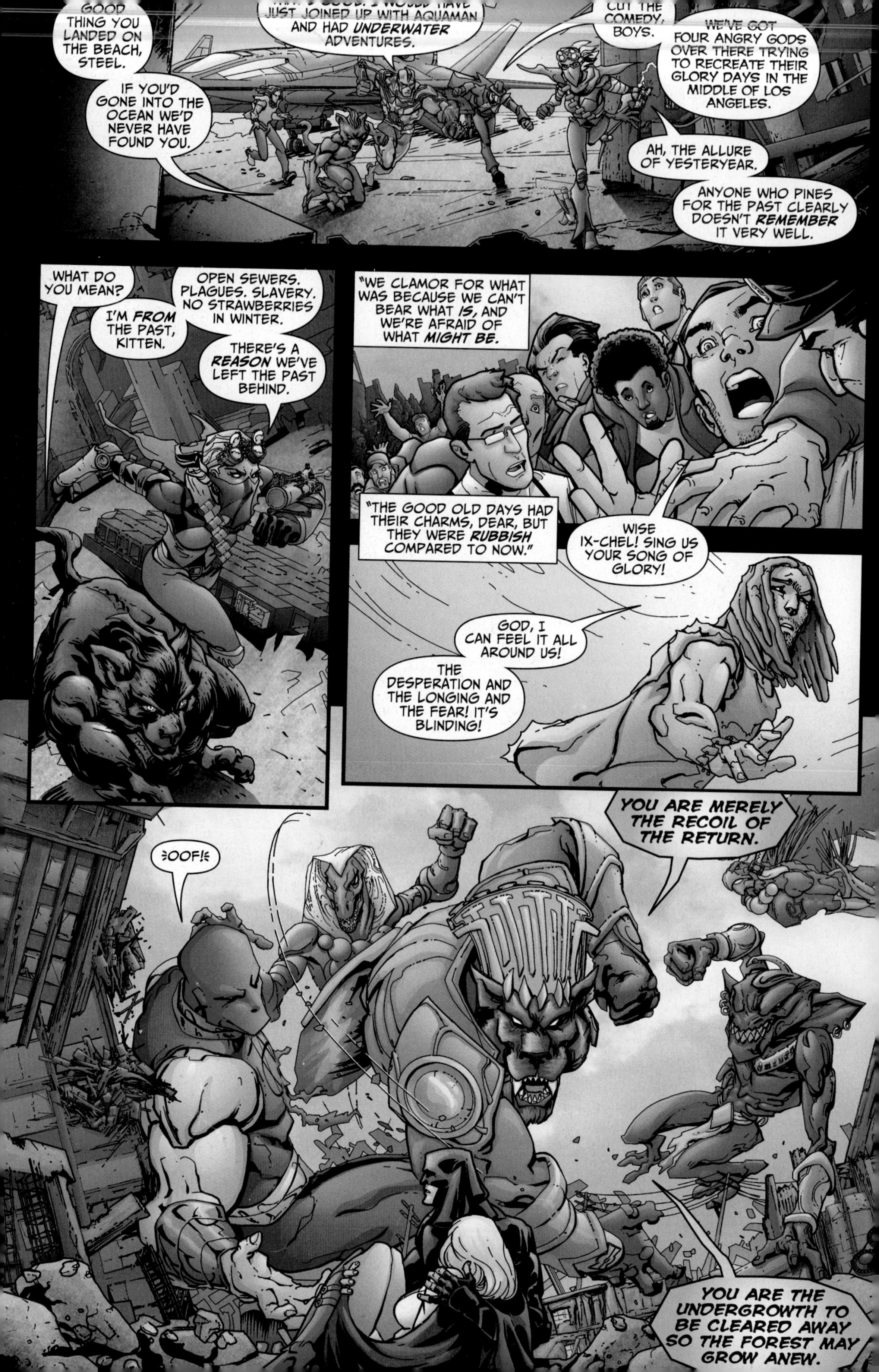

GOOD THING YOU LANDED ON THE BEACH, STEEL.
IF YOU'D GONE INTO THE OCEAN WE'D NEVER HAVE FOUND YOU.
JUST JOINED UP WITH AQUAMAN AND HAD *UNDERWATER* ADVENTURES.
CUT THE COMEDY, BOYS.
WE'VE GOT FOUR ANGRY GODS OVER THERE TRYING TO RECREATE THEIR GLORY DAYS IN THE MIDDLE OF LOS ANGELES.
AH, THE ALLURE OF YESTERYEAR.
ANYONE WHO PINES FOR THE PAST CLEARLY DOESN'T *REMEMBER* IT VERY WELL.
WHAT DO YOU MEAN?
I'M *FROM* THE PAST, KITTEN.
OPEN SEWERS. PLAGUES. SLAVERY. NO STRAWBERRIES IN WINTER.
THERE'S A *REASON* WE'VE LEFT THE PAST BEHIND.
"WE CLAMOR FOR WHAT WAS BECAUSE WE CAN'T BEAR WHAT *IS*, AND WE'RE AFRAID OF WHAT *MIGHT BE*.
"THE GOOD OLD DAYS HAD THEIR CHARMS, DEAR, BUT THEY WERE *RUBBISH* COMPARED TO NOW."
WISE IX-CHEL! SING US YOUR SONG OF GLORY!
GOD, I CAN FEEL IT ALL AROUND US!
THE DESPERATION AND THE LONGING AND THE FEAR! IT'S BLINDING!
OOF!
YOU ARE MERELY THE RECOIL OF THE RETURN.
YOU ARE THE UNDERGROWTH TO BE CLEARED AWAY SO THE FOREST MAY GROW ANEW.

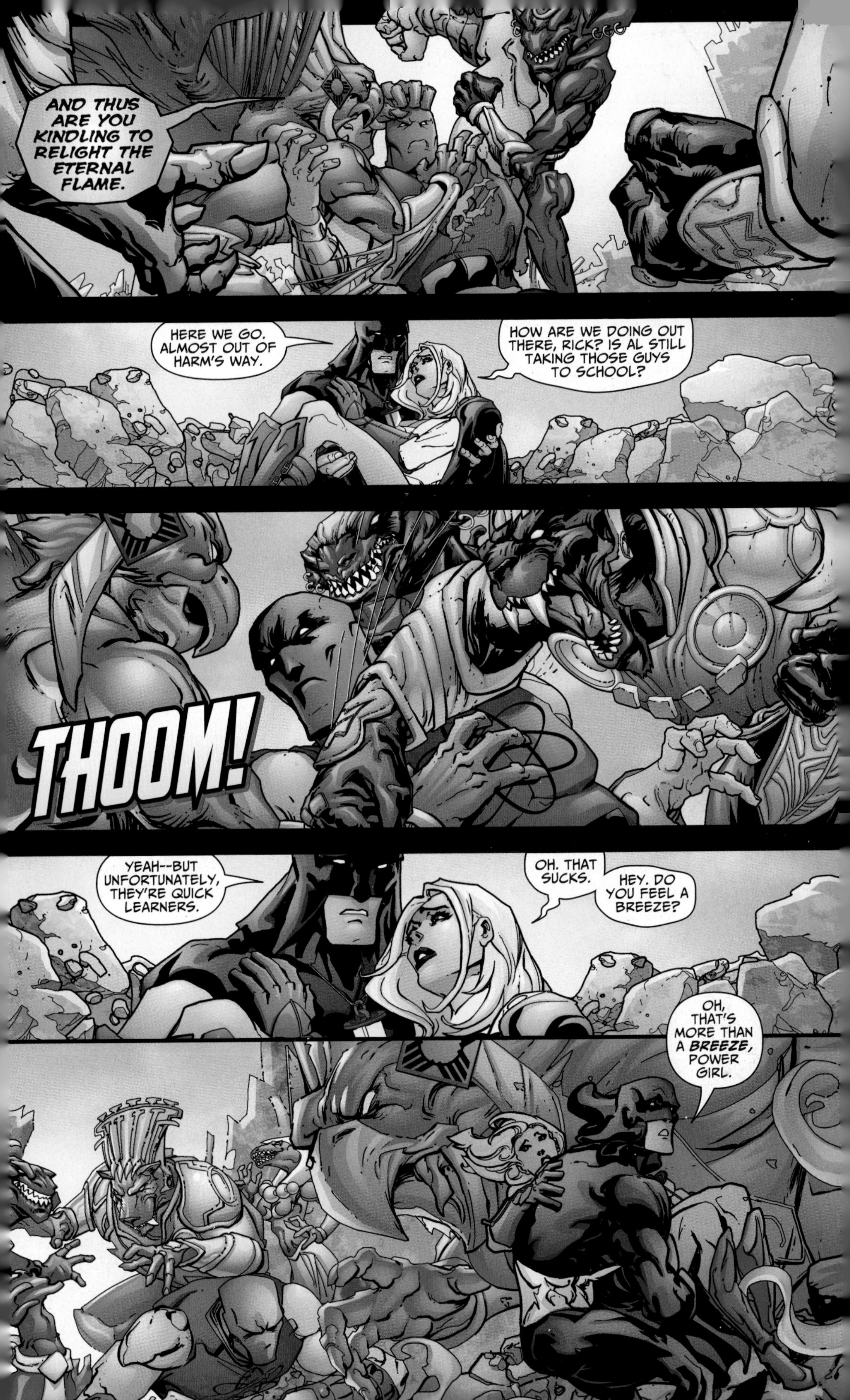
AND THUS ARE YOU KINDLING TO RELIGHT THE ETERNAL FLAME.
HERE WE GO. ALMOST OUT OF HARM'S WAY.
HOW ARE WE DOING OUT THERE, RICK? IS AL STILL TAKING THOSE GUYS TO SCHOOL?
THOOM!
YEAH--BUT UNFORTUNATELY, THEY'RE QUICK LEARNERS.
OH. THAT SUCKS.
HEY. DO YOU FEEL A BREEZE?
OH, THAT'S MORE THAN A BREEZE, POWER GIRL.

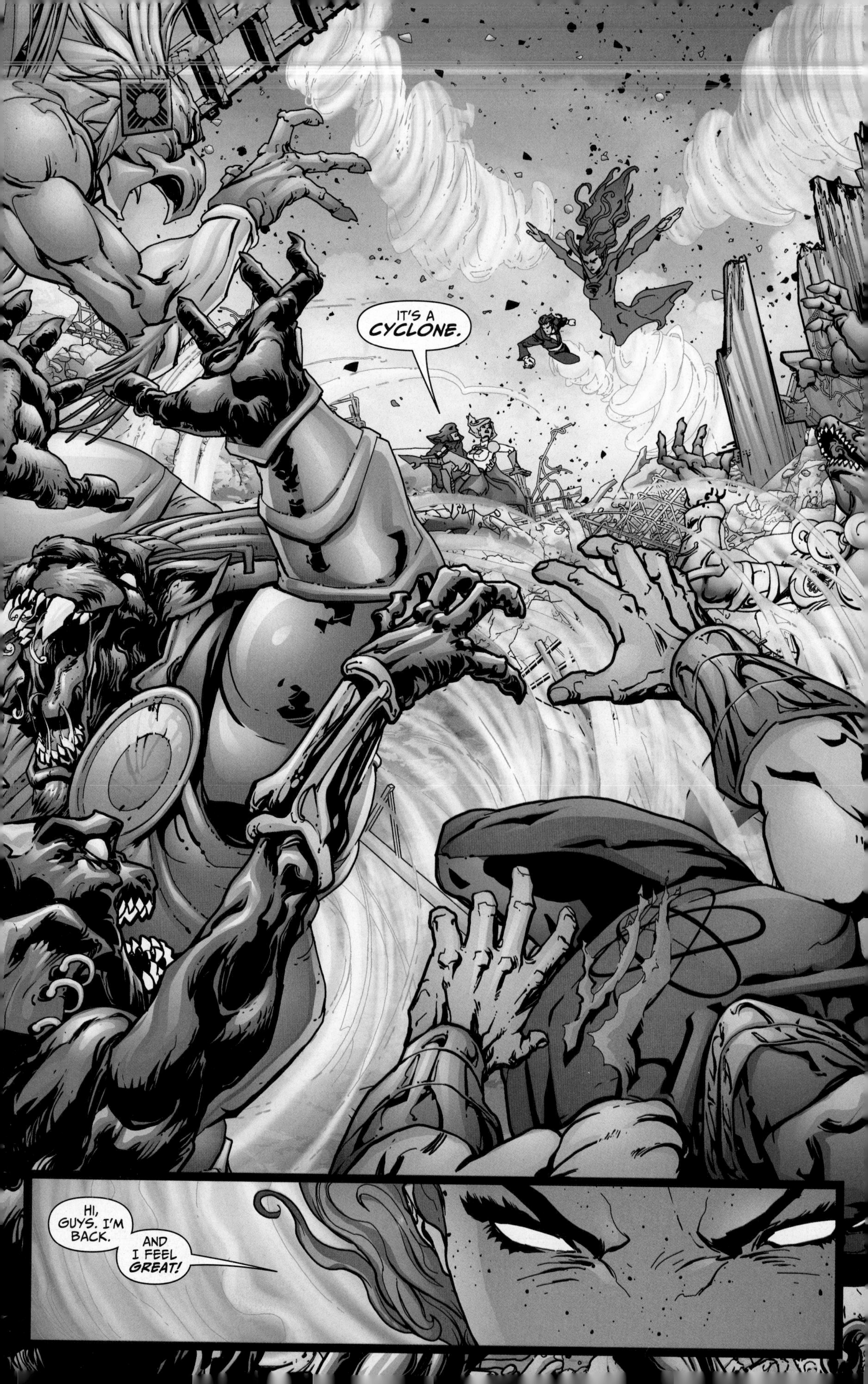
IT'S A CYCLONE.
HI, GUYS. I'M BACK.
AND I FEEL GREAT!

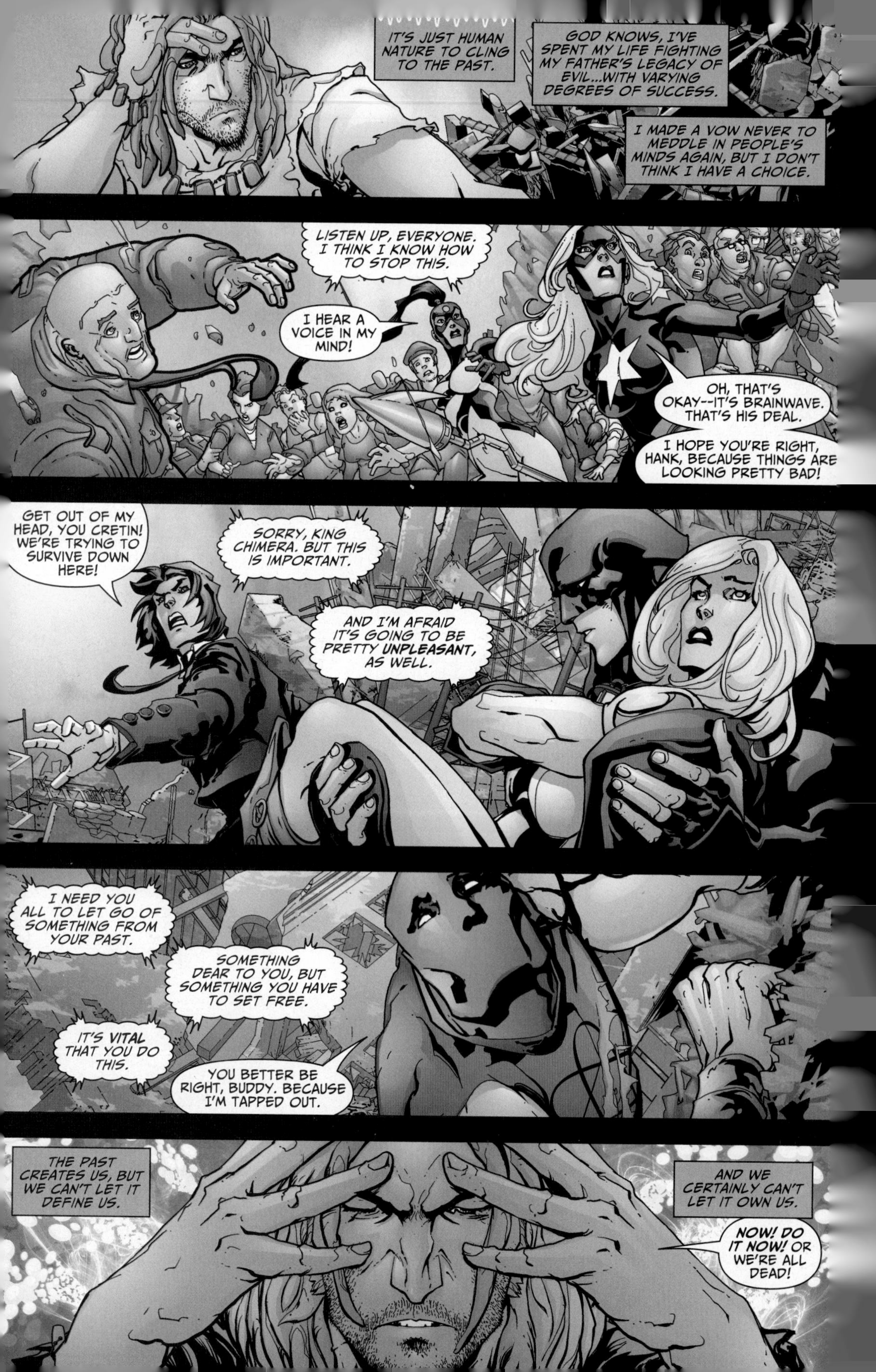
IT'S JUST HUMAN NATURE TO CLING TO THE PAST.
GOD KNOWS, I'VE SPENT MY LIFE FIGHTING MY FATHER'S LEGACY OF EVIL...WITH VARYING DEGREES OF SUCCESS.
I MADE A VOW NEVER TO MEDDLE IN PEOPLE'S MINDS AGAIN, BUT I DON'T THINK I HAVE A CHOICE.
LISTEN UP, EVERYONE. I THINK I KNOW HOW TO STOP THIS.
I HEAR A VOICE IN MY MIND!
OH, THAT'S OKAY--IT'S BRAINWAVE. THAT'S HIS DEAL.
I HOPE YOU'RE RIGHT, HANK, BECAUSE THINGS ARE LOOKING PRETTY BAD!
GET OUT OF MY HEAD, YOU CRETIN! WE'RE TRYING TO SURVIVE DOWN HERE!
SORRY, KING CHIMERA. BUT THIS IS IMPORTANT.
AND I'M AFRAID IT'S GOING TO BE PRETTY UNPLEASANT, AS WELL.
I NEED YOU ALL TO LET GO OF SOMETHING FROM YOUR PAST.
SOMETHING DEAR TO YOU, BUT SOMETHING YOU HAVE TO SET FREE.
IT'S VITAL THAT YOU DO THIS.
YOU BETTER BE RIGHT, BUDDY. BECAUSE I'M TAPPED OUT.
THE PAST CREATES US, BUT WE CAN'T LET IT DEFINE US.
AND WE CERTAINLY CAN'T LET IT OWN US.
NOW! DO IT NOW! OR WE'RE ALL DEAD!

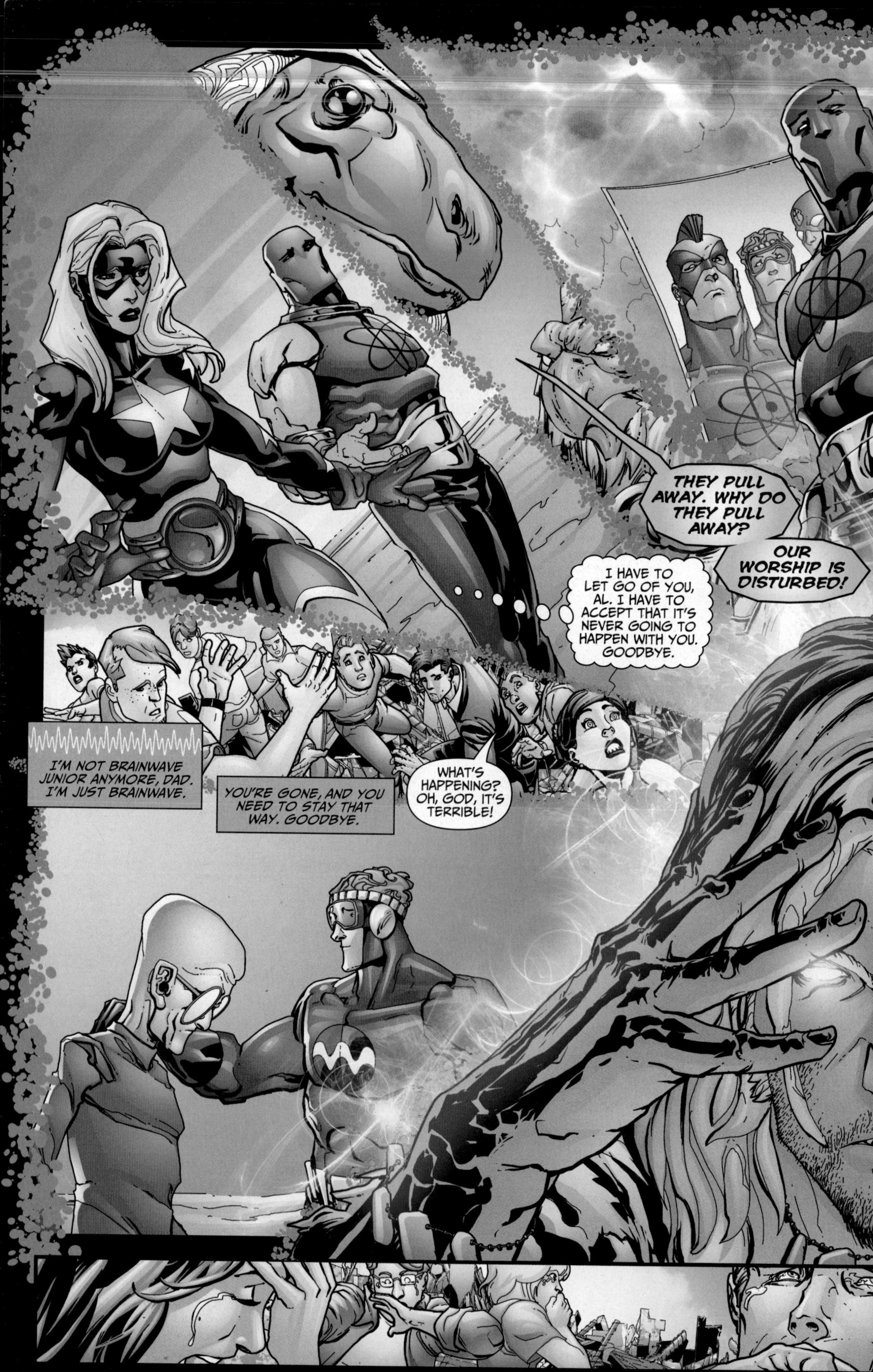
THEY PULL AWAY. WHY DO THEY PULL AWAY?
OUR WORSHIP IS DISTURBED!
I HAVE TO LET GO OF YOU, AL. I HAVE TO ACCEPT THAT IT'S NEVER GOING TO HAPPEN WITH YOU. GOODBYE.
I'M NOT BRAINWAVE JUNIOR ANYMORE, DAD. I'M JUST BRAINWAVE.
YOU'RE GONE, AND YOU NEED TO STAY THAT WAY. GOODBYE.
WHAT'S HAPPENING? OH, GOD, IT'S TERRIBLE!

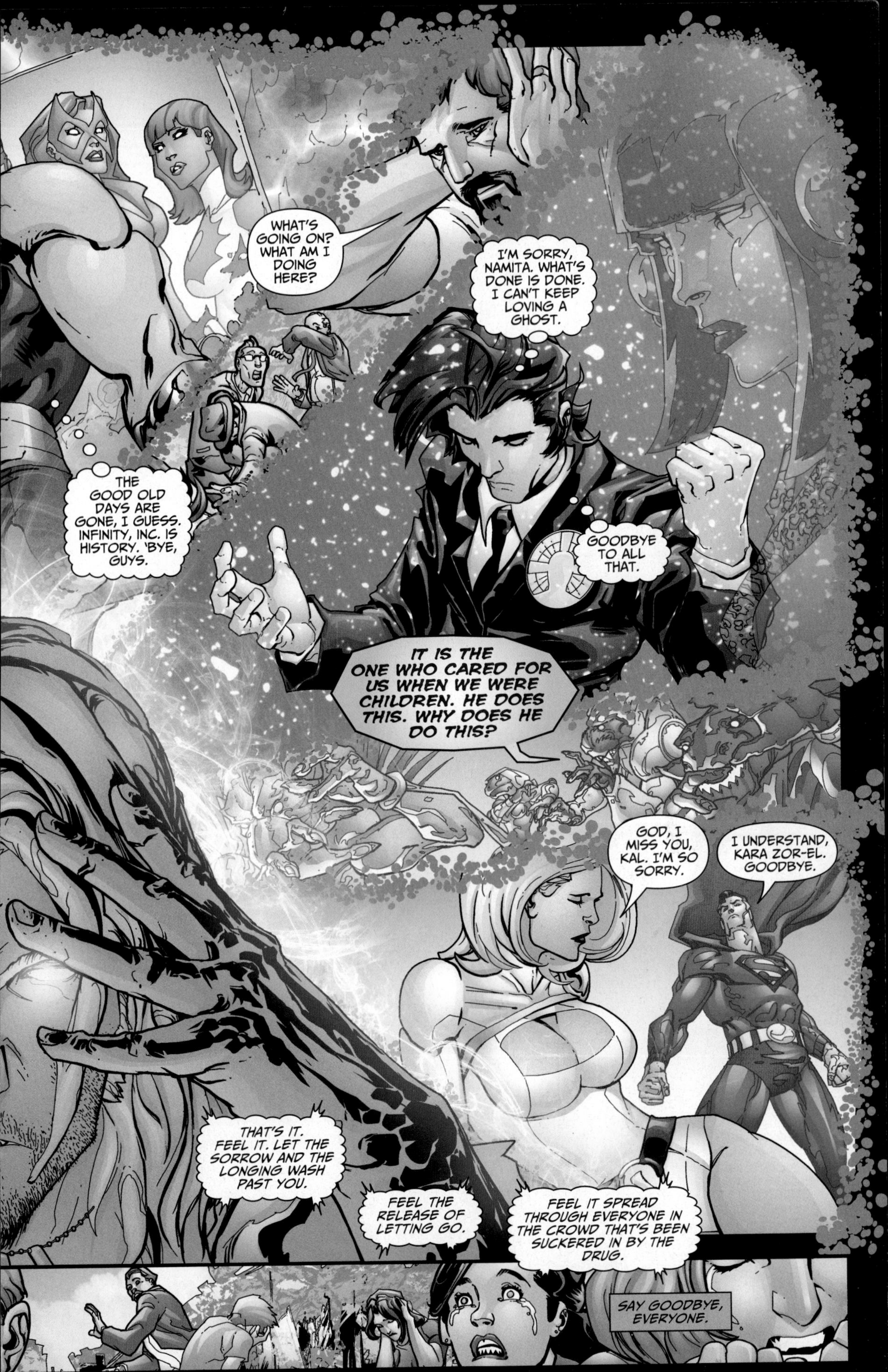
WHAT'S GOING ON? WHAT AM I DOING HERE?
I'M SORRY, NAMITA. WHAT'S DONE IS DONE. I CAN'T KEEP LOVING A GHOST.
THE GOOD OLD DAYS ARE GONE, I GUESS. INFINITY, INC. IS HISTORY. 'BYE, GUYS.
GOODBYE TO ALL THAT.
IT IS THE ONE WHO CARED FOR US WHEN WE WERE CHILDREN. HE DOES THIS. WHY DOES HE DO THIS?
GOD, I MISS YOU, KAL. I'M SO SORRY.
I UNDERSTAND, KARA ZOR-EL. GOODBYE.
THAT'S IT. FEEL IT. LET THE SORROW AND THE LONGING WASH PAST YOU.
FEEL THE RELEASE OF LETTING GO.
FEEL IT SPREAD THROUGH EVERYONE IN THE CROWD THAT'S BEEN SUCKERED IN BY THE DRUG.
SAY GOODBYE, EVERYONE.

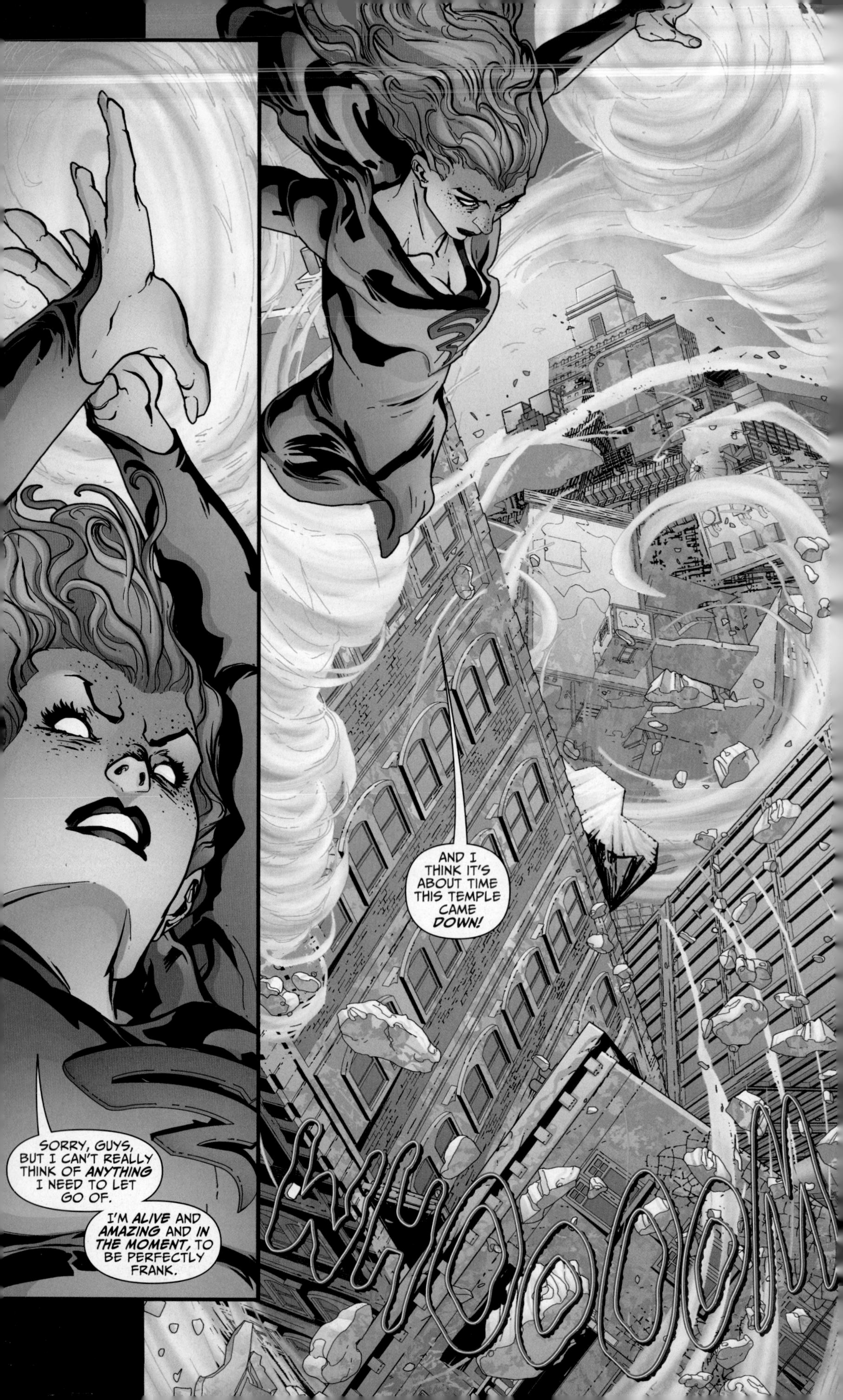
SORRY, GUYS, BUT I CAN'T REALLY THINK OF ANYTHING I NEED TO LET GO OF.
I'M ALIVE AND AMAZING AND IN THE MOMENT, TO BE PERFECTLY FRANK.
AND I THINK IT'S ABOUT TIME THIS TEMPLE CAME DOWN!
WHOOOOOM

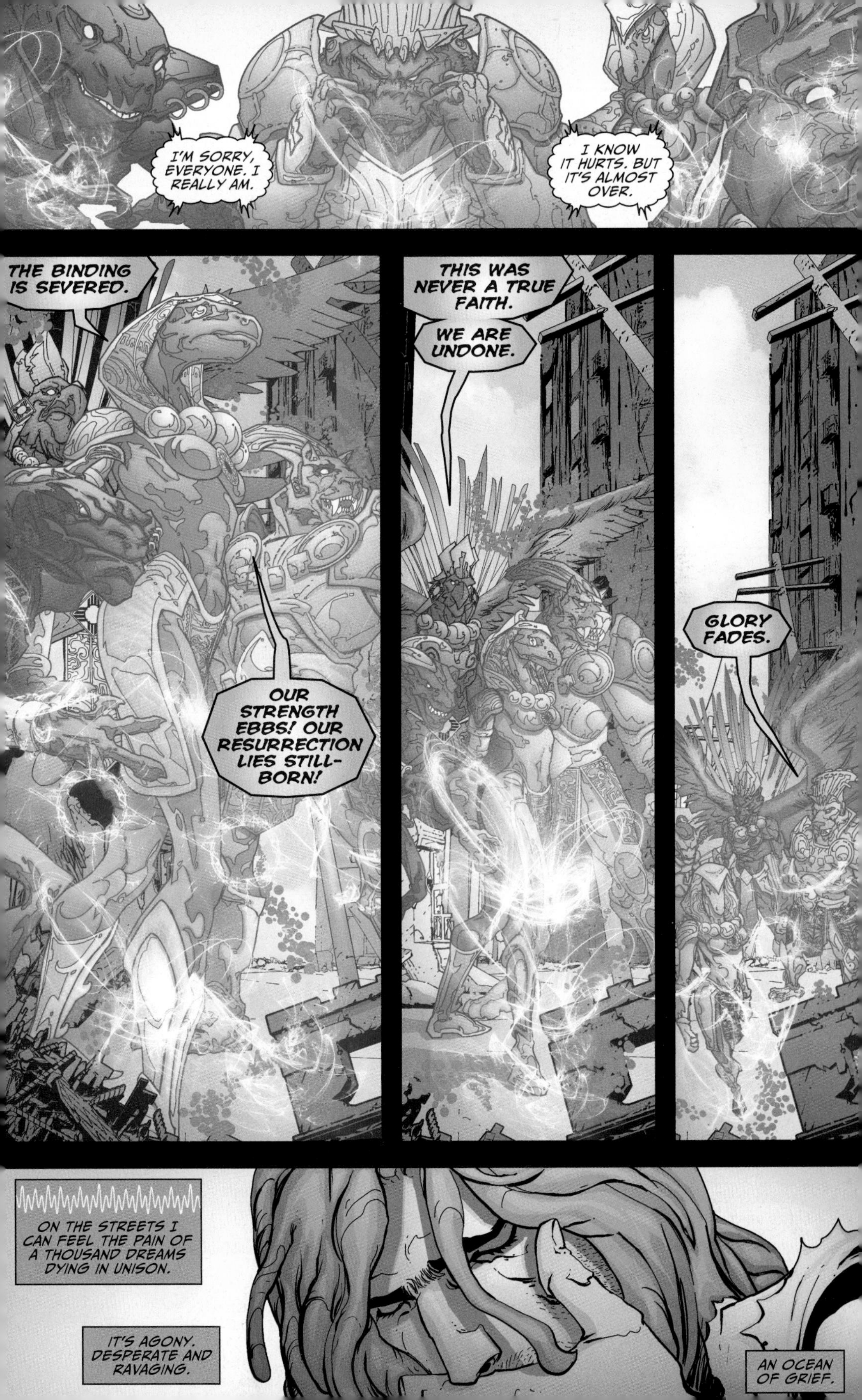
I'M SORRY, EVERYONE. I REALLY AM.
I KNOW IT HURTS. BUT IT'S ALMOST OVER.
THE BINDING IS SEVERED.
OUR STRENGTH EBBS! OUR RESURRECTION LIES STILL-BORN!
THIS WAS NEVER A TRUE FAITH.
WE ARE UNDONE.
GLORY FADES.
ON THE STREETS I CAN FEEL THE PAIN OF A THOUSAND DREAMS DYING IN UNISON.
IT'S AGONY. DESPERATE AND RAVAGING.
AN OCEAN OF GRIEF.

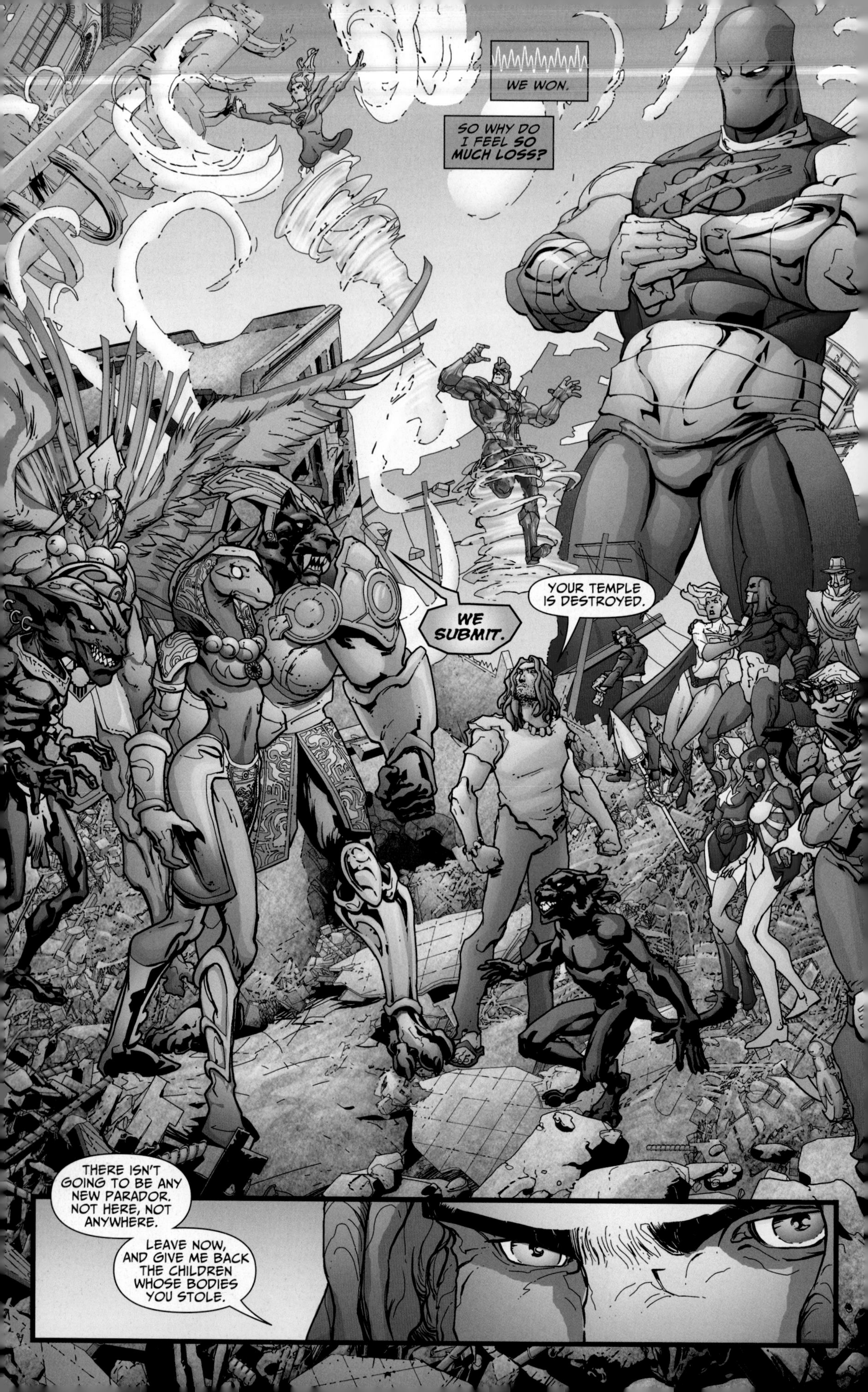
WE WON.
SO WHY DO I FEEL SO MUCH LOSS?
YOUR TEMPLE IS DESTROYED.
WE SUBMIT.
THERE ISN'T GOING TO BE ANY NEW PARADOR. NOT HERE, NOT ANYWHERE.
LEAVE NOW, AND GIVE ME BACK THE CHILDREN WHOSE BODIES YOU STOLE.

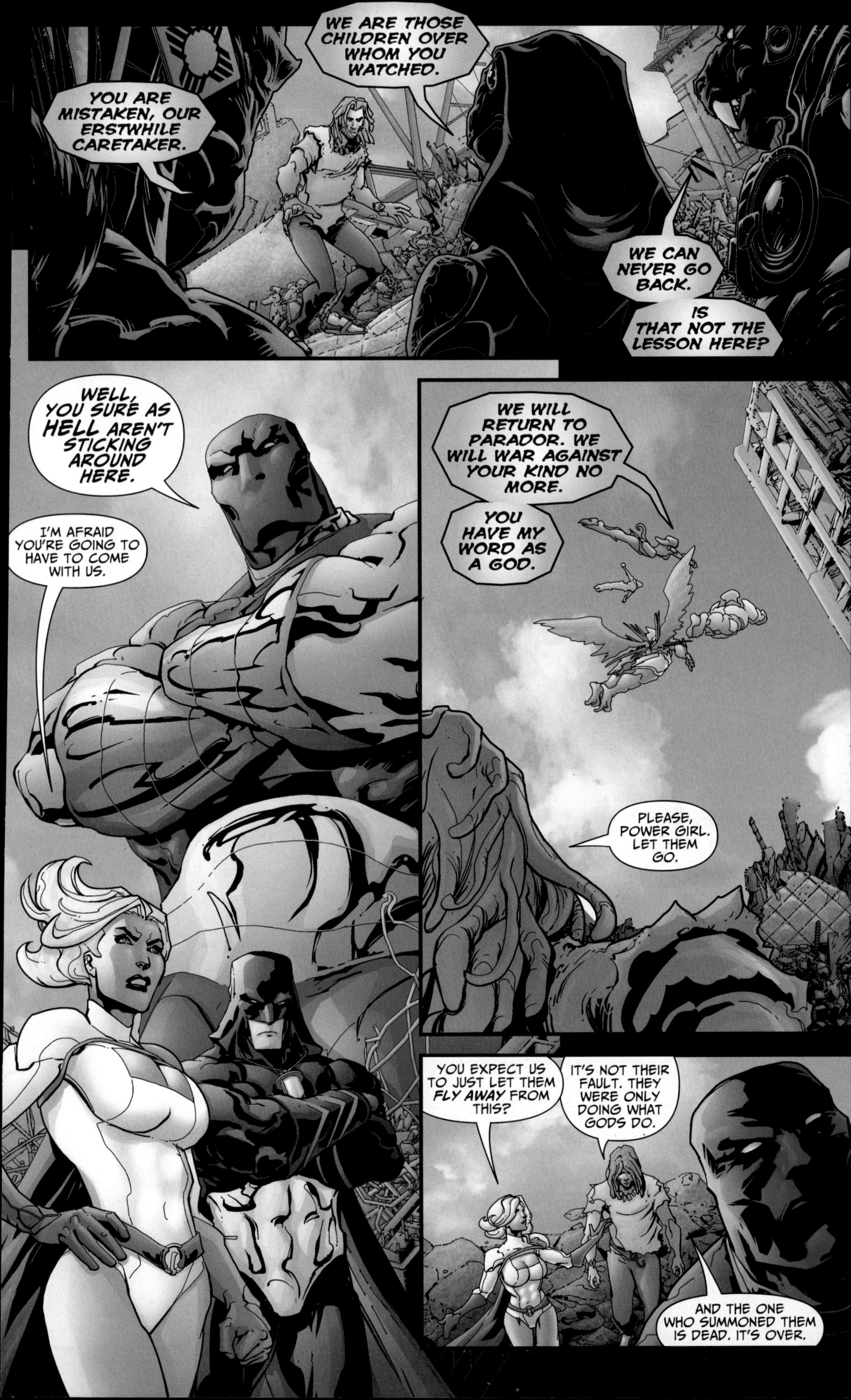
YOU ARE MISTAKEN, OUR ERSTWHILE CARETAKER.
WE ARE THOSE CHILDREN OVER WHOM YOU WATCHED.
WE CAN NEVER GO BACK.
IS THAT NOT THE LESSON HERE?
WELL, YOU SURE AS HELL AREN'T STICKING AROUND HERE.
I'M AFRAID YOU'RE GOING TO HAVE TO COME WITH US.
WE WILL RETURN TO PARADOR. WE WILL WAR AGAINST YOUR KIND NO MORE.
YOU HAVE MY WORD AS A GOD.
PLEASE, POWER GIRL. LET THEM GO.
YOU EXPECT US TO JUST LET THEM FLY AWAY FROM THIS?
IT'S NOT THEIR FAULT. THEY WERE ONLY DOING WHAT GODS DO.
AND THE ONE WHO SUMMONED THEM IS DEAD. IT'S OVER.

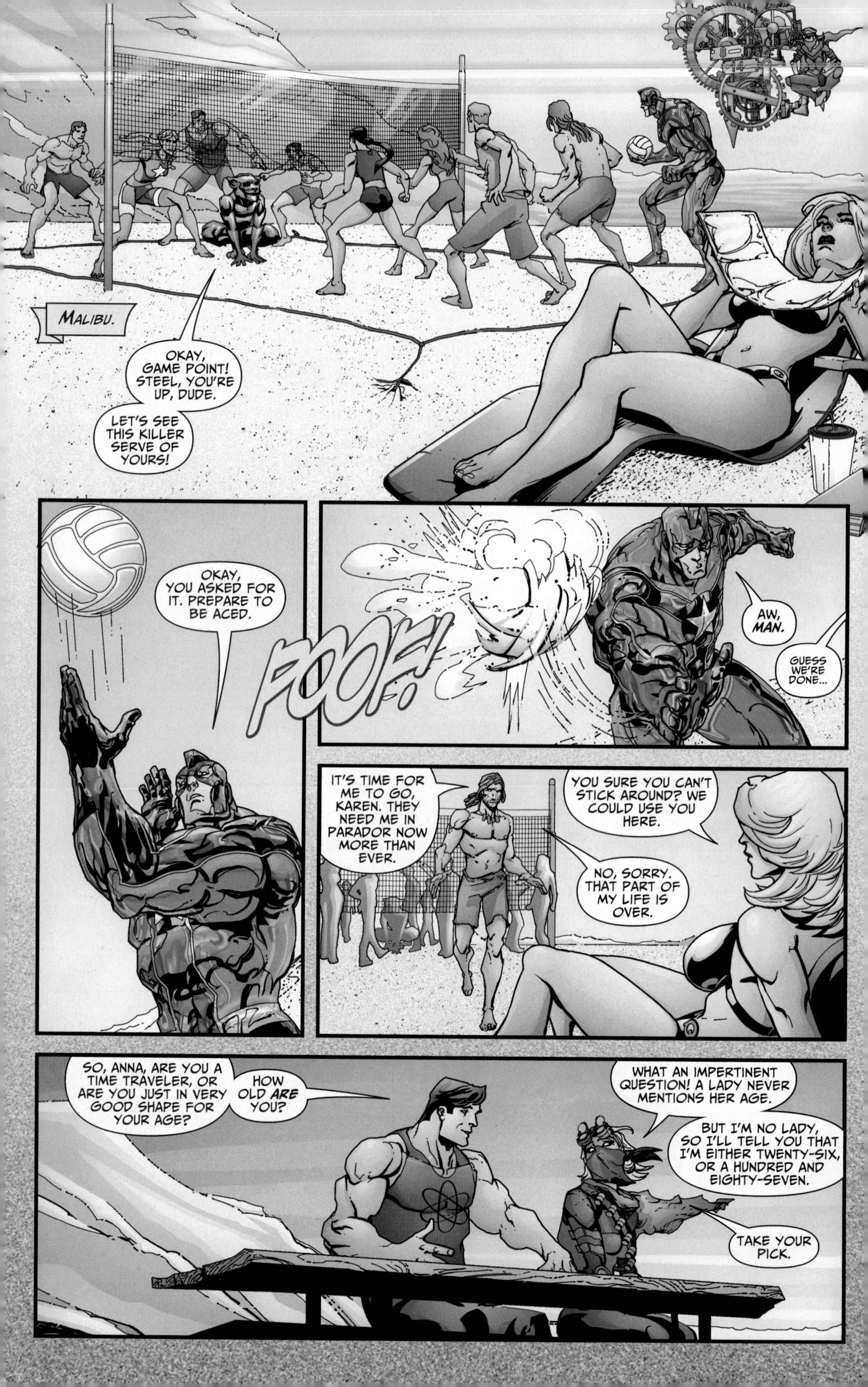
MALIBU.
OKAY, GAME POINT! STEEL, YOU'RE UP, DUDE.
LET'S SEE THIS KILLER SERVE OF YOURS!
OKAY, YOU ASKED FOR IT. PREPARE TO BE ACED.
FOOF!
AW, MAN.
GUESS WE'RE DONE...
IT'S TIME FOR ME TO GO, KAREN. THEY NEED ME IN PARADOR NOW MORE THAN EVER.
YOU SURE YOU CAN'T STICK AROUND? WE COULD USE YOU HERE.
NO, SORRY. THAT PART OF MY LIFE IS OVER.
SO, ANNA, ARE YOU A TIME TRAVELER, OR ARE YOU JUST IN VERY GOOD SHAPE FOR YOUR AGE?
HOW OLD ARE YOU?
WHAT AN IMPERTINENT QUESTION! A LADY NEVER MENTIONS HER AGE.
BUT I'M NO LADY, SO I'LL TELL YOU THAT I'M EITHER TWENTY-SIX, OR A HUNDRED AND EIGHTY-SEVEN.
TAKE YOUR PICK.

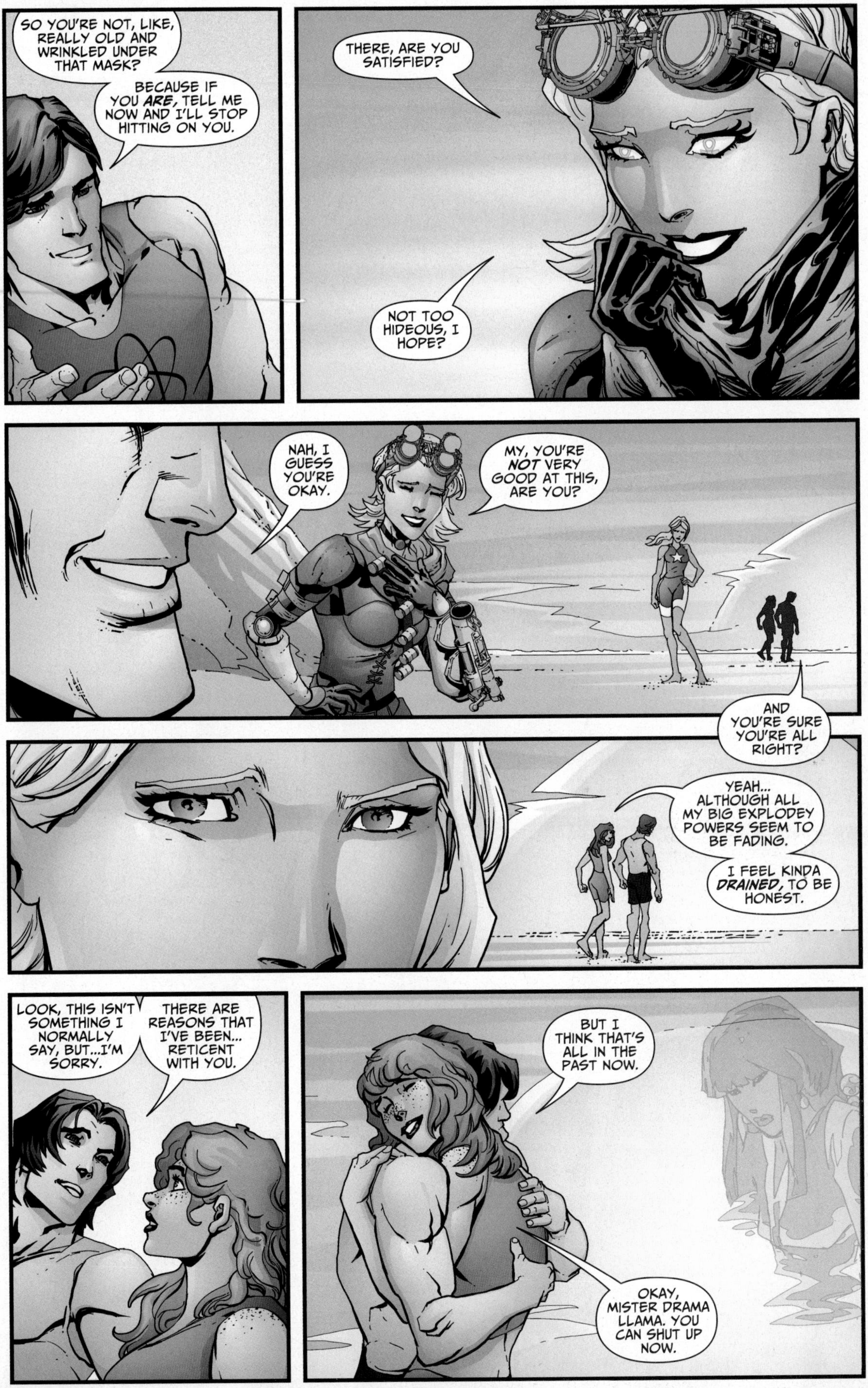
SO YOU'RE NOT, LIKE, REALLY OLD AND WRINKLED UNDER THAT MASK?
BECAUSE IF YOU *ARE*, TELL ME NOW AND I'LL STOP HITTING ON YOU.
THERE, ARE YOU SATISFIED?
NOT TOO HIDEOUS, I HOPE?
NAH, I GUESS YOU'RE OKAY.
MY, YOU'RE *NOT* VERY GOOD AT THIS, ARE YOU?
AND YOU'RE SURE YOU'RE ALL RIGHT?
YEAH... ALTHOUGH ALL MY BIG EXPLODEY POWERS SEEM TO BE FADING.
I FEEL KINDA *DRAINED*, TO BE HONEST.
LOOK, THIS ISN'T SOMETHING I NORMALLY SAY, BUT...I'M SORRY.
THERE ARE REASONS THAT I'VE BEEN... RETICENT WITH YOU.
BUT I THINK THAT'S ALL IN THE PAST NOW.
OKAY, MISTER DRAMA LLAMA. YOU CAN SHUT UP NOW.

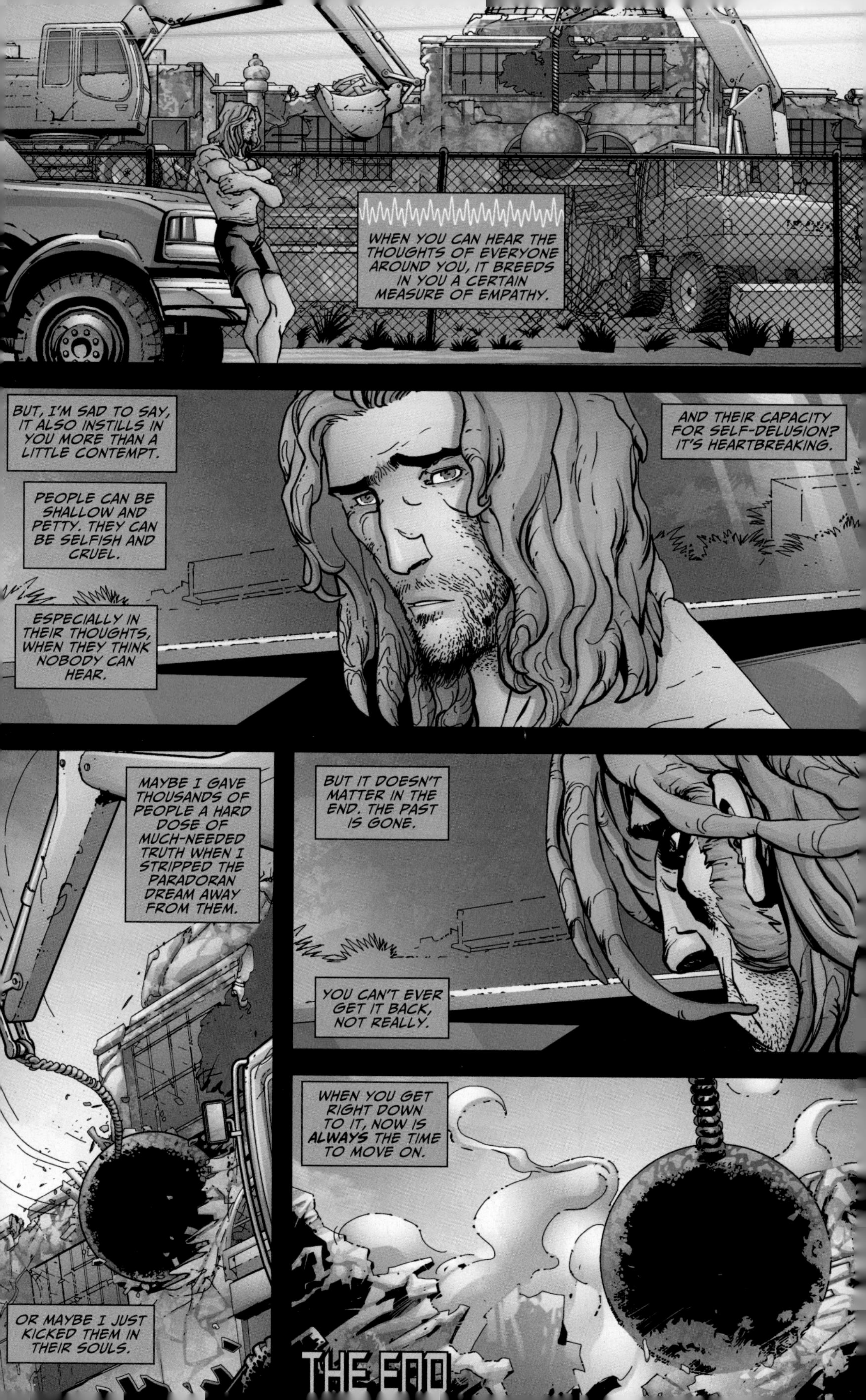

WHEN YOU CAN HEAR THE THOUGHTS OF EVERYONE AROUND YOU, IT BREEDS IN YOU A CERTAIN MEASURE OF EMPATHY.
BUT, I'M SAD TO SAY, IT ALSO INSTILLS IN YOU MORE THAN A LITTLE CONTEMPT.
PEOPLE CAN BE SHALLOW AND PETTY. THEY CAN BE SELFISH AND CRUEL.
ESPECIALLY IN THEIR THOUGHTS, WHEN THEY THINK NOBODY CAN HEAR.
AND THEIR CAPACITY FOR SELF-DELUSION? IT'S HEARTBREAKING.
MAYBE I GAVE THOUSANDS OF PEOPLE A HARD DOSE OF MUCH-NEEDED TRUTH WHEN I STRIPPED THE PARADORAN DREAM AWAY FROM THEM.
OR MAYBE I JUST KICKED THEM IN THEIR SOULS.
BUT IT DOESN'T MATTER IN THE END. THE PAST IS GONE.
YOU CAN'T EVER GET IT BACK, NOT REALLY.
WHEN YOU GET RIGHT DOWN TO IT, NOW IS ALWAYS THE TIME TO MOVE ON.
THE END

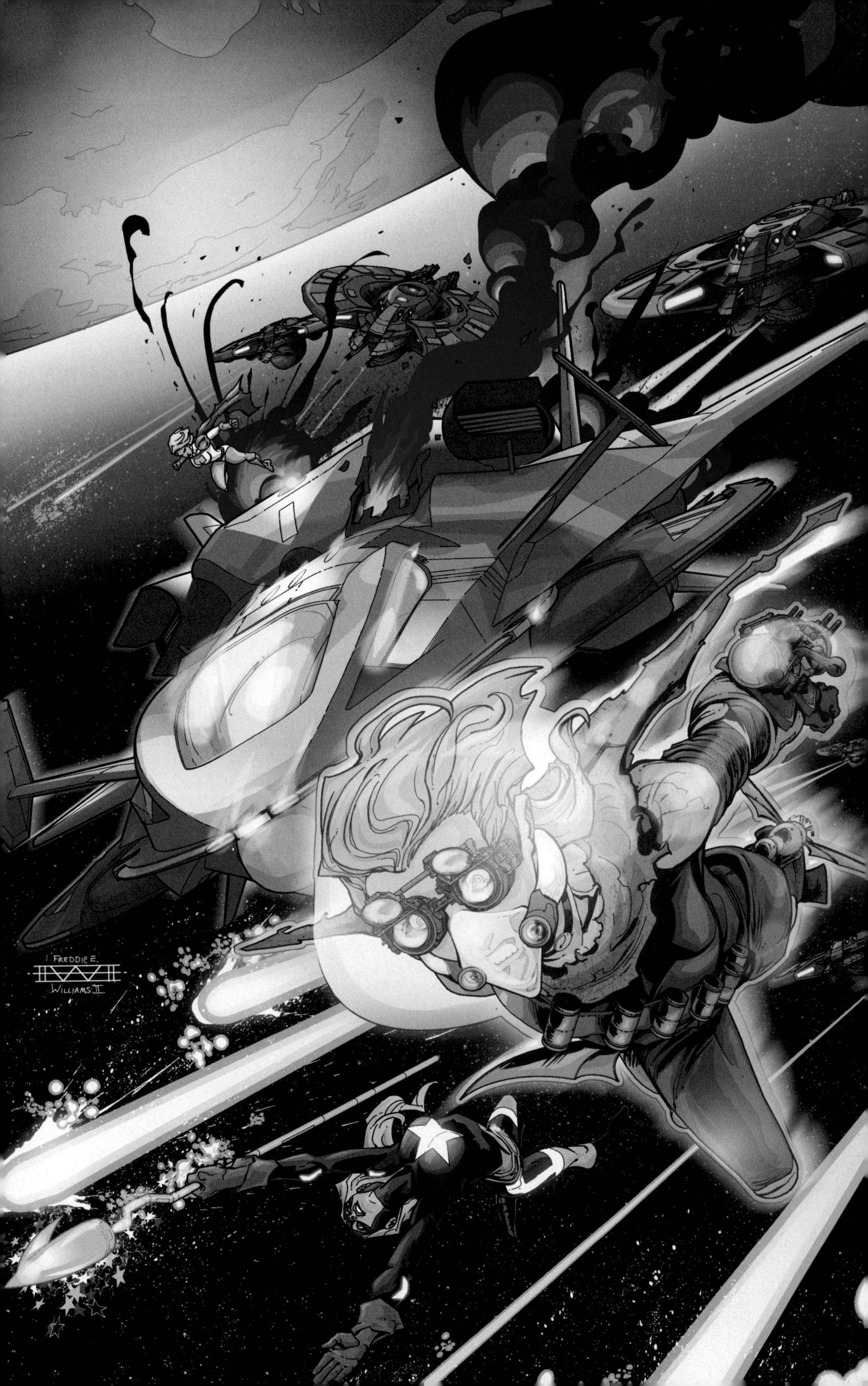
FREDDIE E.
WILLIAMS II

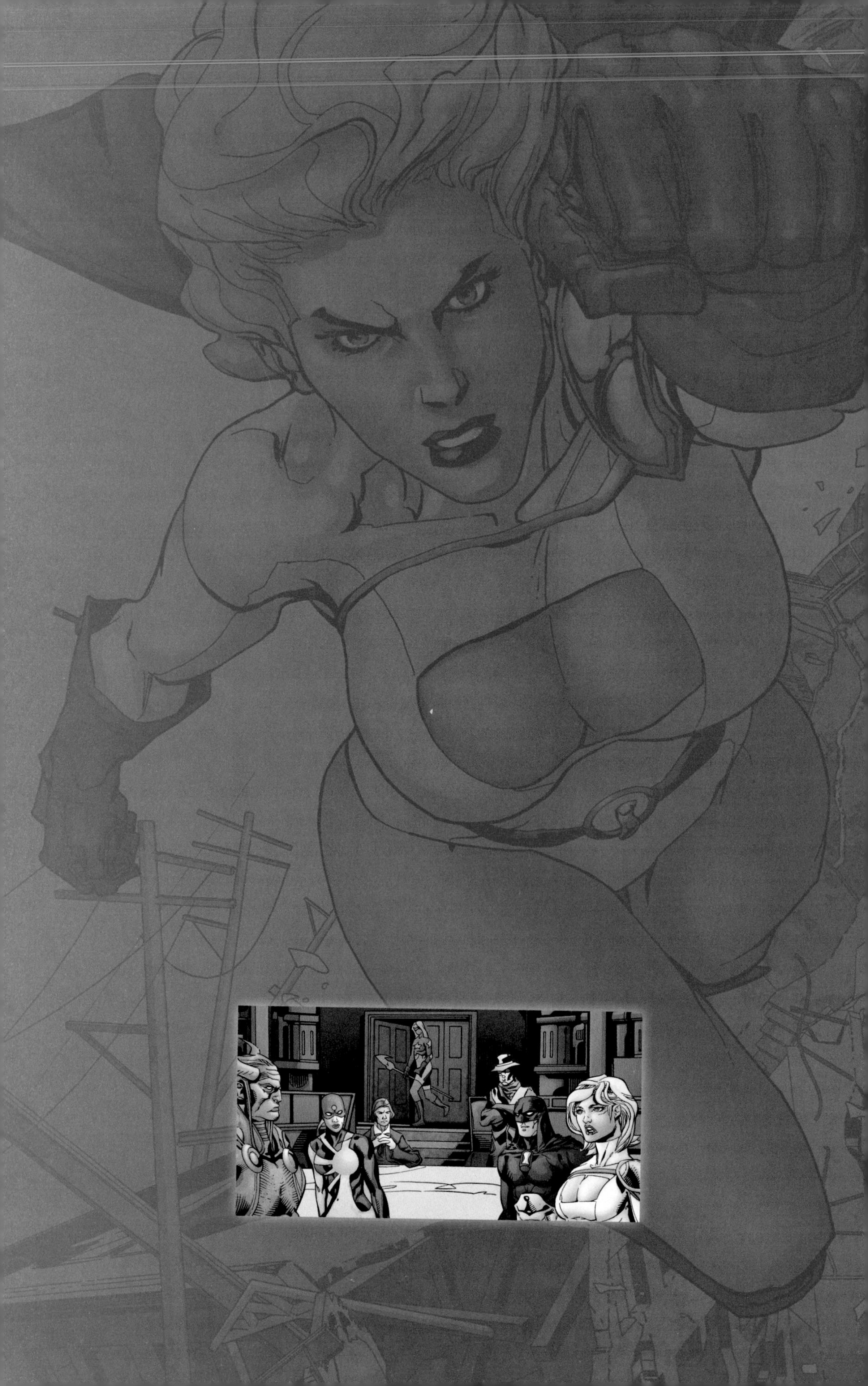

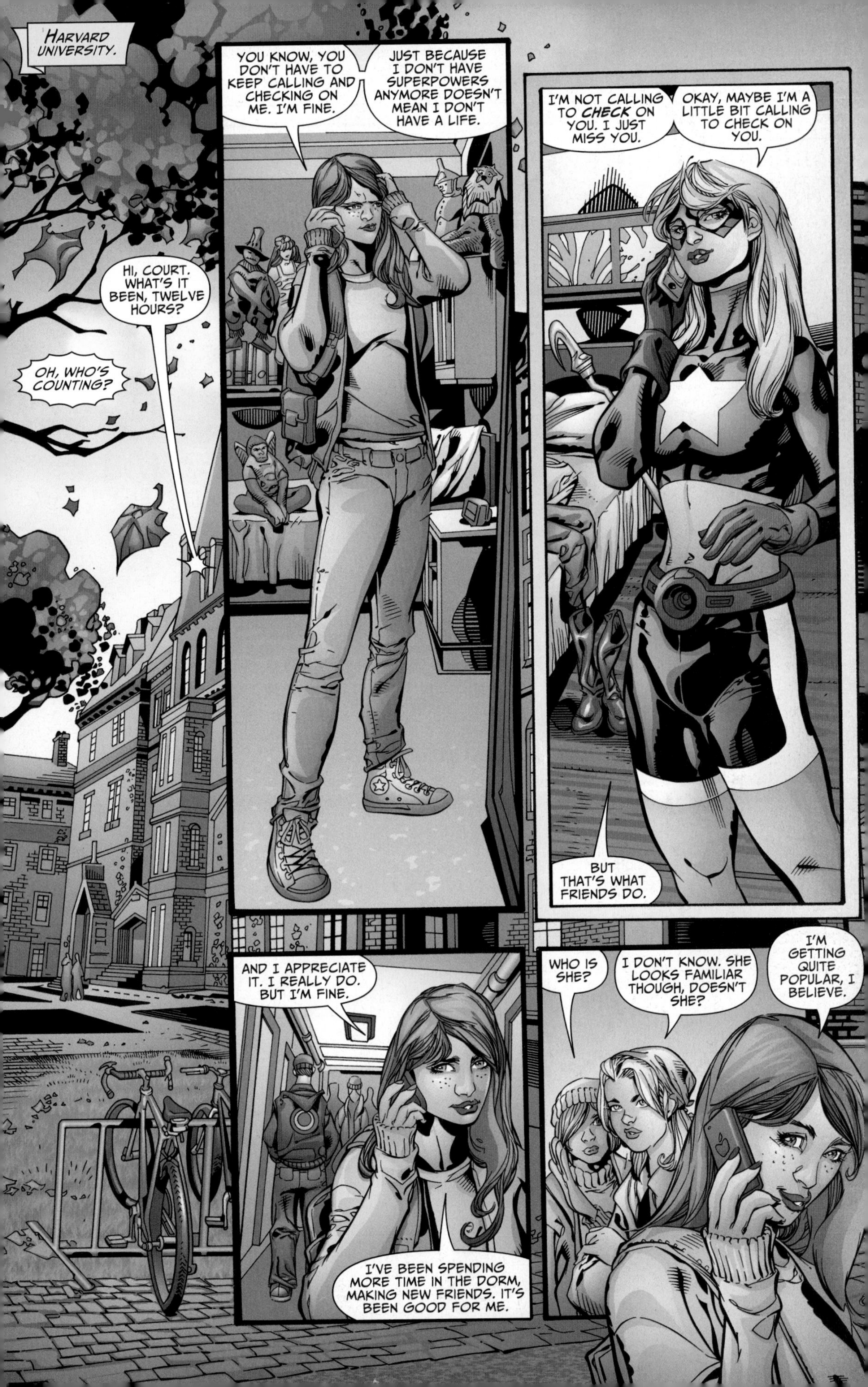
HARVARD UNIVERSITY.
HI, COURT. WHAT'S IT BEEN, TWELVE HOURS?
OH, WHO'S COUNTING?
YOU KNOW, YOU DON'T HAVE TO KEEP CALLING AND CHECKING ON ME. I'M FINE.
JUST BECAUSE I DON'T HAVE SUPERPOWERS ANYMORE DOESN'T MEAN I DON'T HAVE A LIFE.
I'M NOT CALLING TO CHECK ON YOU. I JUST MISS YOU.
OKAY, MAYBE I'M A LITTLE BIT CALLING TO CHECK ON YOU.
BUT THAT'S WHAT FRIENDS DO.
AND I APPRECIATE IT. I REALLY DO. BUT I'M FINE.
I'VE BEEN SPENDING MORE TIME IN THE DORM, MAKING NEW FRIENDS. IT'S BEEN GOOD FOR ME.
WHO IS SHE?
I DON'T KNOW. SHE LOOKS FAMILIAR THOUGH, DOESN'T SHE?
I'M GETTING QUITE POPULAR, I BELIEVE.

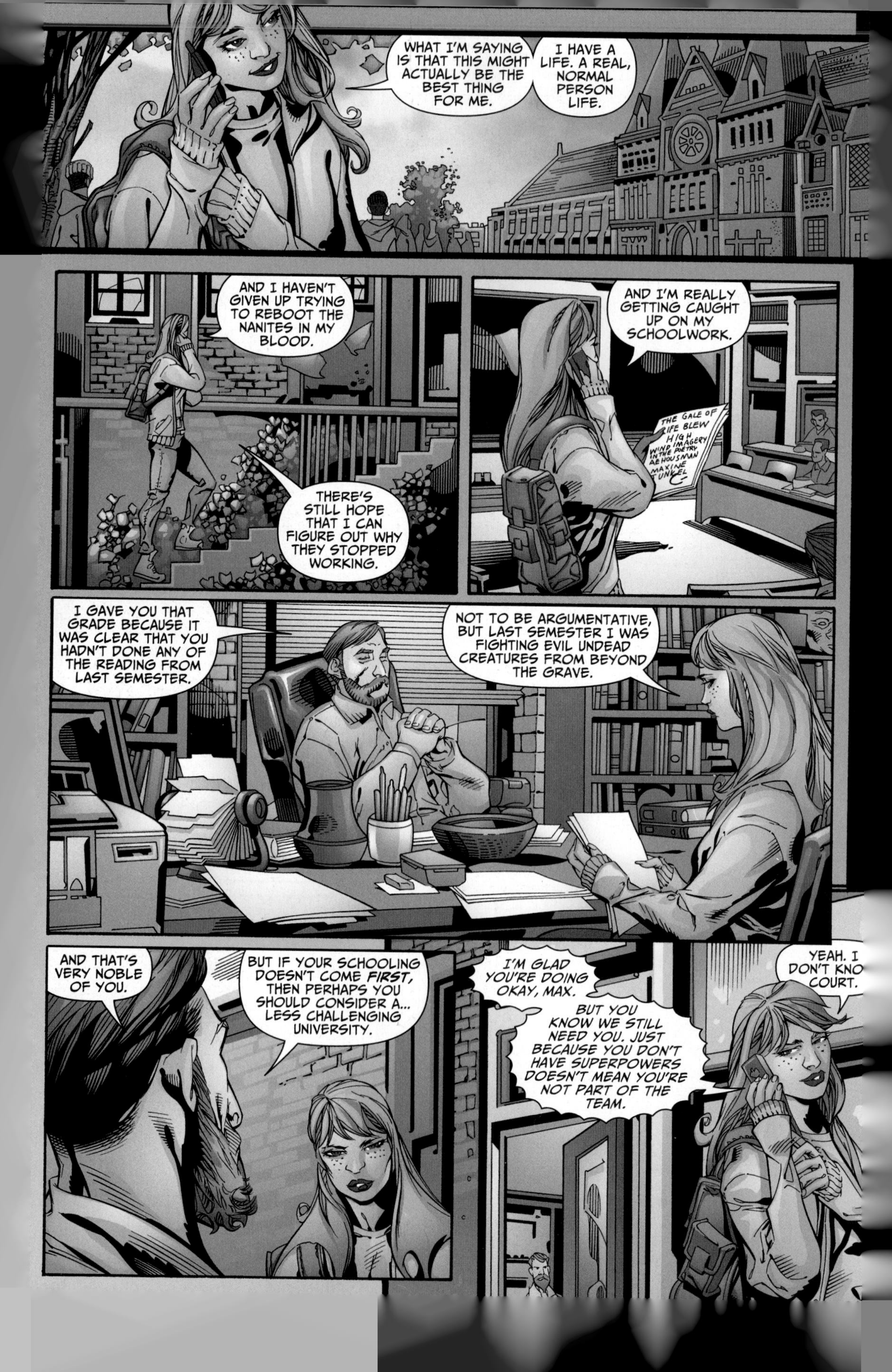
WHAT I'M SAYING IS THAT THIS MIGHT ACTUALLY BE THE BEST THING FOR ME.
I HAVE A LIFE. A REAL, NORMAL PERSON LIFE.
AND I HAVEN'T GIVEN UP TRYING TO REBOOT THE NANITES IN MY BLOOD.
THERE'S STILL HOPE THAT I CAN FIGURE OUT WHY THEY STOPPED WORKING.
AND I'M REALLY GETTING CAUGHT UP ON MY SCHOOLWORK.
THE GALE OF LIFE BLEW HIGH
WIND IMAGERY IN THE POETRY AE HOUSMAN
MAXINE UNKEL
I GAVE YOU THAT GRADE BECAUSE IT WAS CLEAR THAT YOU HADN'T DONE ANY OF THE READING FROM LAST SEMESTER.
NOT TO BE ARGUMENTATIVE, BUT LAST SEMESTER I WAS FIGHTING EVIL UNDEAD CREATURES FROM BEYOND THE GRAVE.
AND THAT'S VERY NOBLE OF YOU.
BUT IF YOUR SCHOOLING DOESN'T COME FIRST, THEN PERHAPS YOU SHOULD CONSIDER A... LESS CHALLENGING UNIVERSITY.
I'M GLAD YOU'RE DOING OKAY, MAX.
BUT YOU KNOW WE STILL NEED YOU. JUST BECAUSE YOU DON'T HAVE SUPERPOWERS DOESN'T MEAN YOU'RE NOT PART OF THE TEAM.
YEAH. I DON'T KNO COURT.

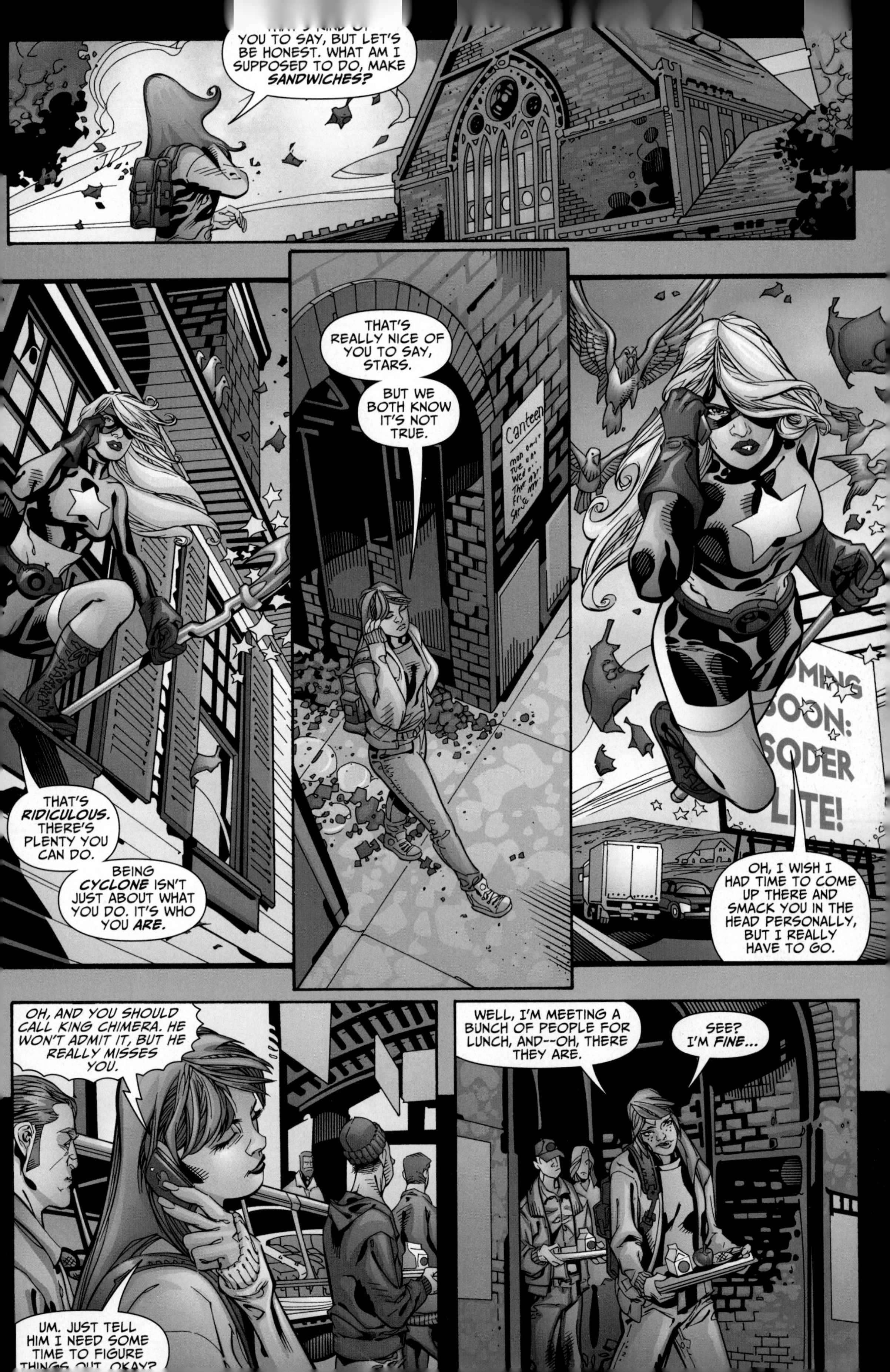
YOU TO SAY, BUT LET'S BE HONEST. WHAT AM I SUPPOSED TO DO, MAKE SANDWICHES?
THAT'S RIDICULOUS. THERE'S PLENTY YOU CAN DO.
BEING CYCLONE ISN'T JUST ABOUT WHAT YOU DO. IT'S WHO YOU ARE.
THAT'S REALLY NICE OF YOU TO SAY, STARS.
BUT WE BOTH KNOW IT'S NOT TRUE.
Canteen
OH, I WISH I HAD TIME TO COME UP THERE AND SMACK YOU IN THE HEAD PERSONALLY, BUT I REALLY HAVE TO GO.
SODER
LITE!
OH, AND YOU SHOULD CALL KING CHIMERA. HE WON'T ADMIT IT, BUT HE REALLY MISSES YOU.
UM. JUST TELL HIM I NEED SOME TIME TO FIGURE THINGS OUT, OKAY?
WELL, I'M MEETING A BUNCH OF PEOPLE FOR LUNCH, AND--OH, THERE THEY ARE.
SEE? I'M FINE...

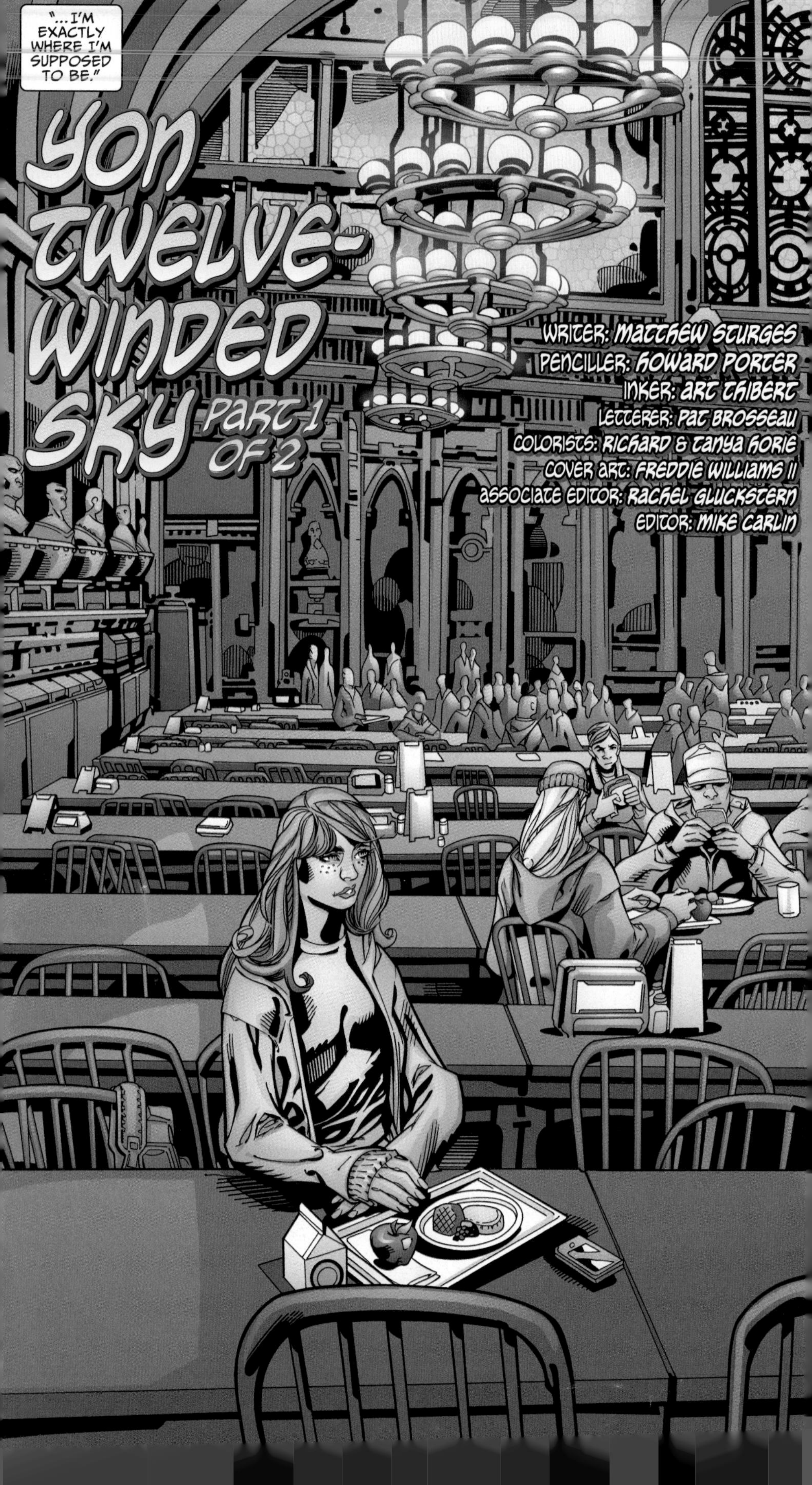
"...I'M EXACTLY WHERE I'M SUPPOSED TO BE."
YON TWELVE-WINDED SKY PART 1 OF 2
WRITER: MATTHEW STURGES
PENCILLER: HOWARD PORTER
INKER: ART THIBERT
LETTERER: PAT BROSSEAU
COLORISTS: RICHARD & TANYA HORIE
COVER ART: FREDDIE WILLIAMS II
ASSOCIATE EDITOR: RACHEL GLUCKSTERN
EDITOR: MIKE CARLIN

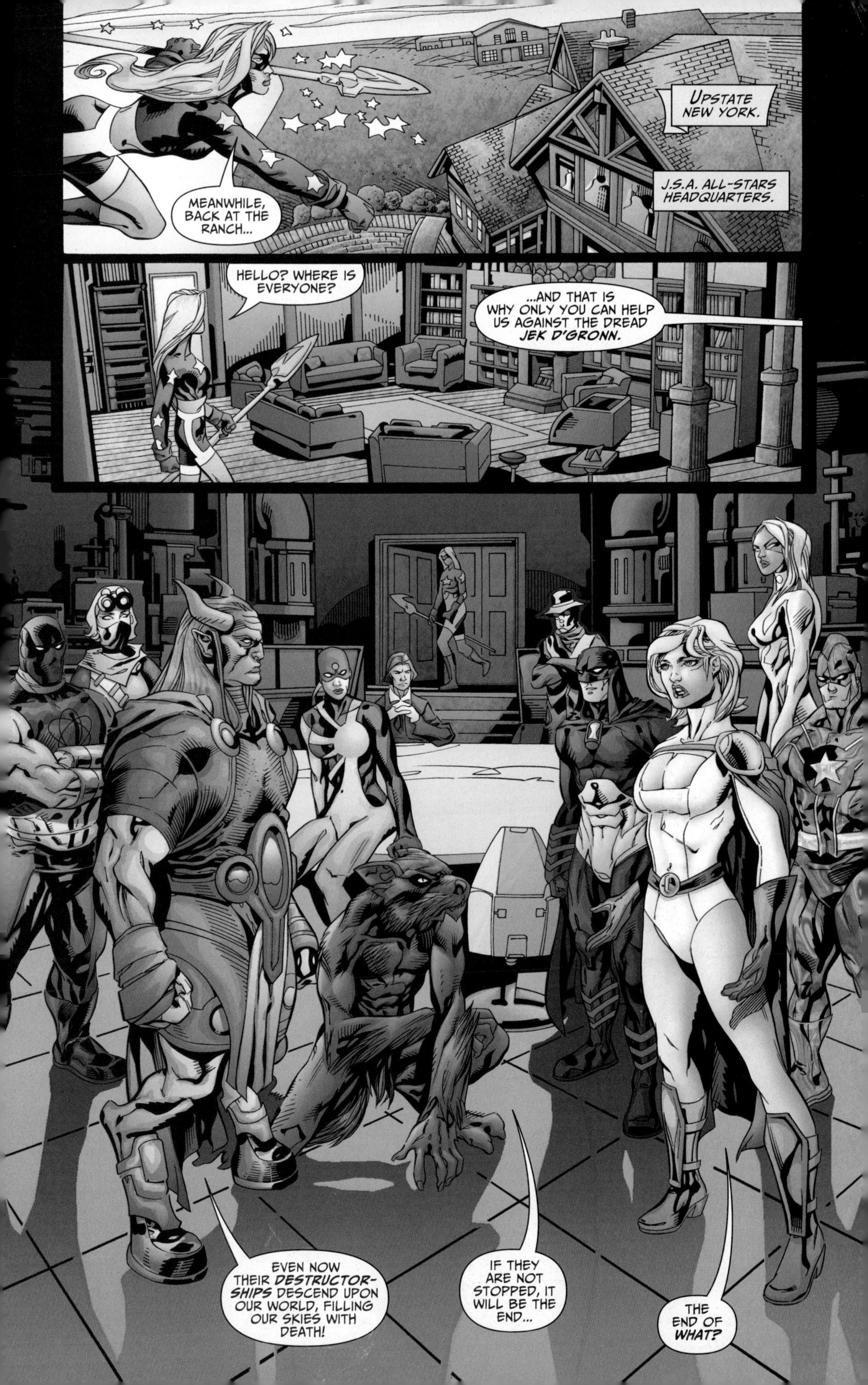
UPSTATE NEW YORK.
MEANWHILE, BACK AT THE RANCH...
J.S.A. ALL-STARS HEADQUARTERS.
HELLO? WHERE IS EVERYONE?
...AND THAT IS WHY ONLY YOU CAN HELP US AGAINST THE DREAD JEK D'GRONN.
EVEN NOW THEIR DESTRUCTOR-SHIPS DESCEND UPON OUR WORLD, FILLING OUR SKIES WITH DEATH!
IF THEY ARE NOT STOPPED, IT WILL BE THE END...
THE END OF WHAT?

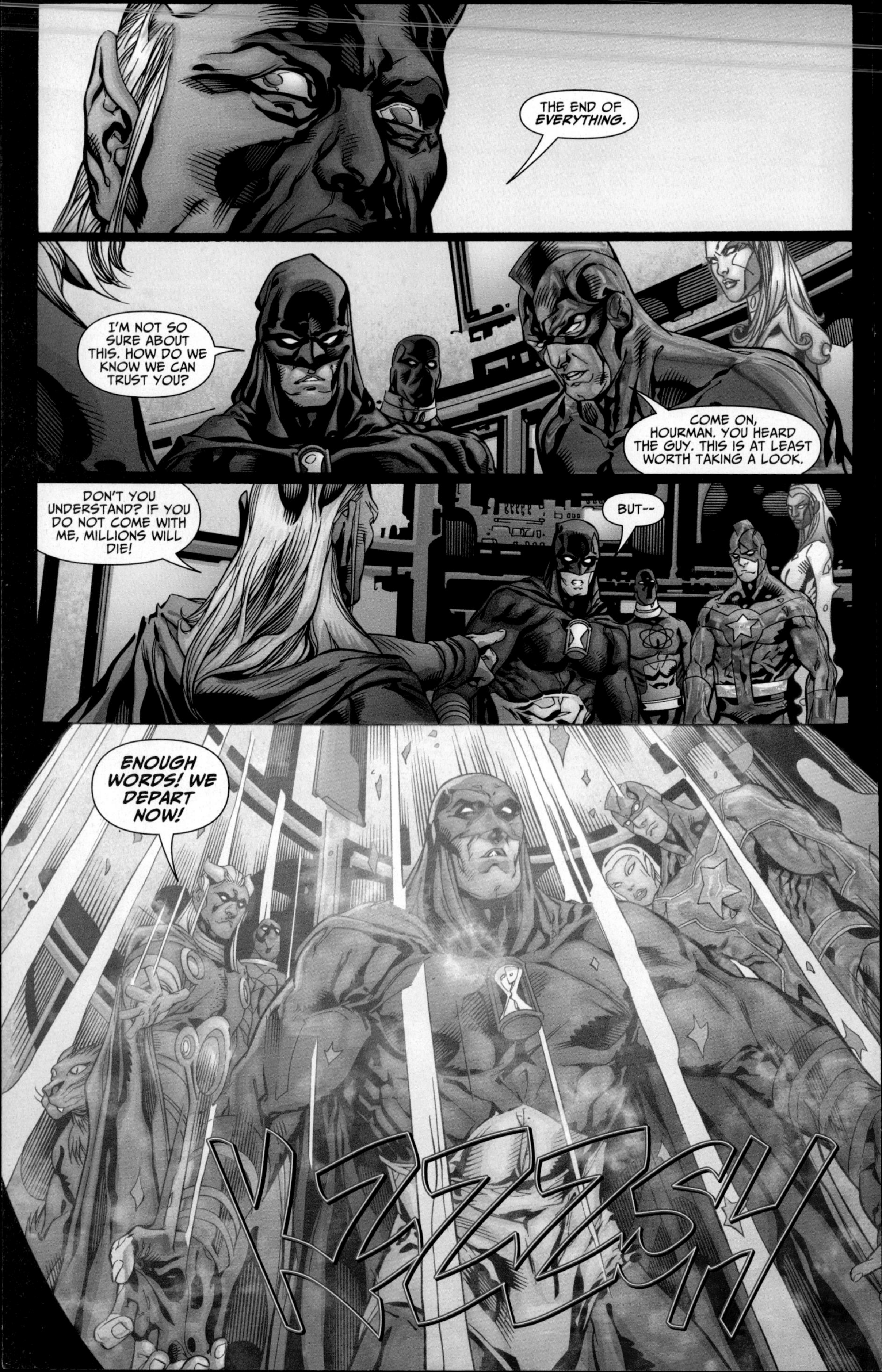
THE END OF *EVERYTHING.*
I'M NOT SO SURE ABOUT THIS. HOW DO WE KNOW WE CAN TRUST YOU?
COME ON, HOURMAN. YOU HEARD THE GUY. THIS IS AT LEAST WORTH TAKING A LOOK.
DON'T YOU UNDERSTAND? IF YOU DO NOT COME WITH ME, MILLIONS WILL DIE!
BUT--
ENOUGH WORDS! WE DEPART NOW!

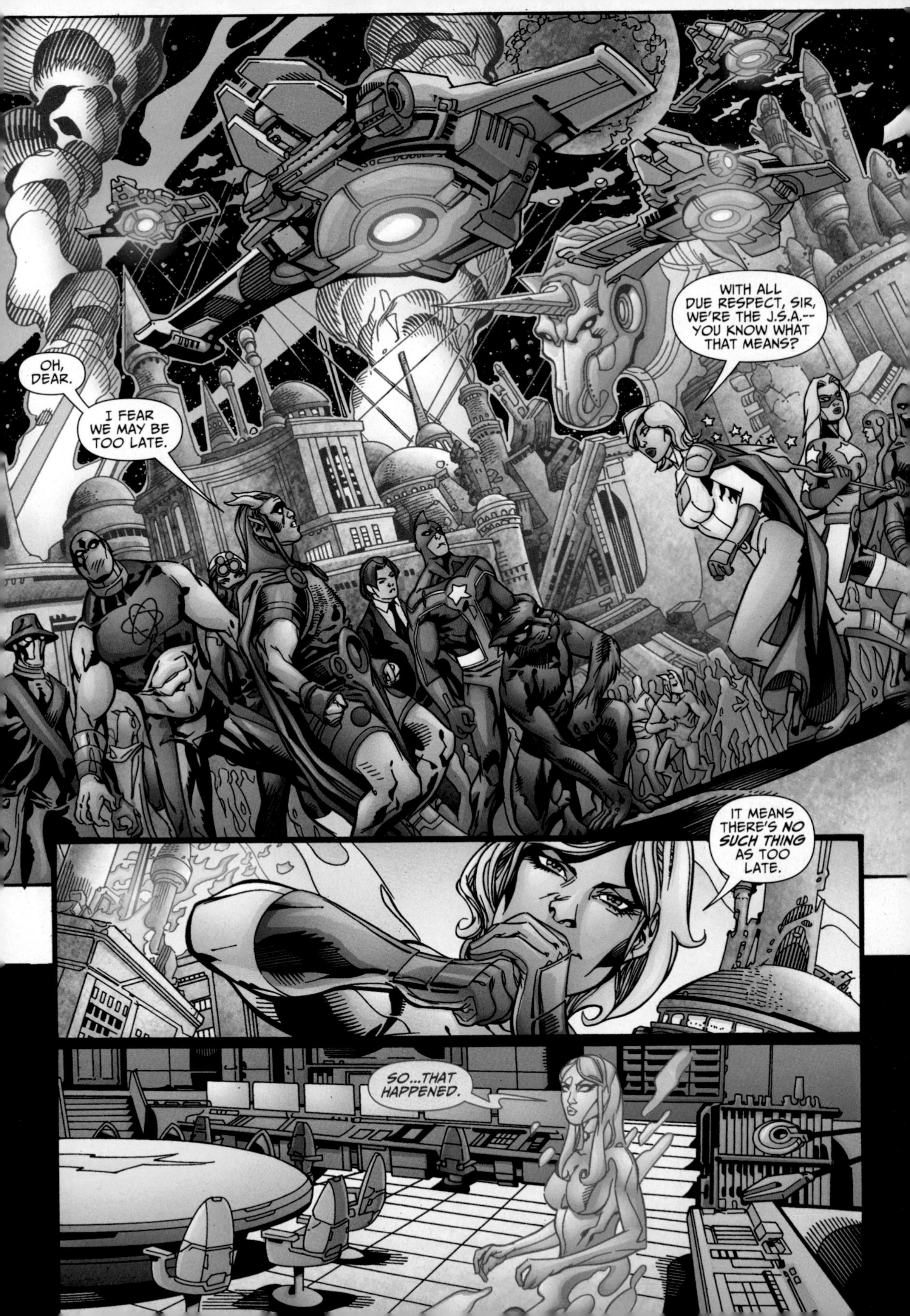
OH, DEAR.
I FEAR WE MAY BE TOO LATE.
WITH ALL DUE RESPECT, SIR, WE'RE THE J.S.A.-- YOU KNOW WHAT THAT MEANS?
IT MEANS THERE'S *NO SUCH THING* AS TOO LATE.
SO...THAT *HAPPENED*.

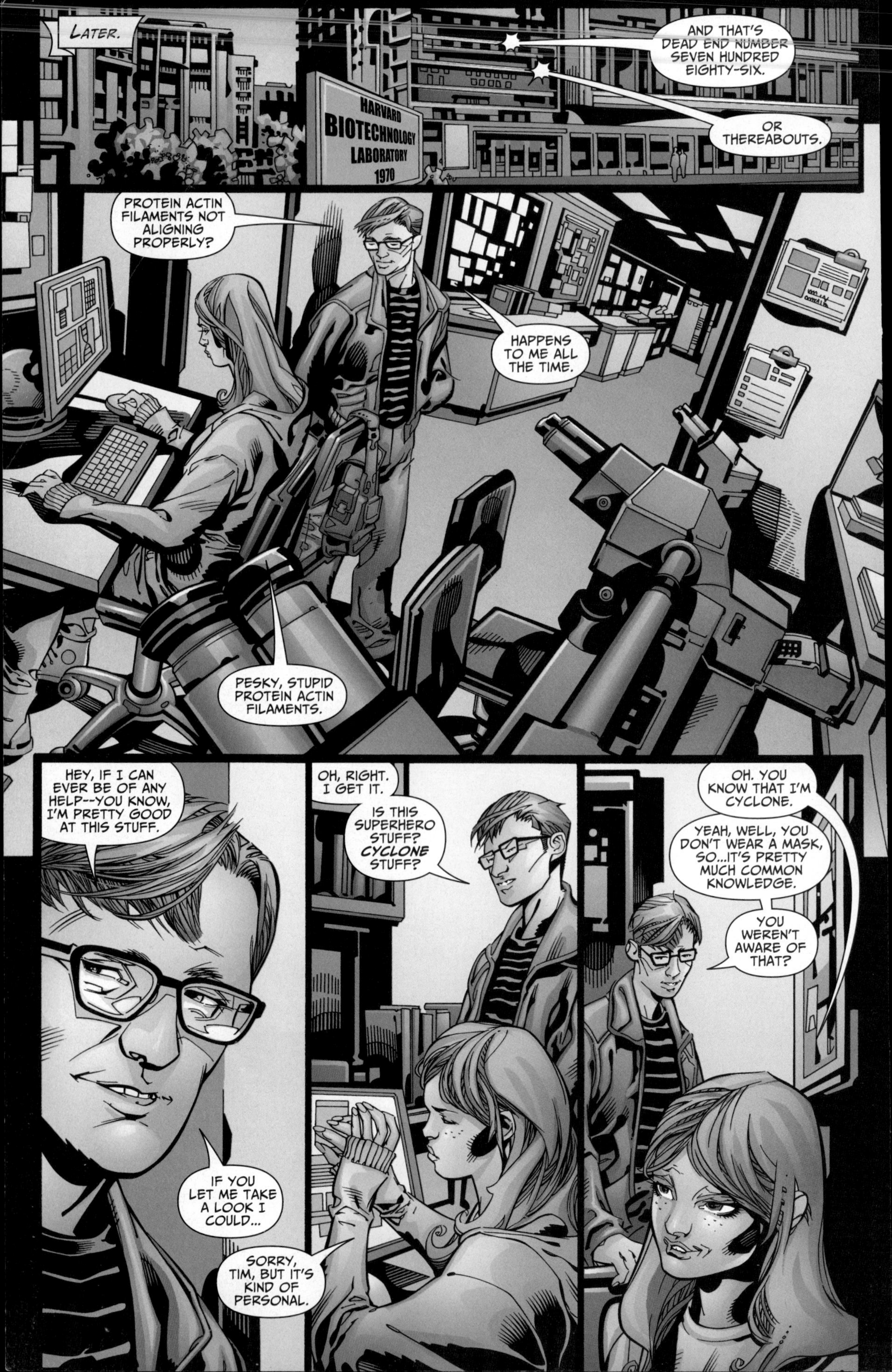
LATER.
HARVARD BIOTECHNOLOGY LABORATORY 1970
AND THAT'S DEAD END NUMBER SEVEN HUNDRED EIGHTY-SIX.
OR THEREABOUTS.
PROTEIN ACTIN FILAMENTS NOT ALIGNING PROPERLY?
HAPPENS TO ME ALL THE TIME.
PESKY, STUPID PROTEIN ACTIN FILAMENTS.
HEY, IF I CAN EVER BE OF ANY HELP--YOU KNOW, I'M PRETTY GOOD AT THIS STUFF.
IF YOU LET ME TAKE A LOOK I COULD...
SORRY, TIM, BUT IT'S KIND OF PERSONAL.
OH, RIGHT. I GET IT.
IS THIS SUPERHERO STUFF? *CYCLONE* STUFF?
OH. YOU KNOW THAT I'M CYCLONE.
YEAH, WELL, YOU DON'T WEAR A MASK, SO...IT'S PRETTY MUCH COMMON KNOWLEDGE.
YOU WEREN'T AWARE OF THAT?

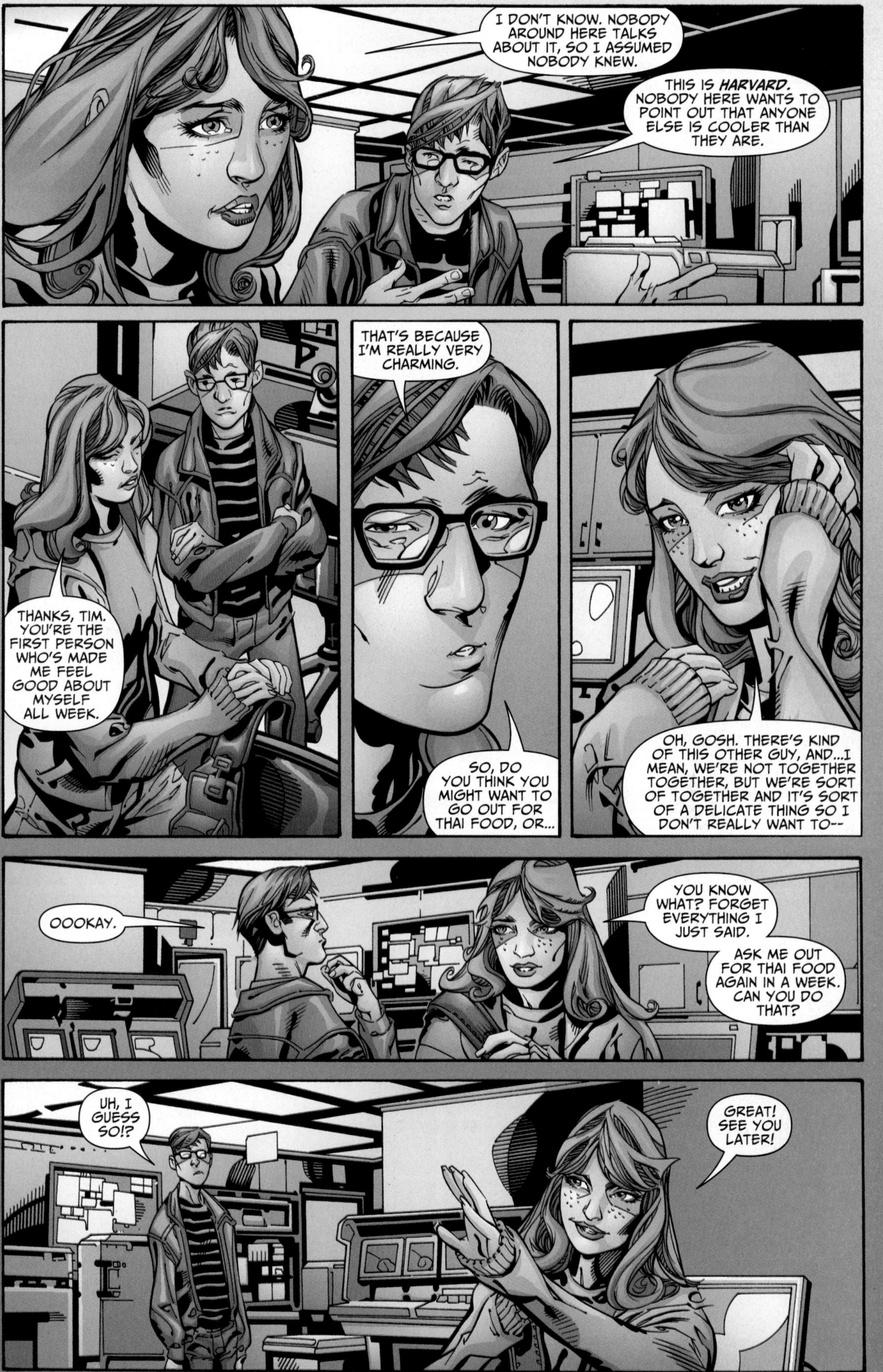
I DON'T KNOW. NOBODY AROUND HERE TALKS ABOUT IT, SO I ASSUMED NOBODY KNEW.
THIS IS *HARVARD.* NOBODY HERE WANTS TO POINT OUT THAT ANYONE ELSE IS COOLER THAN THEY ARE.
THANKS, TIM. YOU'RE THE FIRST PERSON WHO'S MADE ME FEEL GOOD ABOUT MYSELF ALL WEEK.
THAT'S BECAUSE I'M REALLY VERY CHARMING.
SO, DO YOU THINK YOU MIGHT WANT TO GO OUT FOR THAI FOOD, OR...
OH, GOSH. THERE'S KIND OF THIS OTHER GUY, AND...I MEAN, WE'RE NOT TOGETHER TOGETHER, BUT WE'RE SORT OF TOGETHER AND IT'S SORT OF A DELICATE THING SO I DON'T REALLY WANT TO--
OOOKAY.
YOU KNOW WHAT? FORGET EVERYTHING I JUST SAID.
ASK ME OUT FOR THAI FOOD AGAIN IN A WEEK. CAN YOU DO THAT?
UH, I GUESS SO!?
GREAT! SEE YOU LATER!

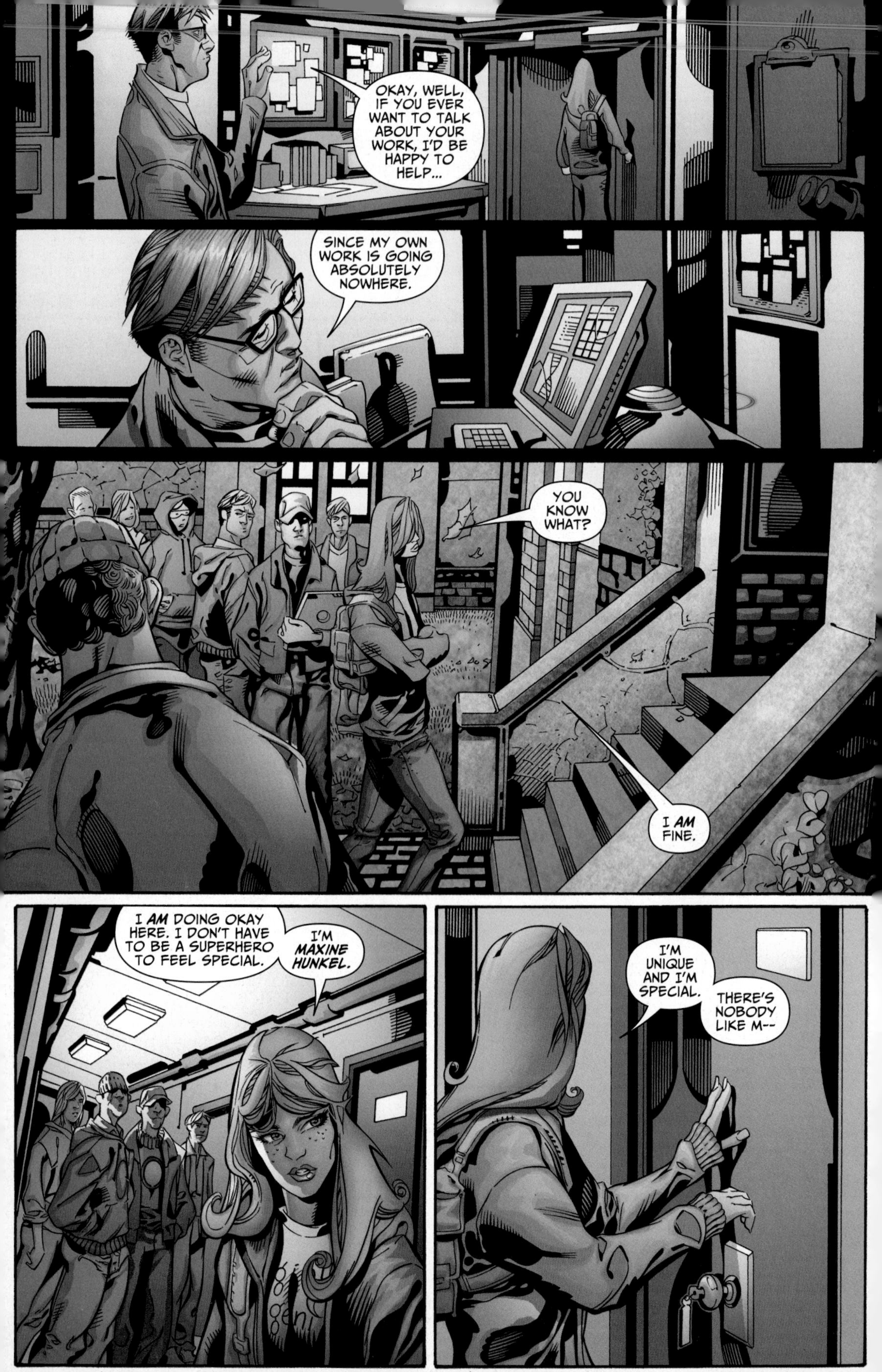
OKAY, WELL, IF YOU EVER WANT TO TALK ABOUT YOUR WORK, I'D BE HAPPY TO HELP...
SINCE MY OWN WORK IS GOING ABSOLUTELY NOWHERE.
YOU KNOW WHAT?
I AM FINE.
I AM DOING OKAY HERE. I DON'T HAVE TO BE A SUPERHERO TO FEEL SPECIAL.
I'M MAXINE HUNKEL.
I'M UNIQUE AND I'M SPECIAL.
THERE'S NOBODY LIKE M--

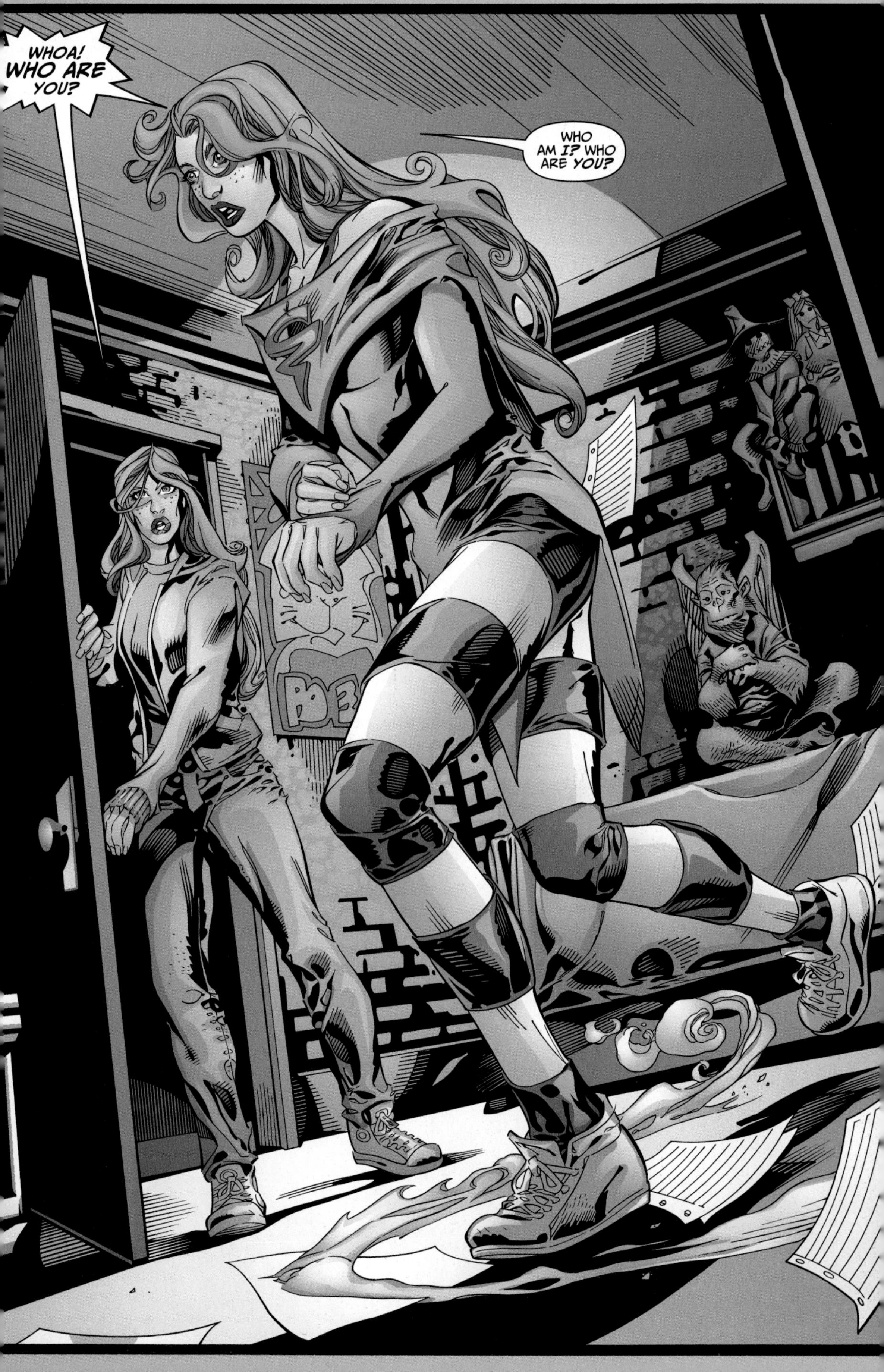
WHOA! WHO ARE YOU?
WHO AM I? WHO ARE YOU?

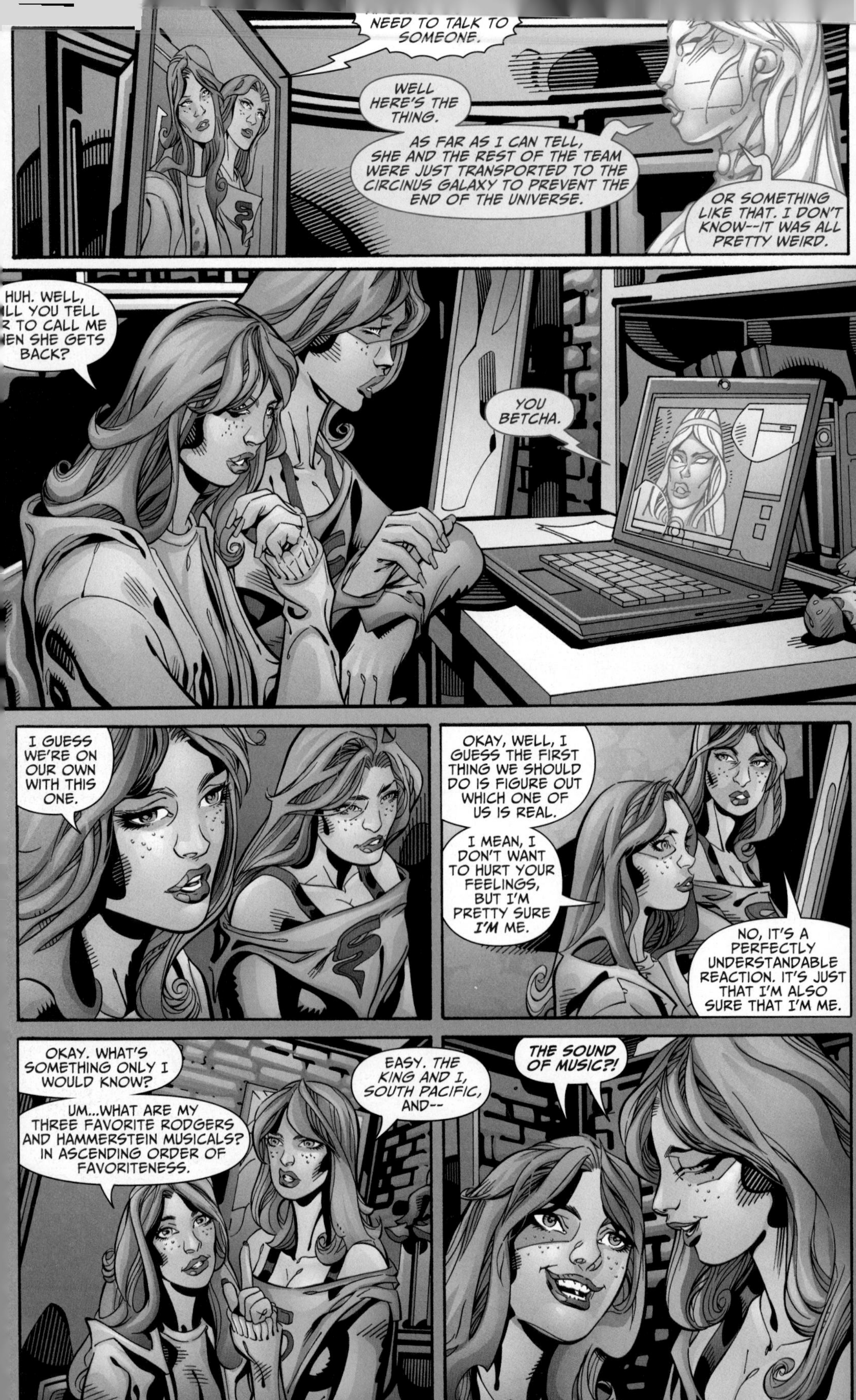
NEED TO TALK TO SOMEONE.
WELL HERE'S THE THING.
AS FAR AS I CAN TELL, SHE AND THE REST OF THE TEAM WERE JUST TRANSPORTED TO THE CIRCINUS GALAXY TO PREVENT THE END OF THE UNIVERSE.
OR SOMETHING LIKE THAT. I DON'T KNOW--IT WAS ALL PRETTY WEIRD.
HUH. WELL, ILL YOU TELL R TO CALL ME EN SHE GETS BACK?
YOU BETCHA.
I GUESS WE'RE ON OUR OWN WITH THIS ONE.
OKAY, WELL, I GUESS THE FIRST THING WE SHOULD DO IS FIGURE OUT WHICH ONE OF US IS REAL.
I MEAN, I DON'T WANT TO HURT YOUR FEELINGS, BUT I'M PRETTY SURE I'M ME.
NO, IT'S A PERFECTLY UNDERSTANDABLE REACTION. IT'S JUST THAT I'M ALSO SURE THAT I'M ME.
OKAY. WHAT'S SOMETHING ONLY I WOULD KNOW?
UM...WHAT ARE MY THREE FAVORITE RODGERS AND HAMMERSTEIN MUSICALS? IN ASCENDING ORDER OF FAVORITENESS.
EASY. THE KING AND I, SOUTH PACIFIC, AND--
THE SOUND OF MUSIC?!

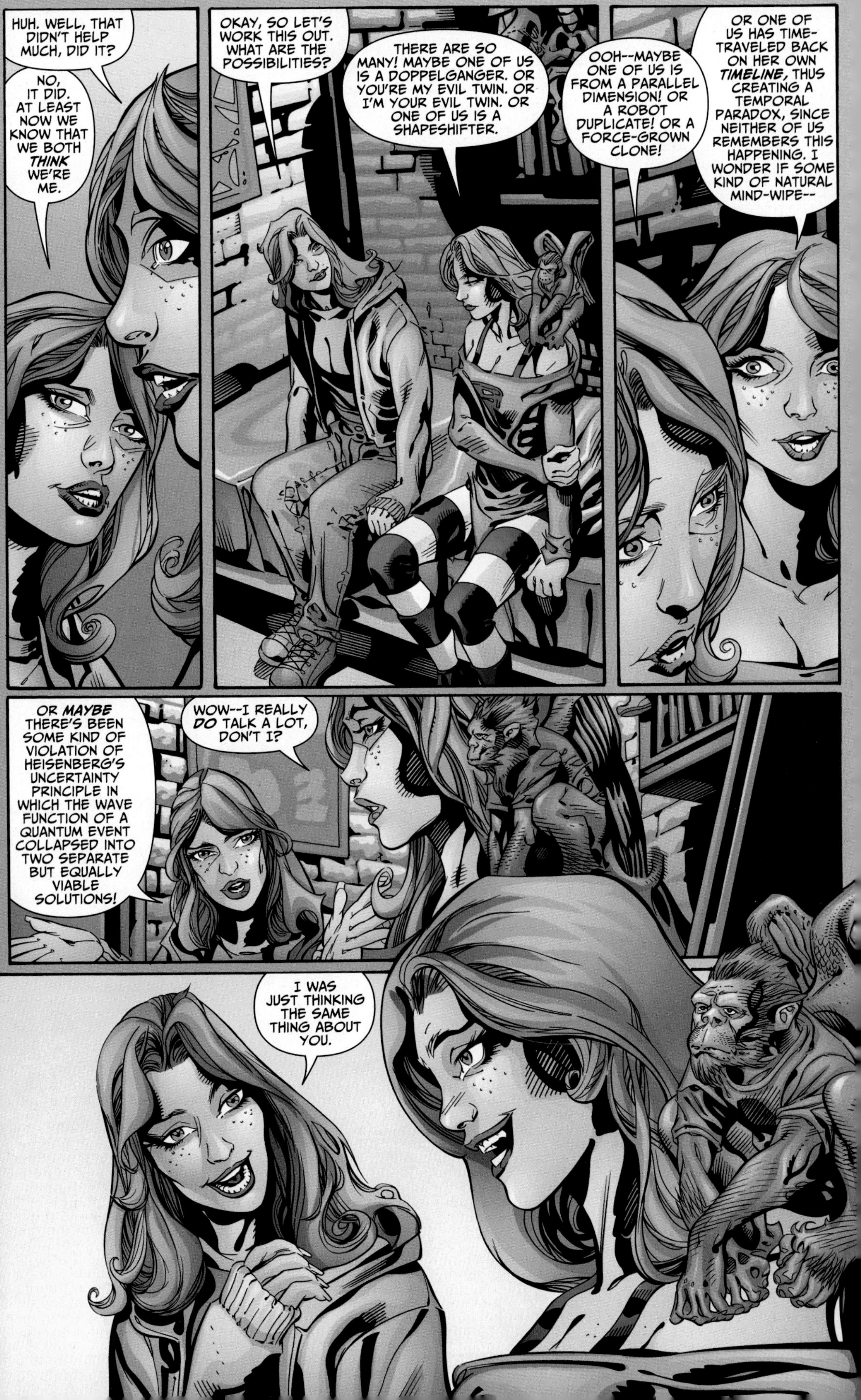
HUH. WELL, THAT DIDN'T HELP MUCH, DID IT?
NO, IT DID. AT LEAST NOW WE KNOW THAT WE BOTH *THINK* WE'RE ME.
OKAY, SO LET'S WORK THIS OUT. WHAT ARE THE POSSIBILITIES?
THERE ARE SO MANY! MAYBE ONE OF US IS A DOPPELGANGER. OR YOU'RE MY EVIL TWIN. OR I'M YOUR EVIL TWIN. OR ONE OF US IS A SHAPESHIFTER.
OOH--MAYBE ONE OF US IS FROM A PARALLEL DIMENSION! OR A ROBOT DUPLICATE! OR A FORCE-GROWN CLONE!
OR ONE OF US HAS TIME-TRAVELED BACK ON HER OWN *TIMELINE,* THUS CREATING A TEMPORAL PARADOX, SINCE NEITHER OF US REMEMBERS THIS HAPPENING. I WONDER IF SOME KIND OF NATURAL MIND-WIPE--
OR *MAYBE* THERE'S BEEN SOME KIND OF VIOLATION OF HEISENBERG'S UNCERTAINTY PRINCIPLE IN WHICH THE WAVE FUNCTION OF A QUANTUM EVENT COLLAPSED INTO TWO SEPARATE BUT EQUALLY VIABLE SOLUTIONS!
WOW--I REALLY *DO* TALK A LOT, DON'T I?
I WAS JUST THINKING THE SAME THING ABOUT YOU.

DAMMIT!

THIS ISN'T WORKING!

I'M DOOMED. I'M *DOOMED.*

I'M GOING TO *LOSE* MY FUNDING AND I'M *NOT* GOING TO GET TENURE--

--AND I'M GOING TO END UP *HOMELESS* AND SLEEPING ON THE *STREET.*

BUT I'M NOT GOING TO LOOK AT MAXINE'S RESEARCH, EVEN THOUGH SHE LEFT HER MACHINE LOGGED ON.

NO WAY. I WOULDN'T DO THAT.

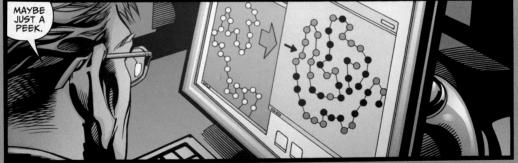

MAYBE JUST A PEEK.

WHOA.

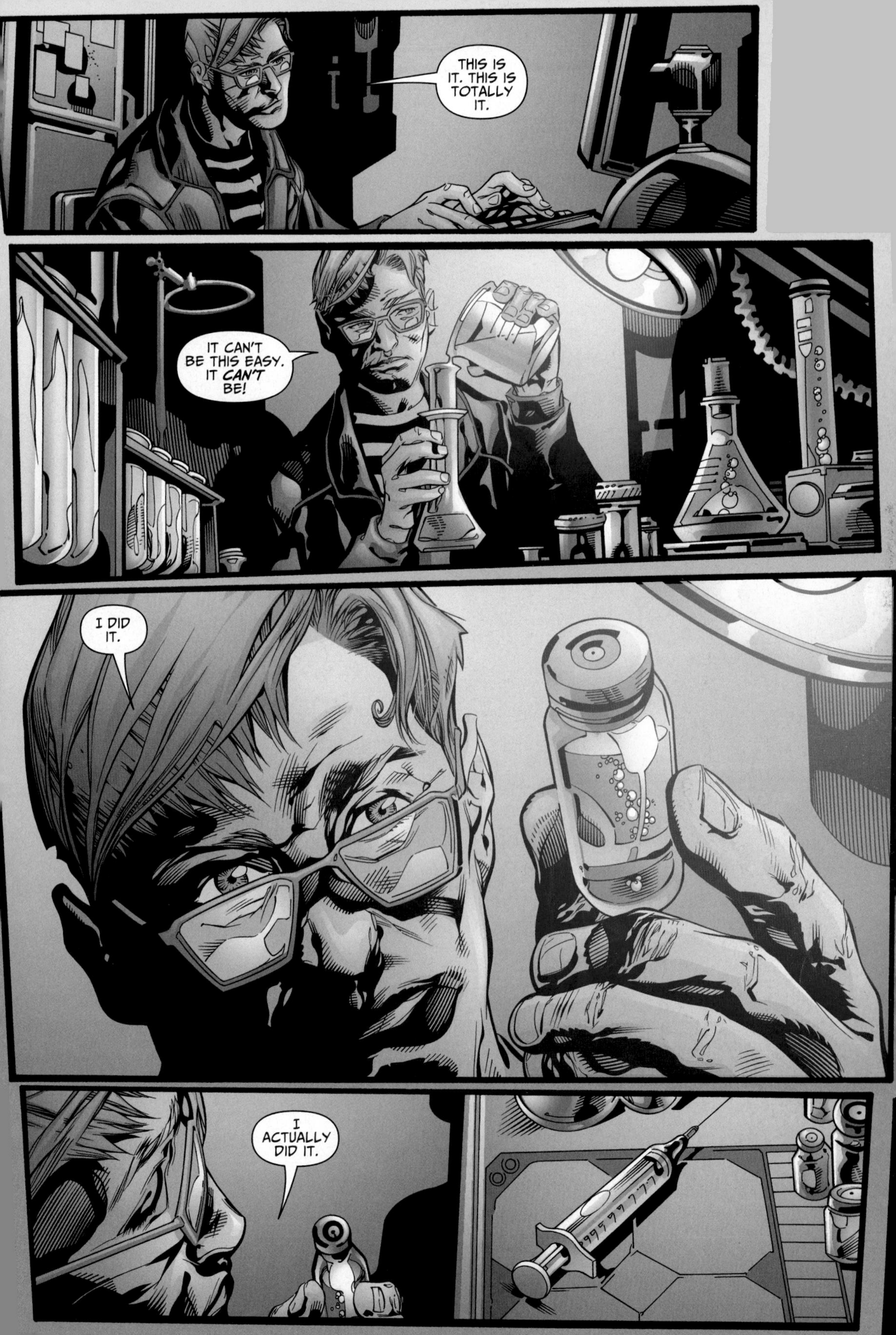
THIS IS IT. THIS IS TOTALLY IT.
IT CAN'T BE THIS EASY. IT *CAN'T* BE!
I DID IT.
I ACTUALLY DID IT.

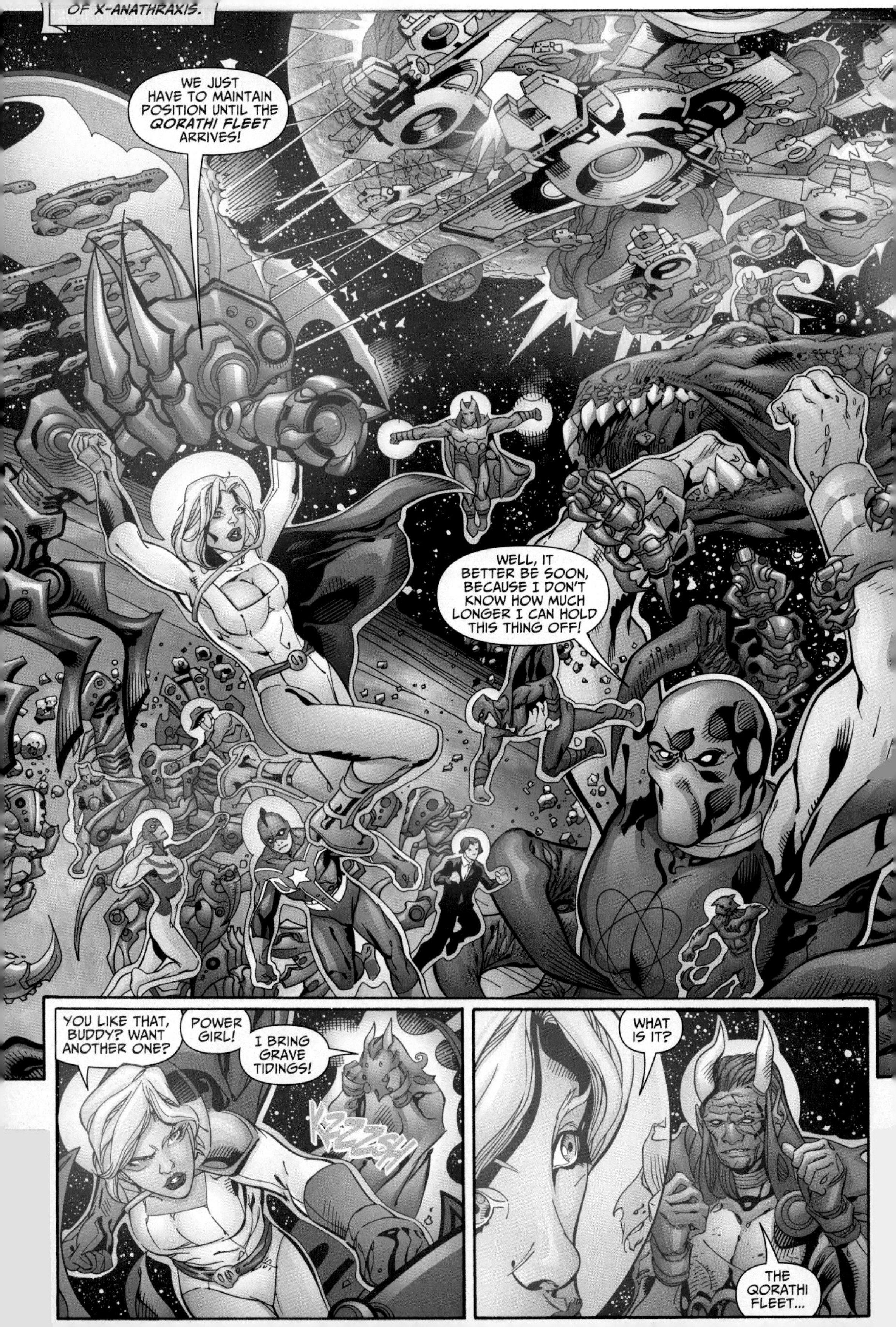
OF X-ANATHRAXIS.
WE JUST HAVE TO MAINTAIN POSITION UNTIL THE QORATHI FLEET ARRIVES!
WELL, IT BETTER BE SOON, BECAUSE I DON'T KNOW HOW MUCH LONGER I CAN HOLD THIS THING OFF!
YOU LIKE THAT, BUDDY? WANT ANOTHER ONE?
POWER GIRL!
I BRING GRAVE TIDINGS!
KZZZSH
WHAT IS IT?
THE QORATHI FLEET...

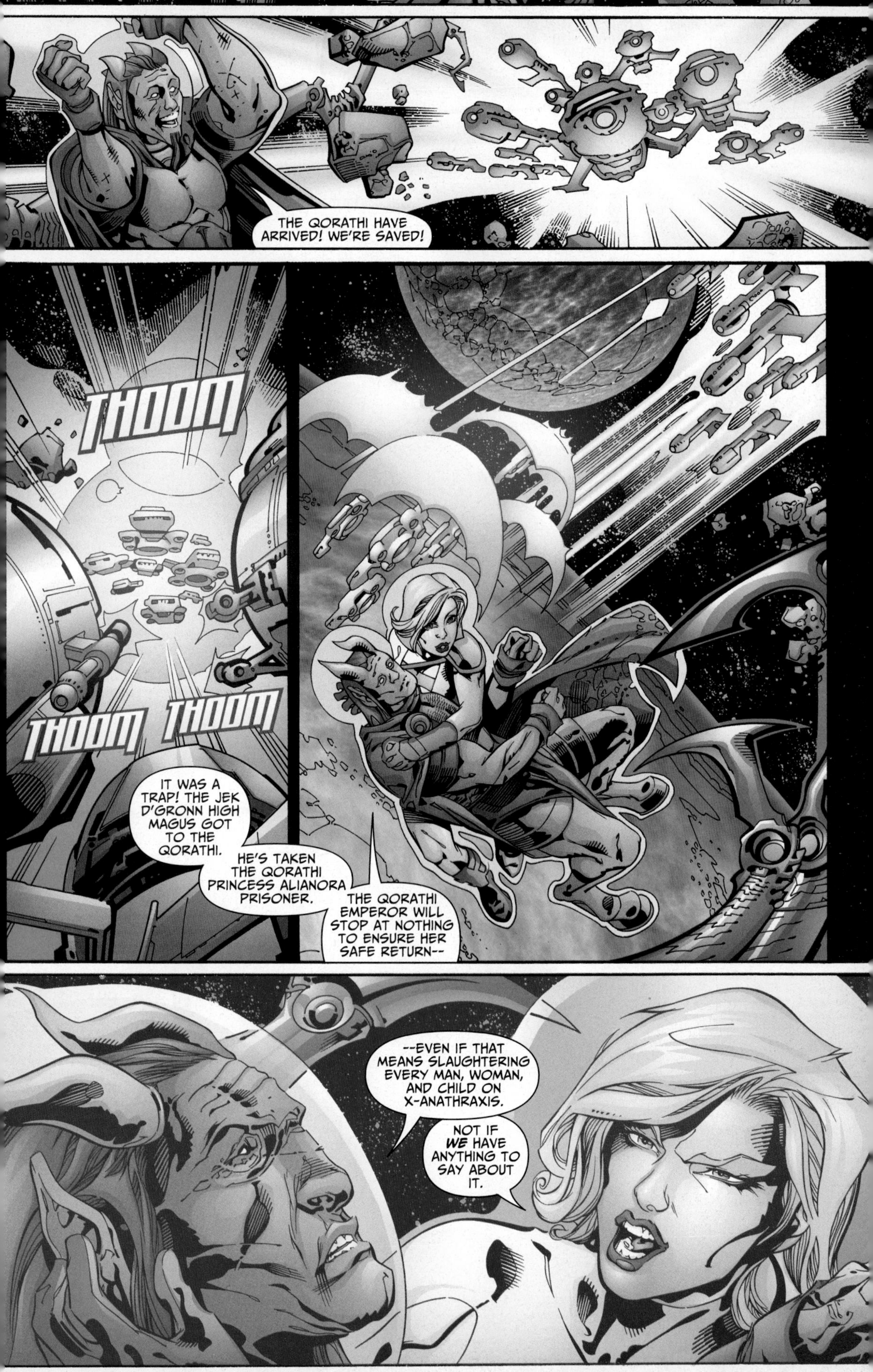
THE QORATHI HAVE ARRIVED! WE'RE SAVED!
THOOM
THOOM THOOM
IT WAS A TRAP! THE JEK D'GRONN HIGH MAGUS GOT TO THE QORATHI.
HE'S TAKEN THE QORATHI PRINCESS ALIANORA PRISONER.
THE QORATHI EMPEROR WILL STOP AT NOTHING TO ENSURE HER SAFE RETURN--
--EVEN IF THAT MEANS SLAUGHTERING EVERY MAN, WOMAN, AND CHILD ON X-ANATHRAXIS.
NOT IF *WE* HAVE ANYTHING TO SAY ABOUT IT.

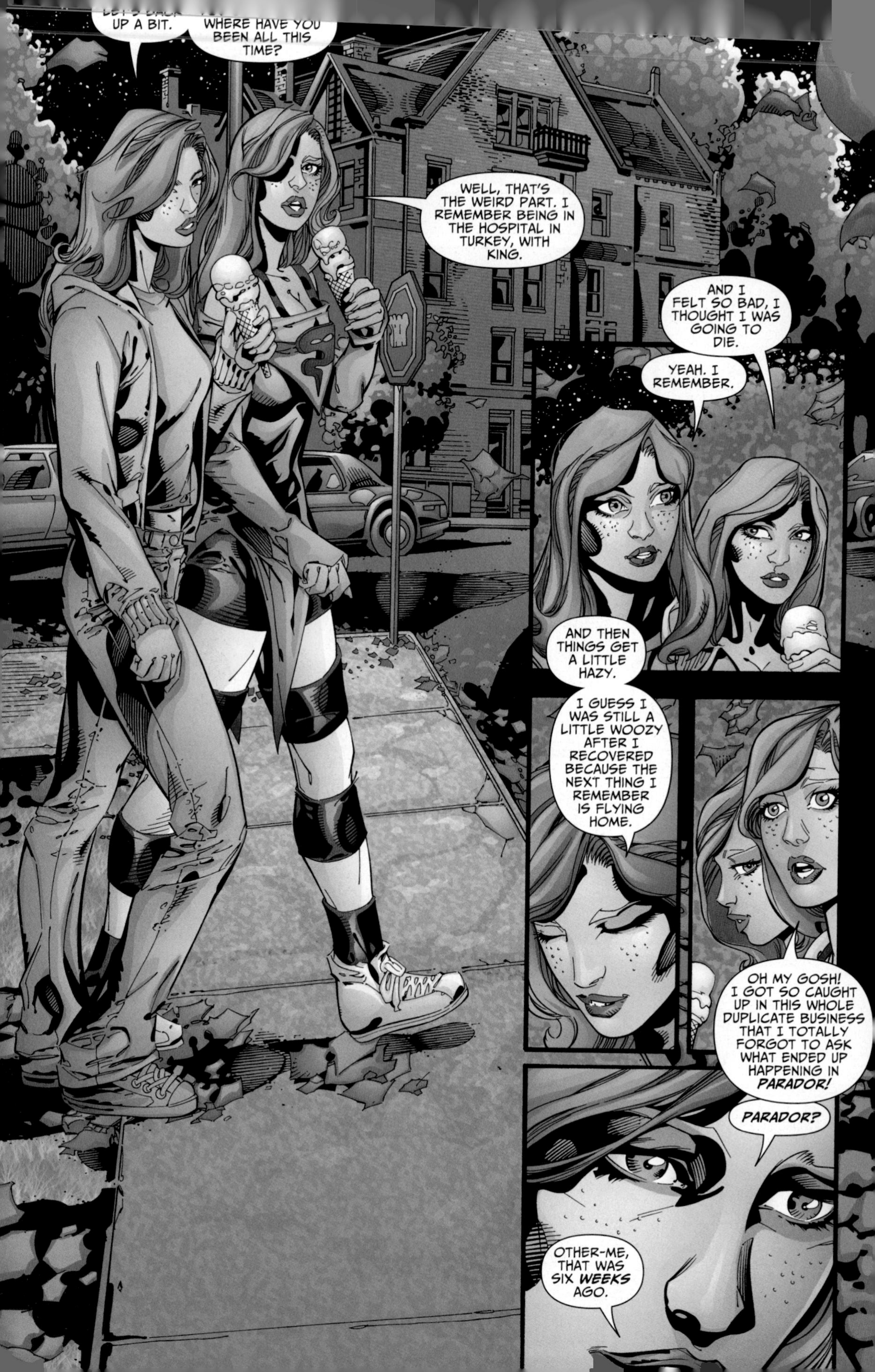

UP A BIT.
WHERE HAVE YOU BEEN ALL THIS TIME?
WELL, THAT'S THE WEIRD PART. I REMEMBER BEING IN THE HOSPITAL IN TURKEY, WITH KING.
AND I FELT SO BAD, I THOUGHT I WAS GOING TO DIE.
YEAH. I REMEMBER.
AND THEN THINGS GET A LITTLE HAZY.
I GUESS I WAS STILL A LITTLE WOOZY AFTER I RECOVERED BECAUSE THE NEXT THING I REMEMBER IS FLYING HOME.
OH MY GOSH! I GOT SO CAUGHT UP IN THIS WHOLE DUPLICATE BUSINESS THAT I TOTALLY FORGOT TO ASK WHAT ENDED UP HAPPENING IN PARADOR!
PARADOR?
OTHER-ME, THAT WAS SIX WEEKS AGO.

...AND THEN THERE WAS A VOLLEYBALL GAME AND WE HUGGED--

--AND THEN MY POWERS JUST WENT *KERFLOOEY!*

MAXINE! MAXINE! I FOUND YO!

I HAVE INCREDIBLE NEWS! I FIGURED IT OUT! I *FIGURED IT OUT!*

WHOA, OW OWN.

ARE YOU OKAY? YOU LOOK REALLY OUT OF IT.

I FIGURED OUT HOW TO ENGAGE A.T.P. GENERATION WITHIN THE PROTEIN ACTIN FILAMENT MATRIX!

I'M REALLY SORRY, MAXINE. I PEEKED AT YOUR RESEARCH. I COULDN'T HELP MYSELF.

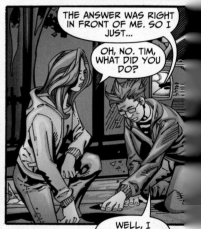

THE ANSWER WAS RIGHT IN FRONT OF ME. SO I JUST...

OH, NO. TIM, WHAT DID YOU DO?

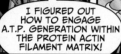

OH, GOD--WHAT'S *HAPPENING?*

I CAN'T STOP IT! MAXINE, TELL ME HOW TO--

WELL, I HAD TO TEST IT, DIDN'T I?

YOU HAVE TO UNDERSTAND, ALL I EVER WANTED WAS TO HAVE POWERS LIKE--

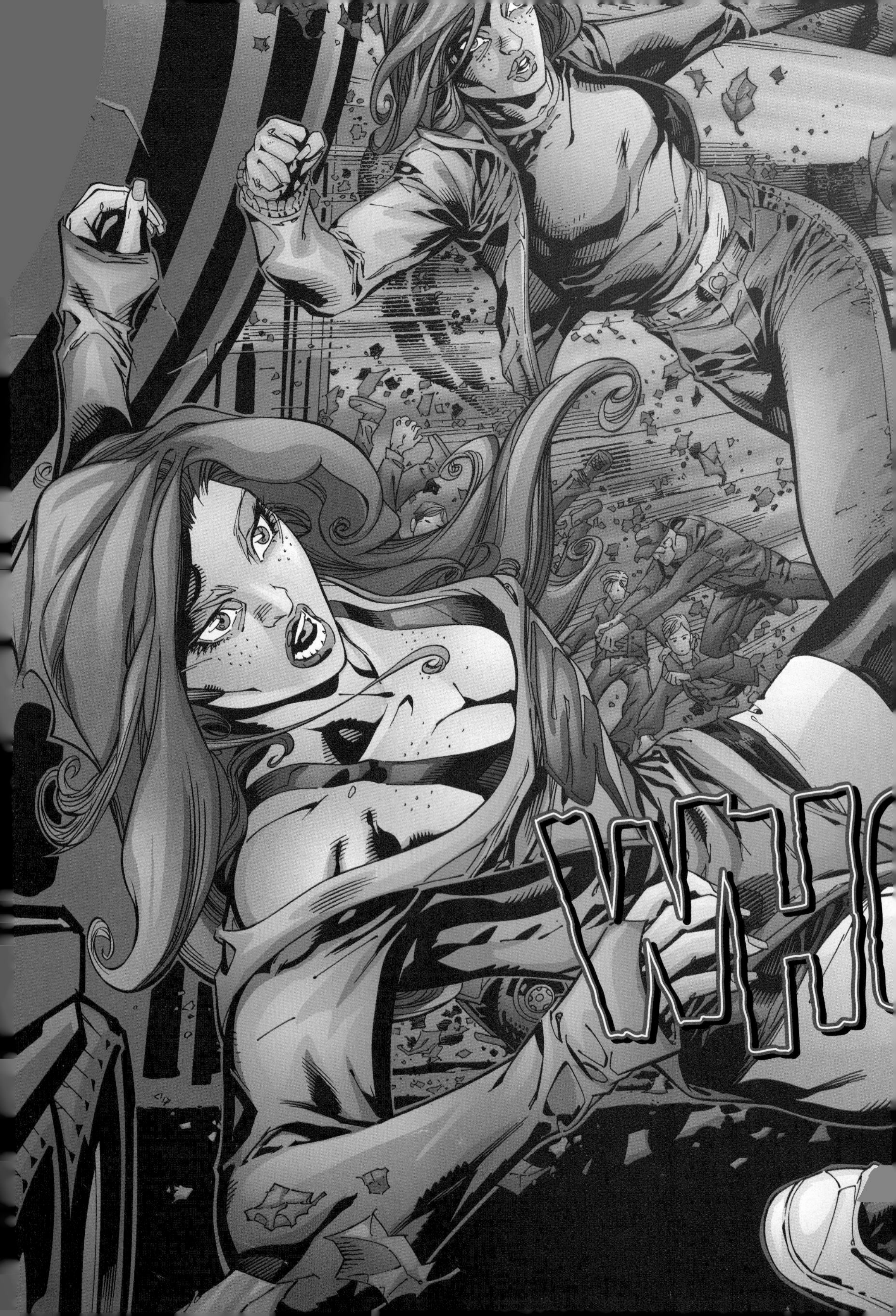

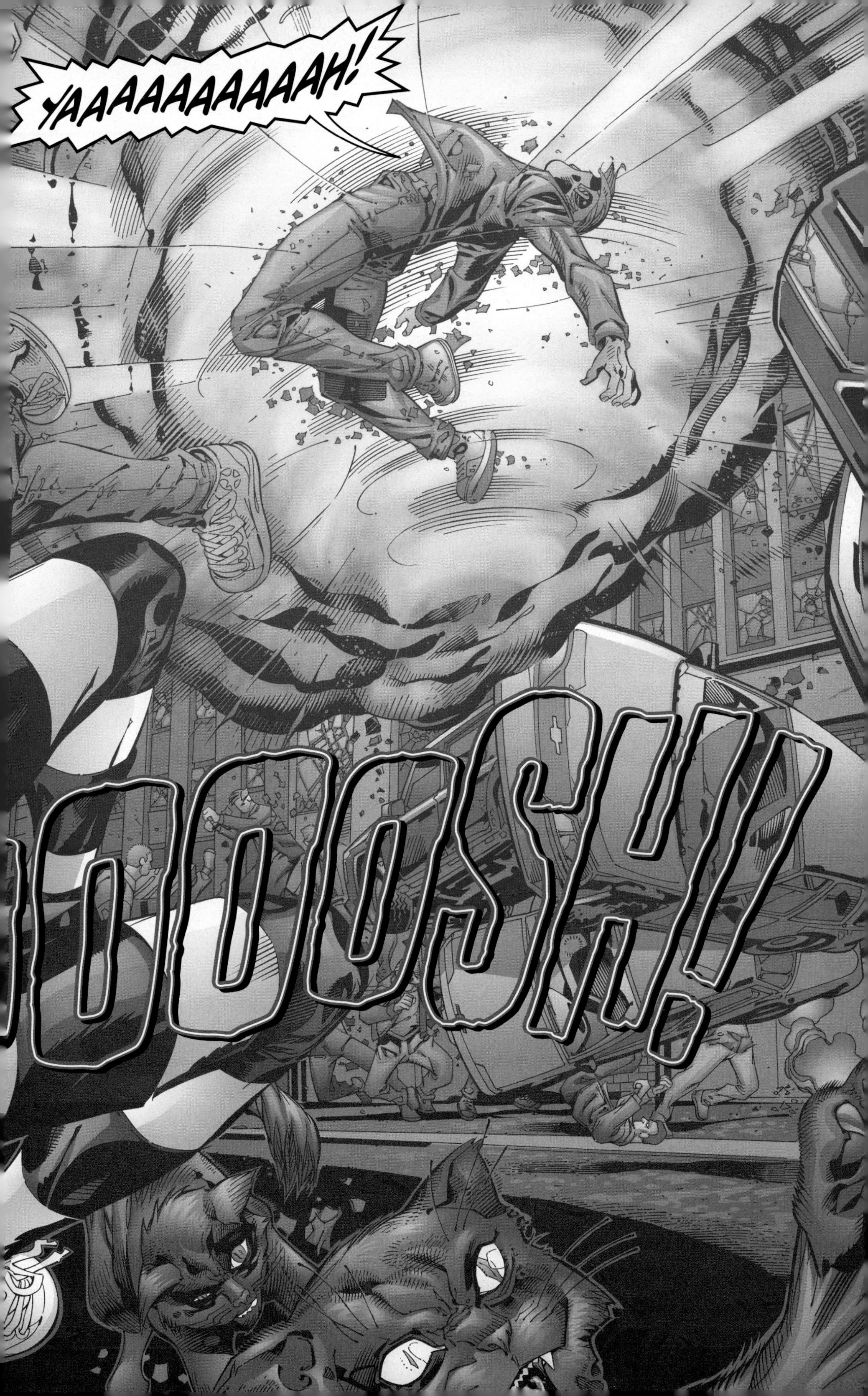
YAAAAAAAAAAH!
OOOSH!

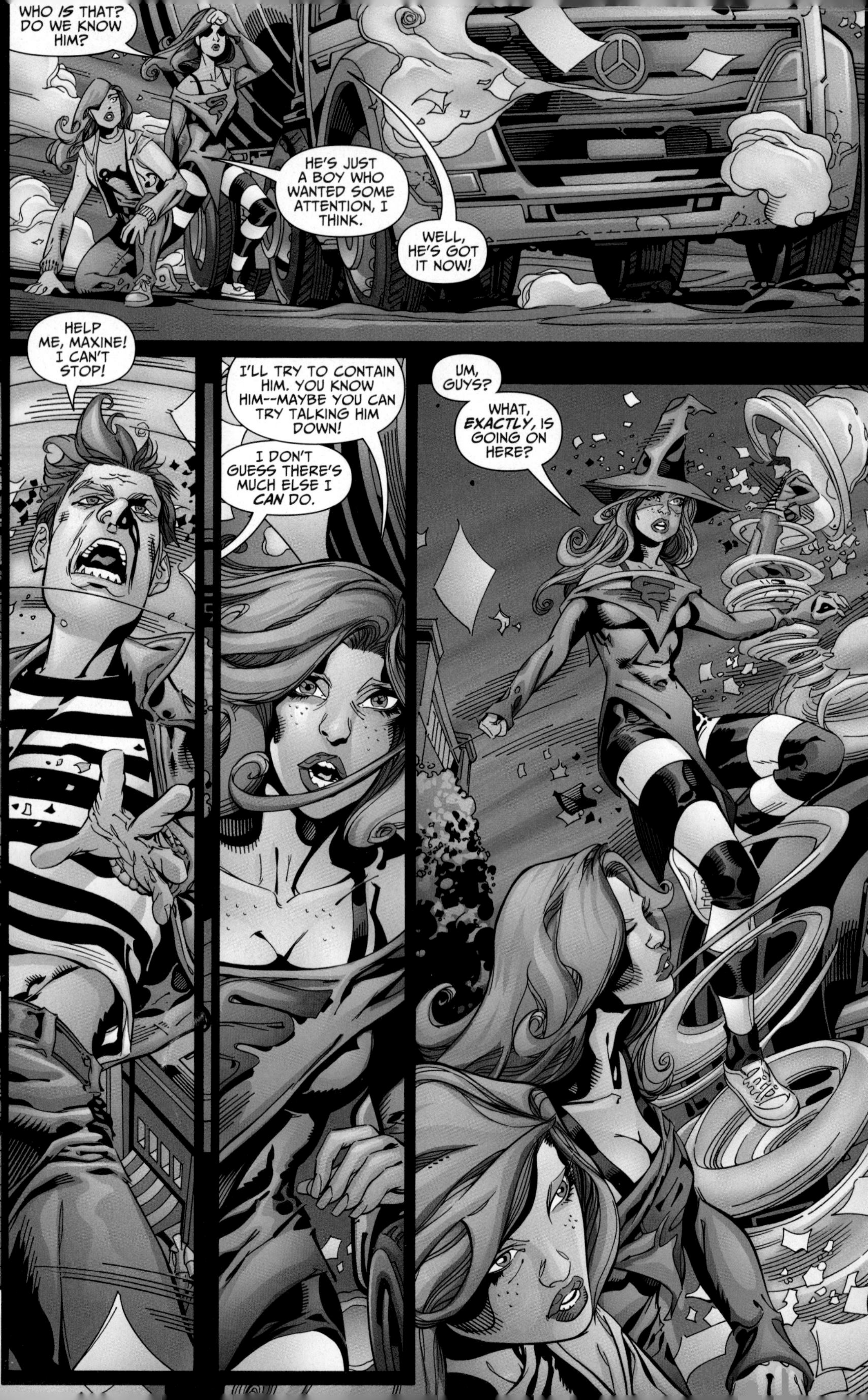
WHO *IS* THAT? DO WE KNOW HIM?
HE'S JUST A BOY WHO WANTED SOME ATTENTION, I THINK.
WELL, HE'S GOT IT NOW!
HELP ME, MAXINE! I CAN'T STOP!
I'LL TRY TO CONTAIN HIM. YOU KNOW HIM--MAYBE YOU CAN TRY TALKING HIM DOWN!
I DON'T GUESS THERE'S MUCH ELSE I *CAN* DO.
UM, GUYS?
WHAT, *EXACTLY*, IS GOING ON HERE?

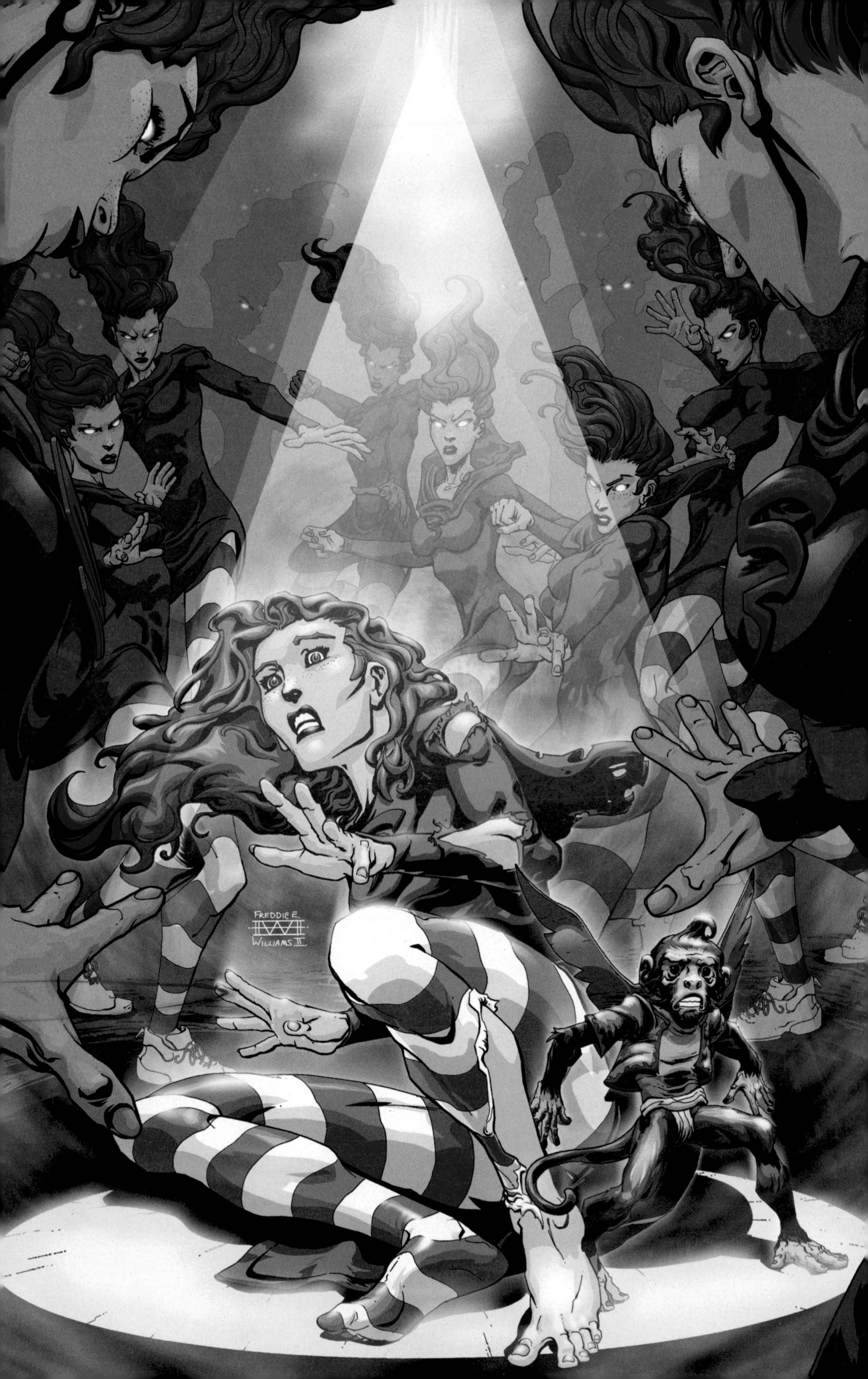
FREDDIE E.
WILLIAMS II

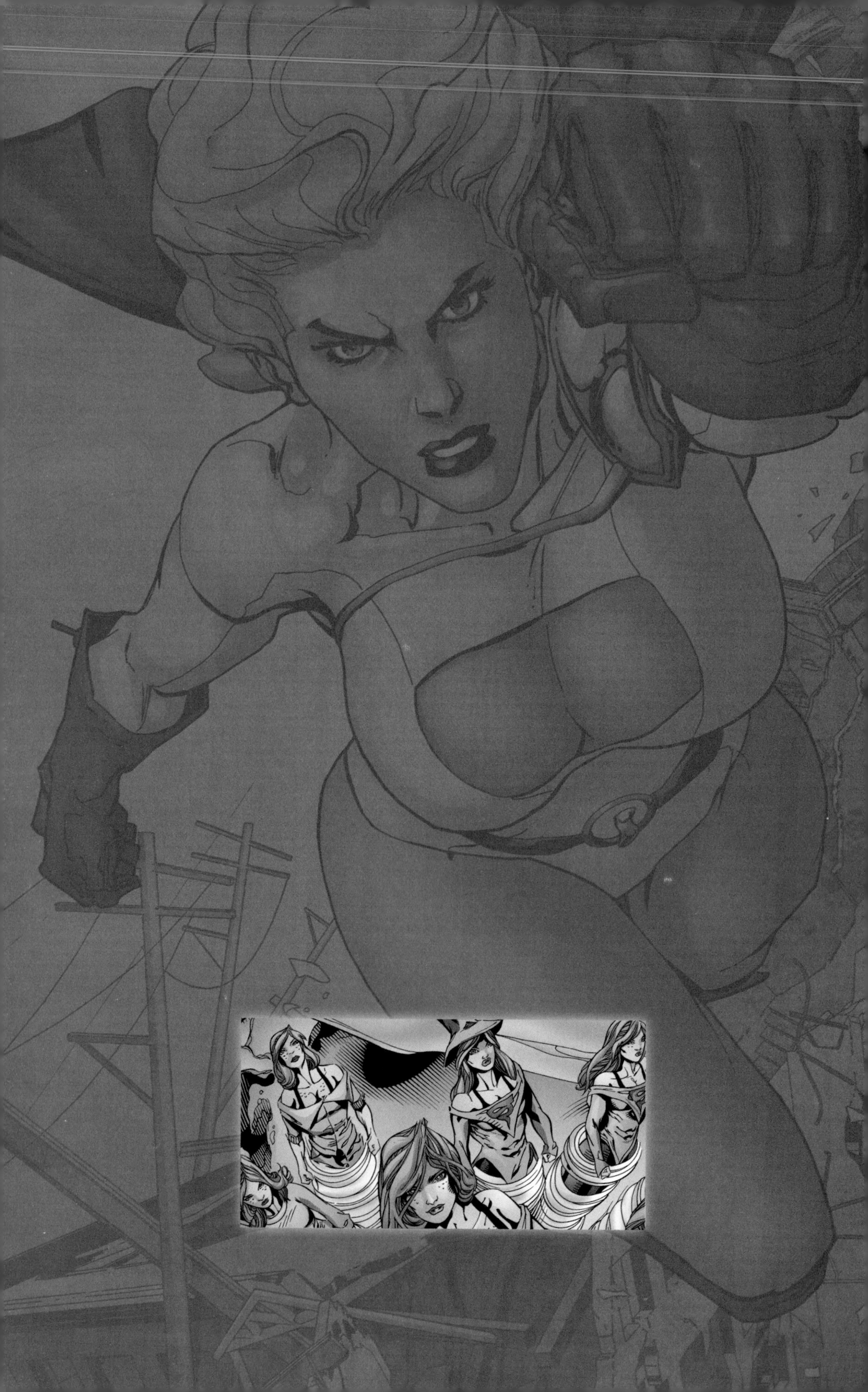

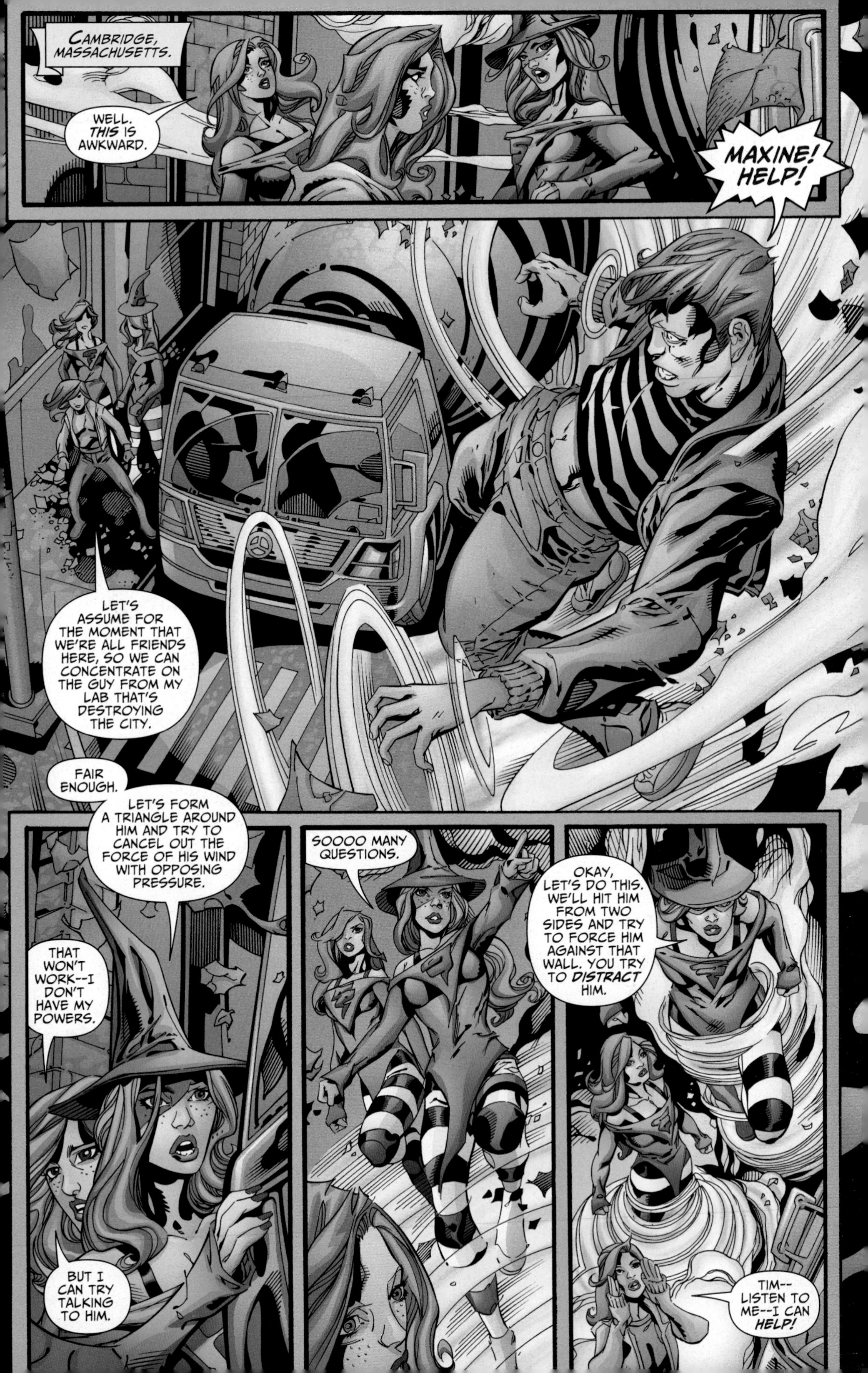
CAMBRIDGE, MASSACHUSETTS.
WELL. *THIS* IS AWKWARD.
MAXINE! HELP!
LET'S ASSUME FOR THE MOMENT THAT WE'RE ALL FRIENDS HERE, SO WE CAN CONCENTRATE ON THE GUY FROM MY LAB THAT'S DESTROYING THE CITY.
FAIR ENOUGH.
LET'S FORM A TRIANGLE AROUND HIM AND TRY TO CANCEL OUT THE FORCE OF HIS WIND WITH OPPOSING PRESSURE.
THAT WON'T WORK--I DON'T HAVE MY POWERS.
BUT I CAN TRY TALKING TO HIM.
SOOOO MANY QUESTIONS.
OKAY, LET'S DO THIS. WE'LL HIT HIM FROM TWO SIDES AND TRY TO FORCE HIM AGAINST THAT WALL. YOU TRY TO *DISTRACT* HIM.
TIM-- LISTEN TO ME--I CAN *HELP!*

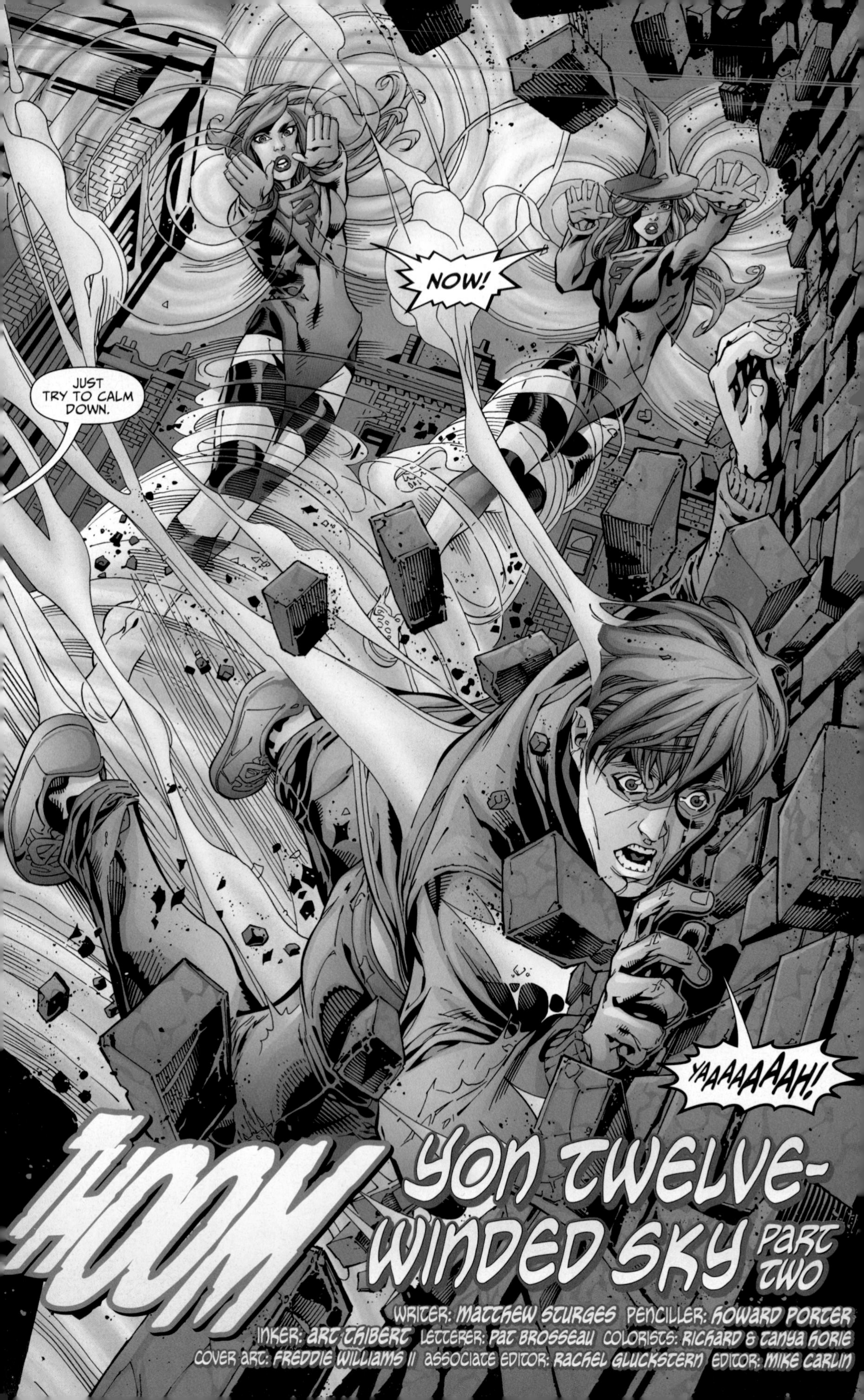
NOW!
JUST TRY TO CALM DOWN.
YAAAAAAAH!
FOOM
YON TWELVE-WINDED SKY PART TWO
WRITER: MATTHEW STURGES PENCILLER: HOWARD PORTER
INKER: ART THIBERT LETTERER: PAT BROSSEAU COLORISTS: RICHARD & TANYA HORIE
COVER ART: FREDDIE WILLIAMS II ASSOCIATE EDITOR: RACHEL GLUCKSTERN EDITOR: MIKE CARLIN

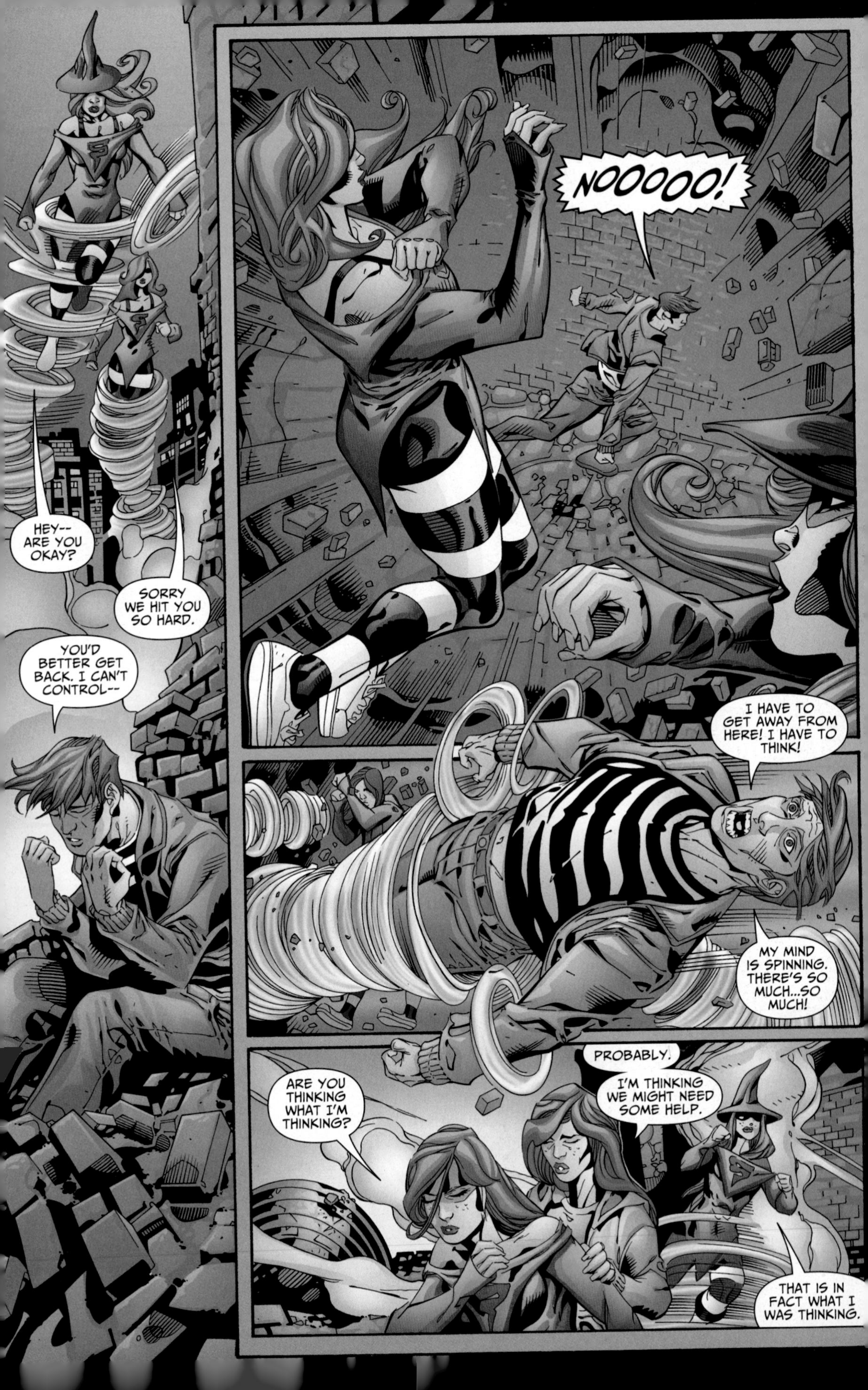
HEY-- ARE YOU OKAY?
SORRY WE HIT YOU SO HARD.
YOU'D BETTER GET BACK. I CAN'T CONTROL--
NOOOOO!
I HAVE TO GET AWAY FROM HERE! I HAVE TO THINK!
MY MIND IS SPINNING. THERE'S SO MUCH...SO MUCH!
ARE YOU THINKING WHAT I'M THINKING?
PROBABLY.
I'M THINKING WE MIGHT NEED SOME HELP.
THAT IS IN FACT WHAT I WAS THINKING.

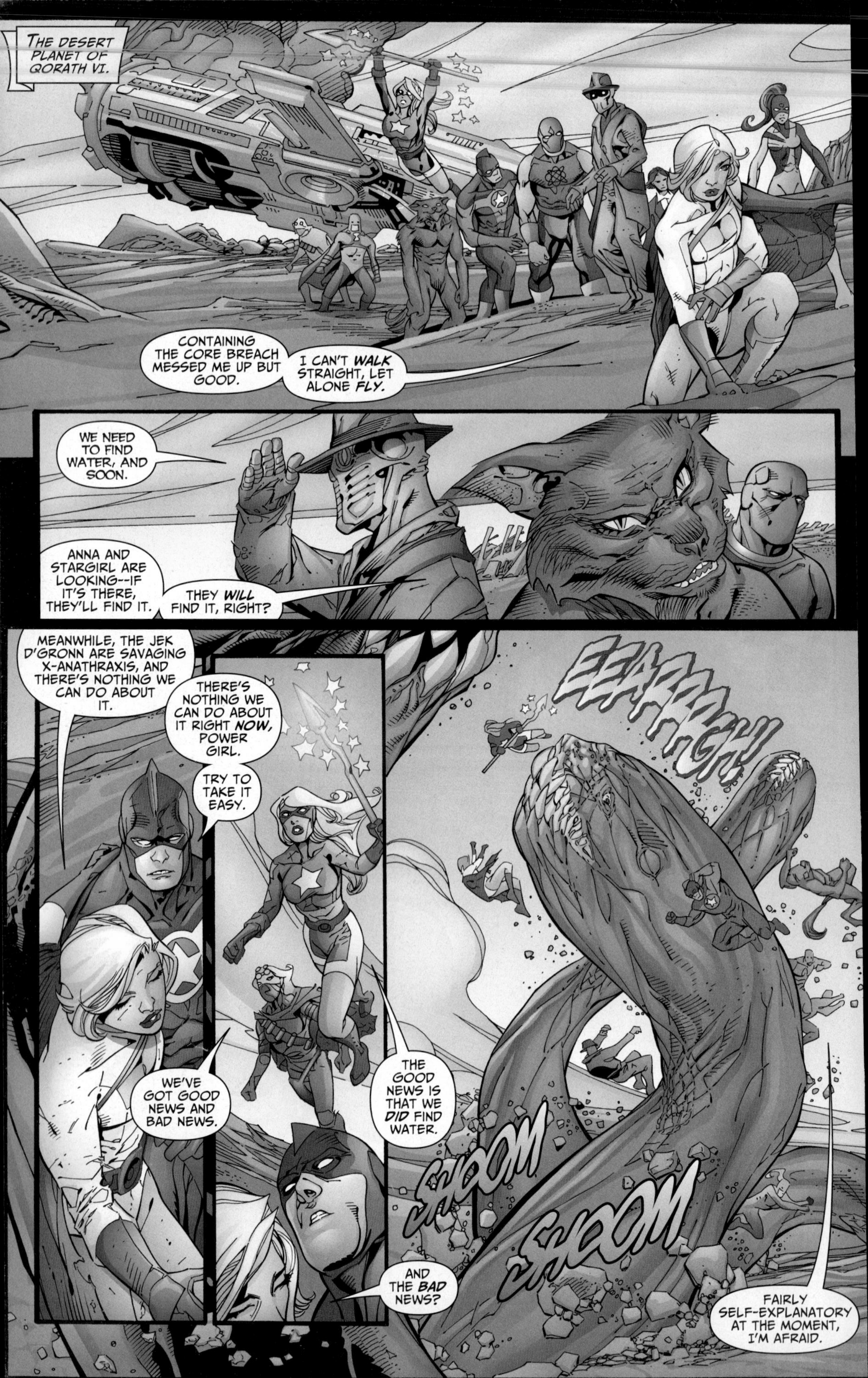
THE DESERT PLANET OF QORATH VI.
CONTAINING THE CORE BREACH MESSED ME UP BUT GOOD.
I CAN'T WALK STRAIGHT, LET ALONE FLY.
WE NEED TO FIND WATER, AND SOON.
ANNA AND STARGIRL ARE LOOKING--IF IT'S THERE, THEY'LL FIND IT.
THEY WILL FIND IT, RIGHT?
MEANWHILE, THE JEK D'GRONN ARE SAVAGING X-ANATHRAXIS, AND THERE'S NOTHING WE CAN DO ABOUT IT.
THERE'S NOTHING WE CAN DO ABOUT IT RIGHT NOW, POWER GIRL.
TRY TO TAKE IT EASY.
WE'VE GOT GOOD NEWS AND BAD NEWS.
THE GOOD NEWS IS THAT WE DID FIND WATER.
AND THE BAD NEWS?
EEAAAAGH!
SHOOM
SHOOM
FAIRLY SELF-EXPLANATORY AT THE MOMENT, I'M AFRAID.

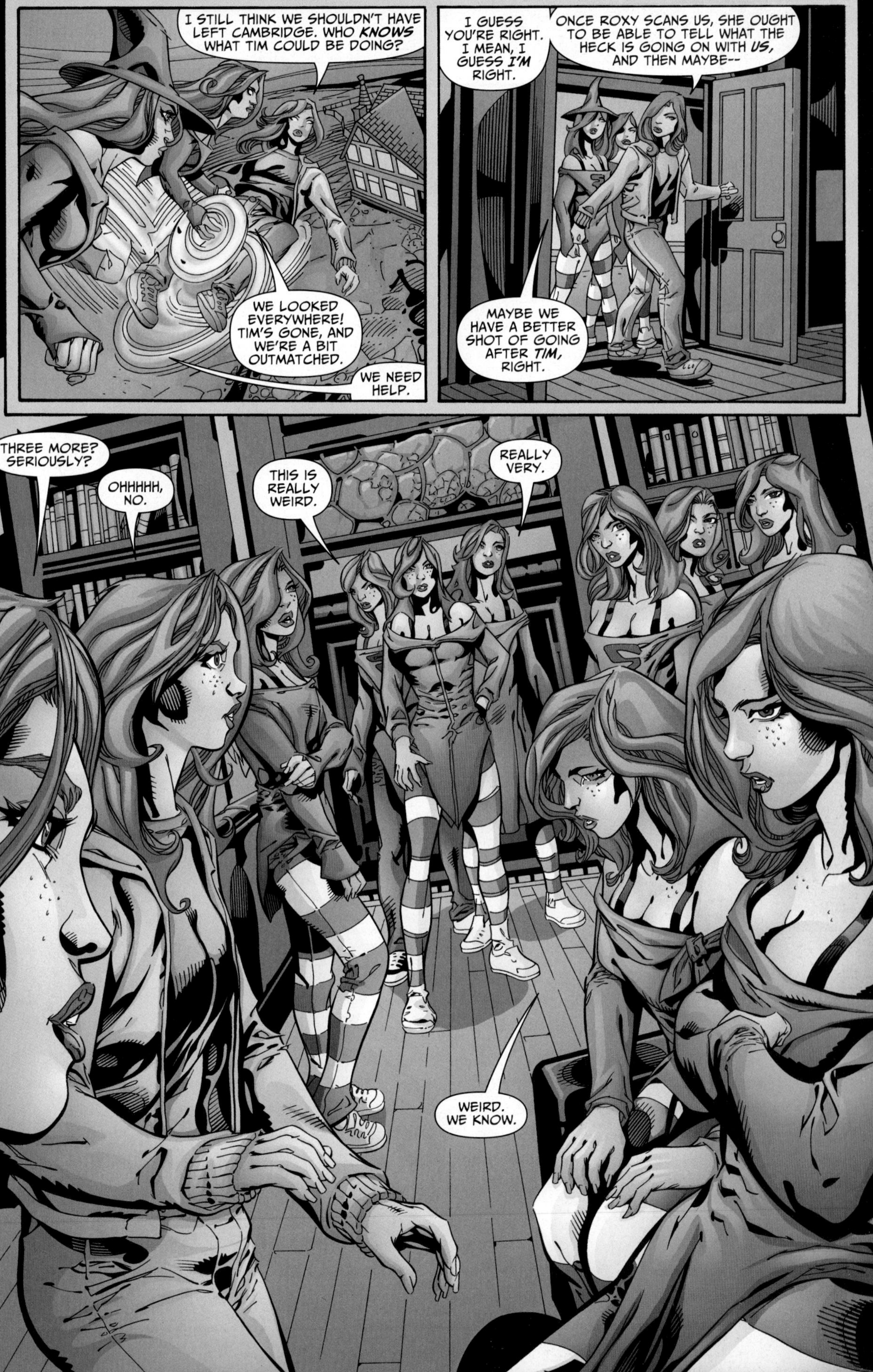
I STILL THINK WE SHOULDN'T HAVE LEFT CAMBRIDGE. WHO KNOWS WHAT TIM COULD BE DOING?
WE LOOKED EVERYWHERE! TIM'S GONE, AND WE'RE A BIT OUTMATCHED.
WE NEED HELP.
I GUESS YOU'RE RIGHT. I MEAN, I GUESS I'M RIGHT.
ONCE ROXY SCANS US, SHE OUGHT TO BE ABLE TO TELL WHAT THE HECK IS GOING ON WITH US, AND THEN MAYBE--
MAYBE WE HAVE A BETTER SHOT OF GOING AFTER TIM, RIGHT.
THREE MORE? SERIOUSLY?
OHHHHH, NO.
THIS IS REALLY WEIRD.
REALLY VERY.
WEIRD. WE KNOW.

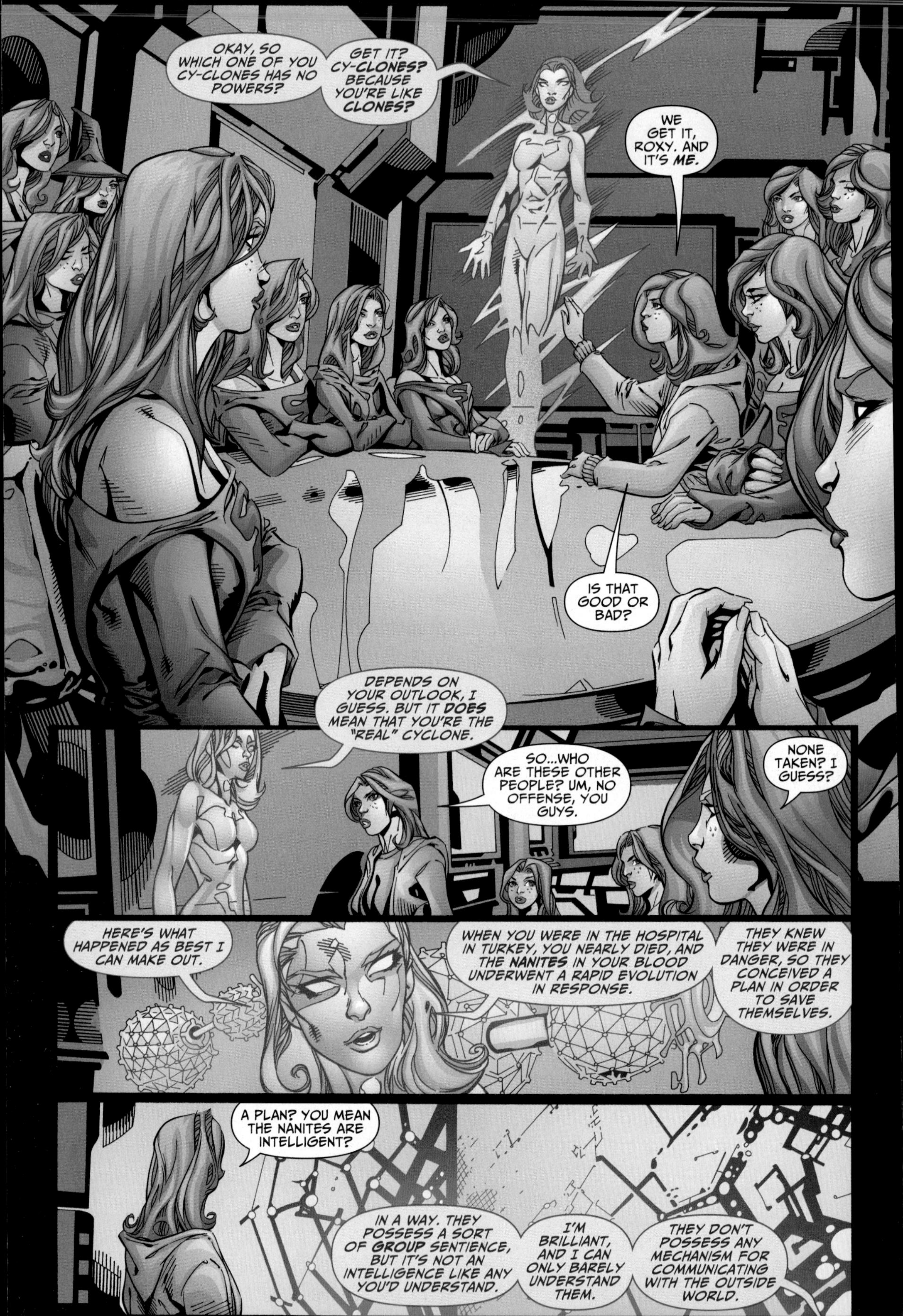
OKAY, SO WHICH ONE OF YOU CY-CLONES HAS NO POWERS?
GET IT? CY-CLONES? BECAUSE YOU'RE LIKE CLONES?
WE GET IT, ROXY. AND IT'S ME.
IS THAT GOOD OR BAD?
DEPENDS ON YOUR OUTLOOK, I GUESS. BUT IT DOES MEAN THAT YOU'RE THE "REAL" CYCLONE.
SO...WHO ARE THESE OTHER PEOPLE? UM, NO OFFENSE, YOU GUYS.
NONE TAKEN? I GUESS?
HERE'S WHAT HAPPENED AS BEST I CAN MAKE OUT.
WHEN YOU WERE IN THE HOSPITAL IN TURKEY, YOU NEARLY DIED, AND THE NANITES IN YOUR BLOOD UNDERWENT A RAPID EVOLUTION IN RESPONSE.
THEY KNEW THEY WERE IN DANGER, SO THEY CONCEIVED A PLAN IN ORDER TO SAVE THEMSELVES.
A PLAN? YOU MEAN THE NANITES ARE INTELLIGENT?
IN A WAY. THEY POSSESS A SORT OF GROUP SENTIENCE, BUT IT'S NOT AN INTELLIGENCE LIKE ANY YOU'D UNDERSTAND.
I'M BRILLIANT, AND I CAN ONLY BARELY UNDERSTAND THEM.
THEY DON'T POSSESS ANY MECHANISM FOR COMMUNICATING WITH THE OUTSIDE WORLD.

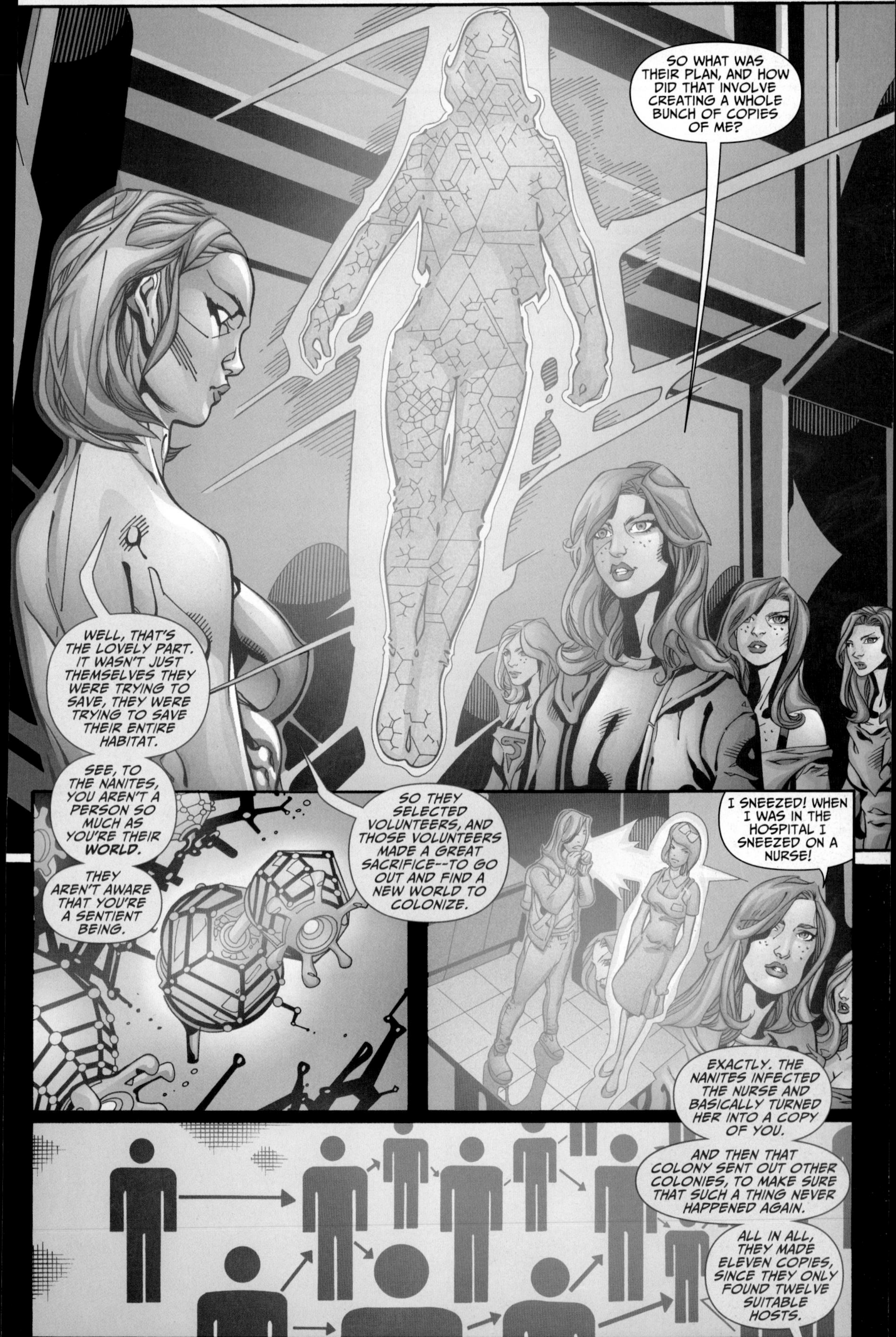

SO WHAT WAS THEIR PLAN, AND HOW DID THAT INVOLVE CREATING A WHOLE BUNCH OF COPIES OF ME?
WELL, THAT'S THE LOVELY PART. IT WASN'T JUST THEMSELVES THEY WERE TRYING TO SAVE, THEY WERE TRYING TO SAVE THEIR ENTIRE HABITAT.
SEE, TO THE NANITES, YOU AREN'T A PERSON SO MUCH AS YOU'RE THEIR WORLD.
THEY AREN'T AWARE THAT YOU'RE A SENTIENT BEING.
SO THEY SELECTED VOLUNTEERS, AND THOSE VOLUNTEERS MADE A GREAT SACRIFICE--TO GO OUT AND FIND A NEW WORLD TO COLONIZE.
I SNEEZED! WHEN I WAS IN THE HOSPITAL I SNEEZED ON A NURSE!
EXACTLY. THE NANITES INFECTED THE NURSE AND BASICALLY TURNED HER INTO A COPY OF YOU.
AND THEN THAT COLONY SENT OUT OTHER COLONIES, TO MAKE SURE THAT SUCH A THING NEVER HAPPENED AGAIN.
ALL IN ALL, THEY MADE ELEVEN COPIES, SINCE THEY ONLY FOUND TWELVE SUITABLE HOSTS.

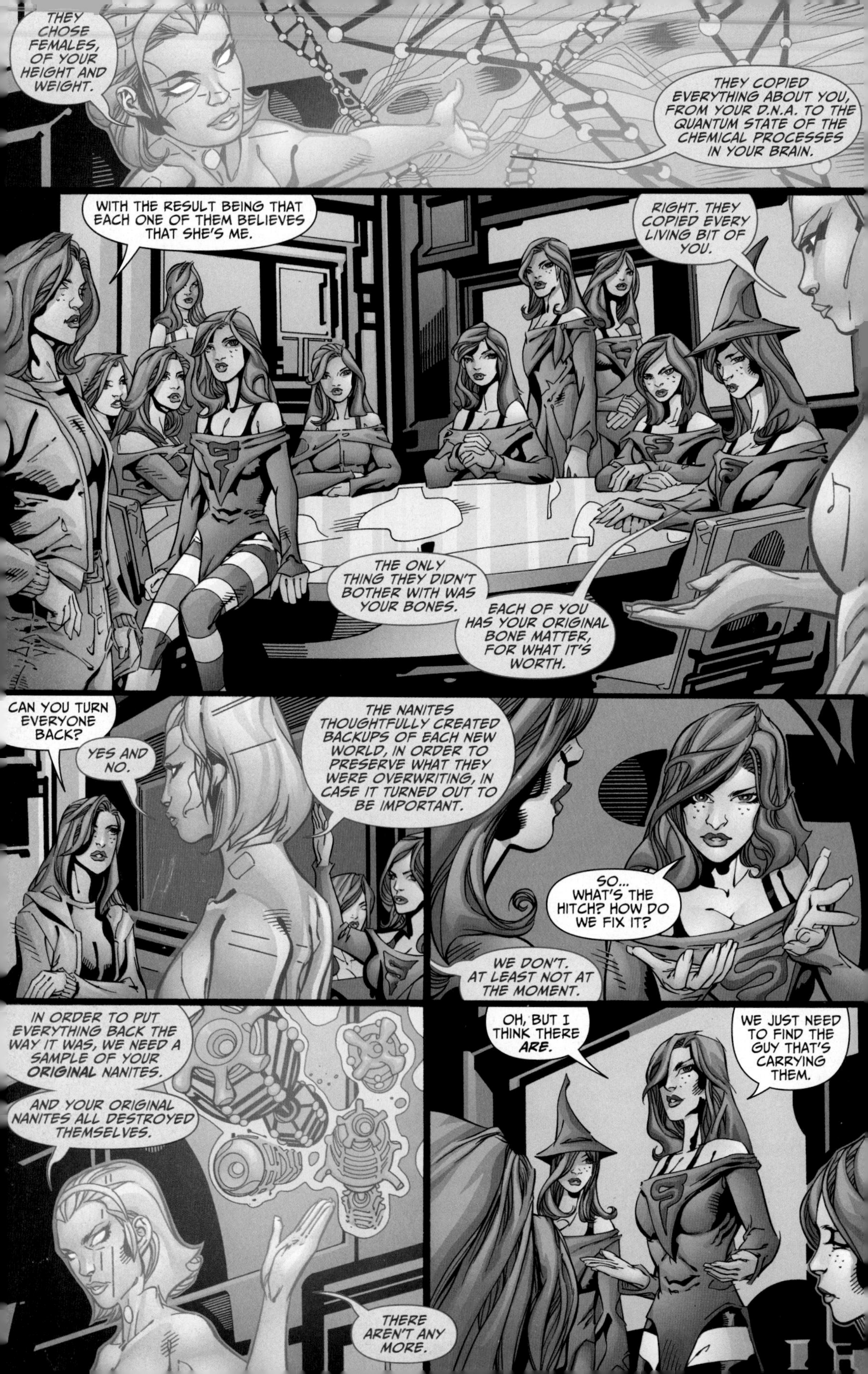
THEY CHOSE FEMALES, OF YOUR HEIGHT AND WEIGHT.
THEY COPIED EVERYTHING ABOUT YOU, FROM YOUR D.N.A. TO THE QUANTUM STATE OF THE CHEMICAL PROCESSES IN YOUR BRAIN.
WITH THE RESULT BEING THAT EACH ONE OF THEM BELIEVES THAT SHE'S ME.
RIGHT. THEY COPIED EVERY LIVING BIT OF YOU.
THE ONLY THING THEY DIDN'T BOTHER WITH WAS YOUR BONES.
EACH OF YOU HAS YOUR ORIGINAL BONE MATTER, FOR WHAT IT'S WORTH.
CAN YOU TURN EVERYONE BACK?
YES AND NO.
THE NANITES THOUGHTFULLY CREATED BACKUPS OF EACH NEW WORLD, IN ORDER TO PRESERVE WHAT THEY WERE OVERWRITING, IN CASE IT TURNED OUT TO BE IMPORTANT.
SO... WHAT'S THE HITCH? HOW DO WE FIX IT?
WE DON'T. AT LEAST NOT AT THE MOMENT.
IN ORDER TO PUT EVERYTHING BACK THE WAY IT WAS, WE NEED A SAMPLE OF YOUR ORIGINAL NANITES.
AND YOUR ORIGINAL NANITES ALL DESTROYED THEMSELVES.
THERE AREN'T ANY MORE.
OH, BUT I THINK THERE ARE.
WE JUST NEED TO FIND THE GUY THAT'S CARRYING THEM.

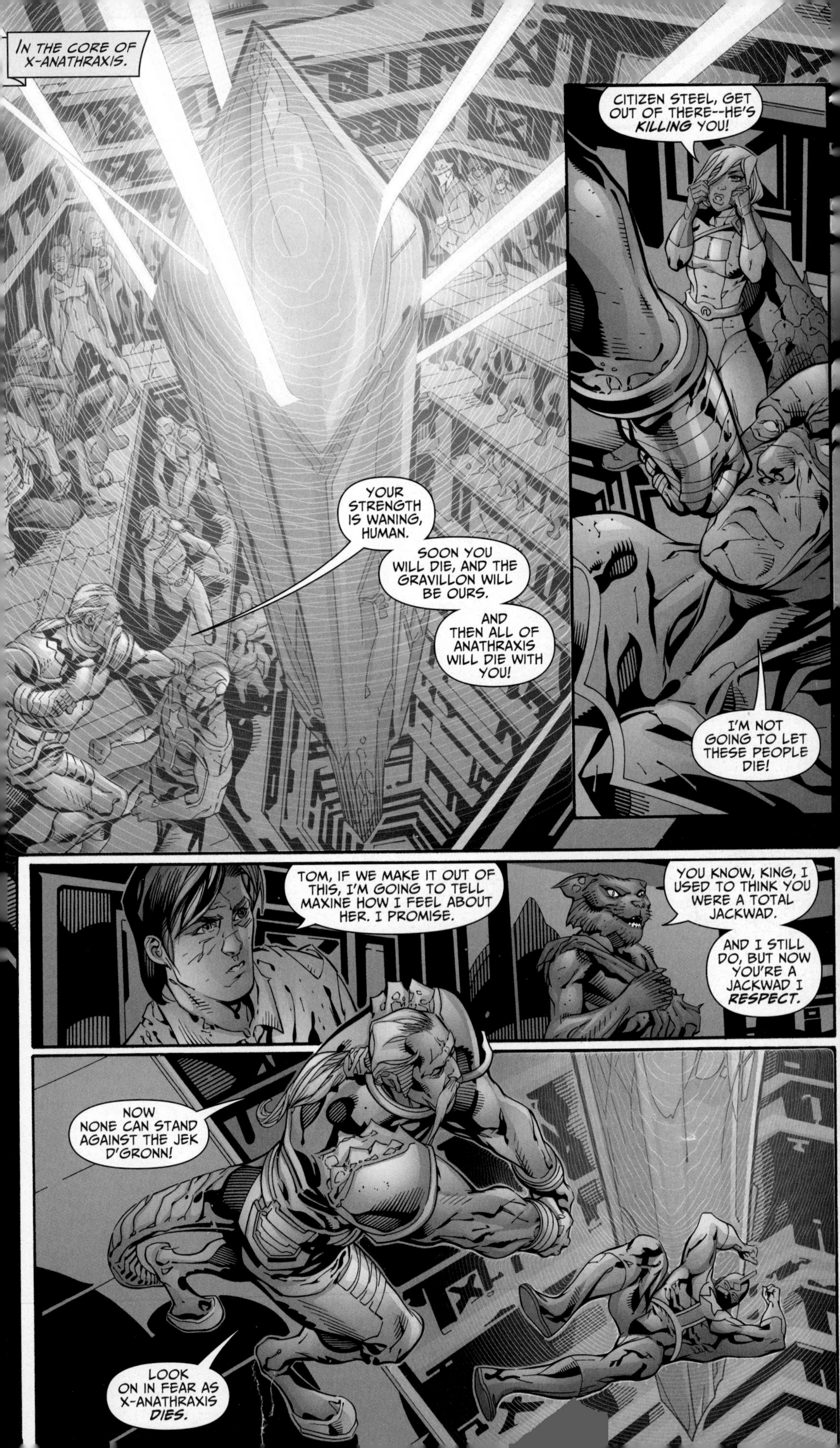
IN THE CORE OF X-ANATHRAXIS.
YOUR STRENGTH IS WANING, HUMAN.
SOON YOU WILL DIE, AND THE GRAVILLON WILL BE OURS.
AND THEN ALL OF ANATHRAXIS WILL DIE WITH YOU!
CITIZEN STEEL, GET OUT OF THERE--HE'S KILLING YOU!
I'M NOT GOING TO LET THESE PEOPLE DIE!
TOM, IF WE MAKE IT OUT OF THIS, I'M GOING TO TELL MAXINE HOW I FEEL ABOUT HER. I PROMISE.
YOU KNOW, KING, I USED TO THINK YOU WERE A TOTAL JACKWAD.
AND I STILL DO, BUT NOW YOU'RE A JACKWAD I RESPECT.
NOW NONE CAN STAND AGAINST THE JEK D'GRONN!
LOOK ON IN FEAR AS X-ANATHRAXIS DIES.

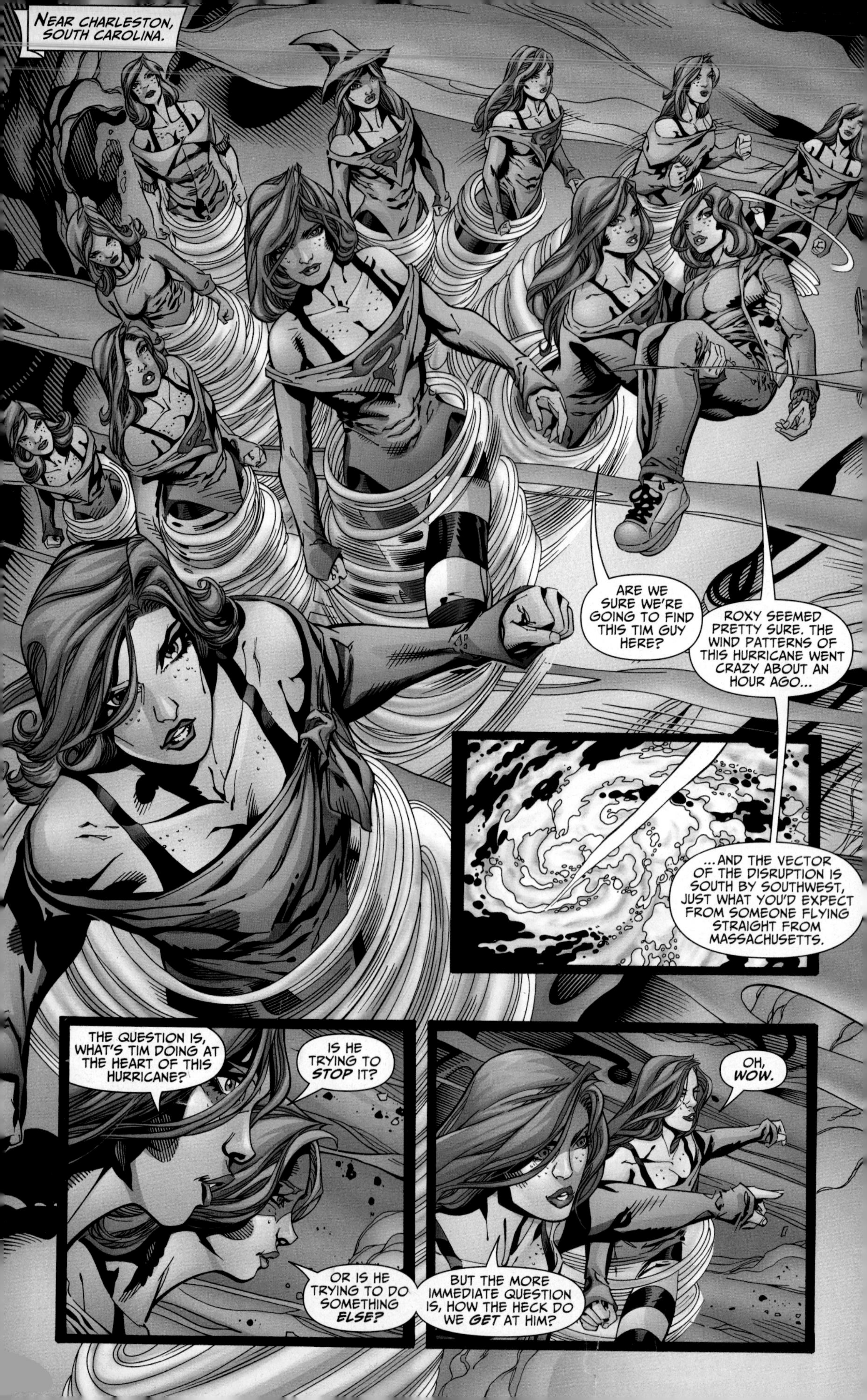
NEAR CHARLESTON, SOUTH CAROLINA.
ARE WE SURE WE'RE GOING TO FIND THIS TIM GUY HERE?
ROXY SEEMED PRETTY SURE. THE WIND PATTERNS OF THIS HURRICANE WENT CRAZY ABOUT AN HOUR AGO...
...AND THE VECTOR OF THE DISRUPTION IS SOUTH BY SOUTHWEST, JUST WHAT YOU'D EXPECT FROM SOMEONE FLYING STRAIGHT FROM MASSACHUSETTS.
THE QUESTION IS, WHAT'S TIM DOING AT THE HEART OF THIS HURRICANE?
IS HE TRYING TO *STOP* IT?
OR IS HE TRYING TO DO SOMETHING *ELSE?*
OH, *WOW.*
BUT THE MORE IMMEDIATE QUESTION IS, HOW THE HECK DO WE *GET* AT HIM?

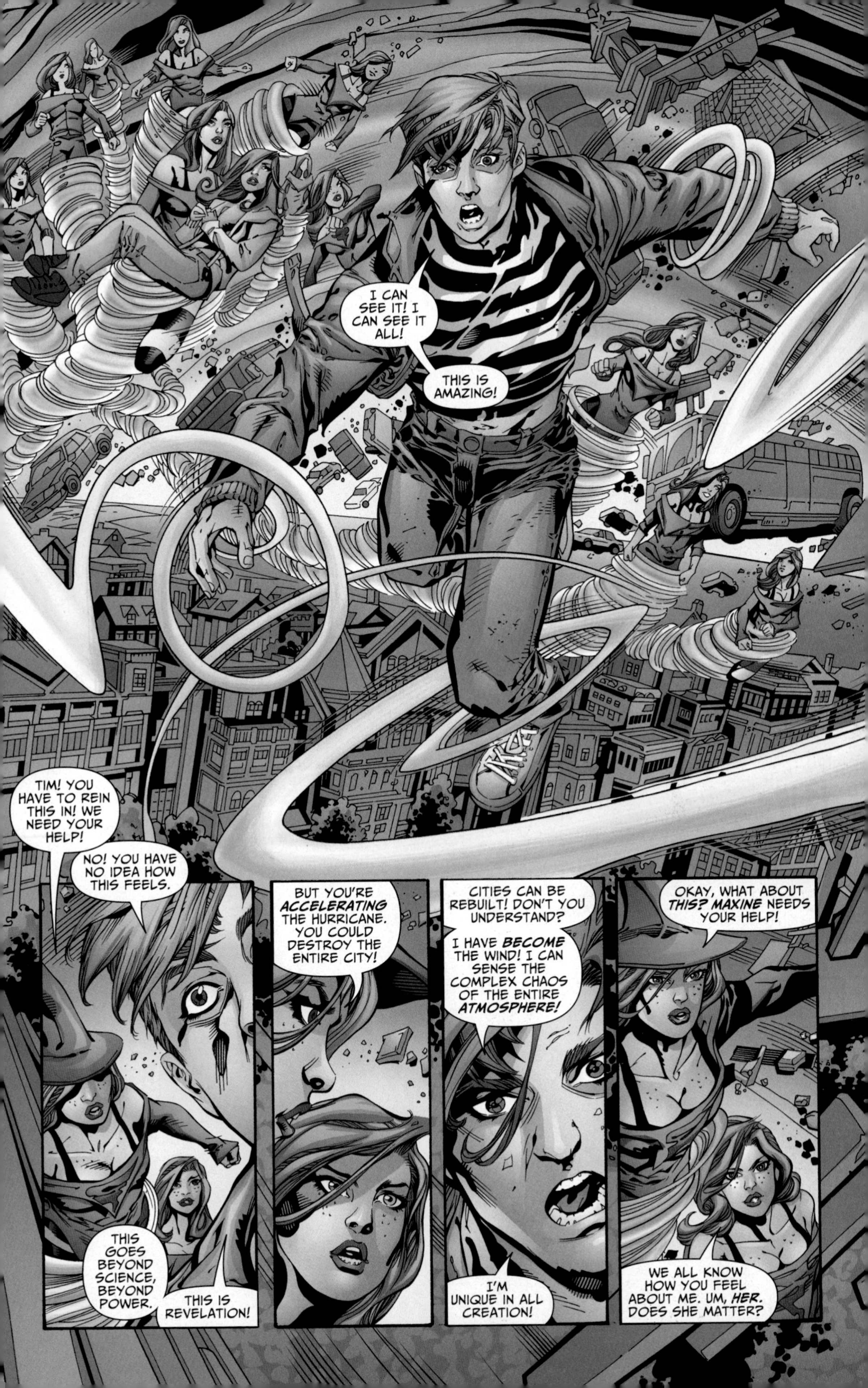

I CAN SEE IT! I CAN SEE IT ALL!
THIS IS AMAZING!
TIM! YOU HAVE TO REIN THIS IN! WE NEED YOUR HELP!
NO! YOU HAVE NO IDEA HOW THIS FEELS.
THIS GOES BEYOND SCIENCE, BEYOND POWER.
THIS IS REVELATION!
BUT YOU'RE ACCELERATING THE HURRICANE. YOU COULD DESTROY THE ENTIRE CITY!
CITIES CAN BE REBUILT! DON'T YOU UNDERSTAND?
I HAVE BECOME THE WIND! I CAN SENSE THE COMPLEX CHAOS OF THE ENTIRE ATMOSPHERE!
I'M UNIQUE IN ALL CREATION!
OKAY, WHAT ABOUT THIS? MAXINE NEEDS YOUR HELP!
WE ALL KNOW HOW YOU FEEL ABOUT ME. UM, HER. DOES SHE MATTER?

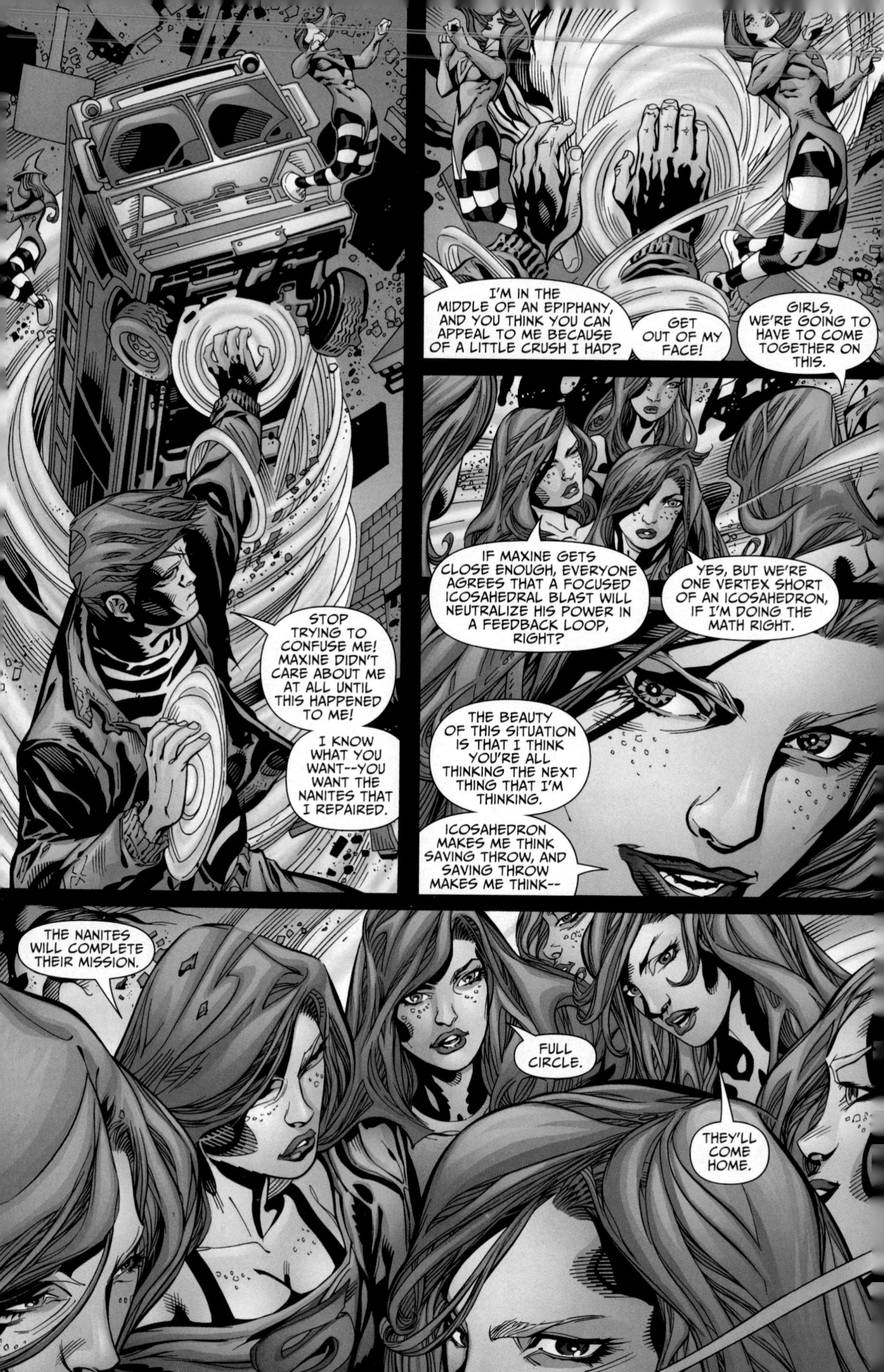
STOP TRYING TO CONFUSE ME! MAXINE DIDN'T CARE ABOUT ME AT ALL UNTIL THIS HAPPENED TO ME!
I KNOW WHAT YOU WANT--YOU WANT THE NANITES THAT I REPAIRED.
I'M IN THE MIDDLE OF AN EPIPHANY, AND YOU THINK YOU CAN APPEAL TO ME BECAUSE OF A LITTLE CRUSH I HAD?
GET OUT OF MY FACE!
GIRLS, WE'RE GOING TO HAVE TO COME TOGETHER ON THIS.
IF MAXINE GETS CLOSE ENOUGH, EVERYONE AGREES THAT A FOCUSED ICOSAHEDRAL BLAST WILL NEUTRALIZE HIS POWER IN A FEEDBACK LOOP, RIGHT?
YES, BUT WE'RE ONE VERTEX SHORT OF AN ICOSAHEDRON, IF I'M DOING THE MATH RIGHT.
THE BEAUTY OF THIS SITUATION IS THAT I THINK YOU'RE ALL THINKING THE NEXT THING THAT I'M THINKING.
ICOSAHEDRON MAKES ME THINK SAVING THROW, AND SAVING THROW MAKES ME THINK--
THE NANITES WILL COMPLETE THEIR MISSION.
FULL CIRCLE.
THEY'LL COME HOME.

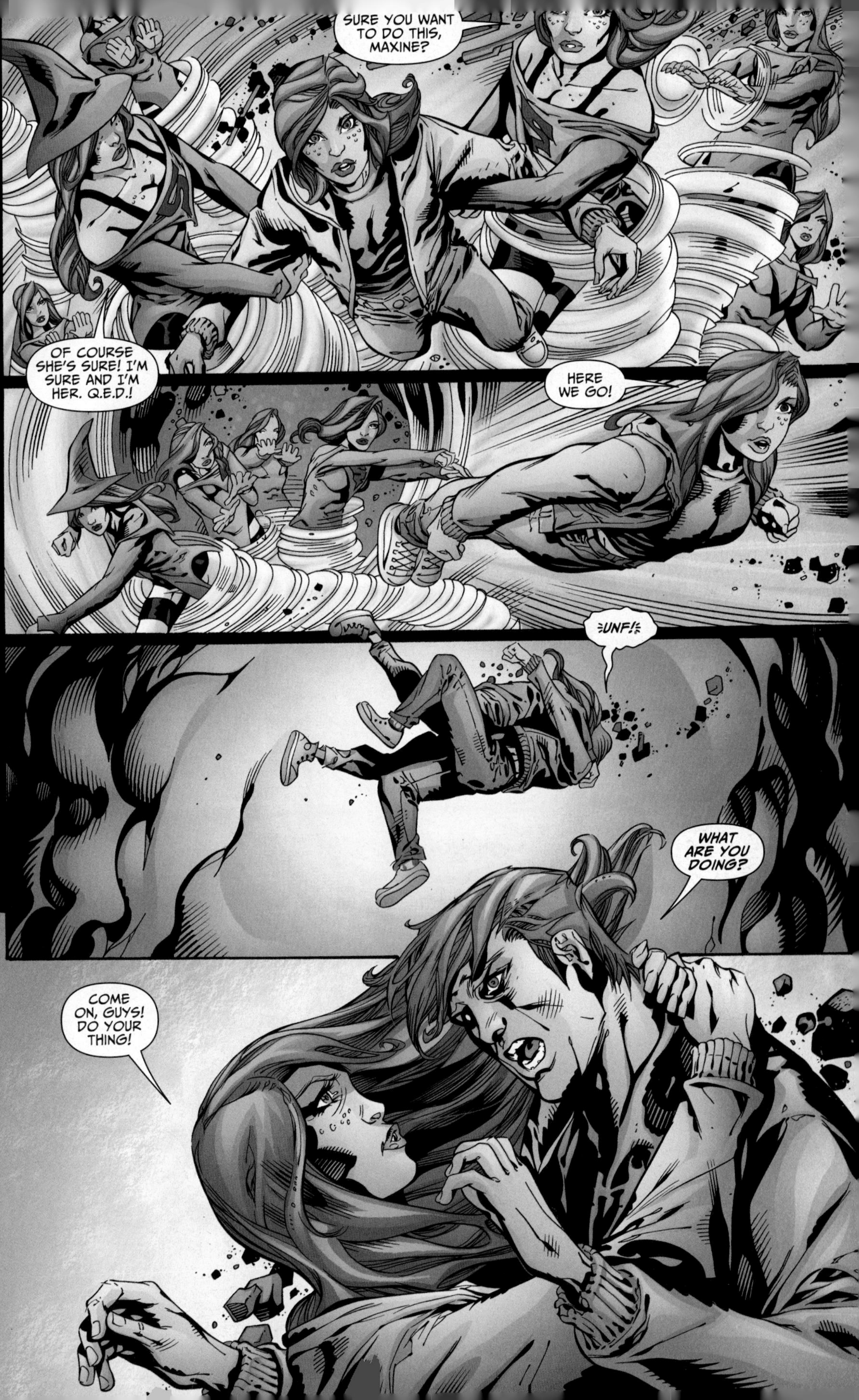
SURE YOU WANT TO DO THIS, MAXINE?
OF COURSE SHE'S SURE! I'M SURE AND I'M HER. Q.E.D.!
HERE WE GO!
UNF!
WHAT ARE YOU DOING?
COME ON, GUYS! DO YOUR THING!

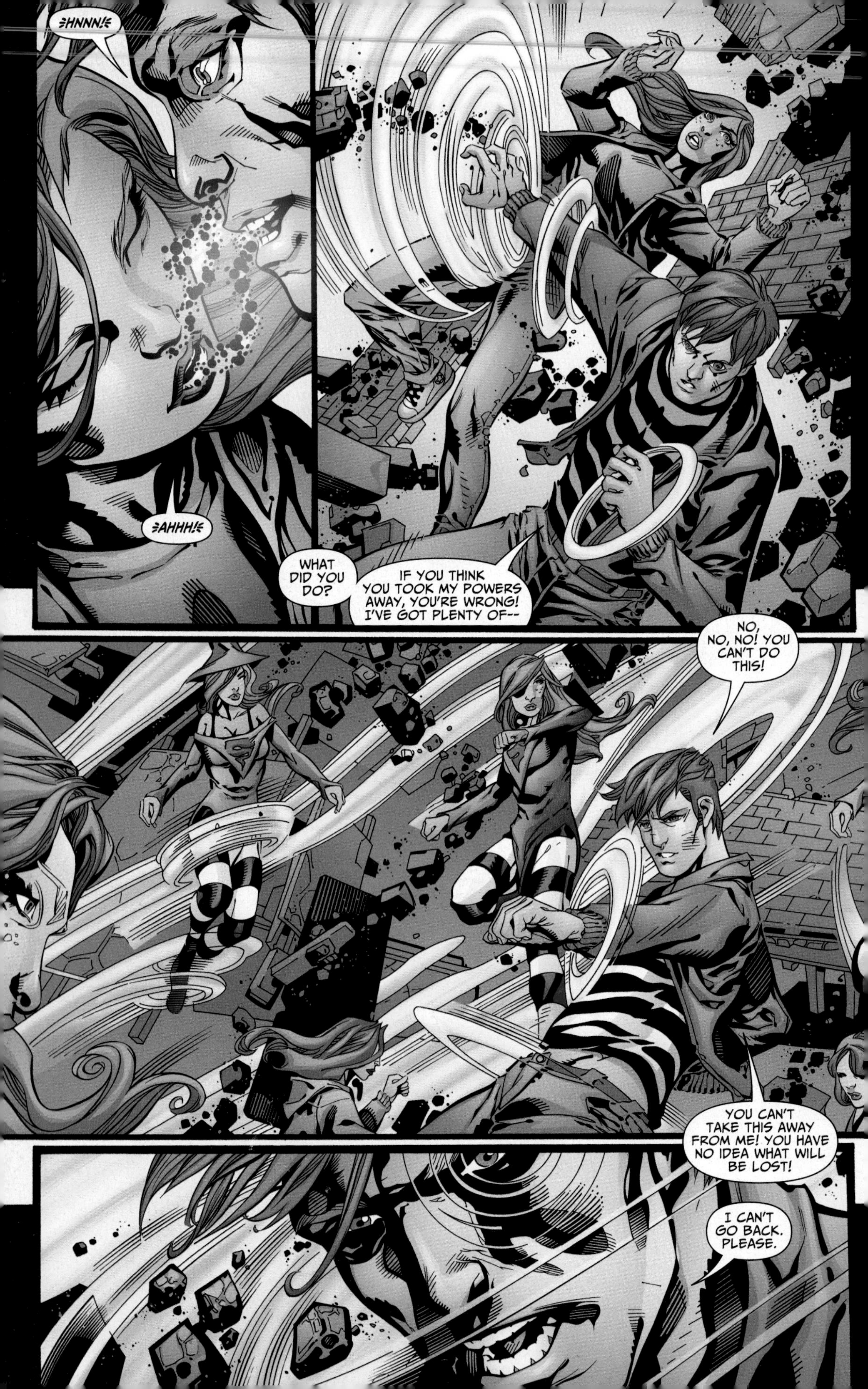
HNNN!
AHHH!
WHAT DID YOU DO?
IF YOU THINK YOU TOOK MY POWERS AWAY, YOU'RE WRONG! I'VE GOT PLENTY OF--
NO, NO, NO! YOU CAN'T DO THIS!
YOU CAN'T TAKE THIS AWAY FROM ME! YOU HAVE NO IDEA WHAT WILL BE LOST!
I CAN'T GO BACK. PLEASE.

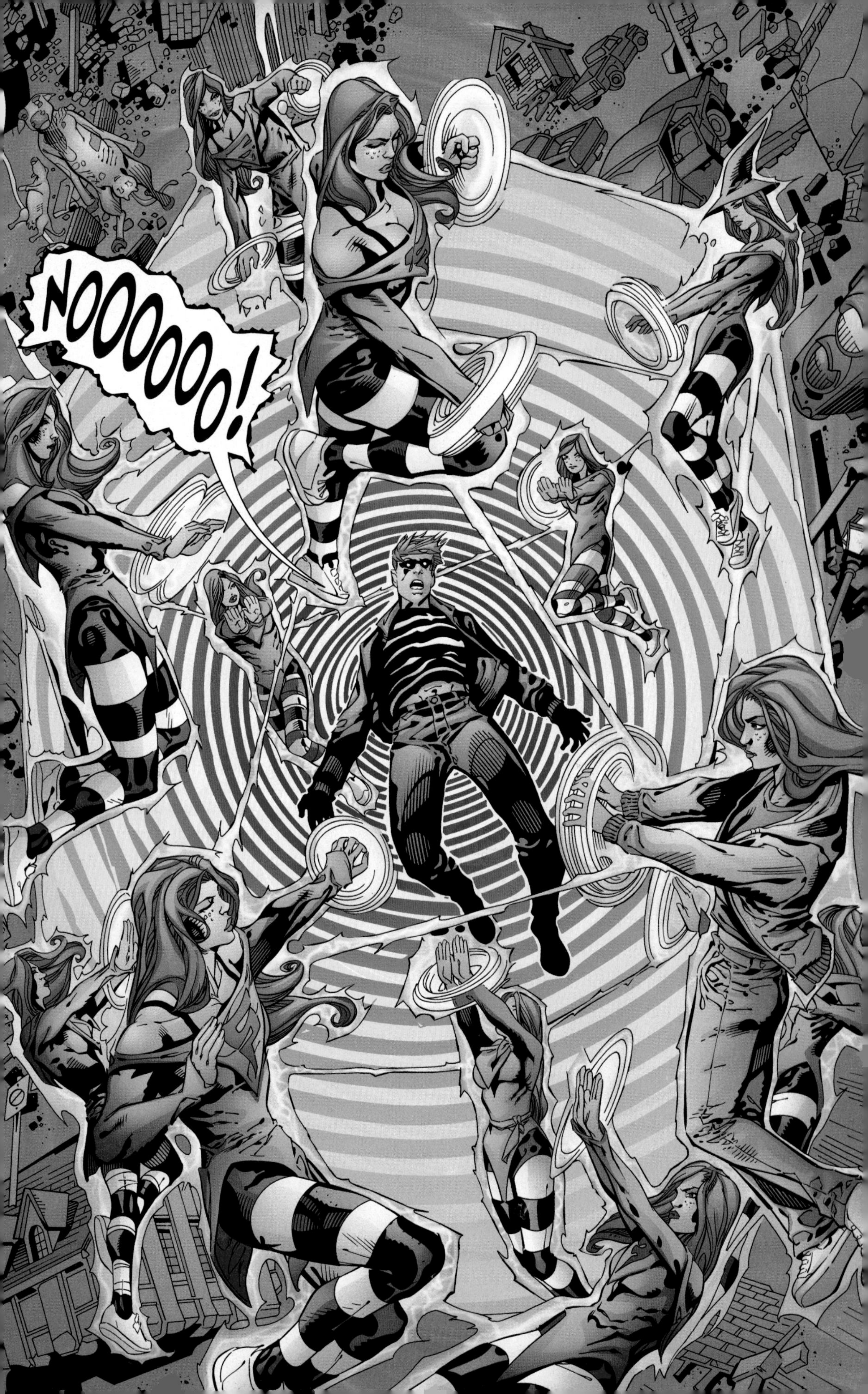
NOOOOOO!

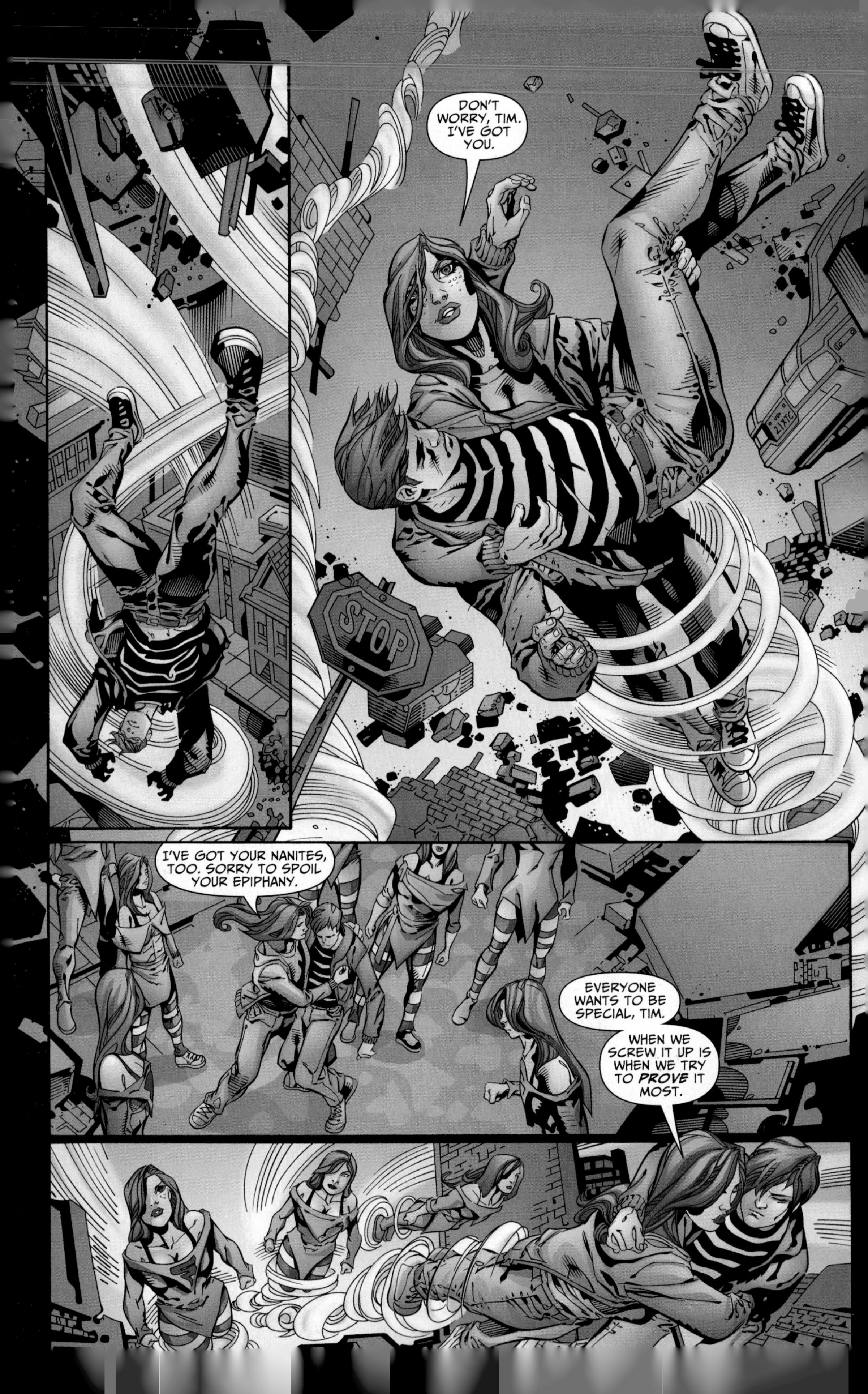
DON'T WORRY, TIM. I'VE GOT YOU.
STOP
I'VE GOT YOUR NANITES, TOO. SORRY TO SPOIL YOUR EPIPHANY.
EVERYONE WANTS TO BE SPECIAL, TIM.
WHEN WE SCREW IT UP IS WHEN WE TRY TO PROVE IT MOST.

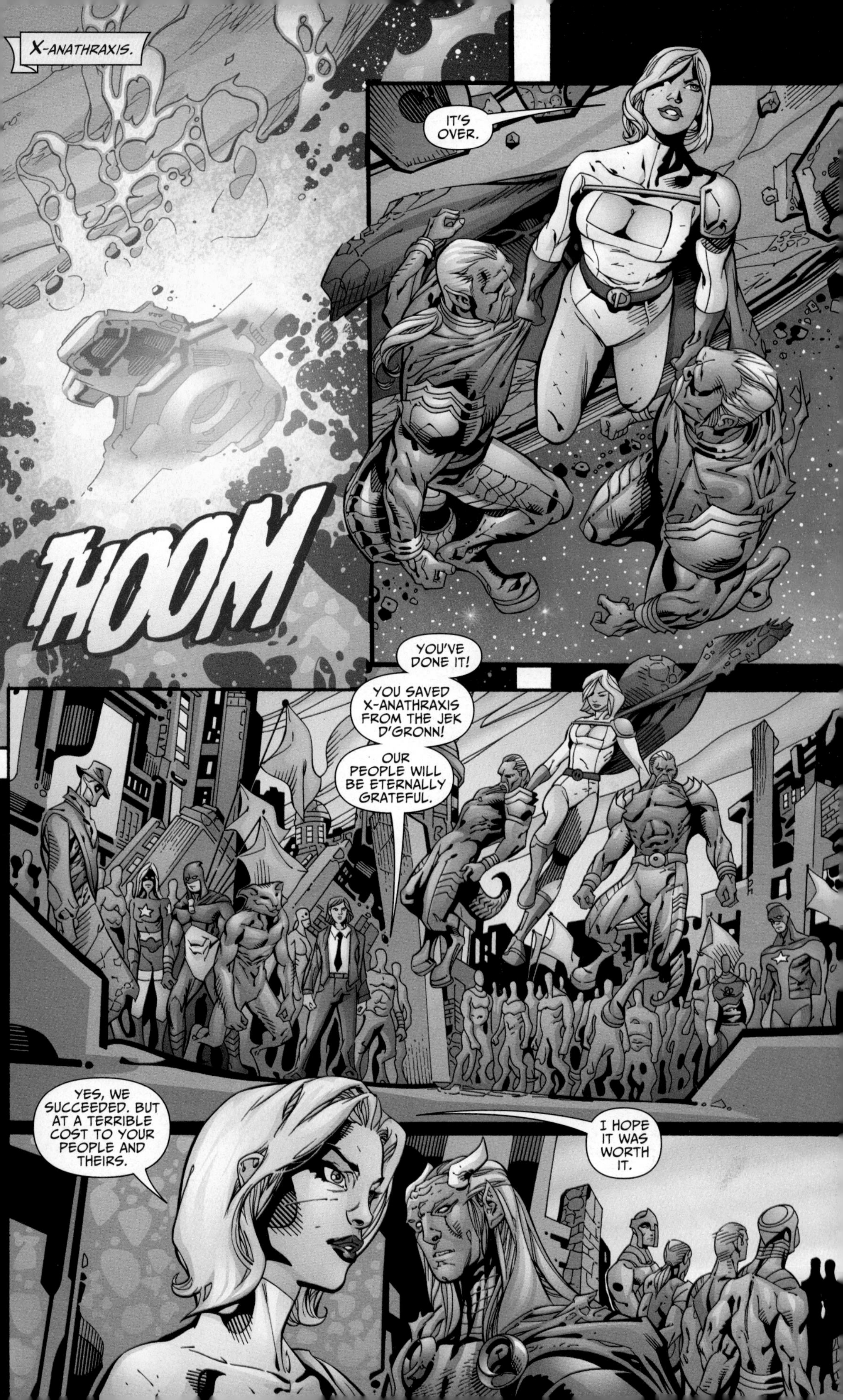
X-ANATHRAXIS.
THOOM
IT'S OVER.
YOU'VE DONE IT!
YOU SAVED X-ANATHRAXIS FROM THE JEK D'GRONN!
OUR PEOPLE WILL BE ETERNALLY GRATEFUL.
YES, WE SUCCEEDED. BUT AT A TERRIBLE COST TO YOUR PEOPLE AND THEIRS.
I HOPE IT WAS WORTH IT.

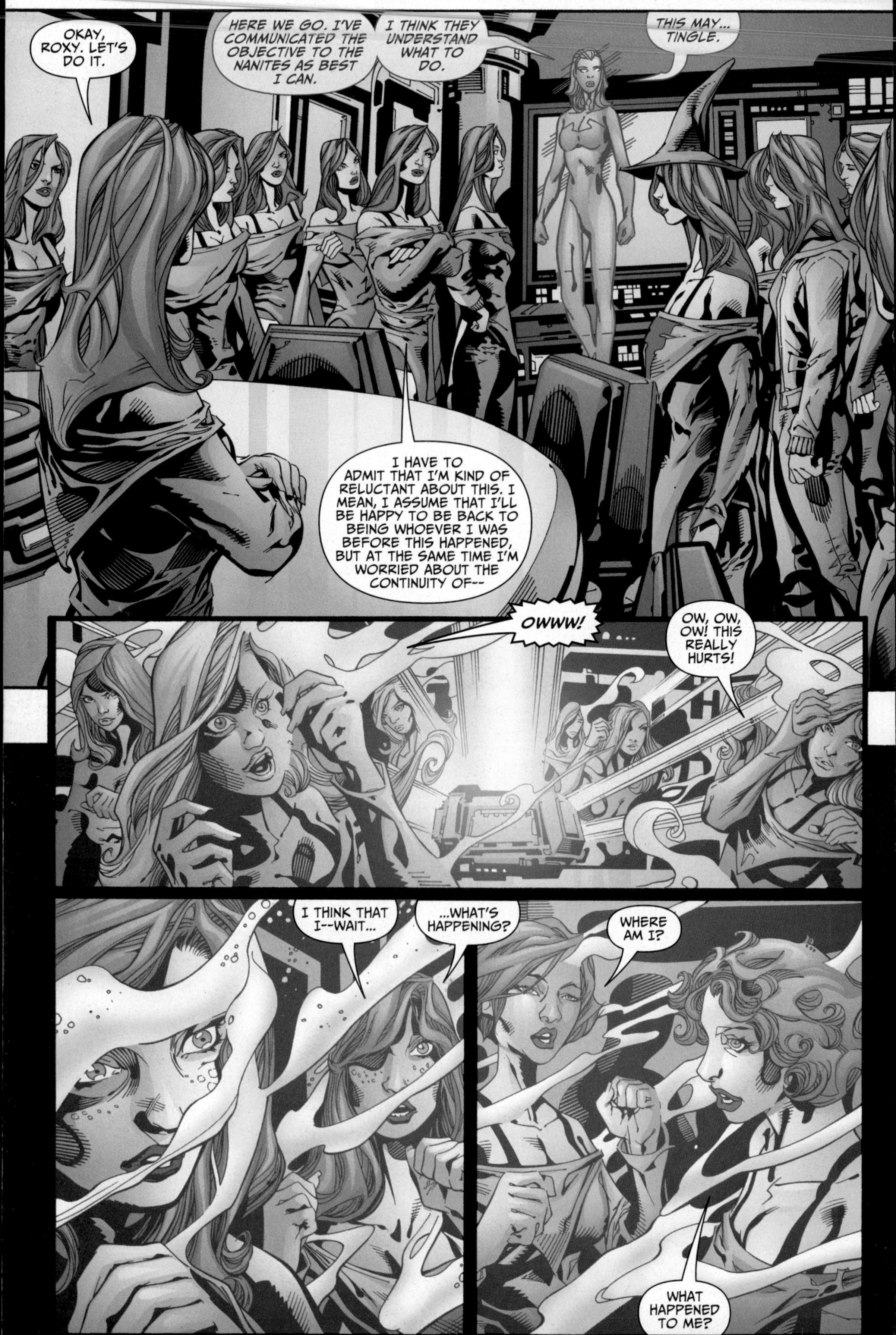
OKAY, ROXY. LET'S DO IT.
HERE WE GO. I'VE COMMUNICATED THE OBJECTIVE TO THE NANITES AS BEST I CAN.
I THINK THEY UNDERSTAND WHAT TO DO.
THIS MAY... TINGLE.
I HAVE TO ADMIT THAT I'M KIND OF RELUCTANT ABOUT THIS. I MEAN, I ASSUME THAT I'LL BE HAPPY TO BE BACK TO BEING WHOEVER I WAS BEFORE THIS HAPPENED, BUT AT THE SAME TIME I'M WORRIED ABOUT THE CONTINUITY OF--
OWWW!
OW, OW, OW! THIS REALLY HURTS!
I THINK THAT I--WAIT...
...WHAT'S HAPPENING?
WHERE AM I?
WHAT HAPPENED TO ME?

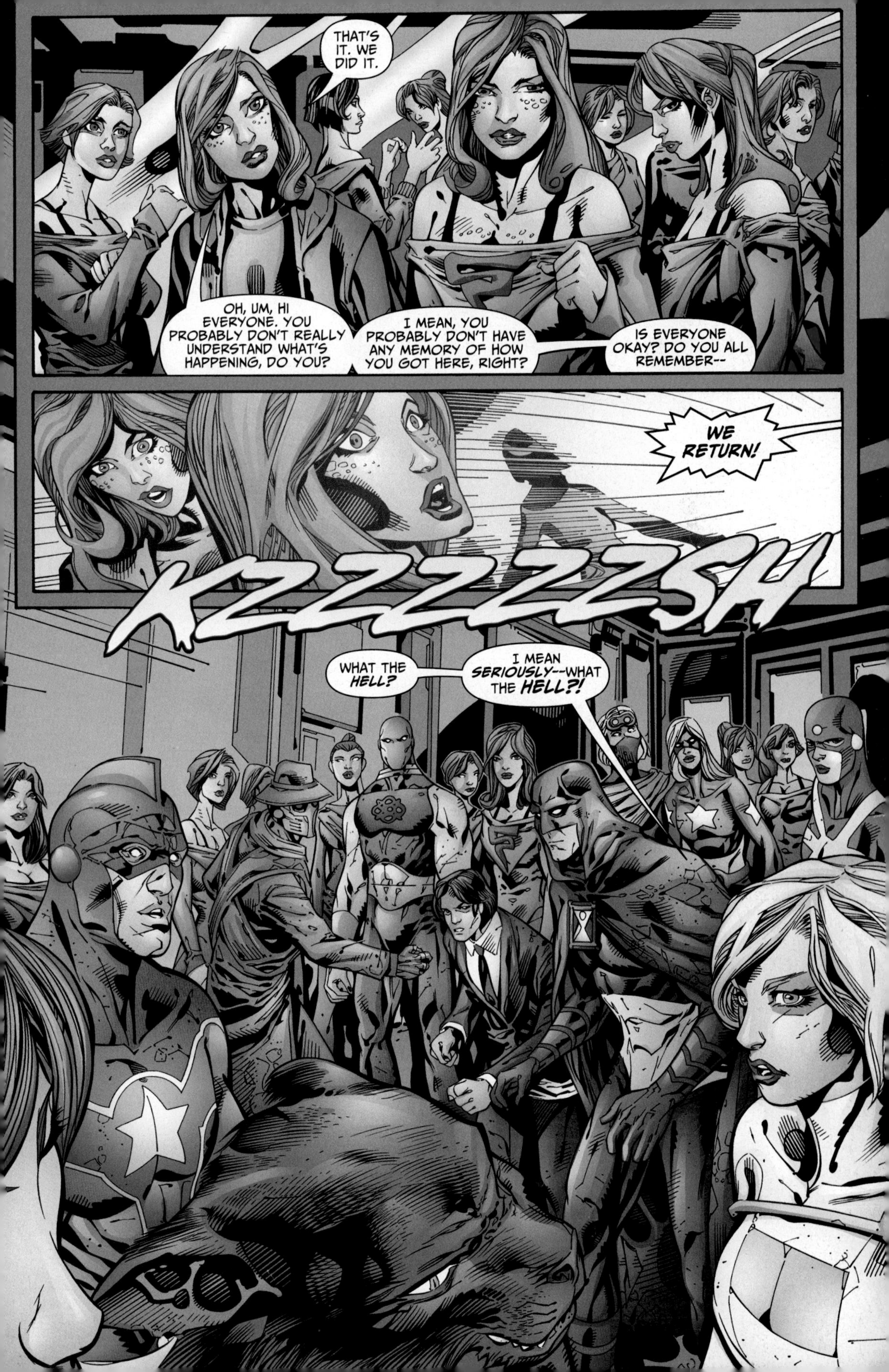
THAT'S IT. WE DID IT.
OH, UM, HI EVERYONE. YOU PROBABLY DON'T REALLY UNDERSTAND WHAT'S HAPPENING, DO YOU?
I MEAN, YOU PROBABLY DON'T HAVE ANY MEMORY OF HOW YOU GOT HERE, RIGHT?
IS EVERYONE OKAY? DO YOU ALL REMEMBER--
WE RETURN!
KZZZZZZSH
WHAT THE HELL?
I MEAN SERIOUSLY--WHAT THE HELL?!

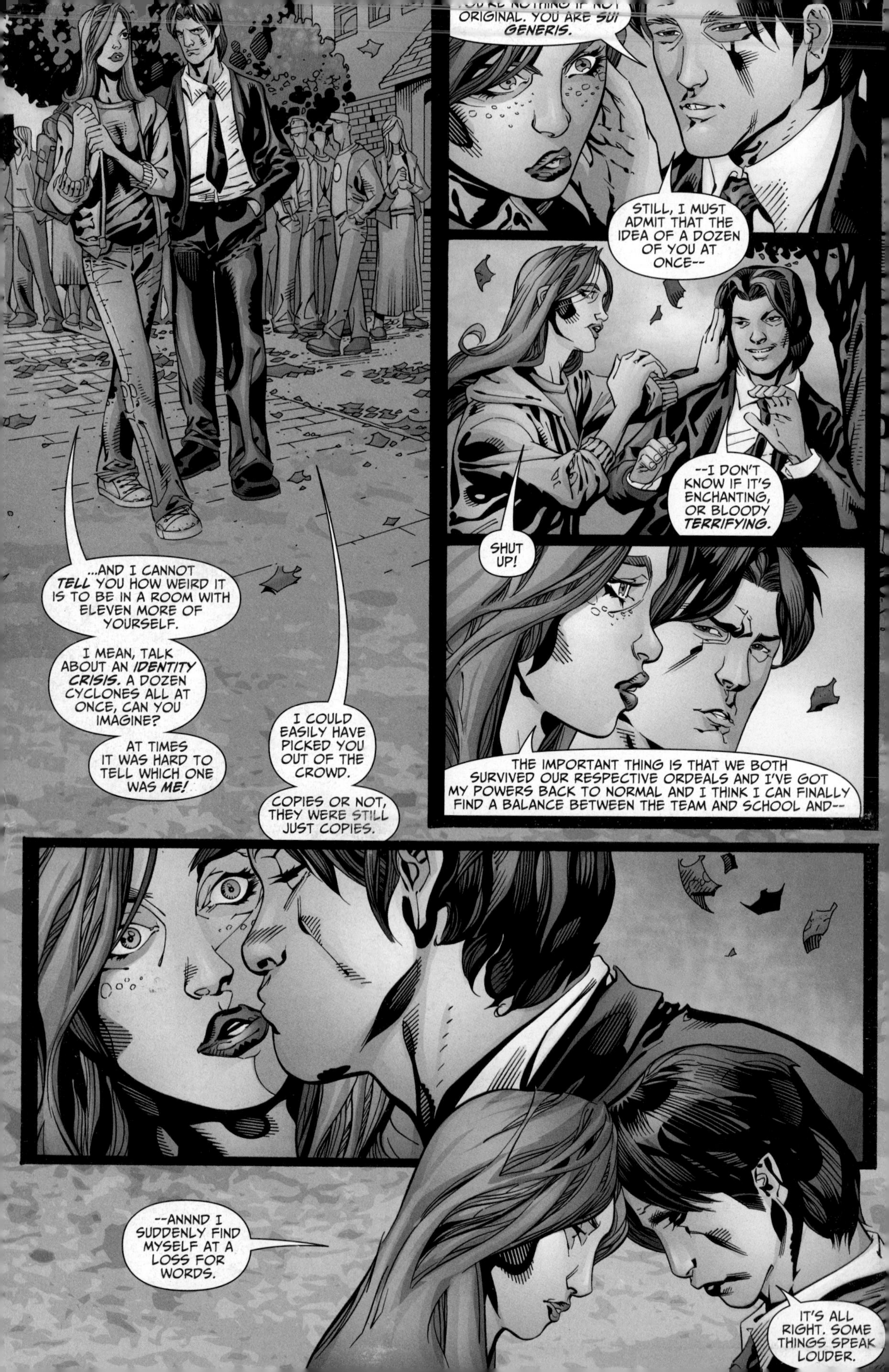
...AND I CANNOT TELL YOU HOW WEIRD IT IS TO BE IN A ROOM WITH ELEVEN MORE OF YOURSELF.
I MEAN, TALK ABOUT AN IDENTITY CRISIS. A DOZEN CYCLONES ALL AT ONCE, CAN YOU IMAGINE?
AT TIMES IT WAS HARD TO TELL WHICH ONE WAS ME!
I COULD EASILY HAVE PICKED YOU OUT OF THE CROWD.
COPIES OR NOT, THEY WERE STILL JUST COPIES.
ORIGINAL. YOU ARE SUI GENERIS.
STILL, I MUST ADMIT THAT THE IDEA OF A DOZEN OF YOU AT ONCE--
--I DON'T KNOW IF IT'S ENCHANTING, OR BLOODY TERRIFYING.
SHUT UP!
THE IMPORTANT THING IS THAT WE BOTH SURVIVED OUR RESPECTIVE ORDEALS AND I'VE GOT MY POWERS BACK TO NORMAL AND I THINK I CAN FINALLY FIND A BALANCE BETWEEN THE TEAM AND SCHOOL AND--
--ANNND I SUDDENLY FIND MYSELF AT A LOSS FOR WORDS.
IT'S ALL RIGHT. SOME THINGS SPEAK LOUDER.

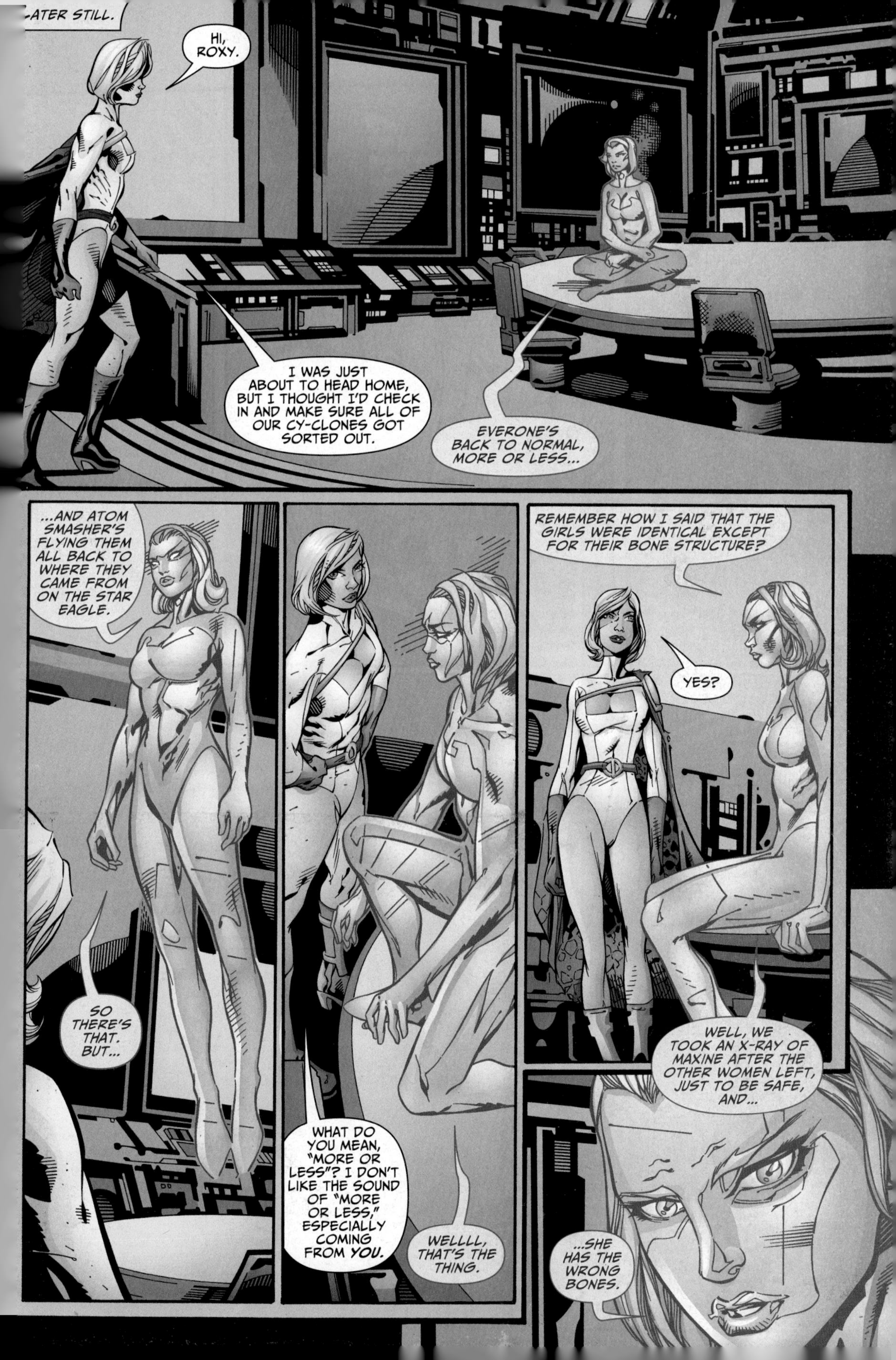
LATER STILL.
HI, ROXY.
I WAS JUST ABOUT TO HEAD HOME, BUT I THOUGHT I'D CHECK IN AND MAKE SURE ALL OF OUR CY-CLONES GOT SORTED OUT.
EVERONE'S BACK TO NORMAL, MORE OR LESS...
...AND ATOM SMASHER'S FLYING THEM ALL BACK TO WHERE THEY CAME FROM ON THE STAR EAGLE.
SO THERE'S THAT. BUT...
WHAT DO YOU MEAN, "MORE OR LESS"? I DON'T LIKE THE SOUND OF "MORE OR LESS," ESPECIALLY COMING FROM YOU.
WELLLL, THAT'S THE THING.
REMEMBER HOW I SAID THAT THE GIRLS WERE IDENTICAL EXCEPT FOR THEIR BONE STRUCTURE?
YES?
WELL, WE TOOK AN X-RAY OF MAXINE AFTER THE OTHER WOMEN LEFT, JUST TO BE SAFE, AND...
...SHE HAS THE WRONG BONES.

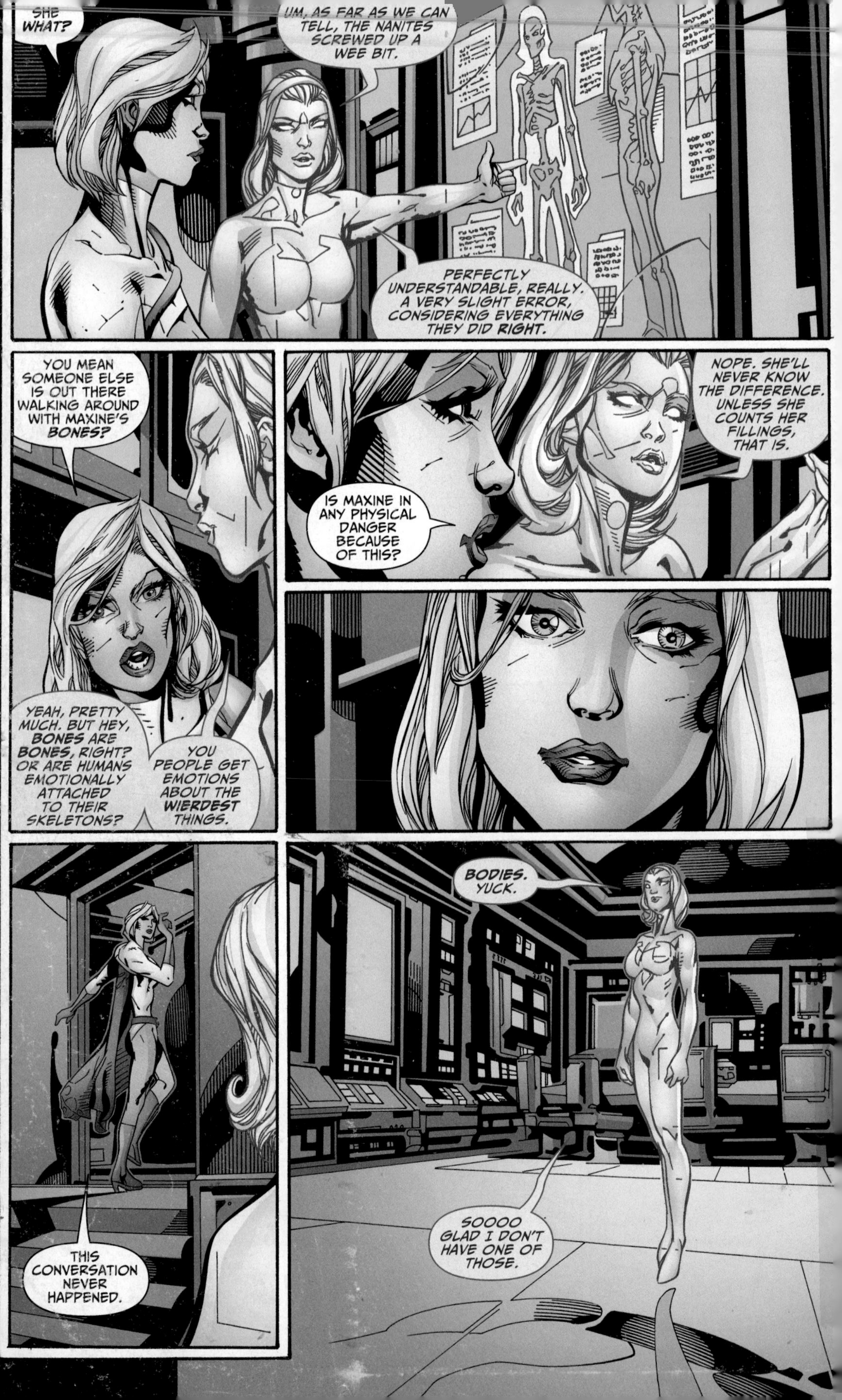
SHE WHAT?
UM, AS FAR AS WE CAN TELL, THE NANITES SCREWED UP A WEE BIT.
PERFECTLY UNDERSTANDABLE, REALLY. A VERY SLIGHT ERROR, CONSIDERING EVERYTHING THEY DID RIGHT.
YOU MEAN SOMEONE ELSE IS OUT THERE WALKING AROUND WITH MAXINE'S BONES?
IS MAXINE IN ANY PHYSICAL DANGER BECAUSE OF THIS?
NOPE. SHE'LL NEVER KNOW THE DIFFERENCE. UNLESS SHE COUNTS HER FILLINGS, THAT IS.
YEAH, PRETTY MUCH. BUT HEY, BONES ARE BONES, RIGHT? OR ARE HUMANS EMOTIONALLY ATTACHED TO THEIR SKELETONS?
YOU PEOPLE GET EMOTIONS ABOUT THE WIERDEST THINGS.
THIS CONVERSATION NEVER HAPPENED.
BODIES. YUCK.
SOOOO GLAD I DON'T HAVE ONE OF THOSE.